The Social Media Reader

The Social Media Reader

EDITED BY

Michael Mandiberg

NEW YORK UNIVERSITY PRESS
New York and London

NEW YORK UNIVERSITY PRESS
New York and London
www.nyupress.org

References to Internet websites (URLs) were accurate at the time of writing. Neither the author nor New York University Press is responsible for URLs that may have expired or changed since the manuscript was prepared.

Library of Congress Cataloging-in-Publication Data

The social media reader / edited by Michael Mandiberg.
p. cm.
Includes bibliographical references and index.
ISBN 978-0-8147-6405-3 (cl : alk. paper)
ISBN 978-0-8147-6406-0 (pb : alk. paper)
ISBN 978-0-8147-6407-7 (ebook)
ISBN 978-0-8147-6302-5 (ebook)
1. Social media. 2. Technological innovations—Social aspects.
I. Mandiberg, Michael.
HM742.S6284   2012
302.23'1—dc23   2011038308

New York University Press books are printed on acid-free paper, and their binding materials are chosen for strength and durability. We strive to use environmentally responsible suppliers and materials to the greatest extent possible in publishing our books.

Manufactured in the United States of America

Contents

Acknowledgments   ix

Introduction   1
Michael Mandiberg

PART I: MECHANISMS

1 The People Formerly Known as the Audience   13
   Jay Rosen

2 Sharing Nicely: On Shareable Goods and the Emergence   17
   of Sharing as a Modality of Economic Production
   Yochai Benkler

3 Open Source as Culture/Culture as Open Source   24
   Siva Vaidhyanathan

4 What Is Web 2.0? Design Patterns and Business Models   32
   for the Next Generation of Software
   Tim O'Reilly

5 What Is Collaboration Anyway?   53
   Adam Hyde, Mike Linksvayer, kanarinka,
   Michael Mandiberg, Marta Peirano, Sissu Tarka,
   Astra Taylor, Alan Toner, Mushon Zer-Aviv

PART II: SOCIALITY

6 Participating in the Always-On Lifestyle   71
   danah boyd

7 From Indymedia to Demand Media: Journalism's Visions   77
   of Its Audience and the Horizons of Democracy
   C. W. Anderson

   PART III: HUMOR

8 Phreaks, Hackers, and Trolls: The Politics of   99
   Transgression and Spectacle
   E. Gabriella Coleman

9 The Language of Internet Memes   120
   Patrick Davison

   PART IV: MONEY

10 The Long Tail   137
   Chris Anderson

   PART V: LAW

11 REMIX: How Creativity Is Being Strangled by the Law   155
   Lawrence Lessig

12 Your Intermediary Is Your Destiny   170
   Fred von Lohmann

13 On the Fungibility and Necessity of Cultural Freedom   178
   Fred Benenson

14 Giving Things Away Is Hard Work: Three Creative   187
   Commons Case Studies
   Michael Mandiberg

   PART VI: LABOR

15 Quentin Tarantino's *Star Wars*? Grassroots Creativity   203
   Meets the Media Industry
   Henry Jenkins

16 Gin, Television, and Social Surplus   236
        Clay Shirky

17 Between Democracy and Spectacle: The Front-End and   242
    Back-End of the Social Web
        Felix Stalder

18 DIY Academy? Cognitive Capitalism, Humanist Scholarship,   257
    and the Digital Transformation
        Ashley Dawson

    About the Contributors   275

    Index   279

Acknowledgments

First and foremost, I thank the many authors who contributed to this volume. I thank both those who created new essays and those who gave their works a Creative Commons license that permitted me to use them here. If it were not for the freedom offered by these freely licensed texts, I would never have had the ability or inspiration to take on this project. Thank you for sharing.

I conceived of this anthology while preparing a seminar on social media. The absence of any critical anthology prompted me to collect the writings that I thought were most important. The realization that many of these were Creative Commons licensed inspired me to transform this reading list into a table of contents for this book. I wish to thank the Department of Media Culture at the College of Staten Island, City University of New York, for its support of this project: C. W. Anderson, Cynthia Chris, Jeanine Corbet, David Gerstner, Janet Manfredonia, Tara Mateik, Edward D. Miller, Sherry Millner, Jason Simon, Matthew Solomon, Valerie Tevere, Cindy Wong, Bilge Yesil, and Ying Zhu. I am indebted to my colleagues at the CUNY Graduate Center: Steve Brier, Ashley Dawson, and Matthew Gold. I am grateful to the provost, William J. Fritz, for the support of the Provost's Research Grant and to Dean Christine Flynn Saulnier and former dean Francisco Soto for their support of my research leaves and for the Dean's Summer Research Assistantship.

I edited this anthology during a leave as a senior fellow at Eyebeam Center for Art and Technology, and I am deeply indebted to Eyebeam for the material support for this period of research and for the context from which to produce such a collection. Amanda McDonald Crowley offered me such a generous period of serious creative research, and Steve Lambert constantly pushed me to live, act, and create in line with my beliefs. I want to thank everyone at Eyebeam, including Ayah Bdeir, Jacob Ciocci, Jon Cohrs, Sarah Cook, Jeff Crouse, Patrick Davison, Jennifer Dopazo, Stephen Duncombe, Clara Jo, John Johnson, Simon Jolly, Emma Lloyd, Qimei Luo, Marisa Olson, Stephanie Pereira, Marc Schiller, Roddy Schrock, Brooke Singer, Marko Tandefelt, and Addie Wagenknecht.

Adam Hyde, Mike Linksvayer, kanarinka, Marta Peirano, Sissu Tarka, Astra Taylor, Alan Toner, and Mushon Zer-Aviv have been inspirational past and future collaborators. Grace M. Cho, Cynthia Chris, Mary Flanagan, Alex Galloway, Tiffany Holmes, and Marita Sturken provided invaluable guidance on the practicalities of publishing. Many thanks to my editors, Eric Zinner and Ciara McLaughlin, who saw the merits in this project.

Thanks to Creative Commons for creating the legal framework that has made this collection possible: Lawrence Lessig for making this kind of sharing conceivable and for sharing his own work, Fred Benenson for being a personal inspiration for my own engagement with this process, and Mike Linksvayer again, though this time in his role at Creative Commons, where he provided information and references about Creative Commons licenses.

Many thanks always to Sherry Millner, Ernie Larsen, and Nadja Millner-Larsen, xtine burrough, Stephen Mandiberg, Joseph Mandiberg, and Linda Mandiberg.

Introduction

MICHAEL MANDIBERG

Beginning with the printing press, technological innovations have enabled the dissemination of more and more media forms over broader and broader audiences. This mass media built and maintained a unidirectional relationship between a few trained professional media producers and many untrained media consumers. This model, which reached its peak in the middle to late twentieth century, began to shift in the 1980s with the widespread use of photocopiers, home video cameras, and mixtapes and evolved further with desktop publishing, home computing, and increased Internet access. By the early 2000s, the cost of computers, software, and Internet access decreased, allowing individuals access to the same tools of production used by professionals. In this period, new media forms such as blogs and social networking sites have focused squarely on active audience participation, uprooting the established relationship between media producer and media consumer. At the end of this first decade of the twenty-first century, the line between media producers and consumers has blurred, and the unidirectional broadcast has partially fragmented into many different kinds of multidirectional conversations.

Access to tools and the invention of new media forms allow formerly passive media consumers to make and disseminate their own media. New technological frameworks have arisen that center on enabling this media creation: message boards, audience-driven review sites, blogs and comment systems, photo- and video-sharing websites, social networks, social news sites, bookmark-sharing sites, and microblogging platforms, to name some of the more prominent ones. These new frameworks have become more and more focused on enabling media creation, as this so-called amateur media becomes the raison d'être of these very professional media organizations. These sites are pointless without audience participation: from the audience's perspective, in order to experience the site you *have to become a media producer*, and from the organizations' perspective, without audience production their sites will fail. These media forms include a spectrum of engagement from elaborate videos uploaded to YouTube to a simple "like" on Facebook. While old forms coexist with these new audience-driven forms and hybrids of the two, media participation is now part of media consumption.

Despite the widespread participant engagement and scholarly interest in this phenomenon, it has no definitive name. It has been given many names, a selection of the most prevalent of which include the corporate media favorite "user-generated content," Henry Jenkins's media-industries-focused "convergence culture," Jay Rosen's "the people formerly known as the audience," the politically infused "participatory media," Yochai Benkler's process-oriented "peer production," and Tim O'Reilly's computer-programming-oriented "Web 2.0." Each of these terms defines one separate aspect of the phenomenon and does so from the specific point of view of the different actors in this system. In order to understand the system as a whole, it is necessary to understand each of these separate terms and the perspective it comes from.

"User-generated content" stands out in this list of terms, as it refers to the material product, not the tools or process of this product's creation; it does address the author but only as an effect of its focus on the product, and it seems to retain a vision of a passive audience in which the users who are generating the content are not synonymous with the audience as a whole but are merely individual members of the audience that step into an intermediate role. This corporate term is very popular with commercial media organizations looking to explain their business plans to investors, but it is reviled by many of these so-called users, foregrounding a general conflict over the line in the sand between amateurs and professionals. Derek Powazek deconstructs the term in his 2006 post "Death to User-Generated Content":

> *User:* One who uses. Like, you know, a junkie.
> *Generated:* Like a generator, engine. Like, you know, a robot.
> *Content:* Something that fills a box. Like, you know, packing peanuts.
>
> So what's user-generated content? Junkies robotically filling boxes with packing peanuts. Lovely.[1]

He then proposes yet another term for the phenomenon, "authentic media." His deconstruction is intentionally cartoonish, but it expresses its point: the term is machine-like and disregards the personal nature of the media these individuals are creating.

As Henry Jenkins has argued in *Convergence Culture*, these new media forms converge with existing forms and with the media industries built around those forms, in an often uneasy coexistence.[2] These inversions of the traditional amateur/professional dialectic blur clearly defined author and audience roles. Powazek's critique is rooted in a proindividual, anticorporate ethos that privileges the authenticity of the individual amateur creator, but four years after his post, professional content has become a much larger part of the social media ecosystem. One marker of this transition is the makeup of the all-time most viewed videos on YouTube: in July 2010 only three of the top-twenty videos were nonprofessional, and the majority of the professional videos were studio-produced, high-budget music videos added to the site in the previous eighteen months. This inversion is well represented by "Lonelygirl15," a series of *amateur-style* videos of a fictional teenage girl named Bree; though the main character was played by an actor, led by a team of independent directors/producers, for the first four months the YouTube channel claimed the videos to be the authentic work of a individual amateur.[3] The goal for many of these media creators, including the creators of "Longelygirl15," is to become professionals through their amateur participation in these social media platforms.

Jay Rosen has theorized this phenomenon as a shift in audience and has contextualized this shift in terms of democratic theory. In his blog post of the same name, he speaks in the voice of "the people formerly known as the audience," who want to announce their active presence to the media and to let the media know that they are not going away (see Rosen, chapter 1 in this volume). Rosen closes his missive with a warning from "the people formerly known as the audience" that they are not just "eyeballs" that can be owned. Rather than thinking of "the people formerly known as the audience" as a market, Rosen wants the media to think of them as the public made real; in referring to the public, and the political processes that it implies, Rosen is engaging the same principles behind the term "participatory media." "Participatory media," and the closely related "citizen journalism," focus on news reporting and the political power involved with destabilizing the one-directional broadcast from a reporter to an audience into a multivoiced conversation among participants.[4] In discussions of "participatory media," participation in the media-creation process is often correlated with participation in the political process. Yochai Benkler's term "peer production" refers to the collaborative process of creating media over software-mediated platforms of the networked information economy, such as Wikipedia, Digg, and Slashdot.[5] Benkler's focus is on the process itself, including the presence of socially or technologically mediated rules and the possibility that these new processes are inherently more democratic.

The term "Web 2.0" is derived from O'Reilly Media's Web 2.0 Conference, first held in 2004. Tim O'Reilly, in his follow-up article "What Is Web

2.0?" defines "Web 2.0" as an upgraded computer-programming model that has enabled a set of participatory websites built on lightweight server-based applications that move rich data across platforms. The dense computer-programming jargon in this last sentence highlights the industry white-paper origins of the term. The term "Web 2.0" describes the tools for making this new media; it does not address the process, product, author, or audience. Though it was coined to describe a specific type of web programming, its prevalence outside the coterie of geeks shows how influential the term has become. This popular buzzword has been widely adopted by the marketing departments of Internet startups (supplanting the tainted "dot-com"), media outlets, and academics analyzing the phenomenon. In the process, the term has lost its tether to the web-programming models it espoused and has become just as closely linked to a design aesthetic and a marketing language. Emptied of its referent, it is an empty signifier: it is a brand. The many "Web 2.0 Bullshit Generator" web pages are poignant critiques of Web 2.0 as brand.[6] These simple applications generate random short sets of Web 2.0 terms. These phrases, such as "reinvent rss-capable communities," "incentivize citizen-media blogospheres," and "beta-test embedded wikis," combine these buzzwords to create meaningless, but convincing, marketing materials for a hypothetical Web 2.0 site. The phrases seem to work by deploying the signs of hip inclusive social-mediraness, and yet they don't actually mean anything: they are the manifestation of Web 2.0 as branding material.

Each of these terms encapsulates a different aspect of, and comes from the different perspectives of the multiple actors of, the phenomenon of social media. This book uses the term "social media," both in the title and in this introduction. The goal of this book is not to argue for the term "social media" at the expense of all these other terms. The goal of this book is to bring examples from the multiple disciplines, perspectives, and agendas into one space. "Social media" is a broad enough term that it can encompass, while preserving, each of these perspectives and their respective terms.

The essays in this book are divided into six thematic parts: "Mechanisms," "Sociality," "Humor," "Money," "Law," and "Labor." The one question that runs through every one of these essays is whether social media is a good thing: is it beneficial for democracy, culture, law, labor, and creative expression? The field of technology studies asks this question of every new technology; the implicit and explicit answers to this question often veer to the extremes of techno-utopia and techno-dystopia, and social media is no exception. Notable examples at the extreme ends of this dialectic include beatific works like *What Would Google Do?*[7] which walks through the hypothetical application wisdom of crowds-based algorithms to every possible area of society, to predictions of social destruction in works like *The Cult of the Amateur: How Today's Internet Is Killing Our Culture*.[8] While all the essays in this book address this theme in some way, some focus on it more than others. The hope for sharing, expression, and the power of new web tools appears strongest in the writings of Chris Anderson, Tim O'Reilly, Jay Rosen, and Clay Shirky. Conversely, C. W. Anderson, Ashley Dawson, Henry Jenkins, and Felix Stalder argue that the unfettered information flow, without the means to control it, turns into a spectacle that does anything but build meaningful political, social, or labor relationships between individuals.

The essays in part 1 provide analyses of the technical and social practices that lay the groundwork for social media. As discussed earlier, Jay Rosen speaks in the voice of "the people formerly known as the audience," who wish for the media makers to know that they exist and are not going away. In doing so, Rosen highlights the change in audience participation, with is the central shift in social practices; this social shift is enabled by technical shifts that are discussed by Tim O'Reilly. Yochai Benkler theorizes the social practice of sharing, a fundamental requirement for social media. Benkler offers models for what can be shared and asserts that these sharing economies can self-organize the use of these surpluses better than an exchange economy can. Siva Vaidhyanathan charts the cultural influence of the open-source software model, touching on the power of copyrights and alternative licenses, which is discussed at length in the section on the law. Tim O'Reilly describes the software models that have enabled the creation of social media platforms. As described earlier, a change in software-development practices, from isolated desktop application to a collaborative web-based platform, defines Web 2.0. In the collaboratively written essay "What Is Collaboration?," Adam Hyde, Mike Linksvayer, kanarinka, Marta Peirano, Sissu Tarka, Astra Taylor, Alan Toner, Mushon Zer-Aviv, and I trace the contours and processes of collaboration from the weak associations to the strong bonds.[9] The essay argues that sharing is a necessary precondition for collaboration but that strong collaboration requires intentionality and coordination.

Part 2 addresses how social media changes the social dynamics of its participants. danah boyd weighs the merits of being perpetually connected to a wireless network, and the information overload and responsibility that results from the deluge of information. boyd accepts the negative aspects of being always on in exchange for the positives, as many of us do, though psychologists and neuroscientists are beginning to reach different conclusions.[10] C. W. Anderson looks at journalism's changing perception of its audience and how that reflects both journalism's and the audience's relationship to democracy. The rise of the algorithmic journalism performed by content farms may satisfy the search-query-based needs of its readership, but it undermines the democratic effect of journalism.

"Lulz" is the term of choice to describe the pleasure of the ends-justify-the-means pranks and humor that pervades chatrooms and image boards. E. Gabriella Coleman traces an alternate genealogy of hackers that does not start at MIT and end with open-source software but, rather, moves from phone phreakers through countercultural politics and ends with "Anonymous," the lulz-seeking Internet trolls on 4chan's infamous /b/ board. This alternate history presents a subculture of computer hackers birthed outside the university and invested in politics and transgression. Patrick Davison traces the evolution of the meme from its origins in Richard Dawkins's writings on evolutionary biology to the fast-track transformations of Internet memes on the anonymous image boards of 4chan. For Davison, the key to the success of Internet memes and their generative nature is the explicit removal of authorship, which he calls the "nonattribution meme."

In most histories, the Internet began as a self-defense mechanism for communicating during a nuclear war.[11] In the late '80s and early '90s it became a haven for academics, geeks, and other subcultures of the command line. By the mid-'90s money and profit had taken over; the dot-com bubble and crash, the current Web 2.0 balloon, and the Great Recession have marked the Internet alternately as a profit machine and an epic failure as such. Though money appears at the edges of many of the essays here as an explicit goal, a constraining factor, or an effect to be eliminated, Chris Anderson's "The Long Tail" takes it on directly, identifying one of the new business models of online retailers. These retailers stock inventories many times larger than those of brick-and-mortar stores. These long-tail businesses manage to make money off books, records, and other goods that were much too obscure for any previous retailer to stock, leading to a previously unimaginable number of audience choices. On the flip side, recent studies suggest that, though these businesses can profit from selling a very small amount of media objects from each of a very large number of creators, those creators may be worse off in this new system.[12] Other repercussions reverberate from these shifts in what we value and how we value it—including Anderson's exploration of free (as in beer) services in his book *Free! Why $0.00 Is the Future of Business*—the exponential growth in the cost of unique objects, and the rise of real economies for virtual goods.[13]

Lawrence Lessig and Fred von Lohmann address the way that the law impacts the creation of social media. Lessig's essay describes a shift in how our culture writes, and the way that copyright law is at odds with this shift. Lessig compellingly argues that "writing" has evolved to include sound and moving image but that the copyright law governing writing has not evolved to reflect this cultural shift. This conflict between social practice and legal precedent criminalizes these new forms of expression. Lessig calls for legal reform and for the embrace of the licenses created by Creative Commons, an organization he helped found. Creative Commons licenses allow creators to exercise the rights guaranteed to them under their copyright: instead of "all rights reserved," these works have "some rights reserved." This book and all its essays are Creative Commons licensed. Fred von Lohmann approaches this legal conflict by looking at the different way the Digital Millennium Copyright Act (DMCA) treats these new forms of expression and how that affects their transmission. Existing laws governing non-Internet-based media distribution allow large monetary penalties for breaking "strict liability" copyright law, preventing the distribution of works that relies on fair-use provisions, unless the creator can prove compliance *before* distribution. The DMCA has a safe-harbor provision that allows sites like YouTube to publish these works and requires them to maintain a mechanism to adjudicate claims by copyright holders *after* distribution. This has allowed an explosion of online content and has allowed some creators to identify who is not going to sue them, but it has also led to massive removals of media from sites such as YouTube. Fred Benenson and I consider the shifts in ideology and methodology when applying these licenses to cultural works. Benenson looks at the intricacies of applying software-derived free-culture ideology to non-fungible creative works. In arguing that not all cultural works should have the same license, Benenson identifies a key difference between the utilitarian software tools that pioneered these license models and nonfungible works that are not intended to be further modified. Extending this discussion, I present three case studies that explore the failures and successes of applying open-source methodologies to Creative Commons–licensed noncode projects. Though this process takes its cues from software development, the arts and design communities have a different set of challenges in the process of creating peer-produced works.

The creation of a participatory audience foregrounds labor dynamics; when an audience participates in creating the media that it consumes, it links audience dynamics and labor relations and sometimes renders them interchangeable. Though these labor dynamics are more central in social media's production model, they are not new. Henry Jenkins has written extensively about fan culture and the tensions between creative fans and the proprietary media empires they are fanatical about. In his essay here, which comes from his book *Convergence Culture*, Jenkins articulates some of the pitfalls of fan culture online and the instability of the trust between creative *Star Wars* fans and LucasArts' wavering support for fan fiction online. Clay Shirky considers the untold possibilities of our coming cognitive surplus. Cognitive surplus is the excess thought power available to society when we convert passive spectatorship into participation in social media. To put this massive capacity in context, the amount of time it has taken to create the entirety of Wikipedia is one hundred million hours, which is equivalent to the amount of time the population of the United States spends watching advertisements on television on any one weekend. Shirky sees this cognitive surplus, released from the drudgery of passive spectatorship, as a force (a *workforce*) that will transform media and society in ways we cannot yet conceive. Conversely, Felix Stalder considers the pitfalls of how our labor accumulates in databases and server farms. Stalder articulates how our labor is often exploited by the "surveillance economy" of analytics software and server logs. Lastly, Ashley Dawson self-reflexively returns us to the very enterprise of this book: academic publishing. Starting from a letter from his editor at University of Michigan Press announcing its digital publication initiative, Dawson asks whether the shift to digitally published scholarship and other forms of computationalism can really provide an escape from the dystopian reality of contemporary academic labor's reduced budgets, informal labor exacerbated by the asymmetry of power-law relationships, pressures of publishing conglomerates exacted through journal subscriptions, and the outcomes-focused mandate on professors to publish or perish. Dawson does see potential in some initiatives but warns that academics are unprepared for digital transformations. He emphasizes that technology, without changing the social context of its implementation, merely reinforces existing inequalities.

The process by which this book was created could never have happened without the use of social media as a tool for creation. Most of the essays in this volume exist on the Internet in one form or another; they are included here by virtue of their Creative Commons licenses. It is because these works have been licensed with free-culture licenses that I can bring them together in this collection, excerpting a few, editing others for print, and remixing Lessig's *Remix* talk into a written essay. In other cases, I was able to ask authors to extend shorter blog posts or to codify informal presentations documented by online video. The print form of these digital texts is but one of their transformations, transformations that you, the people formerly known as the audience, are free to continue: it is social media after all.

Copyright and licensing is powerful but never simple: the chapters in this book are mostly licensed with Attribution ShareAlike (CC BY-SA) licenses,[14] and after a thorough discussion, NYU Press agreed to license the book with an Attribution NonCommercial ShareAlike (CC BY-NC-SA) license.[15] You are free to transmit the whole book, to remix the book, to abridge or amend the book with more essays, or to translate the whole book into other languages or other media platforms, so long as you do so for noncommercial purposes and the work retains this same license. As each individual chapter has a license that permits commercial use, you can use all the chapters except this introduction and Henry Jenkins' chapter in any of the aforementioned ways, without the restriction on commercial use. You may use the Jenkins chapter, the title of the book, and this introduction for noncommercial uses. What form will your remix take?

NOTES

1. Derek Powazek, "Death to User-Generated Content," *Powazek: Just a Thought* (blog), April 4, 2006, http://powazek.com/2006/04/000576.html (accessed July 20, 2010).

2. Henry Jenkins, *Convergence Culture: Where Old and New Media Collide* (New York: NYU Press, 2006).

3. Miles Beckett, Mesh Flinders, and Greg Goodfried, "Lonelygirl15's Channel," YouTube, http://www.youtube.com/user/lonelygirl15 (accessed July 20, 2010).

4. Dan Gillmor, *We the Media* (Sebastopol, CA: O'Reilly, 2004); Derrick Jensen, *The Immediast Underground Pamphlet Series: Seizing the Media* (New York: Immediast International, 1992), available online at http://deoxy.org/seize_it.htm (accessed January 30, 2011).

5. Yochai Benkler, *The Wealth of Networks: How Social Production Transforms Markets and Freedom* (New Haven: Yale University Press, 2006).

6. The most blogged example is "Bullshitr," http://emptybottle.org/bullshit/ (accessed July 20, 2010).

7. Jeff Jarvis, *What Would Google Do?* (New York: HarperBusiness, 2009).

8. Andrew Keen, *The Cult of the Amateur: How Today's Internet Is Killing Our Culture* (New York: Crown Business, 2007).

9. For more on the "Collaborative Futures" process, see Adam Hyde et al., "How This Book Is Written," in *Collaborative Futures*, FLOSSmanuals.net, http://www.booki.cc/collaborativefutures/about-this-book/ (accessed July 20, 2010).

10. Matt Richtel, "Digital Devices Deprive Brain of Needed Downtime," *New York Times*, August 24, 2010, http://www.nytimes.com/2010/08/25/technology/25brain.html (accessed August 31, 2010).

11. Roy Rosenzweig, "Wizards, Bureaucrats, Warriors and Hackers: Writing the History of the Internet," *American Historical Review*, December 1998, available online at http://www-personal.si.umich.edu/~pne/PDF/ahrcwreview.pdf.

12. Krzysztof Wiszniewski, "The Paradise That Should Have Been," *The Cynical Musician* (blog), January 21, 2010, http://thecynicalmusician.com/2010/01/the-paradise-that-should-have-been/ (accessed July 20, 2010).

13. James Gleick, "Keeping It Real," *New York Times*, January 6, 2008; Julian Dibbell, "The Life of the Chinese Gold Farmer," *New York Times*, June 17, 2007, http://www.nytimes.com/2007/06/17/magazine/17lootfarmers-t.html (accessed July 20, 2010).

14. Yochai Benkler's chapter is licensed with an Attribution license, and Henry Jenkins's chapter is licensed with an Attribution NonCommercial ShareAlike license.

15. Please see http://creativecommons.org/licenses/ for more information and the full text of these licenses. Because this is a collection of independent works, the ShareAlike licenses on those works do not trigger copyleft, allowing the NonCommercial license on the collection. As per all NonCommercial licenses, commercial rights can be licensed from the publisher.

PART I

Mechanisms

The People Formerly
Known as the Audience

JAY ROSEN

That's what I call them. Recently I received this statement.

The people formerly known as the audience wish to inform media people of our existence, and of a shift in power that goes with the platform shift you've all heard about.

Think of passengers on your ship who got a boat of their own. The writing readers. The viewers who picked up a camera. The formerly atomized listeners who with modest effort can connect with each other and gain the means to speak— to the world, as it were.

Now we understand that met with ringing statements like these many media people want to cry out in the name of reason herself: *If all would speak, who shall be left to listen? Can you at least tell us that?*

The people formerly known as the audience do not believe this problem— too many speakers!—is our problem. Now for anyone in your circle still wondering who we are, a formal definition might go like this:

The people formerly known as the audience are those who were on the receiving end of a media system that ran one way, in a broadcasting pattern, with high entry fees and a few firms competing to speak very loudly while the rest of the population listened in isolation from one another—and who today are not in a situation like that *at all*.

- Once they were your printing presses; now that humble device, the blog, has given the press to us. That's why blogs have been called little First Amendment machines.[1] They extend freedom of the press to more actors.
- Once it was *your* radio station, broadcasting on *your* frequency. Now that brilliant invention, podcasting, gives radio to us. And we have found more uses for it than you did.

- Shooting, editing and distributing video once belonged to you, Big Media. Only you could afford to reach a TV audience built in your own image. Now video is coming into the user's hands, and audience-building by former members of the audience is alive and well on the web.
- You were once (exclusively) the editors of the news, choosing what ran on the front page. Now we can edit the news, and our choices send items to our own front pages.[2]
- A highly centralized media system had connected people "up" to big social agencies and centers of power but not "across" to each other. Now the horizontal flow, citizen-to-citizen, is as real and consequential as the vertical one.

The "former audience" is Dan Gillmor's term for us.[3] (He's one of our discoverers and champions.) It refers to the owners and operators of tools that were once exclusively used by media people to capture and hold their attention.

Jeff Jarvis, a former media executive, has written a law about us. "Give the people control of media, they will use it. The corollary: Don't give the people control of media, and you will lose. Whenever citizens can exercise control, they will."[4]

Look, media people. We are still perfectly content to listen to our radios while driving, sit passively in the darkness of the local multiplex, watch TV while motionless and glassy-eyed in bed, and read silently to ourselves as we always have.

Should we attend the theater, we are unlikely to storm the stage for purposes of putting on our own production. We feel there is nothing wrong with old-style, one-way, top-down media consumption. Big Media pleasures will not be denied us. You provide them, we'll consume them, and you can have yourselves a nice little business.

But we're not on your clock anymore.[5] Tom Curley, CEO of the Associated Press, has explained this to his people. "The users are deciding what the point of their engagement will be—what application, what device, what time, what place."[6]

We graduate from wanting media when we want it to wanting it without the filler, to wanting media to be way better than it is, to publishing and broadcasting ourselves when it meets a need or sounds like fun.[7]

Mark Thompson, director general of the BBC, has a term for us: The Active Audience ("who doesn't want to just sit there but to take part, debate, create, communicate, share").[8]

Another of your big shots, Rupert Murdoch, told American newspaper editors about us: "They want control over their media, instead of being controlled by it."[9]

Dave Winer, one of the founders of blogging, said it back in 1994: "Once the users take control, they never give it back."[10]

Online, we tend to form user communities around our favorite spaces. Tom Glocer, head of your Reuters, recognized it: "If you want to attract a community around you, you must offer them something original and of a quality that they can react to and incorporate in their creative work."[11]

We think you're getting the idea, media people. If not from us, then from your own kind describing the same shifts.

The people formerly known as the audience would like to say a special word to those working in the media who, in the intensity of their commercial vision, had taken to calling us "eyeballs," as in: "There is always a new challenge coming along for the eyeballs of our customers" (John Fithian, president of the National Association of Theater Owners in the United States).[12]

Or: "We already own the eyeballs on the television screen. We want to make sure we own the eyeballs on the computer screen" (Ann Kirschner, vice president for programming and media development for the National Football League).[13]

Fithian, Kirschner, and company should know that such fantastic delusions ("we own the eyeballs . . .") were the historical products of a media system that gave its operators an exaggerated sense of their own power and mastery over others. New media is undoing all that, which makes us smile.[14]

You don't own the eyeballs. You don't own the press, which is now divided into pro and amateur zones. You don't control production on the new platform, which isn't one-way. There's a new balance of power between you and us.

The people formerly known as the audience are simply the public made realer, less fictional, more able, less predictable. You should welcome that, media people. But whether you do or not, we want you to know we're here.

NOTES

1. Jay Rosen, "Bloggers vs. Journalists Is Over," lecture at the Blogging, Journalism & Credibility Conference, Harvard Berkman Center, Cambridge, MA, January 21, 2005, available online at http://archive.pressthink.org/2005/01/21/berk_essy.html (accessed January 30, 2011).

2. Digg.com, "Help & FAQ," http://about.digg.com/faq (accessed January 30, 2011).

3. Dan Gillmor, *We the Media* (Sebastopol, CA: O'Reilly, 2004), accessed online at http://www.authorama.com/we-the-media-8.html (accessed January 30, 2011).

4. Jeff Jarvis, "Argue with Me," *BuzzMachine* (blog), November 11, 2004, http://www.buzzmachine.com/archives/2004_11_11.html#008464 (accessed January 30, 2011).

5. Jay Rosen, "Web Users Open the Gates," *Washington Post*, June 19, 2006, http://www.washingtonpost.com/wp-dyn/content/article/2006/06/18/AR2006061800618.html (accessed January 30, 2011).

6. Tom Curley, keynote address at Online News Association Conference, Hollywood, CA, November 12, 2004, available online at http://conference.journalists.org/2004conference/archives/000079.php (accessed January 30, 2011).

7. Leslie Walker, "In the Face of Catastrophe, Sites Offer Helping Hands," *Washington Post*, September 4, 2005, http://www.washingtonpost.com/wp-dyn/content/article/2005/09/03/AR2005090300226.html (accessed January 30, 2011); Freevlog, "Freevlog Tutorial," http://freevlog.org/tutorial/ (no longer online).

8. Mark Thompson, "BBC Creative Future: Mark Thompson's Speech in Full," *Guardian*, April 25, 2006, http://www.guardian.co.uk/media/2006/apr/25/bbc.broadcasting (accessed January 30, 2011).

9. Rupert Murdoch, address at American Society of Newspaper Editors, Washington, DC, April 13, 2005, available online at http://www.newscorp.com/news/news_247.html (accessed January 30, 2011).

10. Dave Winer, "Bill Gates vs. the Internet," DaveNet, October 18, 1994, http://scripting.com/davenet/1994/10/18/billgatesvstheinternet.html (accessed January 30, 2011).

11. Tom Glocer, "The Two-Way Pipe—Facing the Challenge of the New Content Creators," address at Online Publisher's Association Global Forum, London, March 2, 2006, available online at http://tomglocer.com/blogs/sample_weblog/archive/2006/10/11/97.aspx (accessed January 30, 2011).

12. Rick Lyman, "A Partly Cloudy Forecast for Theater Owners," *New York Times*, March 12, 2001, http://www.nytimes.com/2001/03/12/business/media-a-partly-cloudy-forecast-for-theater-owners.html (accessed January 30, 2011).

13. Stuart Elliot, "Adding to the Annual Spectacle, NBC and the N.F.L. Take the Super Bowl to Cyberspace," *New York Times*, December 18, 1995, http://www.nytimes.com/1995/12/18/business/media-business-advertising-adding-annual-spectacle-nbc-nfl-take-super-bowl.html (accessed January 30, 2011).

14. Vin Crosbie, "What Is 'New Media'?," *Rebuilding Media* (blog), Corante, April 27, 2006, http://rebuildingmedia.corante.com/archives/2006/04/27/what_is_new_media.php (accessed January 30, 2011).

2

Sharing Nicely

On Shareable Goods and the Emergence of
Sharing as a Modality of Economic Production

YOCHAI BENKLER

The world's fastest supercomputer and the second-largest commuter transportation system in the United States function on a resource-management model that is not well specified in contemporary economics. Both SETI@home, a distributed computing platform involving the computers of over four million volunteers, and carpooling, which accounts for roughly one-sixth of commuting trips in the United States, rely on social relations and an ethic of sharing, rather than on a price system, to mobilize and allocate resources. Yet they coexist with, and outperform, price-based and government-funded systems that offer substitutable functionality. Neither practice involves public goods, network goods, or any other currently defined category of economically "quirky" goods as either inputs or outputs. PCs and automobiles are privately owned, rival goods, with no obvious demand-side positive returns to scale when used for distributed computing or carpooling.[1] The sharing practices that have evolved around them are not limited to tightly knit communities of repeat players who know each other well and interact across many contexts. They represent instances when social sharing[2] is either utterly impersonal or occurs among loosely affiliated individuals who engage in social practices that involve contributions of the capacity of their private goods in patterns that combine to form large-scale and effective systems for provisioning goods, services, and resources.

This chapter in its original form serves as the introduction to a longer essay that seeks to do two things. The first three parts of the full essay are dedicated to defining a particular class of physical goods as "shareable goods" that systematically have excess capacity and to combining comparative transaction costs and motivation analysis to suggest that this excess capacity may better be harnessed through sharing relations than through secondary markets. These first three parts extend the analysis I have performed elsewhere regarding sharing of creative labor, like free software and other peer production,[3] to the domain of sharing rival material resources in the production of both rival and nonrival goods and services. The characteristics I use to define shareable goods are sufficient to make social sharing and exchange of material goods feasible as a sustainable social practice. But these characteristics are neither absolutely necessary nor sufficient for sharing to occur. Instead, they define conditions under which, when goods with these characteristics are prevalent in the physical-capital base of an economy, it becomes feasible for social sharing and exchange to become more salient in the overall mix of relations of production in that economy. The fourth part of the full essay is then dedicated to explaining how my observation about shareable goods in the domain of physical goods meshes with the literature on social norms, social capital, and common property regimes, as well as with my own work on peer production. I suggest that social sharing and exchange is an underappreciated modality of economic production, alongside price-based and firm-based market production and state-based production,[4] whose salience in the economy is sensitive to technological conditions. The last part explores how the recognition of shareable goods and sharing as a modality of economic production can inform policy.

Shareable goods are goods that are (1) technically "lumpy" and (2) of "midgrained" granularity. By "lumpy" I mean that they provision functionality in discrete packages rather than in a smooth flow. A PC is "lumpy" in that you cannot buy less than some threshold computation capacity, but once you have provisioned it, you have at a minimum a certain amount of computation, whether you need all of it or not. By "granularity" I seek to capture (1) technical characteristics of the functionality-producing goods, (2) the shape of demand for the functionality in a given society, and (3) the amount and distribution of wealth in that society. A particular alignment of these characteristics will make some goods or resources "midgrained," by which I mean that there will be relatively widespread private ownership of these goods and that these privately owned goods will systematically exhibit slack capacity relative to the demand of their owners. A steam engine is large grained and lumpy. An automobile or PC is midgrained in the United States, Europe, and Japan but large grained in Bangladesh. Reallocating the slack capacity of midgrained goods—say, excess computer cycles or car seats going from A to B—becomes the problem whose solution can be provided by secondary markets, sharing, or management. I offer reasons to think that sharing may have lower transaction costs, improve the information on which agents who own these resources act, and provide better motivation for clearing excess capacity. While economists might prefer to call these goods "indivisible" rather than "lumpy," that terminology is less intuitive to noneconomists, and, more importantly, it emphasizes a concern with how best to price capacity that is indivisible and coarsely correlated to demand, glossing over the way in which the granularity affects the pattern of distribution of investment in these goods in society. My own concern is how a particular subclass of indivisible goods—those that are midgrained as I define them here—creates a feasibility space for social sharing rather than requiring a particular model of second-best pricing. While indivisibilities do create challenges for efficient pricing, in my analysis they create conditions in which social relations may provide a more efficient transactional framework to provision and exchange those goods than would the price system.

In particular, both markets and managerial hierarchies require crisp specification of behaviors and outcomes. Crispness is costly. It is not a characteristic of social relations, which rely on fuzzier definitions of actions required and performed, of inputs and outputs, and of obligations. Furthermore, where uncertainty is resistant to cost-effective reduction, the more textured (though less computable) information typical of social relations can provide better reasons for action than can the persistent (though futile) search for crisply computable courses of action represented by pricing or managerial commands. Moreover, social sharing can capture a cluster of social and psychological motivations that are not continuous with, and may even be crowded out by, the presence of money. Pooling large numbers of small-scale contributions to achieve effective functionality—where transaction costs would be high and per-contribution payments must be kept low—is likely to be achieved more efficiently through social sharing systems than through market-based systems. It is precisely this form of sharing—on a large scale, among weakly connected participants, in project-specific or even ad hoc contexts—that we are beginning to see more of on the Internet; that is my central focus.

Social sharing and exchange is becoming a common modality of producing valuable desiderata at the very core of the most advanced economies—in information, culture, education, computation, and communications sectors. Free software, distributed computing, ad hoc mesh wireless networks, and other forms of peer production offer clear examples of such large-scale, measurably effective sharing practices. I suggest that the highly distributed capital structure[5] of contemporary communications and computation systems is largely responsible for the increased salience of social sharing as a modality of economic production in those environments. By lowering the capital costs required for effective individual action, these technologies have allowed various provisioning problems to be structured in forms amenable to decentralized production based on social relations, rather than through markets or hierarchies.

My claim is not, of course, that we live in a unique moment of humanistic sharing. It is, rather, that our own moment in history suggests a more general observation: that the technological state of a society, particularly the extent to which individual agents can engage in efficacious production activities with material resources under their individual control, affects the opportunities for, and hence the comparative prevalence and salience of, social, market (both price based and managerial), and state production modalities. The capital cost of effective economic action in the industrial economy shunted sharing to its peripheries—to households in the advanced economies and to the global economic peripheries that have been the subject of the anthropology of gift or common property regime literatures. The emerging restructuring of capital investment in digital networks—in particular, the phenomenon of user-capitalized computation and communications capabilities—is at least partly reversing that effect. Technology does not determine the level of sharing. But it does set threshold constraints on the effective domain of sharing as a modality of economic production. Within the domain of the feasible, the actual level of sharing practices will be culturally driven and cross-culturally diverse.

The loose category of "social sharing" that I employ here covers a broad range of social phenomena. Carpooling can largely, though not exclusively, be explained in terms of instrumental exchange. Distributed computing projects look like cases of mass altruism among strangers. What justifies bringing such diverse practices under one umbrella term is that they are instances of productive cooperation that are based neither on the price system nor on managerial commands. Given the focus of current policy debates on improving the institutional conditions for market-based production of various desiderata, even at the expense of substitutable social practices, it becomes important to recognize the presence, sustainability, and relative efficiency of even a loosely defined broad alternative.

Once we come to accept the economic significance of this cluster of social practices, we will have to turn to mapping internal variations and understanding their workings and relationships to each other as economic phenomena. Even from the relatively limited review I offer here, it is clear that social production covers different forms of motivation and organization. There are instrumental and noninstrumental motivations. Instrumental motivations may, in turn, be material—the primary focus of the social norms, social capital, and common property regimes literatures—or social-relational—that is, focused on the production of relations of power within a society, a focus that has been central to the literature on the gift.[6] The gift literature, however, has meshed the instrumental production of social relations with the noninstrumental, mystical, or religious nature of gift giving. This noninstrumental form of motivation—though from a very nonmystical perspective—has also been the focus of the psychological literature on motivation crowding out. Understanding how the motivational and organizational forms of this modality operate will be important whether one seeks to engage in institutional design that takes into consideration the presence of social production as a potential source of welfare, or whether one is concerned with building a business model that harnesses the power of social production—be it for profit, like IBM's relationship with the GNU/Linux development community, or nonprofit, like NASA's relationship with the contributors to SETI@home. For now, however, all we need is to recognize that a broad set of social practices can be sustainable and efficient substitutes for markets, firms, and bureaucracies.

The policy implications of recognizing the relative importance of sharing-based solutions to economic problems are significant. As we manage the transition to a networked information economy, we face diverse questions regarding how best to regulate different areas of this economy: How should we regulate wireless communications systems? How should we regulate music distribution? Should we regulate the design of computers to assure that they are not used to access cultural products without authorization? Usually these policy debates, to the extent they are concerned with efficiency and welfare, assume that the role of policy is to optimize the institutional conditions of attaching prices to marginal actions so as to permit the price system to be the dominant modality of production. This may or may not be wise, but whether it is or is not can only be examined thoughtfully once we have a full picture of the alternatives. If we believe that there are only two alternatives—the price system and some form of hierarchy—we have a very different policy-choice space than if we believe that there is a third modality of production open to us, social production, that may under certain conditions be more efficient.

Radio and communications technologies have reached a point where our policy focus is changing. The Federal Communications Commission is creating an institutional framework to facilitate markets in shareable goods—unlicensed wireless devices and systems—that coproduce wireless transport capacity. Originally, using such devices was prohibited in order to make the world safe for large-grained systems, like broadcast towers or cellular networks, that deliver wireless services on the basis of either the terms of a government license or markets in "spectrum." The music-copyright debate around peer-to-peer file sharing can also be explained in terms of the change in the type of goods used in distribution, from large-scale capital goods to midgrained shareable goods. Understood in these terms, solving this problem by squelching peer-to-peer sharing becomes implausible, both descriptively and prescriptively. Yet current policy analysis largely disregards how institutional changes will affect existing or emerging practices of sharing that may compete with, or substitute for, market-based production. If indeed we live in an economic system made up of price-based, hierarchy-based, and sharing-based modalities of production, if it is true that optimizing our institutional system for price-based production undermines productivity in the sharing modality, and if it is true that our communications, computation, and information sectors are undergoing technological changes that improve the efficiency of social sharing, then we are making systematically mistaken policy choices not on the peripheries of our economies and societies but at their very engines.

NOTES

This chapter was first published as the introduction to *Sharing Nicely: On Shareable Goods and the Emergence of Sharing as a Modality of Economic Production*, Yale Law Journal 114 (2004): 273–358, available at http://www.benkler.org/SharingNicely.html (accessed July 20, 2010). This work is licensed under the Creative Commons Attribution license.
I owe thanks to Bruce Ackerman, Ian Ayres, Bob Ellickson, Dan Kahan, Al Klevorick, Michael Levine, Orly Lobel, Daniel Markovits, Richard McAdams, Robert Post, Judith Resnik, Carol Rose, Susan Rose-Ackerman, Jed Rubenfeld, Alan Schwartz, Henry Smith, and Jim Whitman, who read prior versions of this essay and provided helpful comments.

    1. Computers as communications devices do have demand-side returns to scale, or network externalities. But as processing units, the paramount value of personal computers is the intrinsic value of their computation speed and memory, not the network externalities they enable owners to capture. SETI@home and other distributed computing projects harness these intrinsic-value aspects of personal computers rather than their capacities as communication devices.

    2. "Sharing" is an uncommon usage in the economics literature, though it is common in some of the anthropology literature. I choose it because it is broader in its application than other, more common, but narrower terms for associated phenomena—most importantly, "reciprocity" or "gift." I hesitate to use "reciprocity" because of its focus on more or less directly responsive reciprocated reward and punishment as a mechanism to sustain cooperation in the teeth of the standard assumptions about collective action. See Dan M. Kahan, The Logic of Reciprocity: Trust, Collective Action, and Law (Yale Law Sch., Pub.

Law Research Paper No. 31, and Yale Program for Studies in Law, Econ. & Pub. Policy, Research Paper No. 281, 2002), available at http://ssrn.com/abstract=361400. Given the presence of purely redistributive practices like tolerated theft and demand sharing in the anthropology literature, evidence of nonreciprocal prosocial behavior—see Bruno S. Frey & Stephan Meier, Pro-social Behavior, Reciprocity, or Both? (Inst. for Empirical Research in Econ., Univ. of Zurich, Working Paper No. 107, 2002)—and more generally our intuitive experiences of acts of humanity toward others whom we will never encounter again, I suspect that some forms of redistribution are nonreciprocal except in the broadest sense of the reciprocation of living in a humane society. Mutual aid and cooperation without the possibility of reciprocal exchange likely exists, the "Lion and the Mouse" fable notwithstanding. See, e.g., James Woodburn, *"Sharing Is Not a Form of Exchange": An Analysis of Property-Sharing in Immediate-Return Hunter-Gatherer Societies*, in Property Relations: Renewing the Anthropological Tradition 48 (C. M. Hann ed., Cambridge Univ. Press 1998). I hesitate to use the term "gift exchange" because the highly developed gift literature (see note 6), has focused very heavily on the production and reproduction of social relations through the exchange and circulation of things. As will soon become clear, I am concerned with the production of things and actions/services valued materially, through nonmarket mechanisms of social sharing. "Sharing," then, offers a less freighted name for evaluating mechanisms of social-relations-based economic production.

3. Yochai Benkler, *Coase's Penguin, or, Linux and the Nature of the Firm*, 112 Yale L.J. 369 (2002).

4. In this, my position tracks the tripartite mapping of the universe of organizational forms that resulted from the work on nonprofits in the early 1980s. See Henry B. Hansmann, *The Role of Nonprofit Enterprise*, 89 Yale L.J. 835 (1980); see also Burton A. Weisbrod, The Nonprofit Economy 1–15 (1988); Susan Rose-Ackerman, *Introduction*, in The Economics of Nonprofit Institutions: Studies in Structure and Policy 3, 3–17 (Susan Rose-Ackerman ed., 1986). Unlike the nonprofit literature, my focus is not within the boundaries of firms—whether for profit or nonprofit—but on sharing among individuals in informal associations more resembling markets in the price-based economy than firms.

5. This is different from capital intensity. The activity may be capital intensive—like distributed computing—when you consider the total capital cost of the computers, network connections, and so on required for an effective unit of production, in comparison to the cost of labor involved. The capital is, however, highly distributed, which is the key characteristic that enables individual agency in the production processes.

6. The anthropological literature on sharing and the gift has been vast, starting with Bronislaw Malinowski, Argonauts of the Western Pacific (1922), and Marcel Mauss, The Gift: Forms and Functions of Exchange in Archaic Societies (Ian Cunnison trans., Free Press 1954) (1925). A combination of a broad intellectual history and a major contemporary contribution to this line is Maurice Godelier, The Enigma of the Gift (Nora Scott trans., Univ. of Chi. Press 1999) (1996). See also James G. Carrier, *Property and Social Relations in Melanesian Anthropology*, in Property Relations, *supra* note 2, at 85, 85–97 (providing brief intellectual history of the literature); C. M. Hann, *Introduction: The Embeddedness of Property*, in Property Relations, *supra* note 2, at 1, 23–34 (same). As an alternative antithesis to the competition-of-all-against-all model of human society, an early manifestation of a focus on mutual aid and cooperation as a possible path for contemporary societies was Petr Kropotkin, Mutual Aid: A Factor of Evolution (Extending Horizons Books 1955) (1902).

3

Open Source as Culture/
Culture as Open Source

SIVA VAIDHYANATHAN

The "open source" way of doing things is all the rage. Companies as powerful and established as IBM boast of using Linux operating systems in its servers. Publications as conservative as *The Economist* have pronounced open-source methods "successful" and have pondered their applicability to areas of research and development as different from software as pharmaceutical research.[1]

It is striking that we have to employ phrases like "open source" and "free software" at all.[2] They are significant, powerful phrases simply because they represent an insurgent model of commercial activity and information policy. They challenge the entrenched status quo: the proprietary model of cultural and technological production.

But this has only recently been the case. The "open source" way is closer to how human creativity has always worked. Open source used to be the default way of doing things. The rapid adoption of proprietary information has been so intense and influential since the 1980s that we hardly remember another way or another time. However, through most of human history all information technologies and almost all technologies were "open source." And we have done pretty well as a species with tools and habits unencumbered by high restrictions on sharing, copying, customizing, and improving.

We have become so inured to the proprietary model, so dazzled and intimidated by its cultural and political power, that any commonsense challenge to its assumptions and tenets seems radical, idealistic, or dangerous. But in recent years the practical advantages of the "open source" model of creativity and commerce have become clear. The resulting clamor about the advantages and threats of open-source models have revealed serious faults in the chief regulatory system that governs global flows of culture and information: copyright.

The Rise of Proprietarianism

Copyright gets stretched way out of shape to accommodate proprietary software. Copyright was originally designed to protect books, charts, and maps. Later, courts and legislatures expanded to include recorded music, film, video, translations, public performance, and finally all media that now exist or have yet to be created. Software is special, though. It's not just expression. It is functional. It's not just information. It's action. In some ways, the inclusion of software among the copyrightable forms of creativity has complicated and challenged the intellectual-property tradition. Copyright and proprietary software have metastasized synergistically.

The proprietary model of software production dates to sometime in the 1970s, when mainframe software vendors like AT&T and Digital started asserting control over their source code, thus limiting what computer scientists could do to customize their tools. This was an insult to and offense against these scientists who were acclimated to the academic and scientific ideologies that privilege openness and nonmonetary reward systems. In a much more precise sense we can date the spark of the conflagration between the then-insurgent proprietary model and the then-dominant hacker culture (open source, although they didn't have a name for it then) to Bill Gates's 1976 open letter to the small but growing community of personal-computer hackers warning them that his new company, then spelled "Micro-Soft," would aggressively assert its intellectual-property claims against those who would trade tapes that carry the company's software. Since that date, despite frequently exploiting the gaps and safety valves of copyright protection on their rise to the heights of wealth and power, Microsoft and Gates have worked in correlation if not coordination with the steady valorization of intellectual-property rights as the chief locus of cultural and industrial policy in the world.[3]

According to the proprietary ideology, innovation would not occur without a strong incentive system for the innovator to exploit for commercial gain. "Fencing off" innovations becomes essential for firms and actors to establish markets and bargain away rights. Because innovation so often concerns the ephemeral, trade in the innovation requires excluding others from using, exploiting, or copying data, designs, or algorithms. The Clinton, Bush, and Blair administrations in the United States and United Kingdom embraced the proprietary model as the key to thriving through the deindustrialization of the developed world, thus locking in the advantages that educated, wired nation-states have over those that have been held in technological and economic bondage for centuries. Proprietary models of innovation policy and market relations can be powerful: witness the remarkable successes and wealth of the global pharmaceutical industry or, for that matter, of Microsoft. But they can be just as powerful with limitations that allow for communal creation, revision, criticism, and adaptability: witness the culture of custom cars or the World Wide Web.[4]

In fact, as economist Richard Adkisson argues, the veneration of muscular intellectual-property rights as the foundation of innovation and creativity above all other forms has generated an unhealthy cultural and social condition, one which can generate suboptimal levels of investment, asset allocation, and policy choices. Adkisson indicts the widespread belief that intellectual-property rights are the best (perhaps only) of all possible arrangements for innovation, by alerting us to the "ceremonial status" these rights have assumed. "Ceremonial encapsulation occurs when ceremonial values are allowed to alter or otherwise limit the application of technologies instrumental in the process of social problem solving," Adkisson writes. Specifically, Adkisson warns that blind faith in high levels of intellectual-property protection is of the "future-binding type," in which technology and mythology act synergistically to legitimize elite control over technologies or other innovative or creative processes.[5]

The Return of the Jedi

Richard Stallman took a stand against the proprietary model long before the rest of us even realized its power and trajectory. A computer scientist working in the 1970s and 1980s for the artificial-intelligence project at MIT, Stallman grew frustrated that computer companies were denying him and other hackers access to their source code. Stallman found he was not allowed to improve the software and devices that he had to work with, even when they did not work very well. More important, Stallman grew alarmed that he was becoming contractually bound to be unkind and selfish. The user agreements that accompanied proprietary software forbade him from sharing his tools and techniques with others. As a scientist, he was offended that openness was being criminalized. As a citizen, he was a concerned that freedoms of speech and creativity were being constricted. As a problem solver, he set out to establish the Free Software Foundation to prove that good tools and technologies could emerge from a community of concerned creators. Leveraging the communicative power of technology newsletters and the postal system, Stallman sold tapes with his free (as in liberated) software on them.

By the time enough of his constituency had connected themselves through the Internet, he started coordinating projects and conversations among a diverse and distributed set of programmers.[6]

During the late 1990s a growing team of hackers struggled to build the holy grail of free software: an operating-system kernel that would allow an array of programs to work in coordination. The group, led by Linus Torvalds, created a system that became known as Linux. It has since become the chief threat to the ubiquity and dominance of Microsoft.[7]

While Linux and the GNU (free software) project have garnered the most attention in accounts of open-source development, the protocols and programs that enable and empower e-mail, the World Wide Web, IRC (Internet Relay Chat), and just about every other activity on the Internet all emerged from community-based project teams, often ad hoc and amateur. The resulting protocols are elegant, efficient, effective, and under constant revision. And they have empowered both the growth of the proprietary model and the open-source model of cultural production to reach expansive new markets and audiences.[8]

Each of these projects illuminates what Yochai Benkler calls "peer production." Benkler writes,

> The emergence of free software as a substantial force in the software development world poses a puzzle for [Ronald Coase's] organization theory. Free software projects do not rely either on markets or on managerial hierarchies to organize production. Programmers do not generally participate in a project because someone who is their boss instructed them, though some do. They do not generally participate in a project because someone offers them a price, though some participants do focus on long-term appropriation through money-oriented activities, like consulting or service contracts. But the critical mass of participation in projects cannot be explained by the direct presence of a command, a price, or even a future monetary return, particularly in the all-important microlevel decisions regarding selection of projects to which participants contribute. In other words, programmers participate in free software projects without following the normal signals generated by market-based, firm-based, or hybrid models.[9]

Economists assumed for decades that firms emerged to lower or eliminate transaction costs and coordination problems. But as it turns out, fast, efficient, and dependable communication, guided by protocols both social and digital (a process Benkler calls "integration"), can generate brilliant and powerful tools and expressions. Benkler concludes,

The strength of peer production is in matching human capital to information inputs to produce new information goods. Strong intellectual property rights inefficiently shrink the universe of existing information inputs that can be subjected to this process. Instead, owned inputs will be limited to human capital with which the owner of the input has a contractual—usually employment—relationship. Moreover, the entire universe of peer-produced information gains no benefit from strong intellectual property rights. Since the core of commons-based peer production entails provisioning without direct appropriation and since indirect appropriation—intrinsic or extrinsic—does not rely on control of the information but on its widest possible availability, intellectual property offers no gain, only loss, to peer production. While it is true that free software currently uses copyright-based licensing to prevent certain kinds of defection from peer production processes, that strategy is needed only as a form of institutional jujitsu to defend from intellectual property. A complete absence of property in the software domain would be at least as congenial to free software development as the condition where property exists, but copyright permits free software projects to use licensing to defend themselves from defection. The same protection from defection might be provided by other means as well, such as creating simple public mechanisms for contributing one's work in a way that makes it unsusceptible to downstream appropriation—a conservancy of sorts. Regulators concerned with fostering innovation may better direct their efforts toward providing the institutional tools that would help thousands of people to collaborate without appropriating their joint product, making the information they produce freely available rather than spending their efforts to increase the scope and sophistication of the mechanisms for private appropriation of this public good as they now do.[10]

Benkler's prescriptions seem like predictions. In recent years the governments of nation-states as diverse as South Africa, Brazil, and the People's Republic of China have adopted policies that would encourage the dissemination of open-source software.

More significantly, the open-source model has moved far beyond software. Musician and composer Gilberto Gil, the culture minister of Brazil, has released several albums under a Creative Commons license. Such licenses (under which this chapter lies as well) are modeled off of the GNU General Public License, which locks the content open. It requires all users of the copyrighted material to conform to terms that encourage sharing and building.[11]

Other significant extrasoftware projects based on the open-source model include Wikipedia, a remarkable compilation of fact and analysis written and reviewed by a committed team of peers placed around the world. And the scientific spheres have rediscovered their commitment to openness through the movement to establish and maintain open-access journals, thus evading the proprietary traps (and expenses) of large commercial journal publishers.[12] By 2004 citizen-based journalism, often known as "open-source journalism," had grown in importance and established itself as an important and essential element of the global information ecosystem.[13] Such experiments are sure to proliferate in response to the failures (market and otherwise) of proprietary media forms.[14]

How Open Source Changes Copyright

Copyright is a limited monopoly, granted by the state, meant to foster creativity by generating a system of presumed incentives. The copyright holder must have enough faith in the system to justify his or her investment. And the copyright holder's rights to exclude are limited by some public values such as education and criticism. This is the standard understanding of copyright law's role and scope. But while acknowledging the interests of the public, it omits the voice of the public itself. In other words, the system cannot thrive if the public considers it to be captured, corrupted, irrelevant, or absurd.[15]

The rise and success of open-source models fosters a general understanding that copyright is not a single right bestowed on a brilliant individual author but is instead a "bundle" of rights that a copyright holder (individual, corporation, organization, or foundation) may license. Most important, these experiments and projects show that "all rights reserved" need not be the default state of copyright protection. For many people, "some rights reserved" serves the interests of creators better than the absolutist proprietary model does.

As the rhetoric of open source and the politics of traditional knowledge and culture emerge in starker relief within the topography of copyright and cultural policy debates, their themes tend to converge. As anthropologist Vladimir Hafstein describes the tension between copyright systems as dictated by the industrialized world and modes of communal cultural production that are best (albeit not exclusively) demonstrated in developing nations, he uses terms that could just as easily be applied to technological peer production. "Creativity as a social process is the common denominator of these concepts and approaches," Hafstein writes. "From each of these perspectives, the act of creation is a social act. From the point of view of intertextuality, for example, works of literature are just as much a product of society or of discourse as they are of an individual author or, for that matter, reader." Traditional cultural knowledge, communally composed and lacking distinct marks of individual authorship, is "a node in a network of relations: not an isolated original, but a reproduction, a copy," Hafstein explains.[16] Nothing about Hafstein's descriptions of the politics of traditional knowledge offers a resolution to that particular source of friction in global intellectual-property battles. But the converging rhetorics reveal the extent to which innovation and creativity often (perhaps most often) sit outside the assumptions of incentives and protectionism on which high levels of corporate copyright protection rest.

The open-source model of peer production, sharing, revision, and peer review has distilled and labeled the most successful creative habits into a political movement. This distillation has had costs and benefits. It has been difficult to court mainstream acceptance for such a tangle of seemingly technical ideas when its chief advocates have been hackers and academics. Neither class has much power or influence in the modern global economy or among centers of policy decision-making. On the other hand, the brilliant success of overtly labeled open-source experiments, coupled with the horror stories of attempts to protect the proprietary model, has added common sense to the toolbox of these advocates.

NOTES

This chapter was originally published in *Open Source Annual 2005* (Berlin: Technische Universität). This work is licensed under the Creative Commons Attribution-ShareAlike license.

1. "An Open-Source Shot in the Arm?," *Economist*, 12 June 2004. Also see Steve Weber, *The Success of Open Source* (Cambridge: Harvard University Press, 2004).

2. Throughout this essay and in all of my work I intentionally conflate these two terms while being fully aware of the political distinction that Richard Stallman emphasizes in his defense of "free software." Stallman's point—that "open source" invites an emphasis on convenience and utility rather than freedom and community—was important to make in the 1990s. He lost the battle to control the terms, just as he has had to concede the rhetorical convenience and ubiquity of "LINUX" instead of the more accurate "GNU/LINUX." I am confident that anyone who peers into the history or politics of the open-source movement will encounter Stallman's persuasive case for freedom and the GNU project's central contribution to the growth of the operating system we now call LINUX. See Richard Stallman, "The GNU Operating System and the Free Software Movement," in *Open Sources: Voices of the Open Source Revolution*, ed. Chris DiBona, Sam Ockman, and Mark Stone (Sebastopol, CA: O'Reilly, 1999).

3. Siva Vaidhyanathan, *Copyrights and Copywrongs: The Rise of Intellectual Property and How It Threatens Creativity* (New York: NYU Press, 2001). Also see Peter Wayner, *Free for All: How Linux and the Free Software Movement Undercut the High-Tech Titans* (New York: HarperBusiness, 2000); Eric S. Raymond, "A Brief History of Hackerdom," in *Open Sources: Voices of the Open Source Revolution*, ed. Chris DiBona, Sam Ockman, and Mark Stone (Sebastopol, CA: O'Reilly, 1999).

4. Siva Vaidhyanathan, *The Anarchist in the Library: How the Clash between Freedom and Control Is Hacking the Real World and Crashing the System* (New York: Basic Books, 2004). Also see Lawrence Lessig, *The Future of Ideas: The Fate of the Commons in a Connected World* (New York: Random House, 2001); Lawrence Lessig, *Free Culture: How Big Media Uses Technology and the Law to Lock Down Culture and Control Creativity* (New York: Penguin, 2004).

5. Richard Adkisson, "Ceremonialism, Intellectual Property Rights, and Innovation Activity," *Journal of Economic Issues* 38, no. 2 (2004): 460.

6. Stallman, "The GNU Operating System and the Free Software Movement." Also see Sam Williams, *Free as in Freedom: Richard Stallman's Crusade for Free Software* (Sebastopol, CA: O'Reilly, 2002).

7. Linus Torvalds et al., *Revolution OS: Hackers, Programmers & Rebels UNITE!* (Los Angeles: Wonderview Productions; distributed by Seventh Art Releasing, 2003), video recording. Also see Eric S. Raymond, *The Cathedral and the Bazaar: Musings on Linux and Open Source by an Accidental Revolutionary*, rev. ed. (Sebastopol, CA: O'Reilly, 2001).

8. Scott Bradner, "The Internet Engineering Task Force," in *Open Sources: Voices from the Open Source Revolution*, ed. Chris DiBona, Sam Ockman, and Mark Stone (Sebastopol, CA: O'Reilly, 1999). Also see Alexander R. Galloway, *Protocol: How Control Exists after Decentralization* (Cambridge: MIT Press, 2004).

9. Yochai Benkler, "Coase's Penguin, or, Linux and the Nature of the Firm," *Yale Law Journal* 112, no. 3 (2002): 372–373.

10. Ibid., 446.

11. Julian Dibell, "We Pledge Allegiance to the Penguin," *Wired*, November 2004, available online at http://www.wired.com/wired/archive/12.11/linux.html.

12. Jocelyn Kaiser, "Zerhouni Plans a Nudge toward Open Access," *Science*, 3 September 2004.

13. Jay Rosen, "Top Ten Ideas of '04: Open Source Journalism, or 'My Readers Know More Than I Do,'" *PressThink* (blog), 28 December 2004, http://journalism.nyu.edu/pubzone/weblogs/pressthink/2004/12/28/tptn04_opsc.html. Also see Dan Gillmor, *We the Media: Grassroots Journalism by the People, for the People* (Sebastopol, CA: O'Reilly, 2004).

14. Christopher M. Kelty, "Culture's Open Sources: Software, Copyright, and Cultural Critique," *Anthropological Quarterly* 77, no. 3 (2004).

15. Vaidhyanathan, *The Anarchist in the Library*.

16. Vladimir Hafstein, "The Politics of Origins: Collective Creation Revisited," *Journal of American Folklore* 117 (2004): 307, 303. Also see Pekka Himanen, *The Hacker Ethic and the Spirit of the Information Age* (New York: Random House, 2001).

What Is Web 2.0?

Design Patterns and Business Models
for the Next Generation of Software

TIM O'REILLY

The bursting of the dot-com bubble in the fall of 2001 marked a turning point for the web. Many people concluded that the web was over-hyped, when in fact bubbles and consequent shakeouts appear to be a common feature of all technological revolutions.[1] Shakeouts typically mark the point at which an ascendant technology is ready to take its place at center stage. The pretenders are given the bum's rush, the real success stories show their strength, and there begins to be an understanding of what separates one from the other.

The concept of "Web 2.0" began with a conference brainstorming session between O'Reilly Media and MediaLive International. Dale Dougherty, web pioneer and O'Reilly vice president, noted that far from having "crashed," the web was more important than ever, with exciting new applications and sites popping up with surprising regularity. What's more, the companies that had survived the collapse seemed to have some things in common. Could it be that the dot-com collapse marked some kind of turning point for the web, such that a call to action such as "Web 2.0" might make sense? We agreed that it did, and so the Web 2.0 Conference was born.[2]

In the year and a half since, the term "Web 2.0" has clearly taken hold, with more than 9.5 million citations in Google. But there's still a huge amount of disagreement about just what "Web 2.0" means,[3] with some people decrying it as a meaningless marketing buzzword and others accepting it as the new conventional wisdom.

This essay is an attempt to clarify just what we mean by "Web 2.0." In our initial brainstorming, we formulated our sense of Web 2.0 by example (see table 4.1). The list went on and on. But what was it that made us identify one application or approach as "Web 1.0" and another as "Web 2.0"? (The question is particularly urgent because the Web 2.0 meme has become so

TABLE 4.1

Web 1.0	Web 2.0
DoubleClick	Google AdSense
Ofoto	Flickr
Akamai	BitTorrent
mp3.com	Napster
Britannica Online	Wikipedia
personal websites	blogging
evite	upcoming.org and EVDB
domain name speculation	search engine optimization
page views	cost per click
screen scraping	web services
publishing	participation
content management systems	wikis
directories (taxonomy)	tagging ("folksonomy")
stickiness	syndication

widespread that companies are now pasting it on as a marketing buzzword, with no real understanding of just what it means. The question is particularly difficult because many of those buzzword-addicted start-ups are definitely *not* Web 2.0, while some of the applications we identified as Web 2.0, like Napster and BitTorrent, are not even properly web applications!) We began trying to tease out the principles that are demonstrated in one way or another by the success stories of Web 1.0 and by the most interesting of the new applications.

1. The Web as Platform

Like many important concepts, Web 2.0 doesn't have a hard boundary but, rather, a gravitational core. You can visualize Web 2.0 as a set of principles and practices that tie together a veritable solar system of sites that demonstrate some or all of those principles, at a varying distance from that core. Figure 4.1 shows a "meme map" of Web 2.0 that was developed at a brainstorming session during FOO Camp, a conference at O'Reilly Media. It's very much a work in progress, but it shows the many ideas that radiate out from the Web 2.0 core.

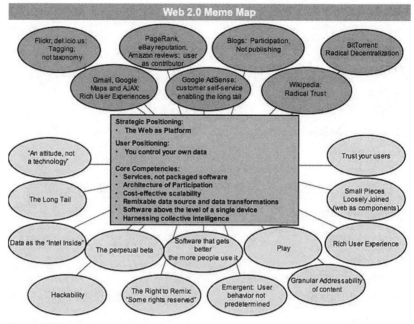

Fig. 4.1. Web 2.0 meme map

For example, at the first Web 2.0 conference, in October 2004, John Battelle and I listed a preliminary set of principles in our opening talk. The first of those principles was "the web as platform." Yet that was also a rallying cry of Web 1.0 darling Netscape, which went down in flames after a heated battle with Microsoft. What's more, two of our initial Web 1.0 exemplars, Double-Click and Akamai, were both pioneers in treating the web as a platform. People don't often think of ad serving as "web services," but in fact, it was the first widely deployed web service and the first widely deployed "mashup" (to use another term that has gained currency of late). Every banner ad is served as a seamless cooperation between two websites, delivering an integrated page to a reader on yet another computer. Akamai also treats the network as the platform, and at a deeper level of the stack, building a transparent caching and content-delivery network that eases bandwidth congestion.

Nonetheless, these pioneers provided useful contrasts because later entrants have taken their solution to the same problem even further, understanding something deeper about the nature of the new platform. Both DoubleClick and Akamai were Web 2.0 pioneers, yet we can also see how it's possible to realize more of the possibilities by embracing additional Web 2.0 design patterns.

Let's drill down for a moment into each of these three cases, teasing out some of the essential elements of difference.

Netscape vs. Google

If Netscape was the standard bearer for Web 1.0, Google is most certainly the standard bearer for Web 2.0, if only because their respective initial public offerings were defining events for each era. So let's start with a comparison of these two companies and their positioning.

Netscape framed "the web as platform" in terms of the old software paradigm: its flagship product was the web browser, a desktop application, and its strategy was to use its dominance in the browser market to establish a market for high-priced server products. Control over standards for displaying content and applications in the browser would, in theory, give Netscape the kind of market power enjoyed by Microsoft in the PC market. Much like the "horseless carriage" framed the automobile as an extension of the familiar, Netscape promoted a "webtop" to replace the desktop and planned to populate that webtop with information updates and applets pushed to the webtop by information providers who would purchase Netscape servers.

In the end, both web browsers and web servers turned out to be commodities, and value moved "up the stack" to services delivered over the web platform.

Google, by contrast, began its life as a native web application, never sold or packaged but delivered as a service, with customers paying, directly or indirectly, for the use of that service. None of the trappings of the old software industry is present. No scheduled software releases, just continuous improvement. No licensing or sale, just usage. No porting to different platforms so that customers can run the software on their own equipment, just a massively scalable collection of commodity PCs running open-source operating systems plus homegrown applications and utilities that no one outside the company ever gets to see.

At bottom, Google requires a competency that Netscape never needed: database management. Google isn't just a collection of software tools; it's a specialized database. Without the data, the tools are useless; without the software, the data is unmanageable.

DoubleClick vs. Overture and AdSense

Like Google, DoubleClick is a true child of the Internet era. It harnesses software as a service, has a core competency in data management, and, as noted earlier, was a pioneer in web services long before web services even had a name. However, DoubleClick was ultimately limited by its business model. It bought into the '90s notion that the web was about publishing, not participation; that advertisers, not consumers, ought to call the shots; that size mattered; and that the Internet was increasingly being dominated by the top websites as measured by MediaMetrix and other web ad-scoring companies.

As a result, DoubleClick proudly cites on its website "over 2000 successful implementations" of its software. Yahoo! Search Marketing (formerly Overture) and Google AdSense, by contrast, already serve hundreds of thousands of advertisers apiece.

Overture's and Google's success came from an understanding of what Chris Anderson refers to as "the long tail," the collective power of the small sites that make up the bulk of the web's content (see chapter 10 in this volume). DoubleClick's offerings require a formal sales contract, limiting its market to the few thousand largest websites. Overture and Google figured out how to enable ad placement on virtually any web page. What's more, they eschewed publisher/ad-agency-friendly advertising formats such as banner ads and popups in favor of minimally intrusive, context-sensitive, consumer-friendly text advertising.

The Web 2.0 lesson: *leverage customer self-service and algorithmic data management to reach out to the entire web, to the edges and not just the center, to the long tail and not just the head.*

Not surprisingly, other Web 2.0 success stories demonstrate this same behavior. eBay enables occasional transactions of only a few dollars between single individuals, acting as an automated intermediary. Napster (though shut down for legal reasons) built its network not by building a centralized song database but by architecting a system in such a way that every downloader also became a server and thus grew the network.

Akamai vs. BitTorrent

Like DoubleClick, Akamai is optimized to do business with the head, not the tail, with the center, not the edges. While it serves the benefit of the individuals at the edge of the web by smoothing their access to the high-demand sites at the center, it collects its revenue from those central sites.

BitTorrent, like other pioneers in the peer-to-peer (P2P) movement, takes a radical approach to Internet decentralization. Every client is also a server; files are broken up into fragments that can be served from multiple locations, transparently harnessing the network of downloaders to provide both band-width and data to other users. The more popular the file, in fact, the faster it can be served, as there are more users providing bandwidth and fragments of the complete file.

BitTorrent thus demonstrates a key Web 2.0 principle: *the service auto-matically gets better the more people use it.* While Akamai must add servers to improve service, every BitTorrent consumer brings his or her own resources to the party. There's an implicit "architecture of participation," a built-in ethic of cooperation, in which the service acts primarily as an intelligent broker, connecting the edges to each other and harnessing the power of the users themselves.

2. Harnessing Collective Intelligence

The central principle behind the success of the giants born in the Web 1.0 era who have survived to lead the Web 2.0 era appears to be this, that they have embraced the power of the web to harness collective intelligence:

Hyperlinking is the foundation of the web. As users add new content, and new sites, it is bound in to the structure of the web by other users discover-ing the content and linking to it. Much as synapses form in the brain, with associations becoming stronger through repetition or intensity, the web of connections grows organically as an output of the collective activity of all web users.

Yahoo!, the first great Internet success story, was born as a catalog, or directory of links, an aggregation of the best work of thousands and then millions of web users. While Yahoo! has since moved into the business of creating many types of content, its role as a portal to the collective work of the net's users remains the core of its value.

Google's breakthrough in search, which quickly made it the undisputed search-market leader, was PageRank, a method of using the link structure of the web rather than just the characteristics of documents to provide better search results.

eBay's product is the collective activity of all its users; like the web itself, eBay grows organically in response to user activity, and the company's role is as an enabler of a context in which that user activity can happen. What's more, eBay's competitive advantage comes almost entirely from the critical mass of buyers and sellers, which makes any new entrant offering similar services significantly less attractive.

Amazon sells the same products as competitors such as Barnesandno-ble.com, and it receives the same product descriptions, cover images, and editorial content from its vendors. But Amazon has made a science of user engagement. It has an order of magnitude more user reviews, invitations to participate in varied ways on virtually every page—and, even more impor-tant, it uses user activity to produce better search results. While a Barne-sandnoble.com search is likely to lead with the company's own products, or sponsored results, Amazon always leads with "most popular," a real-time computation based not only on sales but on other factors that Amazon insid-ers call the "flow" around products. With an order of magnitude more user participation, it's no surprise that Amazon's sales also outpace competitors'.

Now, innovative companies that pick up on this insight and perhaps extend it even further are making their mark on the web:

Wikipedia, an online encyclopedia based on the unlikely notion that an entry can be added by any web user and edited by any other, is a radical experiment in trust, applying Eric Raymond's dictum (originally coined in the context of open-source software) that "with enough eyeballs, all bugs are shallow" to content creation.[4] Wikipedia is already in the top one hun-dred websites, and many people think it will be in the top ten before long. This is a profound change in the dynamics of content creation!

Sites like del.icio.us and Flickr, two companies that have received a great deal of attention of late, have pioneered a concept that some people call "folksonomy" (in contrast to taxonomy), a style of collaborative categoriza-tion of sites using freely chosen keywords, often referred to as tags.[5] Tagging allows for the kind of multiple, overlapping associations that the brain itself uses, rather than rigid categories. In the canonical example, a Flickr photo of a puppy might be tagged both "puppy" and "cute"—allowing for retrieval along natural axes-generated user activity.

Collaborative spam-filtering products like Cloudmark aggregate the indi-vidual decisions of e-mail users about what is and is not spam, outperform-ing systems that rely on analysis of the messages themselves.

It is a truism that the greatest Internet success stories don't advertise their products. Their adoption is driven by "viral marketing"—that is, recommen-dations propagating directly from one user to another. You can almost make the case that if a site or product relies on advertising to get the word out, it isn't Web 2.0.

Even much of the infrastructure of the web—including the Linux, Apache, MySQL, and Perl, PHP, or Python code involved in most web servers—relies on the peer-production methods of open source, in themselves an instance of collective, net-enabled intelligence.[6] There are more than one hundred thousand open-source software projects listed on SourceForge.net. Anyone can add a project, anyone can download and use the code, and new projects migrate from the edges to the center as a result of users putting them to work, an organic software-adoption process relying almost entirely on viral marketing.

The lesson: *network effects from user contributions are the key to market dominance in the Web 2.0 era.*

Software licensing and control over application programming interfaces (APIs)—the lever of power in the previous era—is irrelevant because the software never need be distributed but only performed, and also because without the ability to collect and manage the data, the software is of little use. In fact, *the value of the software is proportional to the scale and dynamism of the data it helps to manage.*

Google's service is not a server, though it is delivered by a massive collection of Internet servers; nor is it a browser, though it is experienced by the user within the browser. Nor does its flagship search service even host the content that it enables users to find. Much like a phone call, which happens not just on the phones at either end of the call but on the network in between, Google happens in the space between browser and search engine and destination content server, as an enabler or middleman between the user and his or her online experience.

While both Netscape and Google could be described as software companies, it's clear that Netscape belonged to the same software world as Lotus, Microsoft, Oracle, SAP, and other companies that got their start in the 1980s software revolution, while Google's fellows are other Internet applications like eBay, Amazon, Napster, and, yes, DoubleClick and Akamai.

Blogging and the Wisdom of Crowds

One of the most highly touted features of the Web 2.0 era is the rise of blogging. Personal home pages have been around since the early days of the web, and the personal diary and daily opinion column have been around much longer than that. So just what is the fuss all about?

A blog, at its most basic, is just a personal home page in diary format. But as Rich Skrenta notes, the chronological organization of a blog "seems like a trivial difference, but it drives an entirely different delivery, advertising and value chain."[7]

One of the things that has made a difference is a technology called RSS.[8] RSS is the most significant advance in the fundamental architecture of the web since early hackers realized that CGI could be used to create database-backed websites. RSS allows someone not just to link to a page but to subscribe to it, with notification every time that page changes. Skrenta calls this "the incremental web." Others call it the "live web."

Now, of course, "dynamic websites" (i.e., database-backed sites with dynamically generated content) replaced static web pages well over ten years ago. What's dynamic about the live web are not just the pages but the links. A link to a weblog is expected to point to a perennially changing page, with "permalinks" for any individual entry and notification for each change. An RSS feed is thus a much stronger link than, say, a bookmark or a link to a single page.

RSS also means that the web browser is not the only means of viewing a web page. While some RSS aggregators, such as Bloglines, are web based, others are desktop clients, and still others allow users of portable devices to subscribe to constantly updated content.

RSS is now being used to push not just notices of new blog entries but also all kinds of data updates, including stock quotes, weather data, and photo availability. This use is actually a return to one of its roots: RSS was born in 1997 out of the confluence of Dave Winer's "Really Simple Syndication" technology, used to push out blog updates, and Netscape's "Rich Site Summary," which allowed users to create custom Netscape home pages with regularly updated data flows. Netscape lost interest, and the technology was carried forward by blogging pioneer Userland, Winer's company. In the current crop of applications, though, we see the heritage of both parents.

But RSS is only part of what makes a weblog different from an ordinary web page. Tom Coates remarks on the significance of the permalink:

> It may seem like a trivial piece of functionality now, but it was effectively the device that turned weblogs from an ease-of-publishing phenomenon into a conversational mess of overlapping communities. For the first time it became relatively easy to gesture directly at a highly specific post on someone else's site and talk about it. Discussion emerged. Chat emerged. And—as a result— friendships emerged or became more entrenched. The permalink was the first—and most successful—attempt to build bridges between weblogs.[9]

In many ways, the combination of RSS and permalinks adds many of the features of NNTP, the Network News Protocol of the Usenet, onto HTTP, the web protocol. The "blogosphere" can be thought of as a new, peer-to-peer equivalent to Usenet and bulletin boards, the conversational watering holes of the early Internet. Not only can people subscribe to each other's sites and easily link to individual comments on a page, but also, via a mechanism known as trackbacks, they can see when anyone else links to their pages and can respond, either with reciprocal links or by adding comments.

Interestingly, two-way links were the goal of early hypertext systems like Xanadu. Hypertext purists have celebrated trackbacks as a step toward two-way links. But note that trackbacks are not properly two way—rather, they are really (potentially) symmetrical one-way links that create the effect of two-way links. The difference may seem subtle, but in practice it is enormous. Social networking systems like Friendster, Orkut, and LinkedIn, which require acknowledgment by the recipient in order to establish a connection, lack the same scalability as the web. As noted by Caterina Fake, cofounder of the Flickr photo-sharing service, attention is only coincidentally reciprocal. (Flickr thus allows users to set watch lists—any user can subscribe to any other user's photostream via RSS. The object of attention is notified but does not have to approve the connection.)

If an essential part of Web 2.0 is harnessing collective intelligence, turning the web into a kind of global brain, the blogosphere is the equivalent of constant mental chatter in the forebrain, the voice we hear in all of our heads. It may not reflect the deep structure of the brain, which is often unconscious, but is instead the equivalent of conscious thought. And as a reflection of conscious thought and attention, the blogosphere has begun to have a powerful effect.

First, because search engines use link structure to help predict useful pages, bloggers, as the most prolific and timely linkers, have a disproportionate role in shaping search-engine results. Second, because the blogging community is so highly self-referential, bloggers' paying attention to other bloggers magnifies their visibility and power. The "echo chamber" that critics decry is also an amplifier.

If blogging were merely an amplifier, it would be uninteresting. But like Wikipedia, blogging harnesses collective intelligence as a kind of filter. What James Surowiecki calls "the wisdom of crowds" comes into play, and much as PageRank produces better results than analysis of any individual document, the collective attention of the blogosphere selects for value.[10]

While mainstream media may see individual blogs as competitors, what is really unnerving is that the competition is with the blogosphere as a whole. This is not just a competition between sites but a competition between business models. The world of Web 2.0 is also the world of what Dan Gillmor calls "we, the media," a world in which "the former audience," not a few people in a back room, decides what's important.[11]

3. Data Is the Next Intel Inside

Every significant Internet application to date has been backed by a specialized database: Google's web crawl, Yahoo!'s directory (and web crawl), Amazon's database of products, eBay's database of products and sellers, MapQuest's map databases, Napster's distributed song database. As Hal Varian remarked in a personal conversation last year, "SQL is the new HTML." Database management is a core competency of Web 2.0 companies, so much so that we have sometimes referred to these applications as "infoware" rather than merely software.[12]

This fact leads to a key question: Who owns the data?

In the Internet era, one can already see a number of cases where control over the database has led to market control and outsized financial returns. The monopoly on domain-name registry initially granted by government fiat to Network Solutions (later purchased by Verisign) was one of the first great moneymakers of the Internet. While we've argued that business advantage via controlling software APIs is much more difficult in the age of the Internet, control of key data sources is not, especially if those data sources are expensive to create or amenable to increasing returns via network effects.

Look at the copyright notices at the base of every map served by MapQuest, maps.yahoo.com, maps.msn.com, or maps.google.com, and you'll see the line "Maps copyright NavTeq, TeleAtlas" or, with the new satellite-imagery services, "Images copyright Digital Globe." These companies made substantial investments in their databases (NavTeq alone reportedly invested $750 million to build its database of street addresses and directions. Digital Globe spent $500 million to launch its own satellite to improve on government-supplied imagery.) NavTeq has gone so far as to imitate Intel's familiar "Intel Inside" logo: cars with navigation systems bear the imprint "NavTeq Onboard." Data is indeed the "Intel Inside" of these applications, a sole source component in systems whose software infrastructure is largely open source or otherwise commodified.

The now hotly contested web-mapping arena demonstrates how a failure to understand the importance of owning an application's core data will eventually undercut its competitive position. MapQuest pioneered the web-mapping category in 1995, yet when Yahoo! and then Microsoft and most recently Google decided to enter the market, they were easily able to offer a competing application simply by licensing the same data.

Contrast, however, the position of Amazon.com. Like competitors such as Barnesandnoble.com, its original database came from ISBN registry provider R. R. Bowker. But unlike MapQuest, Amazon relentlessly enhanced the data, adding publisher-supplied data such as a cover image, a table of contents, an index, and sample material. Even more importantly, it harnessed its users to annotate the data, such that after ten years, Amazon, not Bowker, is the primary source for bibliographic data on books, a reference source for scholars and librarians as well as consumers. Amazon also introduced its own proprietary identifier, the ASIN, which corresponds to the ISBN when one is present and creates an equivalent name space for products without one. Effectively, Amazon "embraced and extended" its data suppliers.

Imagine if MapQuest had done the same thing, harnessing its users to annotate maps and directions, adding layers of value. It would have been much more difficult for competitors to enter the market just by licensing the base data.

The recent introduction of Google Maps provides a living laboratory for the competition between application vendors and their data suppliers. Google's lightweight programming model has led to the creation of numerous value-added services in the form of mashups that link Google Maps with other Internet-accessible data sources. Paul Rademacher's housingmaps.com, which combines Google Maps with Craigslist apartment-rental and home-purchase data to create an interactive housing search tool, is the preeminent example of such a mashup.

At present, these mashups are mostly innovative experiments, done by hackers. But entrepreneurial activity follows close behind. And already one can see that for at least one class of developer, Google has taken the role of data source away from NavTeq and inserted itself as a favored intermediary. We expect to see battles between data suppliers and application vendors in the next few years, as both realize just how important certain classes of data will become as building blocks for Web 2.0 applications.

The race is on to own certain classes of core data: location, identity, calendaring of public events, product identifiers, and name spaces. In many cases, where there is significant cost to create the data, there may be an opportunity for an Intel Inside–style play, with a single source for the data. In others, the winner will be the company that first reaches critical mass via user aggregation and turns that aggregated data into a system service.

For example, in the area of identity, PayPal, Amazon's 1-click, and the millions of users of communications systems may all be legitimate contenders to build a network-wide identity database. (In this regard, Google's recent attempt to use cell-phone numbers as an identifier for Gmail accounts may be a step toward embracing and extending the phone system.) Meanwhile, start-ups like Sxip are exploring the potential of federated identity, in quest of a kind of "distributed 1-click" that will provide a seamless Web 2.0 identity subsystem. In the area of calendaring, EVDB is an attempt to build the world's largest shared calendar via a wiki-style architecture of participation. While the jury's still out on the success of any particular start-up or approach, it's clear that standards and solutions in these areas, effectively turning certain classes of data into reliable subsystems of the "Internet operating system," will enable the next generation of applications.

A further point must be noted with regard to data, and that is user concerns about privacy and their rights to their own data. In many of the early web applications, copyright is only loosely enforced. For example, Amazon lays claim to any reviews submitted to the site, but in the absence of enforcement, people may repost the same review elsewhere. However, as companies begin to realize that control over data may be their chief source of competitive advantage, we may see heightened attempts at control.

Much as the rise of proprietary software led to the Free Software movement, we expect the rise of proprietary databases to result in a Free Data movement within the next decade. One can see early signs of this countervailing trend in open data projects such as Wikipedia, in the Creative Commons, and in software projects like Greasemonkey, which allow users to take control of how data is displayed on their computer.

4. End of the Software Release Cycle

As noted earlier in the discussion of Google versus Netscape, one of the defining characteristics of Internet-era software is that it is delivered as a service, not as a product. This fact leads to a number of fundamental changes in the business model of such a company:

Operations must become a core competency. Google's or Yahoo!'s expertise in product development must be matched by an expertise in daily operations. So fundamental is the shift from software as artifact to software as service that *the software will cease to perform unless it is maintained on a daily basis.* Google must continuously crawl the web and update its indices, continuously filter out link spam and other attempts to influence its results, and continuously and dynamically respond to hundreds of millions of asynchronous user queries, simultaneously matching them with context-appropriate advertisements.

It's no accident that Google's system administration, networking, and load-balancing techniques are perhaps even more closely guarded secrets than are their search algorithms. Google's success at automating these processes is a key part of its cost advantage over competitors.

It's also no accident that scripting languages such as Perl, Python, PHP, and now Ruby play such a large role at Web 2.0 companies. Perl was famously described by Hassan Schroeder, Sun's first webmaster, as "the duct tape of the Internet." Dynamic languages (often called scripting languages and looked down on by the software engineers of the era of software artifacts) are the tool of choice for system and network administrators, as well as for application developers building dynamic systems that require constant change.

Users must be treated as codevelopers, in a reflection of open-source development practices (even if the software in question is unlikely to be released under an open-source license). The open-source dictum, "release early and release often," in fact has morphed into an even more radical position, "the perpetual beta," in which the product is developed in the open, with new features slipstreamed in on a monthly, weekly, or even daily basis. It's no accident that services such as Gmail, Google Maps, Flickr, del.icio.us, and the like may be expected to bear a "Beta" logo for years at a time.

Real-time monitoring of user behavior to see just which new features are used, and how they are used, thus becomes another required core competency. A web developer at a major online service remarked, "We put up two or three new features on some part of the site every day, and if users don't adopt them, we take them down. If they like them, we roll them out to the entire site."

Cal Henderson, the lead developer of Flickr, recently revealed that the company deploys new builds up to every half hour.[13] This is clearly a radically different development model! While not all web applications are developed in as extreme a style as Flickr, almost all web applications have a development cycle that is radically unlike anything from the PC or client-server era. It is for this reason that a recent ZDNet editorial concluded that Microsoft won't be able to beat Google: "Microsoft's business model depends on everyone upgrading their computing environment every two to three years. Google's depends on everyone exploring what's new in their computing environment every day."[14]

While Microsoft has demonstrated enormous ability to learn from and ultimately best its competition, there's no question that this time, the competition will require Microsoft (and by extension, every other existing software company) to become a deeply different kind of company. Native Web 2.0 companies enjoy a natural advantage, as they don't have old patterns (and corresponding business models and revenue sources) to shed.

5. Lightweight Programming Models

Once the idea of web services became au courant, large companies jumped into the fray with a complex web-services stack designed to create highly reliable programming environments for distributed applications.

But much as the web succeeded precisely because it overthrew much of hypertext theory, substituting a simple pragmatism for ideal design, RSS has become perhaps the single most widely deployed web service because of its simplicity, while the complex corporate web-services stacks have yet to achieve wide deployment.

Similarly, Amazon.com's web services are provided in two forms: one adhering to the formalisms of the SOAP (Simple Object Access Protocol) web-services stack, the other simply providing XML data over HTTP, in a lightweight approach sometimes referred to as REST (Representational State Transfer). While high-value business-to-business (B2B) connections (like those between Amazon and retail partners like Toys "R" Us) use the SOAP stack, Amazon reports that 95 percent of the usage is of the lightweight REST service.

This same quest for simplicity can be seen in other "organic" web services. Google's recent release of Google Maps is a case in point. Google Maps' simple AJAX (Javascript and XML) interface was quickly decrypted by hackers, who then proceeded to remix the data into new services.

Mapping-related web services had been available for some time from GIS vendors such as ESRI as well as from MapQuest and Microsoft MapPoint. But Google Maps set the world on fire because of its simplicity. While experimenting with any of the formal vendor-supported web services required a formal contract between the parties, the way Google Maps was implemented left the data for the taking, and hackers soon found ways to creatively reuse that data.

There are several significant lessons here:

Support lightweight programming models that allow for loosely coupled systems. The complexity of the corporate-sponsored web-services stack is designed to enable tight coupling. While this is necessary in many cases, many of the most interesting applications can indeed remain loosely coupled and even fragile. The Web 2.0 mind-set is very different from the traditional IT mind-set!

Think syndication, not coordination. Simple web services, like RSS and REST-based web services, are about syndicating data outward, not controlling what happens when it gets to the other end of the connection. This idea is fundamental to the Internet itself, a reflection of what is known as the end-to-end principle.[15]

Design for "hackability" and remixability. Systems like the original web, RSS, and AJAX all have this in common: the barriers to reuse are extremely low. Much of the useful software is actually open source, but even when it isn't, there is little in the way of intellectual-property protection. The web browser's "View Source" option made it possible for any user to copy any other user's web page; RSS was designed to empower the user to view the content he or she wants, when it's wanted, not at the behest of the information provider; the most successful web services are those that have been easiest to take in new directions unimagined by their creators. The phrase "some rights reserved," which was popularized by the Creative Commons to contrast with the more typical "all rights reserved," is a useful guidepost.

Innovation in Assembly

Lightweight business models are a natural concomitant of lightweight programming and lightweight connections. The Web 2.0 mind-set is good at reuse. A new service like housingmaps.com was built simply by snapping together two existing services. Housingmaps.com doesn't have a business model (yet)—but for many small-scale services, Google AdSense (or perhaps Amazon Associates fees, or both) provides the snap-in equivalent of a revenue model.

These examples provide an insight into another key Web 2.0 principle, which we call "innovation in assembly." When commodity components are abundant, you can create value simply by assembling them in novel or effective ways. Much as the PC revolution provided many opportunities for innovation in assembly of commodity hardware, with companies like Dell making a science out of such assembly, thereby defeating companies whose business model required innovation in product development, we believe that Web 2.0 will provide opportunities for companies to beat the competition by getting better at harnessing and integrating services provided by others.

6. Software above the Level of a Single Device

One other feature of Web 2.0 that deserves mention is the fact that it's no longer limited to the PC platform. Longtime Microsoft developer Dave Stutz pointed out in his parting advice to Microsoft that "useful software written above the level of the single device will command high margins for a long time to come."[16]

Of course, any web application can be seen as software above the level of a single device. After all, even the simplest web application involves at least two computers: the one hosting the web server and the one hosting the browser. And as we've discussed, the development of the web as platform extends this idea to synthetic applications composed of services provided by multiple computers.

But as with many areas of Web 2.0, where the "2.0-ness" is not something new but rather a fuller realization of the true potential of the web platform, this phrase gives us a key insight into how to design applications and services for the new platform.

To date, iTunes is the best exemplar of this principle. This application seamlessly reaches from the handheld device to a massive web back-end, with the PC acting as a local cache and control station. There have been many previous attempts to bring web content to portable devices, but the iPod/iTunes combination is one of the first such applications designed from the ground up to span multiple devices. TiVo is another good example.

iTunes and TiVo also demonstrate many of the other core principles of Web 2.0. They are not web applications per se, but they leverage the power of the web platform, making it a seamless, almost invisible part of their infrastructure. Data management is most clearly the heart of their offering. They are services, not packaged applications (although in the case of iTunes, it can be used as a packaged application, managing only the user's local data). What's more, both TiVo and iTunes show some budding use of collective intelligence, although in both cases, their experiments are at war with those of the intellectual property lobby. There's only a limited architecture of participation in iTunes, though the recent addition of podcasting changes that equation substantially.

This is one of the areas of Web 2.0 where we expect to see some of the greatest change, as more and more devices are connected to the new platform. What applications become possible when our phones and our cars are not consuming data but reporting it? Real-time traffic monitoring, flash mobs, and citizen journalism are only a few of the early warning signs of the capabilities of the new platform.

7. Rich User Experiences

As early as Pei Wei's Viola browser in 1992,[17] the web was being used to deliver "applets" and other kinds of active content within the web browser. Java's introduction in 1995 was framed around the delivery of such applets. JavaScript and then DHTML were introduced as lightweight ways to provide client-side programmability and richer user experiences. Several years ago, Macromedia coined the term "Rich Internet Applications" (which has also been picked up by open-source Flash competitor Laszlo Systems) to highlight the capabilities of Flash to deliver not just multimedia content but also GUI-style application experiences.

However, the potential of the web to deliver full-scale applications didn't hit the mainstream until Google introduced Gmail, quickly followed by Google Maps, web-based applications with rich user interfaces and PC-equivalent interactivity. The collection of technologies used by Google was christened "AJAX," in a seminal essay by Jesse James Garrett of web-design firm Adaptive Path. He wrote,

> Ajax isn't a technology. It's really several technologies, each flourishing in its own right, coming together in powerful new ways. Ajax incorporates:
>
> - standards-based presentation using XHTML and CSS;
> - dynamic display and interaction using the Document Object Model;
> - data interchange and manipulation using XML and XSLT;
> - asynchronous data retrieval using XMLHttpRequest;
> - and JavaScript binding everything together.[18]

AJAX is also a key component of Web 2.0 applications such as Flickr, now part of Yahoo!, 37signals' applications basecamp and backpack, as well as other Google applications such as Gmail and Orkut. We're entering an unprecedented period of user-interface innovation, as web developers are finally able to build web applications as rich as local PC-based applications.

Interestingly, many of the capabilities now being explored have been around for many years. In the late '90s, both Microsoft and Netscape had a vision of the kind of capabilities that are now finally being realized, but their battle over the standards to be used made cross-browser applications difficult. It was only when Microsoft definitively won the browser wars, and there was a single de facto browser standard to write to, that this kind of application became possible. And while Firefox has reintroduced competition to the browser market, at least so far we haven't seen the destructive competition over web standards that held back progress in the '90s.

We expect to see many new web applications over the next few years, both truly novel applications and rich web reimplementations of PC applications. Every platform change to date has also created opportunities for a leadership change in the dominant applications of the previous platform.

Gmail has already provided some interesting innovations in e-mail,[19] combining the strengths of the web (accessible from anywhere, deep database competencies, searchability) with user interfaces that approach PC interfaces in usability. Meanwhile, other mail clients on the PC platform are nibbling away at the problem from the other end, adding instant-messaging (IM) and presence capabilities. How far are we from an integrated communications client combining the best of e-mail, IM, and the cell phone, using Voice over Internet Protocol (VoIP) to add voice capabilities to the rich capabilities of web applications? The race is on.

It's easy to see how Web 2.0 will also remake the address book. A Web 2.0–style address book would treat the local address book on the PC or phone merely as a cache of the contacts you've explicitly asked the system to remember. Meanwhile, a web-based synchronization agent, Gmail style, would remember every message sent or received and every e-mail address and every phone number used and would build social networking heuristics to decide which ones to offer up as alternatives when an answer wasn't found in the local cache. Lacking an answer there, the system would query the broader social network.

A Web 2.0 word processor would support wiki-style collaborative editing, not just standalone documents. But it would also support the rich formatting we've come to expect in PC-based word processors. Writely is a good example of such an application, although it hasn't yet gained wide traction.[20]

Nor will the Web 2.0 revolution be limited to PC applications. Salesforce. com demonstrates how the web can be used to deliver software as a service, in enterprise-scale applications such as Customer Relations Management (CRM).

The competitive opportunity for new entrants is to fully embrace the potential of Web 2.0. Companies that succeed will create applications that learn from their users, using an architecture of participation to build a commanding advantage not just in the software interface but in the richness of the shared data.

Core Competencies of Web 2.0 Companies

In exploring the seven principles discussed in this essay, we've highlighted some of the principal features of Web 2.0. Each of the examples we've explored demonstrates one or more of those key principles but may miss others. Let's close, therefore, by summarizing what we believe to be the core competencies of Web 2.0 companies:

- Services, not packaged software, with cost-effective scalability
- Control over unique, hard-to-re-create data sources that get richer as more people use them
- Trusting users as codevelopers
- Harnessing collective intelligence
- Leveraging the long tail through customer self-service
- Software above the level of a single device
- Lightweight user interfaces, development models, *and* business models

The next time a company claims that it's "Web 2.0," test its features against this list. The more points it scores, the more it is worthy of the name. Remember, though, that excellence in one area may be more telling than some small steps in all seven.

NOTES

This chapter was originally published on September 30, 2005, on *O'Reilly Radar* (blog), at http://www.oreillynet.com/pub/a/oreilly/tim/news/2005/09/30/what-is-web-20.htm (accessed July 17, 2010). This work is licensed under the Creative Commons Attribution-ShareAlike license.

1. Carlota Perez, *Technological Revolutions and Financial Capital: The Dynamics of Bubbles and Golden Ages* (Cheltenham, UK: Elgar, 2002).

2. The first Web 2.0 Conference took place October 5–7, 2004, in San Francisco.

3. Tim O'Reilly, "Not 2.0?," *O'Reilly Radar* (blog), August 5, 2005, http://radar.oreilly.com/archives/2005/08/not-20.html (accessed July 17, 2010).

4. Eric S. Raymond, *The Cathedral and the Bazaar* (Sebastopol, CA: O'Reilly, 2001), http://catb.org/esr/writings/homesteading/cathedral-bazaar/ar01s05.html (accessed July 17, 2010).

5. Thomas Vander Wal, "Folksonomy," *vanderwal.net* (blog), February 2, 2007, http://vanderwal.net/folksonomy.html (accessed July 17, 2010).

6. Yochai Benkler, "Coase's Penguin, or, Linux and the Nature of the Firm," *Yale Law Journal* 369 (2002), available online at http://www.benkler.org/CoasesPenguin.html (accessed July 17, 2010).

7. Rich Skrenta, "The Incremental Web," *topix* (blog), February 12, 2005, http://blog.topix.com/2005/02/the-incremental-web.html (accessed July 17, 2010).

8. Mark Pilgrim, "Dive into XML: What Is RSS," XML.com, December 18, 2002, http://www.xml.com/pub/a/2002/12/18/dive-into-xml.html (accessed July 17, 2010); World Wide Web Consortium, "RSS 2.0 Specification," Fall 2002, http://validator.w3.org/feed/docs/rss2.html (accessed July 17, 2010).

9. Tom Coates, "On Permalinks and Paradigms . . . ," *Plasticbag.org* (blog), June 11, 2003, http://www.plasticbag.org/archives/2003/06/on_permalinks_and_paradigms/.

10. James Surowiecki, *The Wisdom of Crowds* (New York: Doubleday, 2004).

11. Dan Gillmor, *We the Media* (Sebastopol, CA: O'Reilly, 2004), http://www.authorama.com/we-the-media-8.html (accessed July 17, 2010).

12. Tim O'Reilly, "Hardware, Software, and Infoware," in *Open Sources: Voices from the Open Source Revolution*, ed. Chris DiBona, Sam Ockman, and Mark Stone (Sebastopol, CA: O'Reilly, 1999).

13. Tom Coates, "Cal Henderson on 'How We Built Flickr . . . ,'" *Plasticbag.org* (blog), June 20, 2005, http://www.plasticbag.org/archives/2005/06/cal_henderson_on_how_we_built_flickr/ (accessed July 17, 2010); Chris May, "Deploy Every 30 Minutes: Redux," *Secret Plans and Clever Tricks* (blog), August 25, 2005, http://blogs.warwick.ac.uk/chrismay/entry/release_once_every/ (accessed July 17, 2010).

14. Phil Wainewright, "Why Microsoft Can't Best Google," *Software as Services* (blog), ZDNet, August 24, 2005, http://www.zdnet.com/blog/saas/why-microsoft-cant-best-google/13 (accessed July 17, 2010).

15. J. H. Saltzer, D. P. Reed, and D. D. Clark, "End-to-End Arguments in System Design," *ACM Transactions on Computer Systems* 2, no. 4 (1984): 277–288, http://web.mit.edu/Saltzer/www/publications/endtoend/endtoend.pdf (accessed July 17, 2010); M. S Blumenthal and D. D. Clark, "Rethinking the Design of the Internet: The End to End Arguments vs. the Brave New World," *ACM Transactions on Internet Technology* 1, no. 1 (2001): 70–109.

16. David Stutz, "Advice to Microsoft Regarding Commodity Software," *The Synthesist* (blog), February 11, 2003, http://www.synthesist.net/writing/onleavingms.html (accessed July 17, 2010).

17. Viola Web Browser, http://www.viola.org/ (accessed July 17, 2010).

18. Jesse James Garrett, "Ajax: A New Approach to Web Applications," Adaptive Path website, February 18, 2005, http://www.adaptivepath.com/ideas/essays/archives/000385.php (accessed July 17, 2010).

19. Tim O'Reilly, "The Fuss about Gmail and Privacy: Nine Reasons Why It's Bogus," *O'Reilly Net* (blog), April 16, 2004, http://www.oreillynet.com/pub/wlg/4707 (accessed July 17, 2010).

20. *Editor's note*: Writely.com was purchased by Google on March 6, 2006, and has subsequently become Google Docs.

What Is Collaboration Anyway?

ADAM HYDE, MIKE LINKSVAYER, KANARINKA,
MICHAEL MANDIBERG, MARTA PEIRANO,
SISSU TARKA, ASTRA TAYLOR, ALAN TONER,
MUSHON ZER-AVIV

Sharing Is the First Step

Information technology informs and structures the language of networked collaboration. Terms like "sharing," "openness," "user-generated content," and "participation" have become so ubiquitous that too often they tend to be conflated and misused. In an attempt to avoid the misuse of the term "collaboration" we will try to examine what constitutes collaboration in digital networks and how it maps to our previous understanding of the term.

User-generated content and social media create the tendency for confusion between sharing and collaboration. Sharing of content alone does not directly lead to collaboration. A common paradigm in many web services couples identity and content. Examples of this include blogging, microblogging, and video and photo sharing, which effectively say, "This is who I am. This is what I did." The content is the social object, and the author is directly attributed with it. This work is a singularity, even if it is shared with the world via these platforms, and even if it has a free-culture license on it. This body of work stands alone, and alone, this work is not collaborative.

In contrast, the strongly collaborative Wikipedia deemphasizes the tight content-author link. While the attribution of each contribution made by each author is logged on the history tab of each page, attribution is primarily used as a moderation and accountability tool. While most user-generated content platforms offer a one-to-many relationship, in which one user produces and uploads many different entries or media, wikis and centralized code-versioning systems offer a many-to-many relationship, in which many different users can be associated with many different entries or projects.

Social media platforms can become collaborative when they add an additional layer of coordination. On a microblogging platform like Twitter, this layer might take the form of an instruction to "use the #iranelections hashtag on your tweets," or on a photo-sharing platform, it might be an invitation to "post your photos to the LOLcats group." These mechanisms aggregate the content into a new social object. The new social object includes the metadata of each of its constituent objects; the author's name is the most important of this metadata. This creates two layers of content. Each shared individual unit is included in a cluster of shared units. A single shared video is part of an aggregation of demonstration documentation. A single shared bookmark is included in an aggregation of the "inspiration" tag on the social bookmarking service delicious. A single blog post takes its place in a blogosphere discussion, and so on.

This seems similar to a single "commit" to an open-source project or a single edit of a Wikipedia article, but these instances do not maintain the shared unit/collaborative cluster balance. For software in a code-versioning system or a page on Wikipedia, the single unit loses its integrity outside the collaborative context and is indeed created to only function as a part of the larger collaborative social object.

Coordinating Mechanisms Create Contexts

Contributions such as edits to a wiki page or "commits" to a version-control system cannot exist outside the context in which they are made. A relationship to this context requires a coordinating mechanism that is an integral part of the initial production process. These mechanisms of coordination and governance can be both technical and social.

Wikipedia uses several technical coordination mechanisms, as well as strong social mechanisms. The technical mechanism separates each contribution, marks it chronologically, and attributes it to a specific username or IP address. If two users are editing the same paragraph and are submitting contradicting changes, the MediaWiki software will alert these users about the conflict and requires them to resolve it. Version-control systems use similar technical coordination mechanisms, marking each contribution with a time stamp and a username and requiring the resolution of differences between contributions if there are discrepancies in the code due to different versions.

The technical coordination mechanisms of the Wiki software lowers the friction of collaboration tremendously, but it doesn't take it away completely. It makes it much harder to create contributions that are not harmonious with the surrounding context. If a contribution is deemed inaccurate, or not an improvement, a user can simply revert to the previous edit. This new change is then preserved and denoted by the time and user who contributed it.

Academic research into the techno-social dynamics of Wikipedia shows clear emergent patterns of leadership. For example, the initial content and structure outlined by the first edit of an article are often maintained through the many future edits years on.[1] The governance mechanism of the Wiki software does not value one edit over the other. Yet what is offered by the initial author is not just the initiative for the collaboration; it is also a leading guideline that implicitly coordinates the contributions that follow.

Wikipedia then uses social contracts to mediate the relationship of contributions to the collection as a whole. All edits are supposed to advance the collaborative goal—to make the article more accurate and factual. All new articles are supposed to be on relevant topics. All new biographies need to meet specific guidelines of notability. These are socially agreed upon contracts, and their fabric is always permeable. The strength of that fabric is the strength of the community.

An interesting example of leadership and of conflicting social pacts happened on the Wikipedia "Elephants" article. In the TV show *The Colbert Report* Stephen Colbert plays a satirical character of a right-wing television host dedicated to defending Republican ideology by any means necessary. For example, he constructs ridiculous arguments denying climate change. He is not concerned that this completely ignores reality, which he claims "has a liberal bias."

On July 31, 2006, Colbert ironically proposed the term "Wikiality" as a way to alter the perception of reality by editing a Wikipedia article. Colbert analyzed the interface in front of his audience and performed a live edit to the "Elephants" page, adding a claim that the elephant population in Africa had tripled in the past six months.

Colbert proposed his viewers follow a different social pact. He suggested that if enough of them helped edit the article on elephants to preserve his edit about the number of elephants in Africa, then that would become the reality, or the "Wikiality"—the representation of reality through Wikipedia. As he said, "If you're going against what the majority of people perceive to be reality, you're the one who's crazy." He also claimed that this would be a tough "fact" for the environmentalists to compete with, retorting, "Explain that, Al Gore!"[2]

It was great TV, but it created problems for Wikipedia. So many people responded to Colbert's rallying cry that Wikipedia locked the article on elephants to protect it from further vandalism.[3] Furthermore, Wikipedia banned the user Stephencolbert for using an unverified celebrity name, a violation of Wikipedia's terms of use.[4] Colbert's and his viewers' edits were perceived as mere vandalism that was disrespectful of the social contract that the rest of Wikipedia adhered to, thus subverting the underlying fabric of the community. Yet they were following the social contract provided by their leader and his initial edit. It was their own collaborative social pact, enabled and coordinated by their own group. Ultimately, Wikipedia had to push one of its more obscure rules to its edges to prevail against Stephen Colbert and his viewers. The surge of vandals was blocked, but Colbert gave them a run for the money, and everyone else a laugh, all the while making a point about how we define the boundaries of contribution.

Does Aggregation Constitute Collaboration?

Can all contributions coordinated in a defined context be understood as collaboration? In early 2009 Israeli musician Kutiman (Ophir Kutiel) collected video clips posted on YouTube of hobbyist musicians and singers performing to their webcams. He then used one of the many illegal tools available online to extract the raw video files from YouTube. He sampled these clips to create new music videos. He writes of his inspiration,

> Before I had the idea about ThruYou I took some drummers from You-Tube and I played on top of them—just for fun, you know. And then one day, just before I plugged my guitar to play on top of the drummer from YouTube, I thought to myself, you know—maybe I can find a bass and guitar and other players on YouTube to play with this drummer.[5]

The result was a set of seven music-video mashups which he titled "ThruYou—Kutiman Mixes YouTube." Each of these audiovisual mixes is so well crafted it is hard to remind yourself that when David Taub from NextLevelGuitar.com was recording his funk riff he was never planning to be playing it to the Bernard "Pretty" Purdie drum beat or to the user miquelsi's playing with the theremin at the Universeum, in Göteborg. It is also hard to remind yourself that this brilliantly orchestrated musical piece is not the result of a collaboration.

When Kutiman calls the work "ThruYou" does he mean "You" as in "us" his audience? "You" as in the sampled musicians? Or "You" as in YouTube? By subtitling it "Kutiman mixes YouTube" is he referring to the YouTube service owned by Google, or the YouTube users whose videos he sampled?

The site opens with an introduction/disclaimer paragraph:

What you are about to see is a mix of unrelated YouTube videos/clips edited together to create ThruYou. In Other words—what you see is what you get. Check out the credits for each video—you might find yourself.

PLAY ►[6]

In the site Kutiman included an "About" video in which he explains the process and a "Credits" section where the different instruments are credited with their YouTube IDs (like tU8gmozj8xY and 6FX_84iWPLU) and linked to the original YouTube pages.

The user miquelsi did share the video of himself playing the Theremin on YouTube, but he did not intend to collaborate with other musicians. We don't even know if he really thought he was making music: it is very clear from the video that he doesn't really know how to play the Theremin, so when he titled his video "Playing the Theremin" he could have meant playing as music making or playing as amusement. It would be easy to focus on the obvious issues of copyright infringement and licensing, but the aspect of Kutiman's work we're actually interested in is the question of intention.

Is intention essential to collaboration? It seems clear that though these works were aggregated to make a new entity, they were originally shared as discrete objects with no intention of having a relationship to a greater context. But what about works that are shared with an awareness of a greater context, that help improve that context, but are not explicitly shared for that purpose?

Web creators are increasingly aware of "best practices" for search-engine optimization (SEO). By optimizing, web-page creators are sharing objects with a strong awareness of the context in which they are being shared, and in the process they are making the Google PageRank mechanism better and more precise. Their intention is not to make PageRank more precise, but by being aware of the context, they achieve that result. Although reductive, this does fit a more limited definition of collaboration.

The example of PageRank highlights the questions of coordination and intention. Whether or not they are optimizing their content and thus improving PageRank, web-content publishers are not motivated by the same shared goal that motivates Google and its shareholders. These individuals do coordinate their actions with Google's mechanism out of their own self-interest to achieve better search results, but they don't coordinate their actions in order to improve the mechanism itself. The same can be said about most Twitter users, most Flickr users, and the various musicians who have unintentionally contributed to YouTube's success and to Kutiman's ThruYou project.

Collaboration requires goals. There are multiple types of intentionality that highlight the importance of intent in collaboration. The intentional practice is different from the intentional goal. Optimizing a web page is done to intentionally increase search results, but it unintentionally contributes to making Google PageRank better. When we claim that intention is necessary for collaboration, we really are talking about intentional goals. Optimizing your site for Google search is a collaboration with Google only if you define it as your personal goal. Without these shared goals, intentional practice is a much weaker case of collaboration.

Collaborationism

As collaborative action can have more than one intent, it can also have more than one repercussion. These multiple layers are often a source of conflict and confusion. A single collaborative action can imply different and even contrasting group associations. In different group contexts, one intent might incriminate or legitimize the other. This group identity crisis can undermine the legitimacy of collaborative efforts altogether.

Collaboration can mean collaborating with an enemy. In a presentation at the Dictionary of War conference in Novi Sad, Serbia, in January 2008, Israeli curator Galit Eilat described the joint Israeli-Palestinian project "Liminal Spaces":

> When the word "collaboration" appeared, there was a lot of antagonism to the word. It has become very problematic, especially in the Israeli/Palestinian context. I think from the Second World War the word "collaboration" had a special connotation. From Vichy government, the puppet government, and later on the rest of the collaborations with Nazi Germany.[7]

While there was no doubt that "Liminal Spaces" was indeed a collaboration between Israelis and Palestinians, the term itself was not only contested; it was outright dangerous.

The danger of collaboration precedes this project. I remember one night in 1994 when I was a young soldier serving in an Israeli army base near the Palestinian city of Hebron, around 3:30 a.m. a car pulled off just outside the gates of our base. The door opened, and a dead body was dropped from the back seat on the road. The car then turned around and rushed back towards the city. The soldiers that examined the body found it belonged to a Palestinian man. Attached to his back was a sign with the word "Collaborator."

This grim story clearly illustrates how culturally dependent and context-based a collaboration can be. While semantically we will attempt to dissect what constitutes the context of a collaboration, we must acknowledge the inherit conflict between individual identity and group identity. An individual might be a part of several collaborative or noncollaborative networks. Since a certain action like SEO optimization can be read in different contexts, it is often a challenge to distill individual identity from the way it intersects with group identities.

> The nonhuman quality of networks is precisely what makes them so difficult to grasp. They are, we suggest, a medium of contemporary power, and yet no single subject or group absolutely controls a network. Human subjects constitute and construct networks, but always in a highly distributed and unequal fashion. Human subjects thrive on network interaction (kin groups, clans, the social), yet the moments when the network logic takes over—in the mob or the swarm, in contagion or infection—are the moments that are the most disorienting, the most threatening to the integrity of the human ego.[8]

The term "group identity" itself is confusing, as it obfuscates the complexity of different individual identities networked together within the group. This inherent difficulty presented by the nonhuman quality of networks means that the confusion of identities and intents will persist. Relationships between individuals in groups are rich and varied. We cannot assume a completely shared identity and equal characteristics for every group member just by grouping them together.

We cannot expect technology (playing the rational adult) to solve this tension either, as binary computing often leads to an even further reduction (in the representation) of social life. As Ippolita, Geert Lovink, and Ned Rossiter point out, "We are addicted to ghettos, and in so doing refuse the antagonism of 'the political.' Where is the enemy? Not on Facebook, where you can only have 'friends.' What Web 2.0 lacks is the technique of antagonistic linkage."[9]

The basic connection in Facebook is referred to as "friendship" since there is no way for software to elegantly map the true dynamic nuances of social life. While "friendship" feels more comfortable, its overuse is costing us richness of our social life. We would like to avoid these binaries by offering variation and degrees of participation.

Criteria for Collaboration

"Collaboration" is employed so widely to describe the methodology of production behind information goods that it occludes as much as it reveals. In addition, governments, business, and cultural entrepreneurs apparently can't get enough of it, so a certain skepticism is not unwarranted. But even if overuse as a buzzword has thrown a shadow over the term, what follows is an attempt to try and construct an idea of what substantive meaning it could have and distinguish it from related or neighboring ideas such as cooperation, interdependence, or coproduction. This task seems necessary not least because if the etymology of the word is literally "working together," there is a delicate and significant line between "working with" and "being put to work by" . . .

Some products characterized as collaborative are generated simply through people's common use of tools, presence, or performance of routine tasks. Others require active coordination and deliberate allocation of resources. While the results may be comparable from a quantitative or efficiency perspective, a heterogeneity of social relations and design lie behind the outputs.

The intensity of these relationships can be described as sitting somewhere on a continuum from strong ties with shared intentionality to incidental production by strangers, captured through shared interfaces or agents, sometimes unconscious byproducts of other online activity.

Consequently we can set out both strong and weak definitions of collaboration, while remaining aware that many cases will be situated somewhere in between. While the former points toward the centrality of negotiation over objectives and methodology, the latter illustrates the harvesting capacity of technological frameworks where information is both the input and output of production.

Criteria for assessing the strength of a collaboration include:

Questions of Intention
Must the participant actively intend to contribute? Is willful agency needed? Or is a minimal act of tagging a resource with keywords, or mere execution of a command in an enabled technological environment (emergence), sufficient?

Questions of Goals
Is participation motivated by the pursuit of goals shared with other participants or individual interests?

Questions of (Self-)Governance

Are the structures and rules of engagement accessible? Can they be contested and renegotiated? Are participants interested in engaging on this level (control of the mechanism)?

Questions of Coordination Mechanisms

Is human attention required to coordinate the integration of contributions? Or can this be accomplished automatically?

Questions of Property

How is control or ownership organized over the outputs (if relevant)? Who is included and excluded in the division of the benefits?

Questions of Knowledge Transfer

Does the collaboration result in knowledge transfer between participants? Is it similar to a community of practice, described by Etienne Wenger as "groups of people who share a concern, a set of problems, or a passion about a topic, and who deepen their knowledge and expertise in this area by interacting on an ongoing basis."[10]

Questions of Identity

To what degree are individual identities of the participants affected by the collaboration toward a more unified group identity?

Questions of Scale

Questions of scale are key to group management and have a substantial effect on collaboration. The different variables of scale are often dynamic and can change through the process of the collaboration, thus changing the nature and the dynamics of the collaboration altogether.

Size—How big or small is the number of participants?

Duration—How long or short is the time frame of the collaboration?

Speed—How time consuming is each contribution? How fast is the decision-making process?

Space—Does the collaboration take place over a limited or extended geographic scale?

Scope—How minimal or complex is the most basic contribution? How extensive and ambitious is the shared goal?

Questions of Network Topology

How are individuals connected to each other? Are contributions individually connected to each other, or are they all coordinated through a unifying bottle-neck mechanism? Is the participation-network model highly centralized, is it largely distributed, or does it assume different shades of decentralization?

Questions of Accessibility

Can anyone join the collaboration? Is there a vetting process? Are participants accepted by invitation only?

Questions of Equality

Are all contributions largely equal in scope? Does a small group of participants generate a far larger portion of the work? Are the levels of control over the project equal or varied between the different participants?

Continuum Set

The series of criteria just outlined provides a general guide for the qualitative assessment of the cooperative relationship. In what follows, these criteria are used to sketch out a continuum of collaboration. The following clusters of cases illustrate a movement from weakest to strongest connections. This division is crude, as it sidelines the fact that within even apparently weak contexts of interaction there may be a core of people whose commitment is of a higher order (e.g., ReCaptcha).

The Weakest Link . . .

(1) Numerous technological frameworks gather information during use and feed the results back into the apparatus. The most evident example is Google, whose PageRank algorithm uses a survey of links between sites to classify their relevance to a user's query.

Likewise ReCaptcha uses a commonplace authentication in a two-part implementation, first to exclude automated spam and then to digitize words from books that were not recognizable by optical character recognition. Contributions are extracted from participants unconscious of the recycling of their activity into the finessing of the value chain. Website operators who integrate ReCaptcha, however, know precisely what they're doing and choose to transform a necessary defense mechanism for their site into a productive channel of contributions to what they regard as a useful task.

(2) Aggregation services such as delicious and photographic archives such as Flickr, ordered by tags and geographic information, leverage users' self-interests in categorizing their own materials to enhance usability. In these cases the effects of user actions are transparent. Self-interest converges with the usefulness of the aggregated result. There is no active negotiation with the designers or operators of the system but acquiescence to the basic framework.

(3) Distributed computing projects such as SETI and Folding@Home require a one-off choice by users as to how to allocate resources, after which they remain passive. Each contribution is small, and the cost to the user is correspondingly low. Different projects candidate themselves for selection, and users have neither a role in defining the choice available nor an ongoing responsibility for the maintenance of the system. Nonetheless, the aggregated effect generates utility.

Stronger . . .

(4) P2P platforms like BitTorrent, eDonkey, and Limewire constitute a system in which strangers assist one another in accessing music, video, applications, and other files. The subjective preferences of individual users give each an interest in the maintenance of such informal institutions as a whole. Bandwidth contribution to the network guarantees its survival and promises the satisfaction of at least some needs, some of the time. Intention is required, especially in the context of attempts at its suppression through legal action and industry stigmatization. Links between individual users are weak, but uncooperative tendencies are disadvantaged by protocols requiring reciprocity or biasing performance in favor of generous participants (e.g., BitTorrent, emule).

(5) Slashdot, the technology-related news and discussion site, does not actually produce articles at all. Instead, stories are submitted by users, which are then filtered. Those published are either selected by paid staff or voted on by the user base. Following this, the stories are presented on the web page, and the real business of Slashdot begins: voluminous commentary ranging from additional information on the topic covered (of varying levels of accuracy) to analysis (of various degrees of quality) to speculation (of various degrees of pertinence), taking in jokes and assorted trolling along the way. This miasma is then ordered by the users themselves, a changing subset

of whom have evaluation powers over the comments, which they assess for relevance and accuracy on a sliding scale. The number and quality of comments presented is then determined by users themselves by configuring their viewing preferences. User moderations are in turn moderated for fairness by other users, in a process known as metamoderation.[11]

In addition to the news component of the site, Slashdot also provides all users with space for a journal (which predates the blog) and tools to characterize relations with other users as "friends" or "foes" (predating and exceeding Facebook). The software behind the site, slashcode, is free software which is used by numerous other web communities of a smaller scale.

(6) Vimeo, a portal for user-produced video, shelters a wide variety of subcultures/communities under one roof. Two factors stand out which distinguish it from other apparently similar sites: the presence of explicit collective experimentation and a high level of knowledge sharing. Members frequently propose themes and solicit contributions following a defined script and then assemble the results as a collection.

Several channels are explicitly devoted to teaching others techniques in film production and editing, but the spirit of exchange is diffuse throughout the site. Viewers commonly query the filmmaker as to how particular effects were achieved, equipment employed, and so on. The extent to which Vimeo is used for knowledge sharing distinguishes it from YouTube, where commentary regularly collapses into flame wars, and brings it close to Wenger's concept of a "community of practice," previously discussed.

Vimeo is nonetheless a private company whose full-time employees have the final word in terms of moderation decisions, but substantially the community flourishes on a shared set of norms which encourage supportive and constructive commentary and on a willingness to share know-how in addition to moving images.

... Intense

(7) Although there is something of an overreliance on Wikipedia as an example in discussions of collaboration and social media, its unusually evolved structure makes it another salient case. The overall goal is clear: construction of an encyclopedia capable of superseding one of the classical reference books of history.

The highly modular format affords endless scope for self-selected involvement on subjects of a user's choice. Ease of amendment combined with preservation of previous versions (the key qualities of wikis in general) enable both highly granular levels of participation and an effective self-defense mechanism against destructive users who defect from the goal.

At the core of the project lies a group who actively self-identify themselves as Wikipedians and dedicate time to developing and promoting community norms, especially around the arbitration of conflicts. Jimmy Wales, the project's founder, remains the titular head of Wikipedia, and although there have been some conflicts between him and the community, he has in general conceded authority. But the tension remains without conclusive resolution.

(8) FLOSSmanuals, the organization that facilitated the writing of this text you are reading, was originally established to produce documentation for free software projects, a historically weak point of the Free Software community. The method usually involves the assembly of a core group of collaborators who meet face-to-face for a number of days and produce a book during their time together.

Composition of this text takes place on an online collective writing platform called booki, integrating wiki-like versioning history and a chat channel. In addition to those who are physically present, remote participation is actively encouraged. When the work is focused on technical documentation, the functionality of the software in question provides a guide to the shape of the text. When the work is conceptual, as in the case of this text, it is necessary to come to an agreed basic understanding through discussion, which can jumpstart the process. Once under way, both content and structure are continually refined, edited, discussed, and revised. On conclusion, the book is made freely available on the website under a Creative Commons license, and physical copies are available for purchase on demand.

(9) Closed P2P communities for music, film, and text, such as the now-suppressed Oink, build archives and complex databases. These commonly contain technical details about the quality of files (resolution, bit rate), samples to illustrate quality (screenshots), relevant sources of information elsewhere (IMDb links, track listing, artwork), descriptions of the plot, director, musician, or formal significance of the work.

In addition, most have a means of coordinating users such that delivery of the data is ensured. If someone is looking for a file currently unseeded, preceding downloaders are notified, alerting them to the chance to assist. When combined with the fixed rules of protocol operation and community-specific rules such as ratio requirements (whereby one must upload a specified amount in relation to the quantity downloaded), there is an effective scheme to encourage or even oblige cooperation. Numerous other tasks are assumed voluntarily, from the creation of subtitles, in the case of film, to the assembly of thematic collections. All users participate in carrying the data load, and a significant number actively source new materials to share with other members and to satisfy requests.

(10) Debian is built on a clearly defined goal: the development and distribution of a GNU/Linux operating system consistent with the Debian Free Software Guidelines. These guidelines are part of a wider written "social contract," a code embodying the project's ethics, procedural rules, and framework for interaction. These rules are the subject of constant debate, and additions to the code base likewise often give rise to extended debates touching on legal, political, and ethical questions. The social contract can be changed by a general resolution of the developers.

Debian also exemplifies a "recursive community,"[12] in that participants develop and maintain the tools which support their ongoing communication. Developers have specified tasks and responsibilities, and the community requires a high level of commitment and attention. Several positions are appointed by election.

Nonhuman Collaboration

It is interesting to ask ourselves if humans are the only entities which might have agency in the world. Do you need language and consciousness to participate? Donna Haraway has observed that "it isn't humans that produced machines in some unilateral action—the arrow does not move all in one way. . . . There are very important nodes of energy in non-human agency, non-human actions."[13] Bruno Latour suggests it might be possible to extend social agency, rights, and obligations to automatic door closers, sleeping police officers, bacteria, public transport systems, sheep dogs, and fences.[14] Taking this view, perhaps we might begin to imagine ourselves as operating in collaboration with a sidewalk, an egg-and-cheese sandwich, our stomachs, or the Age of Enlightenment.

Most of our conversations about collaboration begin with the presumption of a kind of binary opposition between the individual and social agency. Latour solves this problem by suggesting that there are actor-networks—entities with both structure and agency. We ignore the nonhuman at our own peril, for all manner of nonhuman things incite, provoke, participate in, and author actions in the world. How might it inform and transform our conversations about collaboration if we imagined ourselves to be collaborating not only with people but with things, forces, networks, intellectual history, and bacteria?

This chapter is excerpted from Adam Hyde et al., *Collaborative Futures*, FLOSSmanuals.net, http://www.booki.cc/collaborativefutures/ (accessed July 20, 2010). This work is licensed under the Creative Commons Attribution-ShareAlike license.

1. Aniket Kittur and Robert E. Kraut, "Harnessing the Wisdom of Crowds in Wikipedia: Quality through Coordination," *Proceedings of 2008 ACM Conference on Computer Supported Cooperative Work*, 2004, http://doi.acm.org/10.1145/1460563.1460572 (accessed July 20, 2010).

2. Stephen Colbert, "The Word—Wikiality," Colbert Nation, July 31, 2006, http://www.colbertnation.com/the-colbert-report-videos/72347/july-31-2006/the-word—-wikiality (accessed July 20, 2010).

3. Ral315, "Wikipedia Satire Leads to Vandalism, Protections," Wikipedia Signpost, August 7, 2006, http://en.wikipedia.org/wiki/Wikipedia:Wikipedia_Signpost/2006-08-07/Wikiality (accessed July 20, 2010).

4. Wikipedia, "User:Stephancolbert," Wikipedia user page, https://secure.wikimedia.org/wikipedia/en/wiki/User:Stephencolbert (accessed July 20, 2010).

5. Maham, "thru-you revolution live in wroclove," Radio Wroclove, http://www.radio-wroclove.pl/?p=151 (accessed July 20, 2010).

6. Ophir Kutiel, "ThruYou," http://www.thru-you.com/ (accessed July 20, 2010).

7. Galit Eilat, "Collaboration," lecture at the Dictionary of War conference, Novi Sad, January 25, 2008, available online at http://dictionaryofwar.org/concepts/Collaboration_%282%29 (accessed July 20, 2010).

8. Alexander R. Galloway and Eugene Thacker, *The Exploit: A Theory of Networks* (Minneapolis: University of Minnesota Press, 2007), 5.

9. Ippolita, Geert Lovink, and Ned Rossiter, "The Digital Given—10 Web 2.0 Theses," *net critique* (blog), Institute of Network Cultures, June 15, 2009, http://networkcultures.org/wpmu/geert/2009/06/15/the-digital-given-10-web-20-theses-by-ippolita-geert-lovink-ned-rossiter/ (accessed July 20, 2010).

10. Etienne Wenger, Richard Arnold McDermott, and William Snyder, *Cultivating Communities of Practice: A Guide to Managing Knowledge* (Boston: Harvard Business Press, 2002), 4.

11. See Yochai Benkler, *The Wealth of Networks* (New Haven: Yale University Press, 2007), 76–80.

12. Christopher M. Kelty, *Two Bits: The Cultural Significance of Free Software* (Durham: Duke University Press, 2008).

13. Donna Haraway, "Birth of the Kennel: Cyborgs, Dogs and Companion Species," lecture at the European Graduate School, Leuk-Stadt, Switzerland, August 2000, available online at http://www.egs.edu/faculty/donna-haraway/articles/birth-of-the-kennel/ (accessed July 20, 2010).

14. Bruno Latour, *Reassembling the Social: An Introduction to Actor-Network-Theory* (New York: Oxford University Press, 2005), 63–86.

PART II

Sociality

Participating in the Always-On Lifestyle

DANAH BOYD

I love filling out surveys, but I'm always stumped when I'm asked how many hours per day I spend online. I mean, what counts as online? I try to answer this through subtraction. I start by subtracting the hours that I sleep (~7.5 if I'm lucky). But then a little bird in the back of my brain wonders whether or not sleeping with my iPhone next to my bed really counts. Or maybe it counts when I don't check it, but what about when I check Twitter in the middle of the night when I wake up from a dream? I subtract the time spent in the shower (0.5) because technology and water are not (yet) compatible. But that's as far as I can usually get. I don't *always* check Wikipedia during dinner, but when there's a disagreement, the interwebz are always there to save the day. And, I fully admit, I definitely surf the web while on the toilet.

Y'see . . . I'm part of a cohort who is always-on. I consciously and loudly proclaim offline time through the declaration of e-mail sabbaticals when all content pushed my way is bounced rather than received. (There's nothing more satisfying than coming home from a vacation with an empty inbox and a list of people so desperate to reach me that they actually called my mother.) But this is not to say that I only have "a life" when I'm on digital sabbatical. I spend plenty of time socializing face-to-face with people, watching movies, and walking through cities. And I even spend time doing things that I'd prefer not to—grocery shopping, huffing and puffing on the treadmill, and so on. All of these activities are not in and of themselves "online," but because of technology, the online is always just around the corner. I can look up information, multitask by surfing the web, and backchannel with friends. I'm not really online, in that my activities are not centered on the digital bits of the Internet, but I'm not really offline either. I'm where those concepts break down. It's no longer about on or off really. It's about living in a world where being networked to people and information wherever and whenever you need it is just assumed. I may not be always-on the *Internet* as we think of it colloquially, but I am always connected to the network. And that's what it means to be always-on.

There is an irony to all of this. My always-on-ness doesn't mean that I'm always-accessible-to-everyone. Just because my phone buzzes to tell me that a new message has arrived does not mean that I bother to look at it. This is not because I'm antiphone but because I'm procontext. Different social contexts mean different relationships to being always-on. They are not inherently defined by space but by a social construction of context in my own head. Sometimes I'm interruptible by *anyone* (like when I'm bored out of my mind at the DMV). But more often, I'm not interruptible because connection often means context shift, and only certain context shifts are manageable. So if I'm at dinner, I will look up a Wikipedia entry as a contribution to the conversation without checking my text messages. All channels are accessible, but it doesn't mean I will access them.

I am not alone. Like many others around me, I am perpetually connected to people and information through a series of devices and social media channels. This is often something that's described in generational terms, with "digital natives" being always-on and everyone else hobbling along trying to keep up with the technology. But, while what technology is available to each generation at key life stages keeps changing, being always-on isn't so cleanly generational. There are inequality issues that mean that plenty of youth simply don't have access to the tools that I can afford. But economic capital is not the only factor. Being always-on works best when the people around you are always-on, and the networks of always-on-ers are defined more by values and lifestyle than by generation. In essence, being always-on started as a subcultural practice, and while it is gaining momentum, it is by no means universal. There are plenty of teens who have no interest in being perpetually connected to information and people even if they can. And there are plenty of us who are well beyond our teen years who are living and breathing digital bits for fun. That said, many of the young are certainly more willing to explore this lifestyle than are their techno-fretful parents. So while being young doesn't guarantee deep engagement with technology, it is certainly correlated.

What separates those who are part of the always-on lifestyle from those who aren't is not often the use of specific tools. It's mostly a matter of approach. Instant messaging is a tool used by many but often in different ways and for different purposes. There are those who log in solely to communicate with others. And there are those who use it to convey presence and state of mind. Needless to say, the latter is much more a part of the always-on ethos. Being always-on is not just about consumption and production of content but also about creating an ecosystem in which people can stay peripherally connected to one another through a variety of microdata. It's about creating networks and layering information on top. The goal of being connected is not simply to exchange high-signal content all the time. We also want all of the squishy, gooey content that keeps us connected as people. In our world, phatic content like posting what you had for breakfast on Twitter is AOK. Cuz it can enhance the social context. Of course, some people do go too far. But that's what teasing is meant for.

To an outsider, wanting to be always-on may seem pathological. All too often, it's labeled an addiction. The assumption is that we're addicted to the technology. The technology doesn't matter. It's all about the people and information. Humans are both curious and social critters. We want to understand and interact. Technology introduces new possibilities for doing so, and that's where the passion comes in. We're passionate about technology because we're passionate about people and information, and they go hand in hand. And once you're living in an always-on environment, you really notice what's missing when you're not. There's nothing I hate more than standing in a foreign country with my iPhone in hand, unable to access Wikipedia because roaming on AT&T is so prohibitively expensive as to make the Internet inaccessible. Instead, I find myself making lists of all the things that I want to look up when I can get online.

It's not just about instant gratification either. Sure, I can look up who is buried in the Pantheon later. But the reason that I want to know when I'm standing before it in Italy is because I want to know about the object in front of me whose signs are all in Italian. I want to translate those signs, ask questions about the architecture. And it's 4 a.m., and the guard tells me it's not his job to provide history lessons. What I want is to bring people and information into context. It's about enhancing the experience.

Of course, this doesn't mean it can't get overwhelming. Cuz it does. And I'm not always good at managing the overload. My RSS-feed reader has exploded, and there's no way that I can keep up with the plethora of status updates and Twitter messages posted by friends, colleagues, and intriguing humans that I don't know. E-mail feels like a chore, and I do everything possible to avoid having to log in to dozens of different sites to engage in conversations inside walled gardens. There's more news than I can possibly read on any given day.

So how do I cope? Realistically, I don't. I've started accepting that there's no way that I can manage the onslaught of contact, wade through the mess, and find the hidden gems. I haven't completely thrown my hands up though. Instead, I've decided to take a laissez-faire approach to social media. I do my best, and when that's not good enough, I rely on people bitching loud and clear to make me reprioritize. And then I assess whether or not I can address their unhappiness. And if I can't, I cringe and hope that it won't be too costly. And sometimes I simply declare bankruptcy and start over.

As social media becomes increasingly pervasive in everyday life, more and more people will be overwhelmed by the information surrounding them. And they will have to make choices. Networked technologies allow us to extend our reach, to connect across space and time, to find people with shared interests and gather en masse for social and political purposes. But time and attention are scarce resources. Until we invent the sci-fi doohickey that lets us freeze time, no amount of aggregating and reorganizing will let us overcome the limitations presented by a scarcity of time and attention.

In the meantime, many of us are struggling to find balance. We create artificial structures in an effort to get there. I take digital sabbaticals. Others create technologies that restrict them so that they don't have face hard decisions at points when they're potentially vulnerable. For example, late-night surfing from link to link to link can be so enjoyable that it's easy to forget to sleep. But biology isn't very forgiving, so sometimes a time-out is necessary.

Many from the always-on crowd also try to embrace crazy strategies to optimize time as much as humanly possible. Proponents of polyphasic sleep argue that hacking your circadian rhythm can allow for more wake hours; I just think sleeping in small chunks means more loopy people out in the blogosphere. Of course, I fully admit that I've embraced the cult of GTD in an effort to reduce unnecessary cognitive load by doing inventories of various things.

Hacking time, hacking biology, hacking cognition—these are all common traits of people who've embraced an always-on lifestyle. Many of us love the idea that we can build new synaptic structures through our use of networked technologies. While many old-skool cyberpunks wanted to live in a virtual reality, always-on folks are more interested in an augmented reality. We want to be a part of the network.

There's no formula for embracing always-on practices, and we must each develop our own personal strategies for navigating a world with ever-increasing information. There are definitely folks who fail to find balance, but most of us find a comfortable way to fit these practices into everyday life without consequence. Of course, the process of finding balance may appear like we're feeling our way through a maze while blindfolded. We're all going to bump into a lot of things along the way and have to reassess where we're going when we reach our own personal edges. But, in doing so, we will personalize the media rich environment to meet our needs and desires.

Social media skeptics often look at the output of those who are engaging with the newfangled services and shake their heads. "How can they be so public?" some ask. Others reject digital performances by asking, "Who wants to read what they want anyhow?" Publicness is one of the strange and yet powerful aspects of this new world. Many who blog and tweet are not writing for the world at large; they are writing for the small group who might find it relevant and meaningful. And, realistically, the world at large is not reading the details of their lives. Instead, they are taking advantage of the affordances of these technologies to connect with others in a way that they feel is appropriate.

Each technology has its affordances, and what's powerful about certain technology often stems from these affordances. Consider asynchronicity, an affordance of many social media tools. Years ago, I interviewed an HIV-positive man who started blogging. When I asked him about his decision to start, he told me that it helped him navigate social situations in a more comfortable manner. He did not use his real name on his blog, but his friends all knew where to find the blog. On this site, he wrote about his ups and downs with his illness, and his friends read this. He found that such a mediator allowed him to negotiate social boundaries with friends in new ways. He no longer had to gauge the appropriateness of the situation to suddenly declare his T-cell count. Likewise, his friends didn't have to overcome their uncertainty in social situations to ask about his health. He could report when he felt comfortable doing so, and they could read when they were prepared to know. This subtle shift in how he shared information with friends and how friends consumed it eased all sorts of tensions. Technology doesn't simply break social conventions—it introduces new possibilities for them.

It's also typically assumed that being always-on means facing severe personal or professional consequences. There is fear that participating in a public culture can damage one's reputation or that constant surfing means the loss of focus or that always having information at hand will result in a failure to actually know things. But aren't we living in a world where knowing how to get information is more important than memorizing it? Aren't we moving away from an industrial economy into an information one? Creativity is shaped more by the ability to make new connections than to focus on a single task. And why shouldn't we all have the ability to be craft our identity in a public culture? Personally, I've gained more professionally from being public than I could have dreamed possible when I started blogging in 1997. For example, l'il ol' me had no idea that blogging controversial ideas backed with data might get me an invitation to the White House.

Ironically, the publicness of social media also provides privacy in new ways. Many of those who embrace the public aspects of social media find that the more public they are, the more they can carve off privacy. When people assume you share everything, they don't ask you about what you don't share. There are also ways to embed privacy in public in ways that provide a unique form of control over the setting. Certainly, people have always had private conversations while sitting in public parks. And queer culture is rife with stories of how gay and lesbian individuals signaled to one another in public arenas through a series of jewelry, accessories, and body language. Likewise, in-jokes are only meaningful to those who are in the know, whether they are shared in a group or online. And there are all sorts of ways to say things out loud that are only heard by a handful of people. These become tricks of the trade, skills people learn as they begin fully engaging in an always-on public culture.

Being always-on and living a public life through social media may complicate our lives in new ways, but participating can also enrich the tapestry of life. Those of us who are living this way can be more connected to those whom we love and move in sync with those who share our interests. The key to this lifestyle is finding a balance, a rhythm that moves us in ways that make us feel whole without ripping our sanity to shreds. I've lived my entire adult life in a world of networked information and social media. At times, I'm completely overwhelmed, but when I hit my stride, I feel like an ethereal dancer, energized by the connections and ideas that float by. And there's nothing like being connected and balanced to make me feel alive and in love with the world at large.

From Indymedia to Demand Media

*Journalism's Visions of Its Audience
and the Horizons of Democracy*

C. W. ANDERSON

This chapter focuses on journalism—a particular subcategory of media production where user-generated content has been adopted in significant but contested ways. Underlying the chapter is a more general claim that the tensions within U.S. journalism have relevance for understanding broader categories of media work. Building on earlier ethnographic work in newsrooms, the chapter contends that a fundamental transformation has occurred in journalists' understanding of their relationship to their audiences and that a new level of responsiveness to the agenda of the audience is becoming built into the DNA of contemporary newswork. This new journalistic responsiveness to the "people formerly known as the audience" is often contrasted with an earlier understanding of the news audience by journalists, the so-called traditional or professional view, in which the wants and desires of audience members are subordinated to journalists' expert news judgment about the stories that audience members need to know. In much of the popular rhetoric surrounding "Web 2.0" journalists' newfound audience responsiveness is represented as a democratic advance over older professional models, with the increasing journalistic attention paid to audience wants framed as concomitant with the general democratizing trends afforded by the Internet.

The primary claim of this chapter is that this simple dichotomy between audience ignorance and audience responsiveness obscures as much as it reveals and that multiple, complex, and contradictory visions of the news audience are buried within popular understandings of the relationship between journalism and Web 2.0. The chapter builds on work by writers as diverse as John Battelle[1] and Helen Nissenbaum,[2] who have convincingly argued that diverse socio-material combinations of technology, organizational structure, and human intentionality afford diverse democratic potentialities and prefigure distinct publics; in particular, I argue that diverse materializations of the audience not only afford distinct publics but also stand as an intermediary between *visions* of an audience-as-public and the relationship between audiences and democracy. In short, the manner in which journalists imagine their audience has public consequences, and the relationship between audience responsiveness and democracy involves particular, not necessarily compatible, understandings of what democratic practice actually entails.

To flesh out these arguments, this chapter adopts a method that is primarily historio-critical and, following Max Weber, discusses ideal-types.[3] I trace the conception of audience in three outsider journalistic movements spanning the forty years since Watergate: the public journalism movement, the citizen journalism movement known as Indymedia, and, finally, the quasi-journalistic company Demand Media. While my arguments are primarily synthetic, each of my case studies stems from previous empirical scholarship: four years of newsroom fieldwork in Philadelphia, seven years of participant-observation with Indymedia collectives in New York City, and lengthy research into both the public journalism movement and, more recently, the growth of Demand Media and other so-called news content farms. Elaborating on this analysis, the second section of this chapter ties different visions of the audience into distinct strands of democratic theory. In this section, I hope to demonstrate how an embrace of "the people formerly known as the audience" can mean very different things, depending on the larger social and political context in which this articulation occurs. The chapter concludes with some general reflections on the implications of concepts like algorithmic public and algorithmic democracy, concepts which seem to be key socio-material categories in the digital era.

Journalism and Audiences

The Professional View

The relationship between the audience and the news industry examined here is not one in which media messages "impact" the audience in particular ways; nor is it one in which an audience "interprets" media messages in a variety of ways, depending on a variety of personal and demographic factors. Rather, the newsroom activities in this study are an example of what Joseph Turow has called the "industrial construction" of audiences:[4] "the ways that the people who create [media] materials think of" the people who consume that media, which in turn has "important implications for the texts that viewers and readers receive in the first place."[5] As journalistic visions of the audience for journalism shift, these new visions ultimately affect editorial products.

Herbert Gans's landmark study *Deciding What's News*[6] has shaped the conventional academic wisdom regarding the relationship between journalists and their audiences for several decades. This 1979 ethnographic study of news-making processes at *CBS Evening News*, *NBC Nightly News*, *Newsweek*, and *Time* usefully distinguished between "qualitative" (letters to the editor and to individual journalists) and "quantitative" (audience research studies) forms of feedback.[7] Gans notes,

> I began this study with the assumption that journalists, as commercial employees, take the audience directly into account when selecting and producing news. . . . I was surprised to find, however, that they had little knowledge about the actual audience and rejected feedback from it. Although they had a vague image of the audience, they paid little attention to it; instead, they filmed and wrote for their superiors and themselves, assuming, as I suggested earlier, that what interested them would interest the audience.[8]

Gans argues that multiple factors play a role in journalists' relative disconnect from their audience: an inability to intellectually imagine an audience of millions of people, a distrust of audience news judgment, and the division between the editorial and marketing departments (creating a situation in which business personnel and news editors create a buffer between journalists and their audience). The key values in tension in Gans's study are professional incentives versus commercial imperatives. Journalists, adds Gans, are reluctant to accept any procedure which casts doubt on their professional autonomy. Within the boundaries of his study, professional values remain strong, and the preferences and needs of the audience are largely neglected during the news-making process.

It should be noted that Gans does nuance his observations to some degree. Gans writes that "in the last analysis, news organizations are overseen by corporate executives who are paid to show a profit, . . . [and] if corporate economic well-being is threatened, executives may insist that their news organizations adapt."[9] Additionally, Gans notes that local news production (which was not part of his 1979 study) has always been more sensitive to commercial and audience pressures than has national news. Despite these qualifications, most of the research from what Barbie Zelizer has called the golden era of newsroom ethnography,[10] has echoed Gans's conclusions about the relative unimportance of the news audience to journalistic judgment. "Audience images," James Ettema et al. summarize, "seem to have minor influence on journalistic performance relative to other potential influence sources."[11] And while some scholars[12] have argued that the audience plays a larger role in *shaping* the news than is generally assumed by most ethnographers and media sociologists, even these authors have generally acknowledged that this shaping force is still the product of an "incomplete" understanding of the audience, one which is "not keyed in to demographic information."[13]

"The People Formerly Known as the Audience"

A radically new attitude toward audiences, emerging in recent years alongside the rise of digital technologies, social media, and user-generated content, can be referred to by the helpful new-media maxim[14] "the people formerly known as the audience." First articulated by media theorist and NYU professor Jay Rosen in an influential blogpost, the notion of "the former audience" and its relationship to journalism ultimately revolves around a series of digital technologies that shift the direction of communication from a one-to-many broadcasting system to a many-to-many conversational system. These technologies include social media like online commenting systems and Facebook, media for creative personal expression like blogs and podcasts, and new channels of distribution like Twitter. Rosen argues that this passively receptive audience is no longer the model for thinking about media consumption, especially when this new model treats consumption itself as part of the production of media. He writes that "the people formerly known as the audience . . . are those who were on the receiving end of a media system that ran one way, in a broadcasting pattern, with high entry fees and a few firms competing to speak very loudly while the rest of the population listened in isolation from one another—and who today are not in a situation like that at all."[15] All of these changes, Rosen and many others have argued, are impacting the profession of journalism, a profession whose autonomy was ultimately grounded in the kind of closed, mostly one-way system of communication now being displaced by the old model.[16] Although the notion of professionalized news decisions discussed in detail by Gans and others aren't usually directly cited in discussions of this new image of the audience, it seems likely that the practice of journalists "filming and writing for their superiors and themselves, assuming . . . that what interested them would interest the audience"[17] is one of the professional behaviors under serious stress in the new media environment.

Nevertheless, most of the recent scholarship examining whether the explosion of social media has affected journalism's agenda-setting function presents something of a mixed picture,[18] with a number of studies demonstrating the continued power of professional journalists to "decide what's news."[19] Other research has documented that many journalistic websites, while happy to adopt particular social media tools, have held back from a full-throated embrace of "the people formerly known as the audience."[20]

In light of this emerging class of empirical findings, it is important to add some historical and theoretical nuance to the perhaps overly simplistic dichotomy between a vision of the "people formerly knows as audience" and traditional journalistic professionalism. Two analyses in the pages that follow elaborate on what the audience is and how it has related to news production. First, I trace the conception of audience in three nontraditional journalistic experiments: the public journalism movement, the radical collective-reporting movement known as Indymedia, and, finally, the much-discussed media company Demand Media. Second, I tie these visions of the audience into distinct strands of democratic theory, to show how even an overt embrace of "the people formerly known as the audience" can mean very different things, depending on the context in which this embrace occurs.

Alternative Understandings of News Audiences: Public Journalism, Indymedia, Demand Media

The three organizations and movements I discuss in this section—public journalism, Indymedia, and Demand Media—should not be seen as representative in any meaningful sense. Rather, they might better serve as theoretical ideal types, in which particular characteristics of social reality are emphasized in order to create a class of abstract categories, categories which can then be used as the basis for further, less abstract empirical research. Each of these three institutions and movements has its own large analytical academic literature, and my brief description of them here should not be seen as comprehensive. For further information, readers are encouraged to follow the cited works.

The *public journalism movement* has been called "the best organized social movement inside journalism in the history of the American press" and has an institutional, theoretical, and practical history.[21] Institutionally, public journalism was a professional reform movement that emerged within the American press in the late 1980s, with its heyday in the early to mid-1990s, and which, as a distinct movement, can be said to have ended in the first years of the twenty-first century. Theoretically, public journalism drew on strands of deliberative and participatory democratic theory, arguing that post-Watergate journalism had grown overly concerned with representing the points of view of political insiders, trucked in corrosive cynicism about the meaning and importance of political life, and lacked any meaningful understanding of journalism's relationship to democracy.[22] Critics contended that political journalism was overly obsessed with "horse-race" coverage and polls to the detriment of the coverage of actual public issues. As an antidote, public journalism reformers[23] argued that journalists should acknowledge themselves as democratic actors, should help *create* a public rather than just inform it, and should embrace a thick concept of democratic life centering on political deliberation rather than simply on elections and polls. Practically, public journalists working inside newsrooms undertook a number of professional and reportorial experiments in the heyday of the movement, including sponsoring deliberative forums to help highlight issues that local communities thought worthy of news coverage and sponsoring special election initiatives designed to transcend horse-race political reporting. Public journalism experiments were explicitly adopted at various newspapers, most notably the *Witchita-Eagle*.[24] On the broadest philosophical level, public journalism advocates explicitly cited Jürgen Habermas's notions of deliberative democracy and John Dewey's invocation of community conversation as normative principles that should guide journalistic coverage.

With the popularization and spread of the World Wide Web in the mid-1990s and an upsurge in left-wing social-movement activity in 1999 around the somewhat uneasily titled "antiglobalization movement," a new, less genteel challenge to traditional journalism emerged as a cluster of radically participatory citizen journalism websites grouped under the banner of the Indymedia movement. Indymedia's slogan sums up much of its emphasis during these years: "Don't hate the media, become the media." First launched during the 1999 World Trade Organization protests in Seattle, Indymedia was characterized by its strong political agenda, its decentralized and localized structure (there were Indymedia Centers (IMCs) in more than 150 cities worldwide at the movement's peak), and its notion of radically participatory journalism. As described by Biella Coleman,

> Indymedia centers are run as local collectives that manage and coordinate a news website; some also operate an affiliated media resource center for local activists. These websites give any user of the site (regardless of whether or not they are part of the collective) the ability to create, publish,

and access news reports of various forms—text, photo, video, and audio. The result is a free online source for unfiltered, direct journalism by activists, sometimes uploaded in the heat of the moment during a demonstration or political action. . . . Where traditional journalism holds editorial policies that are hidden in the hands of a few trained experts, Indymedia provides the alternative of "open publishing," a democratic process of creating news that is transparent and accessible to all, challenging the separation between consumers and producers of news.[25]

Unlike the public journalism movement, which was a reform movement primarily directed at journalistic professionals, Indymedia argued for a deprofessionalized vision of citizen journalism in which people would be their own reporters. And unlike the public journalism movement, which was relatively self-reflective about the theoretical underpinnings of various interventions into spheres of journalistic practice, Indymedia spokespeople were more likely to critique the operations of global capitalism from an anarchist or Marxist perspective rather than theorize deeply about their own status as new journalistic actors. Nevertheless, as we will see momentarily, it is certainly possible to reconstruct Indymedia's basic understanding of how it operated as a journalistic reform movement and how it related to its audience.

The first decade of the twenty-first century marks the beginning, but not necessarily the end, of a period of fundamental transformation in the worlds of journalism and digital technology. Starting in 1999 and continuing to the present, many authors and academics have chronicled the virtual disintegration of the American business model for local news under the impact of digital technologies and shifting patterns of advertising,[26] a precipitous decline in the cultural authority of traditional journalists (whose credentials were challenged by journalism thinkers and by an army of so-called citizen journalists),[27] and an explosion in the practices of audience measurement and behavioral tracking afforded by the digital traceability of the Internet. Of these three developments it is the increased ability of news organizations to monitor their audiences which has the most relevance for my discussion of a third outlier: algorithmic journalism.

The material traceability afforded by the web[28] presents journalism with a fundamentally new series of professional challenges and economic opportunities. All user behavior on a website is potentially capturable for analysis by server logfiles, and "whether the audience realizes it or not, their activity is tracked."[29] As journalism analyst Steve Outing noted in 2005, while reporters and editors at the news organizations analyzed by Gans operated largely in ignorance of their audience, "newspaper Web sites . . . have detailed traffic numbers at their disposal. Today's news editors know for a fact if sports articles are the biggest reader draw, or if articles about local crimes consistently outdraw political news. They can know how particular stories fared, and track the popularity of news topics."[30] While a growing body of research has documented the impact online metrics are having on newsrooms, an even more powerful form of quantitative journalistic decision-making has explicitly focused on base audience preferences. These companies learn what the audience searches for online, consider which of these will make them the most money, and choose their subjects solely on these computer-generated metrics. This methodology is powered by *algorithmic intelligence*, and the key practitioners of this new, algorithm-based technique of "deciding what's news" include communications companies like Demand Media, Seed, and Associated Content.[31]

In a widely discussed article, Daniel Roth of *Wired* magazine describes the role played by algorithms in both Demand Media's production and labor-compensation processes:

Demand Media has created a virtual factory that pumps out 4,000 video clips and articles a day. It starts with an algorithm. The algorithm is fed inputs from three sources: *Search terms* (popular terms from more than 100 sources comprising 2 billion searches a day), *The ad market* (a snapshot of which keywords are sought after and how much they are fetching), and *The competition* (what's online already and where a term ranks in search results).

Plenty of other companies—About.com, Mahalo, Answers.com—have tried to corner the market in arcane online advice. But none has gone about it as aggressively, scientifically, and single-mindedly as Demand. Pieces are not dreamed up by trained editors nor commissioned based on submitted questions. Instead they are assigned by an algorithm, which mines nearly a terabyte of search data, Internet traffic patterns, and keyword rates to determine what users want to know and how much advertisers will pay to appear next to the answers.

The process is automatic, random, and endless. . . . It is a database of human needs.[32]

This chapter has argued that the dichotomy between professional and responsive visions of the news audience is overly simplistic and has sought to highlight the actual complexity of news audience visions by discussing three outsider journalistic movements and organizations. Each of these movements can be seen as posing its own vision of journalism's relationship with its audience, visions that deeply complicate simplistic distinctions between audience power and audience irrelevance. In the next section I want to unpack these journalist-audience visions, before concluding with discussion of how these visions ultimately ground themselves in differing notions of communication and democracy.

A Genealogy of the Journalism-Audience Relationship

These four ideal-typical paradigms of journalistic practice—traditional journalism, public journalism, Indymedia journalism, and algorithmic journalism—offer very different models of audience. These models conceive of their audiences and their relationship to democracy in terms that have changed over time. In order to understand this shift, we need to ask how each of them

- thinks about the relationship between the news audience and journalistic institutions;
- thinks about the relationship of the audience to itself; and
- thinks about the relationship between the audience and political institutions.

It is helpful to organize this analysis in a table, with the four paradigms along the left side and the three perspectives on journalism, audiences, and politics along the top (table 7.1). From the perspective of *professional journalism*, news audiences are seen as rather ignorant consumers of media content; they are thus ignorant of both what news really "is" and what journalists do. Under this view, the agenda for what counts as news is determined by professional journalists, who provide it to an audience that can choose to either accept or reject it. The fact that professional journalists envision their audience as both "consumptive" and "easy to ignore" points to a tension that lies at the heart of this vision. Few producers (of media or other forms of consumer products) will operate under a consumption regime and yet argue that the consumers have little role to play in the determining the shape of the products they buy. Yet this is essentially the argument that traditional journalism has made. It is this tension that has periodically manifested itself in the battle between news professionals, who argue that journalism must provide the information citizens need ("citizens must eat their spinach"), and news populists, who argue that journalism must give an audience what it

TABLE 7.1

Journalistic Models and Their Visions of the New Audience

	The audience's relationship to journalism as . . .	The audience's internal relationship to itself as . . .	The audience's relationship to politics as . . .
Professional journalism sees . . .	consumptive, agenda receiving, occasionally as sources	atomistic, consumptive	disengaged, aggregated
Public journalism sees . . .	deliberative, agenda setting	A conversational public	engaged, communicative via deliberation
Indymedia journalism sees . . .	participatory, agenda setting; journalism provides audience with "ammunition"	agonistic, witnessing, and occupying public *sphericules*	engaged, confrontational, witnessing
Algorithmic journalism sees . . .	agenda setting, nonparticipatory, atomized	algorithmic, quantifiable	—

wants (and that any journalism in the public interest needs to coat itself in a wrapper of audience friendliness). The controversy is somewhat overdrawn, yet it speaks to a general truth. Journalists who see themselves as producers of consumer content would be expected to care deeply about what an army of news consumers wants.

In this analytic framework, members of professional journalism's atomized consumptive audience are discrete individuals who, in the tradition of both classic liberalism and market theory, both consume news and relate to each other in an individualized, utilitarian fashion. It is this vision of the audience that was the primary target of reformers in the *public journalism* movement; rather than an aggregate collection of autonomous individuals, the audience should be conceived as relating to itself as a *conversational public*. As Tanni Haas notes, visions of an audience composed of "engaged, responsible 'citizens' who are capable of active, democratic participation"[33] mirror James Carey's argument that "the public will begin to reawaken when they are addressed as conversational partners and are encouraged to join the talk rather than sit passively as spectators before a discussion conducted by journalists and experts."[34] For theorists of public journalism, the audience relates to itself not as a collection of consumptive individuals but as a collection of citizens engaged in public dialogue about the important political issues of the day.

If, according to theorists of public journalism, the audience relates to itself as a deliberative body of citizens, then its relationship to the journalism profession must also be not only deliberative but potentially agenda setting as well. While most of public journalism's early reform efforts were directed at forcing the journalism establishment to see itself as an institution implicated in acts of public "creation" as well as public "inform-ation," questions quickly arose as to how reporters should engage with the agenda of that assembled public. Should local deliberative councils, convened by newspapers as part of public journalism initiatives, determine the topics covered by those newspapers? Or were they simply meant as feel-good exercises in mutual enlightenment? Should the deliberative citizenry be agenda setting? It was this tension that Michael Schudson pointed to when he claimed that public journalism does not remove control over the news from journalists themselves, . . . [and] in this regard, public journalism as a reform movement is conservative. . . . [It] stops short of offering a fourth model of journalism in a democracy, one in which authority is vested not in the market, not in a party, and not in journalists, but in the public. Nothing in public journalism removes the power from the journalists or the corporations they work for.[35]

It seems safe to summarize that the audience envisioned by public journalism theorists was thus both deliberative and *agenda setting in a weak sense*. Ultimately, the relationship between the audience-as-public and the institutions of journalism was mediated by highly formal mechanisms: public meetings, deliberative polls, and special reports. It was this formal character of the journalist-audience relationship that was shattered by the technological affordances[36] enabled by the Internet and the spread of digital production and distribution devices. I have summarized these developments, and the new vision of the audience that emerged with them, under the general category of "Indymedia journalism," although I think this shifting audience conception can be generalized to include many of the early experiments in digital content creation (blogs, citizen journalism websites, and so on). For Indymedia activists and theorists, the audience was not only strongly implicated in setting the news agenda, but the very distinction between a consumptive and agenda-setting audience was blurred to the point of nonexistence.[37] This blurring was the result of Indymedia's highly participatory character. In exhorting activists to "be the media," the promise was that ordinary people would create their own news agenda through the very act of doing journalism itself. The journalism undertaken by Indymedia's presumptive[38] audience, finally, could not be separated from that audience's political activity. It would serve as a weapon in a variety of social-movement struggles and political protests.

This view of journalism as "political ammunition" was closely tied to Indymedia's status as a collection of left-wing social movements. A comparison with the audience envisioned by theorists of public journalism might be instructive here. Rather than a deliberative audience engaged in the civil discussion of political issues in order to advance the public good, Indymedia saw its audience as a rowdy collection of political partisans acting in support of a *particular* (yet still valuable) good. Or as John Durham Peters noted, in reference to the deliberative pretensions of public journalism,

> Public journalism is right to call for better sources of information and fresher forums of debate. But . . . the insistence on dialogue undervalues those modes of action that defy and interrupt conversation. St. Francis and Martin Luther King bore witness; they did not engage in conversation. Any account of democracy has to make room for moral stuntsmanship, for outrageous acts of attention getting employed by an Ezekiel or Gandhi, greens, antinuke activists, or even right-to-lifers. . . . Just as there is a dignity in dialogue, there can be a dignity in refusing to engage in dialog as well.[39]

It was the Indymedia movement which embodied this vision of the "witnessing," "stunt-oriented" public and sought to apply it to journalism. Finally, Indymedia never claimed to represent *the* public, as proponents of public journalism did. Indeed, for Indymedia theorists, the very existence of such a public was an illusion. Following in the tradition of Nancy Fraser and Todd Gitlin, Indymedia activists saw themselves as producing journalism for a particular set of public sphericules[40]—related to, but irreducible to, the larger public as a whole. They were the journalistic mouthpieces of a loosely connected series of "subaltern counterpublics"[41] or, in less formalized language, represented the return of the eighteenth-century party press to the journalistic stage.[42] The Indymedia vision of the audience was of an agonistic, agenda-setting, deeply participatory, fractured public.

With the emergence of Demand Media and its "content-farm" counterparts, the affordances of the Internet have swung from participation to traceability and algorithmically oriented production. These forms of algo-rithmic journalism once again establish the wall between producer and con-sumer. While Demand Media's producers are multitudinous, the relationship between them and the central office is the relationship between a highly pre-carious freelancer and his or her employer, rather than that of the intrinsi-cally motivated creator to the object of his or her temporary affiliation. This reintegration of the producer/consumer wall does not disempower the audi-ence, however, for its wishes and wants are presumed to be understood bet-ter than ever before. As Demand Media founder Richard Rosenblatt noted in an interview with Jay Rosen, "We respect journalists very much. We think they need to use technology to help them figure out what audiences want and how to get value from their content more effectively. And there are big opportunities for them to increase quality by removing inefficiencies in the process of content creation."[43] The agenda-setting vision of the audience, common to both public journalism and Indymedia journalism, is combined with a consumptive, atomistic, and quantifiable vision of the audience taken from the professional model of journalism. Unlike the professional model, however, the tension between the vision of the audience as a consumptive organism and as subject to a professionally determined concept of "what counts" as important content is eliminated, in a direction entirely favorable to the audience. If the audience's needs and wants are entirely knowable, than why should they *not* be catered to, particularly if catering to those wants can lead to the implementation of a highly successful business model? The ulti-mate traceability of audience wants is determined through the algorithm, a complex and mathematically grounded socio-material black box that seems to do far more than simply aggregate preferences. In the vision of the audi-ence embraced by Demand Media and its counterparts, the algorithm is a stand-in for journalistic judgment, and it eviscerates the barriers between content production and consumer demand. According to this new genera-tion of algorithm-based news producers, it is in number crunching that the ultimate guarantor of both communicative democracy and business-model success can be found.

Democratic Horizons of the Journalism-Audience Relationship

In this final section, I want to tie each of the four ideal-typical visions dis-cussed in this essay to particular visions of democracy. In this endeavor, I am inspired by the public journalism movement, which—alone among the mod-els I have discussed—made its normative democratic commitments both transparent and central to its organizing strategy. In this moment of profound journalistic upheaval I am convinced we need to supplement our very understandable debates over newsroom business models with a brief discussion of what kind of democracy we want our business models to serve. As I have articulated in this essay, traditional journalism understands democracy as an aggregative process. Public journalism, in opposition, puts forward a deliberative democratic model, while Indymedia theorists see democracy as a primarily agonistic exercise. Algorithmic journalism embraces an "algorithmic" understanding of democratic processes. It is this algorithmic vision of democracy that might represent the most intellectually interesting, if unsettling, model for both communication and democracy.

Public journalism embraced a strongly normative, deliberative conception of democracy. In it, the legitimacy of political decision-making is assumed to rest only on the force of the superior argument, advanced within a public sphere to which all potential participants have access. It is a process within which legitimation is forged through conversation and the dynamic process of mutual reason giving and preference formation that emerges out of that conversation. Operating from within the tradition of normative political theory, Amy Gutmann and Dennis Thompson define deliberative democracy as

> a form of government in which free and equal citizens (and their representatives) justify decisions in a process in which they give each other reasons that are mutually acceptable and generally acceptable, with the aim of reaching conclusions that are binding in the present on all citizens but open to challenge in the future.[44]

Public journalism advocates, and particularly its practitioners working within newsrooms in the 1980s and '90s, drew on the ideas of John Dewey, Jürgen Habermas, and James Carey in drawing the connection between their journalistic practices and their vision of democracy. As Cole Campbell, editor of the *Virginia-Pilot* and later the *St. Louis Post-Dispatch* told his colleagues at a forum in 1995, "To Dewey, the journalist is, at her best, a catalyst of conversation, and insiders and citizens alike are active participants in that conversation. The conversation in the end is the medium of democracy, not newspapers."[45]

Deliberative democracy, embraced by theorists and practitioners of public journalism, is best understood in contrast to both aggregative democracy (the default democratic vision of news traditionalists) and agonistic democracy, the democratic understanding advanced by Indymedia's citizen-reporters. Gutmann and Thompson define aggregative democracy this way:

The aggregative conception [of democracy], in contrast [to deliberative democracy], takes preferences as a given (though some versions would correct preferences based on misinformation). It requires no justification for the preferences themselves, but seeks only to combine them in ways that are efficient and fair. Under an aggregative conception of democracy, how should governments make decisions? . . . Aggregative theories offer two seemingly different but closely related methods. The first is a form of majoritarianism: put the question to the people and let them vote (or let them record their preferences in public opinion surveys. . . . Under the second method, officials take note of the expressed preferences but put them through an analytic filter.[46]

Unlike the theorists of public journalism, supporters of traditional professional journalism do not typically declare their allegiance to aggregative democracy. As the default democratic setting in both the United States and in journalism itself, they have no need to. Under this democratic vision, journalists are primarily counted on to provide the information, and to correct the misinformation, that is relied on by citizens to register informed preferences that will then be aggregated through either the political processes or in surveys. These traditional journalism institutions, as their primary contribution to democratic processes outside information provision, also occasionally conduct and report on public-opinion polls that provide a "snapshot" of the aggregative preferences of the public. Operating as atomistic individuals, citizens consume both information and media products that they then use to make political choices.

For most of the 1980s and '90s the dominant conceptions of democracy were either conversational or aggregative, and public journalism was the primary challenger to traditional journalistic practice. I want to argue that a third vision of democracy reemerged with the Indymedia movement in the first years of the twenty-first century, a vision that can be generally described as agonistic. Chantal Mouffe has been the primary proponent of this idea of democracy, contrasting it explicitly with Habermasian visions of political consensus achieved via deliberative talk and reason giving. Mouffe writes,

A well-functioning democracy calls for a vibrant clash of democratic political positions. If this is missing there is the danger that this democratic confrontation will be replaced by a confrontation among other forms of collective identification, as is the case with identity politics. Too much emphasis on consensus and the refusal of confrontation lead to apathy and disaffection with political participation. . . . It is for that reason that the ideal of a pluralist democracy cannot be to reach a rational consensus in the public sphere. Such a consensus cannot exist.[47]

For Mouffe, disagreement is an unavoidable aspect of a democratic politics that does not efface difference.

For Indymedia journalists, like generations of political journalists before them, participatory journalism is fused with a vision of contentious politics that deemphasizes deliberation and reason giving (particularly when compared to deliberative notions of politics) and focuses primarily on protest, conflict, and challenge to authority. It is a radical form of citizen journalism far closer to what Peters, quoted earlier, called "[bearing] witness, . . . moral stuntsmanship, [and] outrageous acts of attention getting." As Bonnie Honig has written,

> The radical-pluralist approach finds its justification above all as a critique of political theorists that measure their success by the elimination of dissonance and conflict. Instead of confining politics to the tasks of building consensus or consolidating communities and identities, the radical pluralist approach aims to shift the emphasis of democratic politics to the processes of dislocation, contestation and resistance.[48]

This agonistic vision of democracy has a far greater resonance with highly politicized slices of citizen journalistic practice and "the contentious blogosphere"[49] than do either deliberative or aggregative theories.

The public vision embedded in theories of algorithmic journalism, finally, is not reducible to aggregative, deliberative, or agonistic forms of democratic life. As Daniel Roth noted earlier, Demand Media articles "are not dreamed up by trained editors nor commissioned based on submitted questions. Instead they are assigned by an algorithm" based off of user search requests and the prices that Demand Media can get for advertising on those pages. Roth calls it a "a database of human needs," though it should be added that it is specifically a database only of the profitable human needs. The audience described here is certainly not deliberative in a Habermasian sense,[50] nor is it agonistic in the manner conceived by Indymedia partisans at the dawn of the read-write web. If it is an aggregative audience, it is aggregative in a profoundly new way.

It is certainly possible to argue that companies like Demand Media have no relationship to democracy at all. Their organizational spokespeople would certainly make such a claim. But it seems to me that the vision of an algorithmic audience, as imagined by these emerging journalistic organizations, has deeply political implications. Seen though the window of these new content farms and search engines, the algorithmic audience exists as highly traceable data, its every preference simultaneously known, denuded, and invisible. Its desires are "understood" through a complex assemblage of people, machines, and mathematical formulae. Its essence lies buried inside large-scale data sets. It appears to be endlessly quantifiable. And I would argue that the conception of *the public* that lies at the heart of this algorithmic view of the audience, instantiated at least in a preliminary form by Demand Media and similar companies, is a concept worthy of serious analysis. Though this analysis cannot begin here, I would argue that it is worth undertaking. Such a study would contribute to a "sociology of algorithms," and this sociology of algorithms could, in turn, represent a new analytic horizon for communications scholarship in the twenty-first century.[51]

NOTES

1. J. Battelle, *The Search: How Google and Its Rivals Rewrote the Rules of Business and Transformed Our Culture* (New York: Portfolio, 2005).

2. L. D. Introna and H. Nissenbaum, "Shaping the Web: Why the Politics of Search Engines Matters," *Information Society* 16, no. 3 (2000): 169–185.

3. For Weber, ideal-types represented abstractions useful for their ability to generate generalized images of particular social phenomena. They were not to be confused with descriptions of actual social reality as such. M. Weber, E. Shils, and H. A. Finch, *The Methodology of the Social Sciences* (New York: Free Press, 1949).

4. Joseph Turow, "Audience Construction and Culture Production: Marketing Surveillance in the Digital Age," *Annals of the American Academy of Political and Social Science* 597, no. 1 (2005): 103; also see J. S. Ettema and D. C. Whitney, "The Money Arrow: An Introduction to Audiencemaking," in *Audiencemaking: How the Media Create the Audience*, 1–18 (New York: Sage, 1994).

5. Turow, "Audience Construction and Culture Production," 106.

6. H. J. Gans, *Deciding What's News* (1979; repr., Evanston, IL: Northwestern University Press, 2004).

7. L. Hermans, "Occupational Practices of Dutch Journalists in a Television Newsroom," in *Action Theory and Communication Research: Recent Developments in Europe*, ed. Karsten Renckstorf, Denis McQuail, Judith E. Rosenbaum, and Gabi Schaap, 355–370 (Berlin: Mouton de Gruyter, 2004).

8. Gans, *Deciding What's News*, 229–230.

9. Ibid., 246–247.

10. B. Zelizer, *Taking Journalism Seriously: News and the Academy* (Thousand Oaks, CA: Sage, 2004).

11. James S. Ettema, D. Charles Whitney, and Daniel B. Wackman, "Professional Mass Communicators," in *Social Meanings of News: A Text-Reader*, ed. Dan Berkowitz, 31–50 (Thousand Oaks, CA: Sage, 1997), 40.

12. R. A. Beam, "How Newspapers Use Readership Research," *Newspaper Research Journal* 16, no. 2 (1995): 28–38; J. Hujanen, "RISC Monitor Audience Rating and Its Implications for Journalistic Practice," *Journalism* 9, no. 2 (2008): 182; Ithiel de Sola Pool and Irwin Shulman, "Newsmen's Fantasies, Audiences, and Newswriting," *Public Opinion Quarterly* 23 (1959): 145–148.

13. D. DeWerth-Pallmeyer, *The Audience in the News* (Englewood Cliffs, NJ: Erlbaum, 1997).

14. M. Coddington, "A Quick Guide to the Maxims of New Media," Mark Coddington's website, January 30, 2010, http://markcoddington. com/2010/01/30/a-quick-guide-to-the-maxims-of-new-media/.

15. J. Rosen, "The People Formerly Known as the Audience," *PressThink* (blog), June 27, 2006, http://journalism.nyu.edu/pubzone/weblogs/pressthink/2006/06/27/ppl_frmr.html.

16. C. Shirky, *Here Comes Everybody: The Power of Organizing without Organizations* (New York: Penguin, 2008).

17. H. J. Gans, *Deciding What's News* (1979; repr., Evanston, IL: Northwestern University Press, 2004), 229.

18. A. Delwiche, "Agenda-Setting, Opinion Leadership, and the World of Web Logs," *First Monday* 10, no. 12 (December 2005), http://firstmonday.org/htbin/cgiwrap/bin/ojs/index.php/fm/article/viewArticle/1300/1220.

19. P. J. Boczkowski, "When More Media Equals Less News: Patterns of Content Homogenization in Argentina's Leading Print and Online Newspapers," *Political Communication* 24, no. 2 (2007): 167–180; M. McCombs and D. L. Shaw, "The Agenda-Setting Function of the Press," *The Press* 156 (2006): 149–156.

20. D. Domingo et al., "Participatory Journalism Practices in the Media and Beyond," *Journalism Practice* 2, no. 3 (2008): 326–342; S. C. Lewis, K. Kaufhold, and D. L. Lasorsa, "Thinking about Citizen Journalism: Perspectives on Participatory News Production at Community Newspapers" (paper presented at the International Symposium on Online Journalism, Austin, TX, April 18, 2009).

21. M. Schudson, "What Public Journalism Knows about Journalism but Doesn't Know about 'Public,'" in *The Pursuit of Public Journalism: Theory, Practice, and Criticism*, ed. T. L. Glasser, 118–133 (New York: Guilford, 1999); T. Haas, *The Pursuit of Public Journalism: Theory, Practice, and Criticism* (New York: Routledge, 2007).

22. J. W. Carey, "American Journalism on, before, and after September 11," in *Journalism after September 11*, ed. Barbie Zelizer and Stuart Allan, 71–90 (London and New York: Routledge, 2002).

23. T. L. Glasser, *The Idea of Public Journalism* (New York: Guilford, 1999).

24. J. Rosen, "The Action of the Idea: Public Journalism in Built Form," in *The Idea of Public Journalism*, ed. T. L. Glasser, 21–48 (New York: Guilford, 1999).

25. B. Coleman, "Indymedia's Independence: From Activist Media to Free Software," *PlaNetwork Journal: Source Code for Global Citizenship*, 2005, http://journal.planetwork. net/article.php?lab=coleman0704.

26. J. Doran, "Besieged US Newspaper Journalists Face Final Deadline," *Observer*, June 29, 2008; Leonard Downie, Jr., and Michael Schudson, "The Reconstruction of American Journalism," *Columbia Journalism Review*, October 19, 2009; Free Press, "Strategic Policy Roundtable on Saving Journalism" (presented at the Rockefeller Brothers Fund, New

York, NY, April 7, 2009); Project for Excellence in Journalism, "The State of the News Media 2008," Journalism.org, 2008, http://www.stateofthenewsmedia.org/2008/.

27. N. Lemann, "Amateur Hour," *New Yorker*, August 7, 2006, http://www.newyorker.com/archive/2006/08/07/060807fa_fact1; A. Lenhart and S. Fox, "Bloggers: A Portrait of the Internet's New Storytellers," Pew Internet & American Life Project, July 19, 2006; Lewis, Kaufhold, and Lasorsa, "Thinking about Citizen Journalism"; Project for Excellence in Journalism, "PEJ Report on Citizen Journalism Sites," 2008.

28. B. Latour, "Beware, Your Imagination Leaves Digital Traces," *Times Higher Education Supplement*, April 6, 2007.

29. P. MacGregor, "Tracking the Online Audience," *Journalism Studies* 8, no. 2 (2007): 286.

30. S. Outing, "Sophisticated Web Stats Give Editors Better Idea of Reader Interests," AllBusiness.com, July 26, 2005, http://www.allbusiness.com/services/business-services-miscellaneous-business/4680055-1.html.

31. J. Rosen, "Jay Rosen Interviews Demand Media: Are Content Farms 'Demonic'?," *ReadWriteWeb* (blog), December 16, 2009, http://www.readwriteweb.com/archives/jay_rosen_vs_demand_media_are_content_farms_demoni.php; Daniel Roth, "The Answer Factory: Demand Media and the Fast, Disposable, and Profitable as Hell Media Model," *Wired*, November 2009, http://www.wired.com/magazine/2009/10/ff_demandmedia.

32. Roth, "The Answer Factory."

33. Haas, *The Pursuit of Public Journalism*, 4.

34. J. Carey, "The Press, Public Opinion, and Public Discourse," in *Public Opinion and the Communication of Consent*, ed. T. L. Glasser and Charles Salmon (New York: Guilford, 1995), 374.

35. Schudson, "What Public Journalism Knows about Journalism," 122.

36. L. Graves, "The Affordances of Blogging: A Case Study in Culture and Technological Effects," *Journal of Communication Inquiry* 31, no. 4 (2007): 331.

37. Chris Atton, in *Alternative Media* (Thousand Oaks, CA: Sage, 2002), has argued that few studies of alternative media discuss how media producers conceive of their audiences. This chapter is thus a contribution to his call for more research on the alternative media-audience relationship.

38. A. Bruns, *Blogs, Wikipedia, Second life, and Beyond: From Production to Produsage* (New York: Lang, 2008).

39. J. D. Peters, "Public Journalism and Democratic Theory: Four Challenges," in *The Idea of Public Journalism*, ed. T. Glasser, 99–117 (New York: Guilford, 1999), 105–106.

40. T. Gitlin, "Public Sphere or Public Sphericules?," in *Media, Ritual and Identity*, ed. T. Liebes and J. Curran, 168–174 (London and New York: Routledge, 1998).

41. N. Fraser, "Rethinking the Public Sphere: A Contribution to the Critique of Actually Existing Democracy," *Social Text* 25–26 (1990): 67.

42. Schudson, "What Public Journalism Knows about Journalism."

43. Rosen, "Jay Rosen Interviews Demand Media."

44. A. Gutmann and D. F. Thompson, *Why Deliberative Democracy?* (Princeton: Princeton University Press, 2004), 7.

45. J. Rosen, "The Action of the Idea," 143.

46. Gutmann and Thompson, *Why Deliberative Democracy?*, 13–14.

47. C. Mouffe, "For an Agonistic Model of Democracy," in *The Democratic Paradox* (London: Verso, 2000), 104.

48. B. Honig, "The Politics of Agonism: A Critical Response to 'Beyond Good and Evil: Arendt, Nietzsche, and the Aestheticization of Political Action' by Dana R. Villa," *Political Theory* 21, no. 3 (1993): 532.

49. M. Wall, "'Blogs of War': Weblogs as News," *Journalism* 6, no. 2 (2005): 153.

50. In this discussion I am indebted to R. Stuart Geiger, "Does Habermas Understand the Internet? The Algorithmic Construction of the Blogo/Public Sphere," *gnovis* 10 (Fall 2009), http://gnovisjournal.org/journal/does-habermas-understand-internet-algorithmic-construction-blogopublic-sphere.

51. Such a sociology might begin with science and technology studies generally and quickly expand; relevant starting citations might include Geiger, "Does Habermas Understand the Internet?"; G. Linch, "Why Computational Thinking Should Be the Core of the New Journalism Mindset," *Publish2* (blog), April 30, 2010, http://blog.publish2.com/2010/04/30/computational-thinking-new-journalism-mindset/; F. Muniesa, Y. Millo, and M. Callon, "An Introduction to Market Devices," in "Monograph Series: Market Devices," supplement, *Sociological Review* 55, no. s2 (2007): 1–12; F. Pasquale, "Assessing Algorithmic Authority," Madisonian.net, November 18, 2009, http://madisonian.net/2009/11/18/assessing-algorithmic-authority/; M. Poon, "Scorecards as Devices for Consumer Credit: The Case of Fair, Isaac & Company Incorporated," *Sociological Review* 55, no. 2 (2007): 284–306; C. Shirky, "A Speculative Post on the Idea of Algorithmic Authority," Clay Shirky's blog, November 2009, http://www.shirky.com/weblog/2009/11/a-speculative-post-on-the-idea-of-algorithmic-authority/.

Humor

Phreaks, Hackers, and Trolls

The Politics of Transgression
and Spectacle

E. GABRIELLA COLEMAN

Among academics, journalists, and hackers, it is common to define hackers not only by their inquisitive demeanor, the extreme joy they garner from uninterrupted hacking sprints, and the technological artifacts they create but also by the "hacker ethic." Journalist Steven Levy first defined the hacker ethic in *Hackers: Heroes of the Revolution*, published in 1984. The hacker ethic is shorthand for a mix of aesthetic and pragmatic imperatives: a commitment to information freedom, a mistrust of authority, a heightened dedication to meritocracy, and the firm belief that computers can be the basis for beauty and a better world.[1]

In many respects, the fact that academics, journalists, and many hackers refer to the existence of this ethic is testament not only to the superb account that Levy offers—it is still one of the finest and most thoroughgoing accounts on hacking—but to the fact that the hacker ethic in the most general sense can be said to exist. For example, many of the principles motivating free and open-source software (F/OSS) philosophy reinstantiate, refine, extend, and clarify many of those original precepts.[2]

However, over the years, the concept has been overly used and has become reified. Indeed as I learned more about the contemporary face of hacking and its history during the course of my fieldwork on free and open-source software hacking, I started to see significant problems in positing any simple connection between all hackers and an unchanging ethic. Falling back on the story of the hacker ethic elides tensions and differences that exist among hackers.[3] Although hacker ethical principles may have a common core—one might even say a general ethos—further inquiry soon demonstrates that, similar to any cultural sphere, we can easily identify variance, ambiguity, and, at times, even serious points of contention.

Take for instance the outlandish and probably not entirely serious (but not entirely frivolous) accusation launched by a hacker bearing a spectacular and provocative name, the "UNIX Terrorist." He is featured in the hacker e-zine *Phrack*, which reached its popular zenith in the late 1980s and the early 1990s.[4] The UNIX Terrorist claims that a class of so-called hackers, those who write free and open-source software, such as the Linux operating system and the enormously popular Firefox browser, are not deserving of the moniker "hacker":

> Nowadays, it is claimed that the Chinese and even women are hacking things. Man, am I ever glad I got a chance to experience "the scene" before it degenerated completely. And remember, kids, knowing how to program or wanting really badly to figure out how things work inside doesn't make you a hacker! Hacking boxes makes you a "hacker"! That's right! Write your local representatives at Wikipedia/urbandictionary/OED and let them know that hackers are people that gain unauthorized access/ privileges to computerized systems! Linus Torvalds isn't a hacker! Richard Stallman isn't a hacker! Niels Provos isn't a hacker! Fat/ugly, maybe! Hackers, no! And what is up with the use of the term "cracker"? As far as I'm concerned, that term applies to people that bypass copyright protection mechanisms. Vladimir Levin? hacker. phiber optik? hacker. Kevin Mitnick? OK maybe a gay/bad one, but still was a "hacker." Hope that's clear.[5]

Hackers do not universally invoke this type of policing between "good" and "bad" or "authentic" and "inauthentic."[6] Some hackers recognize the diversity of hacking and also acknowledge that, despite differences, hacking hangs together around a loose but interconnected set of issues, values, experiences, and artifacts. For instance, hackers tend to uphold a value for freedom, privacy, and access; they tend to adore computers—the cultural glue that binds them together; they are trained in highly specialized and technical esoteric arts, including programming, systems administration, and security research; some gain unauthorized access to technologies, though the degree of illegality greatly varies (and much of hacking is fully legal). Despite a parade of similarities, if we are to understand the political and cultural significance of hacking and its role in shaping and influencing segments of contemporary Internet cultures—such as Internet trolling—every effort must be made to address its ethical and social variability.

While Levy, and countless others, locate the birth of hacking at MIT and similar university institutions during the late 1950s, it may be more accurate to identify MIT as the place where *one variant of hacking* got its start. Another variant began in the 1950s with telephone phreakers, who were the direct ancestors to underground hackers like the UNIX Terrorist. Phreakers studied, explored, and entered the phone system by re-creating the audio frequencies that the system used to route calls. Quite distinct from university-bred hackers whose ethical commitments exhibit a hyperextension of academic norms such as their elevation of meritocracy, these phone explorers exhibited other ethical and aesthetic sensibilities rooted in transgression (often by breaking the law or duping humans for information) and spectacle (often by mocking those in power). The institutional independence of phreakers, in combination with some early political influences, such as the Yippies (Youth International Party), made for a class of technologists whose aesthetic sensibilities and linguistic practices proved to be more daring, vivacious, audacious, and brash than what is commonly found in other genres of hacking, such as F/OSS.

As phreaking morphed into computer hacking in the late 1970s and early 1980s, this brash aesthetic tradition and the politics of transgression continued to grow in visibility and importance, especially evident in the literary genres—textfiles and zines—produced by the hacker underground. In recent times, the aesthetics of audaciousness has veritably exploded with Internet trolls—a class of geek whose raison d'être is to engage in acts of merciless mockery/flaming or morally dicey pranking. These acts are often delivered in the most spectacular and often in the most ethically offensive terms possible.[7]

The behavior of trolls cannot, of course, be explained only by reference to the hacker underground or phreakers; nonetheless, as this essay will illustrate, there is a rich aesthetic tradition of spectacle and transgression at play with trolls, which includes the irreverent legacy of phreakers and the hacker underground. This aesthetic tradition demonstrates an important political attribute of spectacle: the marked hyperbole and spectacle among phreakers, hackers, and trollers not only makes it difficult to parse out truth from lies; it has made it difficult to decipher and understand the cultural politics of their actions. This evasiveness sits in marked contrast to other genealogies of hacking that are far easier to culturally decipher.

This drive toward cultural obfuscation is common to other edgy youth subcultures, according to cultural theorist Dick Hebdige. One of his most valuable insights, relevant to phreakers, hackers, and trollers, concerns the way that some subcultural groups have "translate[d] the fact of being under scrutiny into the pleasures of being watched, and the elaboration of surfaces which takes place within it reveals a darker will toward opacity, a drive against classification and control, a desire to exceed."[8] This description, which Hebdige used to describe the "costers," young and impoverished British boys who sold street wares and who flourished a century ago, could have just as well been written about phreakers, hackers, and trollers nearly a century later.

As the example of the UNIX Terrorist exemplifies, and as we will see below with other examples, these technologists "make a 'spectacle' of themselves, respond to surveillance as if they were expecting it, as if it were perfectly natural."[9] Even if they may vilify their trackers, they nonetheless take some degree of pleasure in performing the spectacle that is expected of them. Through forms of aesthetic audacity, a black hole is also created that helps shield these technologists from easy comprehension and provides some inoculation against forms of cultural co-optation and capitalist commodification that so commonly prey on subcultural forms.[10]

In the rest of the essay, I narrow my analysis to phreakers, underground hackers, and Internet trolls. The point here is not to fully isolate them from other types of hacking or tinkering, nor is it to provide, in any substantial manner, the historical connections between them. Rather it provides in broad strokes a basic historical sketch to illustrate the rich aesthetic tradition of spectacle that has existed for decades, all the while growing markedly in importance in recent years with Internet trolling.

1950–1960s: The Birth of Phone Exploration, Freaking, and Phreaking

Currently, the history of phone exploring, freaking, and phreaking exists only in fragments and scraps, although basic details have been covered in various books, public lectures, and Internet sites.[11] Most accounts claim Joe Engressia, also known as Joy Bubbles, as their spiritual father, although others were already experimenting with the phone network in this period. Blind since birth and with perfect pitch, Engressia spent countless hours playing at home with his phone. In 1957, at the age of eight, he discovered he could "stop" the phone by whistling at a certain pitch, later discovered to be a 2600 hertz tone, into the receiver. Eventually, the media showcased this blind whiz kid, and local coverage most likely inspired others to follow in his footsteps.

In the late 1950s, the first glimmerings of phone explorations thus flickered, although only sporadically. Largely due to a set of technological changes, phreaking glimmered more consistently in the 1960s, although it was still well below general public view. By 1961, phreakers—although still not named as such—no longer had to rely on perfect pitch to make their way into the phone system. They were building and using an assortment of small electrical boxes, the most famous of these being the Blue Box. This device was used to replicate the tones used by the telephone switching system to route calls, enabling Blue Box users to act as if they were a telephone operator, facilitating their spelunking of the phone system and, for some, free phone calls. Phreakers drew up and released schematics, or detailed "Box plans," allowing others to construct them at home. Eventually, further technical discoveries enabled phreakers to set up telephone conferences, also known as "party lines," where they congregated together to chat, gossip, and share technological information.[12] By the late 1960s, a "larger, nationwide phone phreak community began to form," notes historian of phreaking Phil Lapsely, and "the term 'phone freak' condensed out of the ambient cultural humidity."[13] Its codes of conduct and technical aesthetics were slowly but surely boiling, thickening into a regularized set of practices, ethics, commitments, and especially jargon—a sometimes impenetrable alphabet soup of acronyms—that no author who has written on phreakers and subsequently hackers has ever left without remark.[14]

Hello World! The 1970s

In was only in the 1970s when phone freaking made its way out of its crevasse and into the public limelight through a trickle of highly influential journalistic accounts that also worked to produce the very technologists represented in these pieces. Thanks in particular to "Secrets of the Little Blue Box," a provocative account published in 1971, mainstream Americans were given a window into the spelunkers of the phone system. The article, authored by Ron Rosenbaum, who coined the term "phreaker,"[15] was an instant sensation, for it revealed, in astonishingly remarkable detail, the practices and sensual world of phreaking. It focused on a colorful cast of characters with "strange" practices, names, and obsessions, who, according to Rosenbaum, were barely able to control their technological urges: "A tone of tightly restrained excitement enters the Captain's voice," wrote Rosenbaum, "when he starts talking about Systems. He begins to pronounce each syllable with the hushed deliberation of an obscene caller."[16] Rosenbaum wrote such a compelling account of phreaking that it inspired a crop of young male teenagers and adults (including two Steves: Wozniak and Jobs) to follow in the footsteps of the phreakers he showcased. The most famous of the featured phreakers was

Captain Crunch, whose name references a toy whistle packaged in the sugary Cap'n Crunch brand cereal. Captain Crunch discovered that this whistle emitted the very 2600 hertz tone that provided one entryway into the phone system.

If journalists were spreading the word about these "renegade" technological enthusiasts throughout the 1970s, many phreakers and eventually hackers also took on literary pursuits of their own. In the 1980s they produced a flood of writing, often quite audacious in its form and content. In the early 1970s, however, the volume was only a steady trickle. In 1971, phreakers published a newsletter as part of their brief affiliation with an existing and well-known countercultural political movement, the Yippies. Founded in 1967, the Yippies, who resided on the far left of the political spectrum, became famous for promoting sexual and political anarchy and for the memorable and outrageous pranks they staged. Originally bearing the title *YIPL* (*Youth International Party Line*), the newsletter was later renamed *TAP* (the *Technical Assistance Program*). Over time, the editors of *TAP* dropped the overt politics, instead deriving "tremendous gut-level satisfaction from the sensation of pure technical power."[17]

For a number of years, however, *YIPL* blended technological knowledge with a clear political call to arms. For instance, the first issue, published in 1971, opens with a brief shout-out of thanks to the phreakers who contributed the technical details that would fill the pages of this DIY/rough-and-tumble newsletter: "We at YIPL would like to offer thanks to all you phreaks out there." And it ends with a clear political statement:

> YIPL believes that education alone cannot affect the System, but education can be an invaluable tool for those willing to use it. Specifically, YIPL will show you why something must be done immediately in regard, of course, to the improper control of the communication in this country by none other than bell telephone company.[18]

Published out of a small storefront office on Bleecker Street in Manhattan's then seedy East Village neighborhood, the YIPL newsletter offered technical advice for making free phone calls, with the aid of hand-drawn schematics on pages also peppered with political slogans and images. For instance, these included a raised fist, a call to "Strike the War Machine," and, important for our purposes here, the identification of AT&T as "Public Enemy Number 1."[19] A group of phreakers, who by and large had pursued their exploitations and explorations in apolitical terms, got married, at least for a brief period of time, to an existing political movement. Although the marriage was brief, the Yippies nonetheless left their imprint on phreaking and eventually hacking.

Although phreakers were already in the habit of scorning AT&T, they had done so with at least a measure of respect.[20] The zines *YIPL*, *TAP*, and eventually *2600* signaled a new history of the phreakers' (and eventually hackers') scornful crusade against AT&T. For example, in 1984, when *TAP* ceased to be, the hacker magazine and organization *2600* got its start. Largely, although not exclusively, focusing on computers, *2600* paid homage to its phone-phreaking roots in choosing its name and spent over two decades lampooning and critiquing AT&T (among other corporations and the government) with notable vigor.

1980s: "To Make a Thief, Make an Owner; to Create Crime, Create Laws"—Ursula Le Guin

Arguably one of the most influential legacies of the Yippies was their role in amplifying the audacious politics of pranking, transgression, and mockery that already existed among phreaks. However, it took another set of legal changes in the 1980s for the politics of transgression and spectacle to reach new, towering heights. By the 1980s, phreaking was still alive and kicking but was increasingly joined by a growing number of computer enthusiasts, many of them preteens and teens, who extended the politics of transgression into new technological terrains. During this decade, the mainstream media also closely yoked the hacker to the figure of the criminal—often in spectacular terms as well—an image buttressed by legal changes that outlawed for the first time certain classes of computer intrusions.[21]

As in the past, other media representations also proved central in sparking the desire to hack, and few examples illustrate this better than the blockbuster 1983 movie *War Games*. Many hackers I interviewed, for example, recounted how watching the movie led to a desire to follow in the footsteps of the happy-go-lucky hacker figure David, whose smarts lead him to unwittingly hack his way into a government computer called WOPR, located at the North American Aerospace Defense Command Center (NORAD). After initiating a game of chess with the computer, David (unintentionally, of course) almost starts World War III. Most of the movie concentrates on his effort to stop the catastrophic end of the world by doing what hackers are famous for: subduing a recalcitrant and disobedient computer.

Apparently the movie appealed to a slew of nerdy types across Europe, Latin America, and the United States, leading them to incessantly demand from their parents a PC and modem, which once they got, commanded their attention while they were logged on for hours on Bulletin Board Systems (BBSes). A BBS is a computerized meeting and announcement system where users could upload and download files, make announcements, play games, and have discussions. BBSes housed a wildly diverse mixture of information, from government UFO coverups to phreaking box schematics, as well as software to ingest.[22] They also functioned like virtual warehouses filled with vast amounts of stand-alone texts, including genres like textfiles and zines, both of which significantly expanded the reach of the hacker underground, often broadcasting their message in audacious tones.

Textfiles, which were especially popular among underground hackers, spanned an enormously versatile subject range: anarchism, bomb building, schematics for electronics, manifestos, humorous tirades, UNIX guides, proper BBS etiquette, anti-Scientology rants, ASCII (text-based) porn, and even revenge tactics. A quite common type of textfile was box plans, schematics for electronics that showed how to use the phone system or other communication devices for unexpected (and sometimes illegal) purposes. Each textfile bears the same sparse aesthetic stamp: ASCII text, at times conjoined with some crude ASCII graphics. This visual simplicity sharply contrasts with the more audacious nature of the content. Take for example a textfile from 1984: "the code of the verbal warrior,or, [sic] barney's bitch war manual," which offered (quite practical) advice on the art of bitching.

```
><><><><><><><><><><><><><><><><><><><><
       the glue ball bbs———————312-465-hack
><><><><><><><><><><><><><><><><><><><><

                barney badass's b-files
       ——————————————————————————-
           /////////////b-file #1/////////////////
            the code of the verbal warrior,or,
                 barney's bitch war manual
```

so you log onto a board and make a bee-line for your favorite sub-board. some people love pirate boards,some people like phreak boards. my passion is the trusty old standby,the bitch board.

so you get in the 'argument den', or 'discussion board',or'nuclear bitchfare'and start looking around for someone who you think you can outrank.you know,insult,cut down,and generally verbally abuse. and so you post,and,next thing you know,somebody appears to hate your guts. you've got an enemy. now what?

the main problem with 85% of all bitching that goes on on boards today, is that people just don't know how to handle the answer to that question. now what? do i keep it up? do i give up? do i insult his mother?

barney's bitch tip #1———-make up yor mind. either take the bitching completely seriously,or do not take it seriously at all. if you find yourself grinning at insults thrown at you by your opponent,then either cut it out immediately,or try grinning even wider when you're typing your reply. the benefit of this is that you can't be affected one way or the other by any thing that your opponent says.if you're taking it seriously,then you just keep glaring at your monitor,and remain determined to grind the little filth into submission. if you're using the lighthearted approach,then it's pretty dif- ficult to get annoyed by any kind of reference towards your mother/some chains/and the family dog,because,remember,you're not taking this seriously![23]

During the 1980s and through the 1990s, hackers were churning out these literary and political texts at rates that made it impossible for any individual to keep up with all of them. As cultural historian of hacking Douglas Thomas has persuasively argued, there was one publication, the electronic zine *Phrack*, that produced a shared footprint of attention among an otherwise sprawling crew of hackers and phreakers.[24] *Phrack* was particularly influential during its first decade of publication, and its style honored and amplified the brash aesthetics of hacking/phreaking as it spread news about the hacker underground.

One of the most important sections of the zine was the hacker "Pro-Phile," an example of which is the UNIX Terrorist's Pro-Phile that appears at the beginning of this essay. Thomas explains its importance in the following terms:

The Pro-Phile feature was designed to enshrine hackers who had "retired" as the elder statesmen of the underground. The Pro-Philes became a kind of nostalgic romanticizing of hacker culture, akin to the write-up one expects in a high school yearbook, replete with "Favorite Things" and "Most Memorable Experiences."[25]

This material was not simply meant for the hacker public to ingest alone. In the case of *Phrack*, the audience included law enforcement, for this was the period when hackers were being watched closely and constantly. Like Hebdige's costers, hackers conveyed the message that they too were watching back. The cat-and-mouse game of surveillance and countersurveillance among underground hackers and law enforcement amplified the existing propensity for hyperbole and trash talking that existed among phreakers and hackers. Their mockery of law enforcement, for example, not only abounded in the content featured in *Phrack* but was reflected in the very form of the zine. For instance, the structure of the Pro-Phile mirrors (and mocks) the FBI's "Most Wanted" poster, listing such attributes as date of birth, height, eye color, and so on.[26]

Hackers' expert command of technology, their ability to so easily dupe humans in their quest for information, and especially their ability to watch the watchers made them an especially subversive force to law enforcement. With society unable to pacify hackers through mere representation or traditional capitalist co-optation, a string of hackers were not simply legally prosecuted but also persecuted, with their punishment often exceeding the nature of their crime.[27]

1990s: "In the United States Hackers Were Public Enemy No 1."—Phiber Optik

Throughout the 1990s, the hacker underground was thriving, but an increasing number of these types of hackers were being nabbed and criminally prosecuted.[28] Although there are many examples to draw on, the most famous case and set of trials concerns hacker and phone phreaker Kevin Mitnick.[29] Throughout the 1980s and 1990s, he was arrested and convicted multiple times for various crimes, including computer fraud and possessing illegal long-distance access cods. Eventually the FBI placed him on the FBI's "Most Wanted" list before they were able to track him down and arrest him in 1995, after a three-year manhunt. He was in jail for five years, although he spent over four of those as a pretrial detainee, during which time he was placed in solitary confinement for a year.[30] Mitnick explained in an interview why this extreme measure was taken: "because a federal prosecutor told the judge that if I got to a phone I could connect to NORAD (North American Aerospace Command) and somehow launch an ICBM (Intercontinental Ballistic Missile)."[31] Mitnick was unquestionably guilty of a string of crimes, although he never gained anything financially from his hacks. The extreme nature of his punishment was received as a warning message within the wider hacker community. "I was the guy pinned up on the cross," Kevin Mitnick told a packed room of hackers a couple of years after his release, "to deter you from hacking."[32]

At the time of Mitnick's arrest, hackers took action by launching a "Free Kevin" campaign. Starting in the mid-1990s and continuing until Mitnick's release in January 2002, the hacker underground engaged in both traditional and inventively new political activities during a vibrant, multiyear campaign: they marched in the streets, wrote editorials, made documentaries, and publicized his ordeal during the enormously popular hacker conference HOPE (Hackers on Planet Earth), held roughly every two years in New York City since 1994.

2000–2010: *Good Grief! The Masses Have Come to Our Internet*

Although the Internet was becoming more accessible throughout the 1990s, it was still largely off-limits, even to most North American and European citizens. By 2000, the floodgates started to open wide, especially with the spread of cheaper Internet connections. A host of new social media technologies, including blogs, wikis, social networking sites, and video-sharing sites, were being built and used by geeks and nongeeks to post messages, to share pictures, to chatter aimlessly, to throw ephemeral thoughts into the virtual wind, and to post videos and other related Internet memes. Internet memes are viral images, videos, and catchphrases under constant modification by users, and with a propensity to travel as fast as the Internet can move them.

During the period when large droves of people were joining the Internet, post-9/11 terrorism laws, which mandated stiff punishments for cybercrimes, and the string of hacker crackdowns of the 1980s and 1990s most likely made for a more reserved hacker underground.[33] Without a doubt, cultural signs and signals of the hacker underground were and are still visible and vibrant. Hacker underground groups, such as Cult of the Dead Cow (CDC), continued to release software. Conferences popular among the underground, such as DEFCON and HOPE, continue to be wildly popular even to this day. Free from jail after two years, Kevin Mitnick delivered his humorous keynote address to an overflowing crowd of hackers at the 2004 HOPE conference, who listened to the figure who had commanded their political attention for over ten years.

Yet, with a few exceptions, the type of hacker Kevin Mitnick represents has become an endangered species in today's North American and European cultural landscape. Trolls, on the other hand, have proliferated beyond their more limited existence prior to this decade. Trolls have transformed what were more occasional and sporadic acts, often focused on virtual arguments called flaming or flame wars, into a full-blown set of cultural norms and set of linguistic practices.[34] These codes are now so well established and documented that many others can, and have, followed in their footsteps.

Trolls work to remind the "masses" that have lapped onto the shores of the Internet that there is still a class of geeks who, as their name suggests, will cause Internet grief, hell, and misery; examples of trolling are legion. Griefers, one particular subset of troll, who roam in virtual worlds and games seeking to jam the normal protocols of gaming, might enact a relatively harmless prank, such as programming flying phalluses to pay a public visit in the popular virtual world Second Life during a high-profile CNET interview.[35] Other pranks are far more morally dicey. During a virtual funeral held in the enormously popular massively multiplayer online game *World of Warcraft*, for a young player who had passed away in real life, griefers orchestrated a raid and mercilessly killed the unarmed virtual funeral entourage.[36]

In the winter of 2007 and 2008, one group of trolls, bearing the name Anonymous, trolled the Church of Scientology after the church attempted to censor an internal video featuring Tom Cruise that had been leaked. (Eventually what was simply done for the sake of trolling grew into a more traditional protest movement.)[37] One participant in the raids describes the first wave of trolling as "ultra coordinated motherfuckary [*sic*]," a description fitting for many instances of trolling:

> The unified bulk of anonymous collaborated though [*sic*] massive chat rooms to engage in various forms of ultra coordinated motherfuckary [*sic*]. For very short periods of time between Jan 15th and 23rd Scientology websites were hacked, DDos'ed to remove them from the Internet, the Dianteics [*sic*] telephone hot line was completely bombarded with prank calls . . . and the "secrets" of their religion were blasted all over the internet, I also personally scanned my bare ass and faxed it to them. Because fuck them.

If hackers in the 1980s and 1990 were "bred by boards," as Bruce Sterling has aptly remarked, trolls have been partly bred in one of the key descendants of boards: wildly popular image forums, like 4chan.org, which was founded in 2003.[38] 4chan houses a series of topic-based forums where participants—all of them anonymous—post and often comment on discussions or images, many of these being esoteric, audacious, creative, humorous, heavily Photoshopped, and often very grotesque or pornographic. In contrast to many websites, the posts on 4chan, along with their commentary, images, and video, are not archived. They are also posted at such an unbelievably fast pace and volume that much of what is produced effectively vanishes shortly after it is posted and viewed. These rapid-fire conditions magnify the need for audacious, unusual, gross, or funny content. This is especially true on the most popular and infamous of 4chan boards, /b/, the "random" board whose reigning logic combines topical randomness with aesthetic, linguistic, and visual extremity. "If you like the upbeat metaphor of the Internet as hive mind," explains Rob Walker, "then maybe /b/ is one of the places where its unruly id lives."[39] This board is a haven for most anything and thus has birthed many acts of trolling.

Like phreakers and hackers, some trolls act as historical archivists and informal ethnographers. They record and commemorate their pranks, trivia, language, and cultural mores in astonishing detail on a website called Encyclopedia Dramatica (ED). ED is written in a style and genre that, like *Phrack*, pays aesthetic homage and tribute to the brashness that the trolls it chronicles constantly spew out. Take for example, the definition of "troll" and "lulz," a plural bastardization of laughing out loud ("lol"); lulz are often cited as the motivating emotional force *and* consequence of an act of trolling:

A troll is more than the embodiment of the internet hate machine, trolls are the ultimate anti-hero, trolls fuck shit up. Trolls exist to fuck with people, they fuck with people on every level, from their deepest held beliefs, to the trivial. They do this for many reasons, from boredom, to making people think, but most do it for the lulz.[40]

Lulz is laughter at someone else's expense. . . . This makes it inherently superior to lesser forms of humor. . . . The term lulz was coined by Jameth, and is the only good reason to do anything, from trolling to consensual sex. After every action taken, you must make the epilogic dubious disclaimer: "I did it for the lulz." Sometimes you may see the word spelled as luls but only if you are reading something written by a faggot. It's also Dutch for cock."[41]

As one will immediately notice, the very definition of "lulz" is a linguistic spectacle—one clearly meant to shock and offend through references to "cocks" and "faggots." Trolls have taken political correctness, which reached its zenith in the 1980s and the 1990s, by the horns and not only tossed it out the window but made a mockery of the idea that language, much like everything virtual, is anything that should be taken seriously.

Clearly, trolls value pranking and offensiveness for the pleasure it affords. But pleasure is not always cut from the same cloth; it is a multivalent emotion with various incarnations and a rich, multifaceted history. Common to F/OSS developers, hacker pleasure approximates the Aristotelian theory of eudaimonia described by philosopher Martha Nussbaum as "the unimpeded performance of the activities that constitute happiness."[42] Hackers, in pushing their personal capacities and technologies to new horizons, experience the joy of what follows from the self-directed realization of skills, goals, and talents—more often than not achieved through computing technologies.

The lulz, on the other hand, celebrates a form of bliss that revels and celebrates in its own raw power and thus is a form of joy that, for the most part, is divorced from a moral hinge—such as the ethical love of technology. If underground hackers of the 1980s and 1990s acted out in brashness often for the pleasure of doing so, and as a way to perform to the watching eyes of the media and law enforcement, it was still largely hinged to the collective love of hacking/building and understanding technology. There was a balance between technological exploration and rude-boy behavior, even within the hacker underground that held an "elitist contempt" for anyone who simply used technological hacks for financial gain, as Bruce Sterling has put it.[43]

At first blush, it thus might seem like trolls and griefers live by no moral code whatsoever, but among trolls and griefers, there is a form of moral restraint at work. However naive and problematic it is, this morality lies in the "wisdom" that one should keep one's pranking ways on the Internet. Nothing represents this better than the definition for "Chronic Troll Syndrome," also from Encyclopedia Dramatica. This entry uses the characteristically offensive and brash style to highlight the existence of some boundaries, although in reality this advice is routinely ignored:

> Chronic Troll Syndrome (CTS) is an internet disease (not to be confused with Internet Disease) that is generally present in trolls. It causes the given troll to be unable to tell the difference between internet and IRL [in real life] limits.
>
> As a result, the troll is no longer able to comprehend what is appropriate to say and do when dealing with IRL people in contrast with the Internets. Symptoms include being inconsiderate and generally asshatty to friends and family, the common offensive use of racial epithets, and a tendency to interfere in other people's business uninvited "for the laughs."[44]

As so many Internet scholars insist, one should question any such tidy division between the virtual world and meatspace; further trolling often exceeds the bounds of speech and the Internet when trolls "dox" (revealing social security numbers, home addresses, etc.) individuals and send unpaid pizzas to target's home, for instance.[45] However problematic their division is, I would like to suggest that when trolls draw this cultural line in the sand, they are also commenting on the massification of the Internet—a position that is quite contemptuous of newcomers. Although trolling has existed in some form since people congregated online,[46] trolling proliferated and exploded at the moment the Internet became populated with non-technologically-minded people. The brash behavior of trolls is especially offensive to people unfamiliar with this world, and even for those familiar with this world, it can still be quite offensive. Their spectacle works in part as a virtual fence adorned with a sign bearing the following message: "keep (the hell) out of here, this is our Homeland."

This geeky commentary on the masses is not entirely new. Take, for instance, "September That Never Ended," an entry from an online glossary of hacker terms, the Jargon File:

All time since September 1993. One of the seasonal rhythms of the Usenet used to be the annual September influx of clueless newbies who, lacking any sense of netiquette, made a general nuisance of themselves. This coincided with people starting college, getting their first internet accounts, and plunging in without bothering to learn what was acceptable. These relatively small drafts of newbies could be assimilated within a few months. But in September 1993, AOL users became able to post to Usenet, nearly overwhelming the old-timers' capacity to acculturate them; to those who nostalgically recall the period before, this triggered an inexorable decline in the quality of discussions on newsgroups. Syn. eternal September. See also AOL![47]

Already by 1993 geeks and hackers who considered the Internet as their particular romping grounds were remarking on the arrival of newcomers. This tradition of lamenting the "lame" behavior of "noobs" continues today; however, the tactics have changed among a class of technologists. Instead of reasoned debate, as is common with university and F/OSS hackers, among trolls, the preferred tactic of performing their "eliteness" is shocking spectacle and the creation of highly specialized and esoteric jargon: argot. As noted folklorist David Maurer has argued, argot functions primarily in three capacities: to encode technical expertise, to create boundaries between insiders and outsiders, and to maintain secrecy.[48]

The behavior of trolls, of course, cannot be explained only by their contempt of newcomers; as this essay has argued, there are multiple sources and a rich historical tradition at play, including the aesthetic legacy of phreakers and the underground, who provided a rich, albeit less shocking, tradition of spectacle and brashness from which to draw on, extend, and reformulate. We must also give due weight to the condition of collective anonymity, which, as the psychosocial literature has so long noted, fans the fire of flaming and rude behavior.[49] Finally, with a number of important exceptions, their antics, while perhaps morally deplorable, are not illegal. The hacker crackdown of the 1980 and 1990s may have subdued illegal hacks, but it certainly did not eliminate the rude-boy behavior that often went along with them; in fact, it might have created a space that allowed trolling to explode as it has in the past few years.

How have underground hackers reacted to this class of technologists? Although there is no uniform assessment, the UNIX Terrorist, who opened this piece, ends his rant by analyzing "epic lulz." Engaging in the "lulz," he notes, provides "a viable alternative" both to the hacker underground and to open-source software development:

> Every day, more and more youngsters are born who are many times more likely to contribute articles to socially useful publications such as Encyclo-pedia Dramatica instead of 2600. Spreading terror and wreaking havoc for "epic lulz" have been established as viable alternatives to contributing to open source software projects. If you're a kid reading this zine for the first time because you're interested in becoming a hacker, fucking forget it. You're better off starting a collection of poached adult website passwords, or hanging out on 4chan. At least trash like this has some modicum of entertainment value, whereas the hacking/security scene had become some kind of fetid sinkhole for all the worst kinds of recycled academic masturbation imaginable. In summary, the end is fucking nigh, and don't tell me I didn't warn you . . . even though there's nothing you can do about it.
>
> Good night and good luck,
>
> the unix terrorist[50]

One obvious question remains: do trolls even deserve any place in the historical halls of hacking? I cannot answer this question here, for it is at once too early to make the judgment and not entirely my place to do the judging. One thing is clear: even if trolls are to be distinguished from underground hackers, they do not reside entirely in different social universes; trolling was common on BBSes, Usenet, and other Internet arenas where underground hacking thrived. There is a small class of the most elite griefers and trolls who use hacking as a weapon for their merciless mockery. Most telling may be the

UNIX Terrorist himself, and especially his rant; as the UNIX Terrorist's final words so clearly broadcast: underground hacking is notoriously irreverent and brash and thus helped to light an aesthetic torch that trolls not only have carried to the present but have also doused with gasoline.

Conclusion: Informational Tricksters or Just "Scum of the Earth Douchebags"?

Even while some of the actions of phreakers, hackers, and trolls may be ethically questionable and profoundly disquieting, there are important lessons to be drawn from their spectacular antics.[51] As political theorist and activist Stephen Duncombe has so insightfully argued, if carried out responsibly, a politics of spectacle can prove to be an invaluable and robust political tactic: "spectacle must be staged in order to dramatize the unseen and expose associations elusive to the eye."[52] The question that remains, of course, is whether there is *any* ethical substance to these spectacular antics, especially those of the troll, whose spectacle is often generated through merciless mocking, irreverent pranking, and at times, harassment.

If we dare consider these informational pranksters in light of the trickster, then perhaps there may be some ethical substance to some, although certainly not all, of their actions. The trickster encompasses a wide range of wildly entertaining and really audacious mythical characters and legends from all over the world, from the Norse god Loki to the North American coyote. Not all tricksters are sanitized and safe, as Disney has led us to believe. Although clever, some are irreverent and grotesque. They engage in acts of cunning, deceitfulness, lying, cheating, killing and destruction, hell raising, and as their name suggests, trickery. Sometimes they do this to quell their insatiable appetite, to prove a point, at times just to cause hell, and in other instances to do good in the world. Tricksters are much like trolls: provocateurs and saboteurs. And according to Lewis Hyde, tricksters help to renew the world, in fact, to renew culture, insofar as their mythological force has worked to "disturb the established categories of truth and property and, by so doing, open the road to possible new worlds."[53]

The mythical notion of the trickster does seem to embody many of the attributes of the phreaker, hacker, and especially the contemporary Internet troll. But is it reasonable to equate the mythical trickster figure Loki and the tricksters in Shakespeare with figures that do not reside in myth (although Internet trolls certainly create myths), do not reside in fiction, but reside in the reality of the Internet? Given that trolls, in certain instances, have caused mayhem in people's lives, does the moniker "trickster" act as an alibi, a defense, or an apology for juvenile, racist, or misogynist behavior?[54] Or is there a positive role for the troll to play on the Internet as site/place of constant play and performance? Is the troll playing the role of the trickster, or is the troll playing, you know, just for the lulz?

NOTES

I would like to thank Patrick Davison, Micah Anderson, Ashley Dawson, Finn Brunton, and especially Michael Mandiberg, who all provided such generous feedback and comments. This work is licensed under the Creative Commons Attribution-ShareAlike license.

1. Steven Levy, *Hackers: Heroes of the Computer Revolution* (New York: Delta, 1984), 39–46.

2. Samir Chopra and Scott Dexter, *Decoding Liberation: The Promise of Free and Open Source Software* (New York: Routledge, 2009); E. Gabriella Coleman, "Code Is Speech: Legal Tinkering, Expertise, and Protest among Free and Open Source Software Developers," *Cultural Anthropology* 24, no. 3 (2009): 420–454. Chris M. Kelty, *Two Bits: The Cultural Significance of Free Software* (Durham: Duke University Press, 2008).

3. E. Gabriella Coleman and Golub Alex, "Hacker Practice: Moral Genres and the Cultural Articulation of Liberalism," *Anthropological Theory* 8, no. 3 (2008): 255–277; Tim Jordan, *Hacking: Digital Media and Technological Determinism* (London: Polity, 2008).

4. Douglas Thomas, *Hacker Culture* (Minneapolis: University of Minnesota Press, 2003).

5. "Phrack Prophile on the UNIX Terrorist," *Phrack*, November 8, 2008, http://phrack. org/issues.html?issue=65&id=2#article (accessed June 27, 2010).

6. It is far more common for hackers who do not engage in transgression to accuse transgressive hackers like the UNIX Terrorist of not being authentic hackers, instead being "crackers." See the entry for "cracker" in the tome of hacker lore, the Jargon File: http://catb.org/jargon/html/C/cracker.html.

7. Julian Dibbell, "Mutilated Furries, Flying Phalluses: Put the Blame on Griefers, the Sociopaths of the Virtual World," *Wired*, January 18, 2008, http://www.wired.com/gaming/ virtualworlds/magazine/16-02/mf_goons (accessed July 10, 2009); Mattathias Schwartz, "Trolls among Us," *New York Times Magazine*, August 3, 2008, http://www.nytimes. com/2008/08/03/magazine/03trolls-t.html (accessed August 3, 2008).

8. Dick Hebdige, "Posing . . . Threats, Striking . . . Poses" (1983), in *The Subcultures Reader*, ed. Ken Gelder and Sarah Thornton (New York: Routledge, 1997), 403.

9. Ibid., 398.

10. Dick Hebdige, "Subculture: The Meaning of Style" (1979), in *The Subcultures Reader*, ed. Ken Gelder and Sarah Thornton, 393–405 (New York: Routledge, 1997).

11. Phil Lapsely is currently writing a comprehensive history of phone phreaking and has given various lectures on the topic. See http://www.historyofphonephreaking.org/.

12. For a presentation about these early phone conferences held in the 1980s and 1990s, see TProphet & Barcode's talk, "Phreaks, Confs and Jail," given at The Last HOPE conference, July 2008, http://securitytube.net/Phreaks,-Confs-and-Jail-(The-Last-HOPE)-video.aspx.

13. Phil Lapsely, "More on the Origin of 'Phreak,'" *The History of Phone Phreaking Blog*, April 4, 2010, http://blog.historyofphonephreaking.org/2010/04/more-on-origin-of-phreak.html (accessed April 4, 2010).

14. See Steven Levy, *Hackers: Heroes of the Computer Revolution* (New York: Delta, 1984), 39–46; Ron Rosenbaum, "Secrets of the Little Blue Box," *Esquire*, October 1971, available online at http://www.lospadres.info/thorg/lbb.html (accessed April 16, 2011); Levy, *Hackers*; and Bruce Sterling, *The Hacker Crackdown: Law and Disorder on the Electronic Frontier* (New York: Bantam, 1992).

15. Lapsely, "More on the Origin of 'Phreak.'"

16. Rosenbaum, "Secrets of the Little Blue Box."

17. Sterling, *The Hacker Crackdown*, 62.

18. "The Youth International Party Lines First Issue," *YIPL*, June 1971, 1 (on file with the author).

19. Ibid.

20. Rosenbaum, "Secrets of the Little Blue Box."

21. Helen Nissenbaum, "Hackers and the Contested Ontology of Cyberspace," *New Media and Society* 6, no. 2 (2004): 195–217.

22. Jason Scott has produced a seminal history of the BBS era in his documentary *BBS: The Documentary*. See http://www.bbsdocumentary.com/.

23. barney badass, "the code of the verbal warrior," http://www.textfiles.com/100/war-bitch.txt (accessed July 10, 2010).

24. Thomas, *Hacker Culture*.

25. Ibid., 92.

26. Ibid., 132.

27. Thomas, *Hacker Culture*; Sterling, *The Hacker Crackdown*. Among underground hackers, media representation and commodification were and still are largely ineffective tools to placate them. However, lucrative information-technology jobs, especially within the security industry, as Andrew Ross has noted, has led "two generations of hackers" to agonize "over accepting lucrative offers of employment within corporate or government IP security." Andrew Ross, *Nice Work If You Can Get It* (New York: NYU Press, 2009), 124.

28. Quotation in section title from Elinor Mills, "Q&A: Mark Abene, from 'Phiber Optik' to Security Guru," CNET News, June 23, 2009, http://news.cnet.com/8301-1009_3-10270582-83.html (accessed July 10, 2010).

29. Kevin Mitnick's case and others are covered in Thomas, *Hacker Culture*.

30. E. Gabriella Coleman and Golub Alex, "Hacker Practice: Moral Genres and the Cultural Articulation of Liberalism," *Anthropological Theory* 8, no. 3 (2008): 255–277; Thomas, *Hacker Culture*.

31. Elinor Mills, "Q&A: Kevin Mitnick, from Ham Operator to Fugitive to Consultant," CNET News, June 22, 2009, http://news.cnet.com/8301-1009_3-10269348-83.html (accessed July 10, 2010).

32. Quotation from Kevin Mitnick's keynote address delivered at the fifth HOPE conference, held in New York City, July 9–11, 2004, available online at http://www.the-fifth-hope.org/mp3/mitnick-1.mp3 and http://www.the-fifth-hope.org/mp3/mitnick-2.mp3 (accessed July 10, 2010).

33. This is difficult to empirically verify, yet it is not unreasonable to surmise that the well-publicized hacker arrests of the 1990s, combined with even stiffer penalties for computer intrusion mandated in the Patriot Act, would work to curb the most flagrant or potentially illegal behaviors or, alternatively, possibly make the underground burrow back into the recesses of its crevasses, away from the watchful eye of law enforcement.

34. Contemporary trolls encompass a wide range of subgroups, each with particular histories and techniques and some also harboring great distaste for other trolling groups.

35. Burci Bakioglu, "Spectacular Interventions of Second Life: Goon Culture, Griefing, and Disruption in Virtual Spaces," in special edition: "Cultures of Virtual Worlds," *Journal of Virtual Worlds Research* 3, no. 1 (2009), https://journals.tdl.org/jvwr/article/view/348; Dibbell, "Mutilated Furries, Flying Phalluses."

36. "WoW Funeral Raid," Playercraft.com, June 13, 2009, http://playercraft.com/famous/wow-funeral-raid/ (accessed June 10, 2009).

37. See http://www.whyweprotest.net/.

38. Sterling, *The Hacker Crackdown.*

39. Rob Walker, "When Funny Goes Viral," *New York Times Magazine,* July 12, 2010, http://www.nytimes.com/2010/07/18/magazine/18ROFL-t.html (accessed July 12, 2010).

40. Encyclopedia Dramatica, s.v. "Troll," http://encyclopediadramatica.com/Troll (accessed October 12, 2009).

41. Encyclopedia Dramatica, s.v. "Lulz," http://encyclopediadramatica.com/Lulz (accessed October 12, 2009).

42. Martha C. Nussbaum, "Mill between Aristotle and Bentham," *Daedalus* 133, no. 2 (2004): 64.

43. Sterling, *The Hacker Crackdown.*

44. Encyclopedia Dramatica, s.v. "Chronic Troll Syndrome," http://encyclopediadramatica.com/Chronic_Troll_Syndrome (accessed October 12, 2009).

45. E. Gabriella Coleman, "Ethnographic Approaches to Digital Media," *Annual Review of Anthropology* 39 (2010): 1–19; David Hakken, *Cyborgs@Cyberspace? An Ethnographer Looks to the Future* (New York: Routledge, 1999); T. L. Taylor, *Play between Worlds: Exploring Online Game Culture* (Cambridge: MIT Press, 2006).

46. Judith S. Donath, "Identity and Deception in the Virtual Community," in *Communities in Cyberspace,* ed. Mark A. Smith and Peter Kollock, 29–59 (London: Routledge, 1999).

47. Jargon File, s.v. "September That Never Ended," http://www.catb.org/~esr/jargon/html/S/September-that-never-ended.html.

48. David Maurer, *Whiz Mob: A Correlation of the Technical Argot of Pickpockets with Their Behavior* (Lanham, MD: Rowman and Littlefield, 1964).

49. Patricia Wallace, *The Psychology of the Internet* (New York: Cambridge University Press, 1999).

50. "Phrack Prophile on the UNIX Terrorist."

51. Quotation in section title from Encyclopedia Dramatica, s.v. "Troll," March 27, 2010, revision, http://web.archive.org/web/20100327134636/http://encyclopediadramatica.com/Troll (accessed July 5, 2011).

52. Stephen Duncombe, *Dream: Re-imagining Progressive Politics in an Age of Fantasy* (New York: New Press, 2007), 156–157.

53. Lewis Hyde, *Trickster Makes This World: Mischief, Myth, and Art* (New York: North Point, 1999), 13.

54. Although I am not answering this question here, I am certainly not posing it rhetorically. It is crucial to interrogate trolling in all its dimensions, roots, and consequences, which I am unable to do here, as the main purpose of this essay is to establish aesthetic linkages between phreakers, hackers, and trolls. Lisa Nakamura has written about online racism extensively. See Lisa Nakamura, *Digitizing Race: Visual Cultures of the Internet* (Minneapolis: University of Minnesota Press, 2008) and *Cybertypes: Race, Ethnicity, and Identity on the Internet* (New York: Routledge, 2002). Recently, she has explored the intersection between racism and griefing in a talk: "Don't Hate the Player, Hate the Game," June 16, 2010, available online at http://blogs.law.harvard.edu/mediaberkman/2010/06/16/lisa-nakamura-dont-hate-the-player-hate-the-game. Legal scholar Danielle Citron has examined cyberharassment of women in terms of discrimination, building on her previous work on legal barriers and opportunities for addressing online abuse. See Danielle Citron, "Law's Expressive Value in Combating Cyber Gender Harassment," *Michigan Law Review* 108 (2009): 373–416; and Danielle Citron, "Cyber Civil Rights," *Boston University Law Review* 89 (2009): 61–125. Not all cases of trolling are relevant to the issues raised by these scholars, but some of them certainly are pertinent.

The Language of Internet Memes

PATRICK DAVISON

In *The Future of the Internet—and How to Stop It,* Jonathan Zittrain describes the features of a *generative* network. A generative network encourages and enables creative production and, as a system, possesses leverage, adaptability, ease of mastery, accessibility, and transferability.[1] Notably absent from this list of characteristics, however, is security. Many of the characteristics that make a system generative are precisely the same ones that leave it vulnerable to exploitation. This zero-sum game between creativity and security implies a divided Internet. Those platforms and communities which value security over creativity can be thought of as the "restricted web," while those that remain generative in the face of other concerns are the "unrestricted web."

The restricted web has its poster children. Facebook and other social networking sites are growing at incredible speeds. Google and its ever-expanding corral of applications are slowly assimilating solutions to all our computing needs. Amazon and similar search-based commerce sites are creating previously unimagined economies.[2] Metaphorically, these sites, and countless others, make up the cities and public works of the restricted web. However, the unrestricted web remains the wilderness all around them, and it is this wilderness that is the native habitat of Internet memes.

The purpose of this essay is twofold. The first is to contribute to a framework for discussing so-called Internet memes. Internet memes are popular and recognizable but lack a rigorous descriptive vocabulary. I provide a few terms to aid in their discussion. The second purpose is to consider Foucault's "author function" relative to Internet memes, many of which are created and spread anonymously.

What Is an Internet Meme?

In 1979 Richard Dawkins published *The Selfish Gene*, in which he discredits the idea that living beings are genetically compelled to behave in ways that are "good for the species." Dawkins accomplishes this by making one point clear: the basic units of genetics are not species, families, or even individuals but rather single genes—unique strands of DNA.[3]

At the end of the book, Dawkins discusses two areas where evolutionary theory might be heading next. It is here that he coins the term "meme." He acknowledges that much of human behavior comes not from genes but from culture. He proposes that any nongenetic behavior be labeled as a meme and then poses a question: can the application of genetic logic to memes be productive? To make the differences between genes and memes clear, I offer a short example of each.

Genes determine an organism's physical characteristics. A certain gene causes an organism to have short legs, or long, for instance. Imagine two zebra. The first has the short-leg gene, and the second the long. A lion attacks them. The short-legged zebra runs more slowly and is eaten. The long-legged zebra runs more quickly (because of its legs) and lives. At this point, there are more long-leg genes in the imaginary ecosystem than short-leg genes. If the long-legged zebra breeds and has offspring, those offspring with long legs will continue to survive at a higher rate, and more offspring of those offspring will contain the long-leg gene. The genes themselves are not thinking beings—the long-leg gene does not know it causes long-leggedness, nor does it care, but given that it bestows a property that interacts with the environment to allow more of itself to be produced, it is *successful*.[4]

Memes determine the behavior of an organism. They are either taught to an organism (you go to school and learn math) or learned through experience (you stick a finger in an outlet, get shocked, understand that outlets should be avoided). Imagine two soccer players. There are genetic factors which might make them better or worse at playing (long or short legs, for instance); however, their ability is also dependent on their understanding of the game. For this example, let us imagine that the two players are physically identical. However, one of them goes to practice, and the other does not. At practice, the coach teaches the attendant player about passing: you pass the ball to other players and increase the chance that your team will score. During a game, the attendant player is likely to pass and to experience success because of it. The truant player, having not learned the passing meme, will not pass, and that player's team will suffer because of it.

While genes rely on the physical process of reproduction to replicate, memes rely on the mental processes of observation and learning. In our example, the truant player comes to the game without the passing meme and suffers. That player is, however, able to observe the attendant player passing, and succeeding, and can decide to imitate the attendant player by passing as well. The passing meme successfully replicates itself in a new organism without the all-or-nothing cycle of life and death. This highlights one of the critical differences between genes and memes: speed of transmission. Compared to genetic changes (which span generations upon generations), memetic changes happen in the blink of an eye. Offline memes, cultural cornerstones like language or religion, are hyperfast when compared to their genetic counterparts. Internet memes are even faster.

The other notable difference between genes and memes is their relative fidelity of form. In our zebra example, a zebra is granted physical characteristics based on a discrete combination of DNA. All the genes that Dawkins discusses are at their most basic made up of sequences of only four chemicals. The memes that I examine in this essay, however, are not made up of chemicals but of ideas and concepts. Our truant player may observe and learn the passing meme, but that process does not transfer an identical chemical "code" for passing. The meme is subject to interpretation and therefore to variation.

In Dawkins's original framing, memes described any cultural idea or behavior. Fashion, language, religion, sports—all of these are memes. Today, though, the term "meme"—or specifically "Internet meme"—has a new, colloquial meaning. While memes themselves have been the subject of entire books, modern Internet memes lack even an accurate definition. There are numerous online sources (Wikipedia, Urban Dictionary, Know Your Meme, Encyclopedia Dramatica) that describe Internet memes as the public perceives them, but none does so in an academically rigorous way. Given this, I have found the following new definition to be useful in the consideration of Internet memes specifically:

> *An Internet meme is a piece of culture, typically a joke, which gains influence through online transmission.*

While not all Internet memes are jokes, comparing them to offline jokes makes it clear what makes Internet memes unique: the speed of their transmission and the fidelity of their form.[5] A spoken joke, for instance, can only be transmitted as quickly as those individuals who know it can move from place to place, and its form must be preserved by memory. A printed joke, in contrast, can be transmitted by moving paper and can be preserved by a physical arrangement of ink. The speed of transmission is no longer limited by the movement of individuals, and the form of the joke is preserved by a medium, not memory.

Now, consider a joke that exists on the Internet. The speed of transmission is increased yet again, in an incredible way. Space is overcome: computers connect to one another through far-reaching networks. Time is overcome: the digitally represented information is available as long as the server hosting it remains online. A joke stored on a website can be viewed by as many people as want to view it, as many times as they want to, as quickly as they can request it.

An online joke's fidelity of form, however, is subject to a unique contradiction. Being digital, the joke is perfectly replicable. Copy and paste functions (or their equivalents) are ubiquitous, expected parts of software platforms.[6] However, a piece of digital media in the modern landscape of robust and varied manipulation software renders it also perfectly malleable. Individual sections of a piece of digital media can be lifted, manipulated, and reapplied with little effort.

Once I say that a piece of media, or a meme, is replicable and malleable, I must specify what *exactly* is being copied or changed. A meme can be separated into components. I propose three: the manifestation, the behavior, and the ideal.

The *manifestation* of a meme is its observable, external phenomena. It is the set of objects created by the meme, the records of its existence. It indicates any arrangement of physical particles in time and space that are the direct result of the reality of the meme.

The *behavior* of a meme is the action taken by an individual in service of the meme. The behavior of the meme creates the manifestation. For instance, if the behavior is photographing a cat and manipulating that photograph with software, the manifestation this creates is the ordered progression of pixels subsequently uploaded to the Internet.

The *ideal* of a meme is the concept or idea conveyed.[7] The ideal dictates the behavior, which in turn creates the manifestation. If the manifestation is a funny image of a cat and the behavior is using software to make it, then the ideal is something like "cats are funny."

When tracking the spread of a particular meme, it is useful to identify which of these three aspects is being replicated and which adapted. Dawkins prefigures this in his original chapter by theorizing that the principal tool for meme identification would be the perception of replication. This is important, because identifying the replication of memes is subjective. Sometimes this identification is easy: one person acts, and another person copies that person exactly. Other times the process of replication is less exact. This is why separating the manifestation, behavior, and ideal is useful. As long as one of the three components is passed on, the meme is replicating, even if mutating and adapting.

Early Internet Memes

In 1982 Scott E. Fahlman proposed a solution to a problem he and other users were experiencing when communicating via the Internet. Members who participated on the bulletin-board system at Carnegie Mellon would on occasion descend into "flame wars"—long threads of communication that are hostile or openly aggressive to other users. Fahlman believed that many of these disagreements arose out of misinterpreted humor. His solution to this problem was to add a specific marker to the end of any message that was a joke.[8] That marker was :-). I am going to assume that anyone reading this has seen this "emoticon" and understands that if rotated ninety degrees clockwise, the colon, hyphen, and close-parenthesis resemble a smiling face, a symbol lifted from pre-Internet time. This practice of contextualizing one's written messages with an emoticon to indicate emotional intent has become widespread. Today there are countless other pseudopictograms of expressions and objects which are regularly added to typed communication. Emoticons are a meme.

To leverage my framework, the manifestation of an emoticon is whatever combination of typed characters is employed as pseudopictogram. These can be in any medium—handwritten or printed on paper, displayed on a screen, any form capable of representing glyphs. The behavior is the act of constructing such an emoticon to contribute emotional meaning to a text. The ideal is that small combinations of recognizable glyphs represent the intent or emotional state of the person transmitting them.

If we analyze the emoticon meme from a genetic point of view which values survival and defines success through continued replication, it proves itself remarkably well situated. Emoticons can be very quickly used. Emoticons are easy to experiment with. The tools for making emoticons are included on every device we use to type. The primary glyphs used for many of the emoticons are glyphs used less often than the upper- and lower-case alphabets. Emoticons reference a previously existing source of meaning (human facial expressions) and therefore can be easily interpreted upon first encounter. More than just re-creating face-to-face meaning in textual communication, emoticons also add the possibility of a new level of meaning—a level impossible without them.

If all these factors were not true, perhaps emoticons would see less use. If keyboards full of punctuation were not already spread across the landscape, or if human facial expressions were not a cultural constant, maybe emoticons would disappear or be relegated to obscurity. As it stands, though, emoticons not only pervade both online and offline communication but have also received significant formal support on many platforms.[9]

Emoticons come from the Internet's childhood, when bulletin boards and e-mails accounted for a bulk of the activity online. Another early meme came from its adolescence—1998, after the widespread adoption of the World Wide Web and during the heyday of GeoCities.[10] Deidre LaCarte, who was a Canadian art student at the time, made a GeoCities-hosted website as part of a contest with a friend to see who could generate the most online traffic. The website she created, popularly known as "Hamster Dance," consisted of row upon row of animated gifs, each one depicting a hamster dancing, all set to a distorted nine-second audio loop. As of January 1999 the site had amassed eight hundred views, total. Once 1999 began, however, without warning or clear cause, the site began to log as many as fifteen thousand views a day.[11] The comparison of these two early memes, Hamster Dance and emoticons, provides an opportunity to expand and clarify some of the vocabulary I use to discuss memes and to make two important distinctions.

Emoticons are a meme that serve a number of functions in the transmission of information. They can be used to frame content as positive or negative, serious or joking, or any number of other things. Hamster Dance essentially serves a single function: to entertain. This difference in function influences the primary modes of access for each of these memes. For the emoticon meme the behavior is to construct any number of emotional glyphs in any number of settings, while for the Hamster Dance meme the behavior is only a single thing: have people (themselves or others) view the Hamster Dance web page. The Hamster Dance page is a singular thing, a spectacle. It gains influence through its surprising centralization. It is a piece of content that seems unsuited given more traditional models of assessment of organizing people around a central location, but yet, that is precisely the function it serves.

Emoticons gain influence in exactly the opposite way. There was an original, single emoticon typed in 1982, but other emoticons do not drive people toward that single iteration. The emoticon has gained influence not by being surprisingly centralized but by being surprisingly distributed. Hamster Dance is big like Mt. Rushmore. Emoticons are big like McDonald's. This first distinction, then, is that the influence gained by memes can be both centralized and distributed.

The second distinction is closely related to the first. Just as Hamster Dance is characterized by many-in-one-location, and emoticons are characterized by individuals-in-many-locations, the two also differ in the nature of

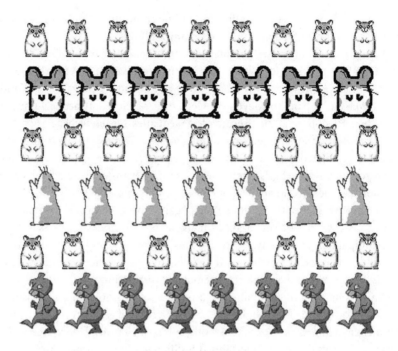

Fig. 9.1. Hamster Dance (http://www.webhamster.com/)

the behavior they replicate. Many more people have used an emoticon, or concocted their own, than have seen the very first emoticon from 1982. In contrast, many more people have seen the original Hamster Dance site than have created their own Hamster Dance site. It is tempting, then, to say that this difference implies two categories of memetic behavior: use and view. It is more useful, though, to treat both of these behaviors as characteristics present in varying degrees for any given meme. These two behaviors connect directly to the previously mentioned states of replicable and malleable.[12] A piece of media's being replicable makes it easier for that media to gain influence through views. A piece of media's being malleable makes it easier for that media to gain influence through use. Engagement with a meme, then, takes the form of either use or viewing or, more in keeping with the terms of malleable and replicable, of transformation or transmission.

These distinctions help to account for the variety of phenomena popularly identified as Internet memes. Working from Dawkins's initial conception, the term "meme" can mean almost anything. By limiting the scope of what is meant by "Internet meme," the goal is not to create a basis for invalidating the widespread use of the term but, rather, to provide an inclusive method for accounting for and relating the various phenomena labeled as such.

Current Internet Memes

All memes (offline and on) are capable of existing in layers. For instance, consider language. The meme of language is communication through speech. There are, however, multiple languages. Each individual language is a meme nested within the larger language meme. Additionally, within each individual language there are even more submemes: dialects, slang, jargon.

Internet memes follow the same structure. One very common, rather large meme is the image macro. An image macro is a set of stylistic rules for adding text to images. Some image macros involve adding the same text to various images, and others involve adding different text to a common image. Just like emoticons, which exist in an environment well suited to supporting their survival, image macros are able to thrive online because the software necessary for their creation and distribution is readily available.

There are countless submemes within the image macro meme, such as LOLcats, FAIL, demotivators. I am going to focus on just one: Advice Dog. The trope of this meme is that Advice Dog, a friendly looking dog at the center of a rainbow-colored background, is offering the viewer whatever advice is contained in the text above and below his head. The formula is simple:

1. Image of dog in center of rainbow
2. First line of advice
3. Second line of advice (usually a punch line)

Iterations of the Advice Dog meme vary not only in the specific text they use to communicate humor but also in the type of humor communicated. When Advice Dog gives someone advice, genuine good advice, it can be humorous simply by virtue of being attached to a bright background and smiling dog. Once it is established that the explicit function of Advice Dog is to give advice, though, having him give bad or unexpected advice is ironic. The text can also be transgressive, giving advice that is intentionally offensive or absurd, accompanied by text that is not advice at all.

In addition to having Advice Dog offer various kinds of advice, one can also have other figures deliver other kinds of messages. These are Advice Dog–like variants. Whether a "genuine" Advice Dog iteration or a simply an Advice Dog–like variant, all of these are contained within the larger Advice

Fig. 9.2. Advice Dog meme

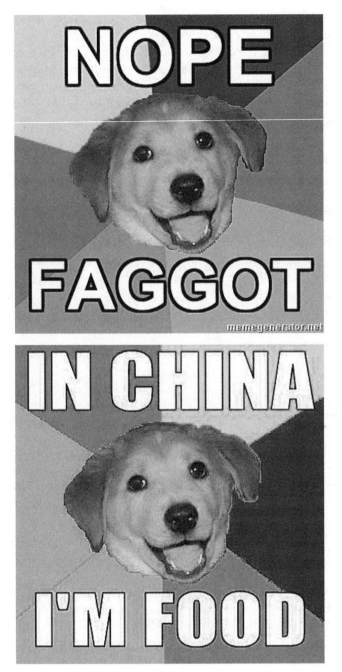

Figs. 9.3–9.5. More Advice Dog memes

Dog meme. The manifestations are the individual images, among which numerous replicated elements are obvious. The style of the background, the square format of the image, the central placement of a cropped figure—all of these remain constant (with consistent variation) from image to image. The behavior of the meme is a varied set of practices. Viewing and linking to various Advice Dog manifestations is part of the meme, as is saving and reposting the same. Creating original iterations with new text is part of the meme, as is creating or contributing to any of the Advice Dog–like variants in the same manner.

The ideal of the Advice Dog meme is harder to describe. The meaning conveyed by any single Advice Dog macro can vary wildly. Some have ironic meanings, while others have aggressive or offensive meanings. The subject can be a dog that gives advice or a child that celebrates success. So we can say that for Advice Dog, the ideal of the meme is not always replicated from instance to instance. With no qualities recognizable from iteration to iteration, it would seem there is no justification for linking them together as part of the same meme. However, what is replicated from instance to instance is the set of formal characteristics. We are able to identify each instance as part of the larger Advice Dog meme because of the similarities in form and regardless of the differences in meaning.

Attribution

The identification of memes relies on the identification of replications. One of the most common replicated elements that sets memes of the unrestricted web apart from memes of the restricted web is attribution. Attribution is the identification of an author for a piece of media. Attribution is central to much of the restricted web: YouTube is host to numerous copyright battles, fueled by rights holders' desire to derive worth from media attributed to them. Wikipedia encourages submissions from anyone but meticulously tracks participation and only allows images to be uploaded by their license holder. Creative Commons offers numerous alternative licenses for content creators, but attribution is common to every one.[13]

It is clear that many of the popular platforms of the Internet preserve and extend a historical prioritizing of attribution and authorship. Foucault, in his essay "What Is an Author?" writes that the author's name "performs a certain role with regard to narrative discourse, assuring a classificatory function. Such a name permits one to group together a certain number of texts, define them, differentiate them from and contrast them to others. In addi-

Figs. 9.6–9.11. Advice Dog variants: Courage Wolf, Politically-Neutral Dog, Depression Dog, Bachelor Frog, Rich Raven, Success Kid

tion, it establishes a relationship between the texts."[14] Foucault's concept of the "author function" is therefore similar in function to modern metadata. The author's name serves to classify and group together separate works, much in the same way tags and keywords allow distributed digital media to be searched and sorted. The Internet is a system filled with an incalculable amount of data. The question of where to find a piece of media has become just as relevant as the question of how to produce a piece of media. Attribution supports this model and fits within the modern practice of prioritizing metadata. Metadata is a meme. It is a meme that existed well before the Internet but that has, like other memes introduced to the Internet, achieved an accelerated rate of growth and change.

Then why do certain memes eschew attribution? The memes of the unrestricted web (Advice Dog is only one example) not only often disregard attribution and metadata; they are also frequently incorporated into systems and among practices that actively prevent and dismantle attribution.[15] Some people might argue that many Internet memes lack attribution because their creators have no stake in claiming ownership over worthless material. However, if the practice of attribution is a meme, then the practice of omitting attribution is also a meme, and insofar as it exists and replicates within certain populations, we must say that it is successful. The nonattribution meme possesses characteristics that make it likely to be replicated in others.

What, then, does the practice of anonymity offer to the individuals who enact it? In many ways, anonymity enables a type of freedom. This freedom can have obvious personal benefits if the material one is generating, sharing, or collecting is transgressive. For those Internet users who revel in the existence of racist, sexist, or otherwise offensive memes, a practice and system of anonymity protects them from the regulation or punishment that peers or authorities might attempt to enact in response to such material. However, there is an additional layer of freedom afforded by a lack of attribution. With no documented authors, there exists no intellectual property. Memes can be born, replicated, transmitted, transformed, and forwarded with no concern for rights management, monetization, citation, or licensing. This takes us full circle back to Zittrain's generative network and to the unrestricted web it implies. The prioritization of creative freedom over security is epitomized by the nonattribution meme.

The question I am left with, that I am as of yet unequipped to answer, is whether this thought process casts the nonattribution meme in the role of a metameme. If the presence of the nonattribution meme in a network makes that network more likely to be generative, and if being generative makes a network a more fertile environment for the production and evolution of memes, then is nonattribution a meme that makes the creation of other memes more likely? Lastly, how important is the effect of this metameme when we consider a network (the Internet) whose platforms can require either attribution or anonymity?

NOTES

This work is licensed under the Creative Commons Attribution-ShareAlike license.

1. Jonathan Zittrain, *The Future of the Internet—and How to Stop It* (New Haven: Yale University Press, 2008).

2. Chris Anderson, *The Long Tail* (New York: Hyperion, 2006).

3. Richard Dawkins, *The Selfish Gene* (New York: Oxford University Press, 1989).

4. The use of the word "successful" here is nontrivial. Dawkins explains that replication is a fundamental process for genetics. The earliest forms of life achieve their status as such by virtue of their ability to create copies of themselves. The process of evolution relies entirely on the particulars of the process of reproduction. The theoretical method of meme identification that Dawkins proposes is one that relies on identifying replications. Given all of this, success is always measured by volume of replication. Insofar as an entity (gene, meme, or otherwise) makes more of itself, it is successful.

5. These are the same two characteristics that differ so greatly between genes and memes. If memes transmit faster and are more adaptable than genes, then Internet memes are the most extreme example of that tendency: they are transmitted the fastest and are the most adaptable.

6. Nilay Patel, "iPhone Finally Gets Copy and Paste!," *engadget*, March 17, 2009, http://www.engadget.com/2009/03/17/iphone-finally-gets-copy-and-paste/ (accessed June 25, 2010).

7. I use "ideal" here specifically to reference a platonic ideal. The historical understanding of a platonic ideal is ultimately centralized. A single, theoretical ideal dictates characteristics down to individual manifestations. The ideals of memes operate in reverse. The ideal of a meme is the aggregate of all manifestations of that meme. This is a bottom-up rather than top-down organization.

8. Scott E. Fahlman, "Smiley Lore :-)," Scott E. Fahlman's Carnegie Mellon University web page, http://www.cs.cmu.edu/~sef/sefSmiley.htm (accessed June 25, 2010).

9. The "Gchat" functionality inside of Google's Gmail, for instance, not only automatically animates any of a number of popular emoticons; it also allows users to select from various styles of animation and provides buttons for inserting emoticons without typing.

10. GeoCities was an early website-hosting service from 1994 which allowed people with no programming knowledge to create their own websites for free. It was later acquired by Yahoo! in 1999 and then closed in 2009 (http://geocities.yahoo.com).

11. "Hamster Dance," Wikipedia, http://en.wikipedia.org/wiki/Hamster_dance (accessed June 25, 2010).

12. When considering the form of any given meme, one must consider how easily the form is copied and how easily the form is changed. As I have said, Internet memes are cultural units that are the most replicable and malleable.

13. Since the initial writing of this essay, Creative Commons has introduced a CC0 license, which does not require attribution.

14. Michel Foucault, "What Is an Author?," in *The Foucault Reader*, ed. Paul Rabinow, 101–120 (New York: Pantheon Books, 1984), 107.

15. 4chan.org is a website which has become the most popular example of a site that eschews attribution. It allows contributions from users with no registration process, which has led to a user base operating largely in anonymity.

PART IV

Money

The Long Tail

CHRIS ANDERSON

In 1988, a British mountain climber named Jo Simpson wrote a book called *Touching the Void*, a harrowing account of near death in the Peruvian Andes. It got good reviews, but, only a modest success, it was soon forgotten. Then, a decade later, a strange thing happened. Jon Krakauer wrote *Into Thin Air*, another book about a mountain-climbing tragedy, which became a publishing sensation. Suddenly *Touching the Void* started to sell again.

Random House rushed out a new edition to keep up with demand. Booksellers began to promote it next to their *Into Thin Air* displays, and sales rose further. A revised paperback edition, which came out in January, spent fourteen weeks on the *New York Times* bestseller list. That same month, IFC Films released a docudrama of the story to critical acclaim. Now, *Touching the Void* outsells *Into Thin Air* more than two to one. What happened? In short, Amazon.com recommendations. The online bookseller's software noted patterns in buying behavior and suggested that readers who liked *Into Thin Air* would also like *Touching the Void*. People took the suggestion, agreed wholeheartedly, wrote rhapsodic reviews. More sales, more algorithm-fueled recommendations, and the positive feedback loop kicked in.

Particularly notable is that when Krakauer's book hit shelves, Simpson's was nearly out of print. A few years ago, readers of Krakauer would never even have learned about Simpson's book—and if they had, they wouldn't have been able to find it. Amazon changed that. It created the *Touching the Void* phenomenon by combining infinite shelf space with real-time information about buying trends and public opinion. The result: rising demand for an obscure book.

This is not just a virtue of online booksellers: it is an example of an entirely new economic model for the media and entertainment industries, one that is just beginning to show its power. Unlimited selection is revealing truths about what consumers want and how they want to get it in service after service, from DVDs at Netflix to music videos on Yahoo! Launch to songs in the iTunes Music Store and Rhapsody. People are going deep into the catalog, down the long, long list of available titles, far past what's available at Blockbuster Video, Tower Records, and Barnes & Noble. And the more they find, the more they like. As they wander further from the beaten path, they discover their taste is not as mainstream as they thought (or as they had been led to believe by marketing, a lack of alternatives, and a hit-driven culture).

An analysis of the sales data and trends from these services and others like them shows that the emerging digital entertainment economy is going to be radically different from today's mass market. If the twentieth-century entertainment industry was about hits, the twenty-first will be equally about misses.

For too long we've been suffering the tyranny of lowest-common-denominator fare, subjected to brain-dead summer blockbusters and manufactured pop. Why? Economics. Many of our assumptions about popular taste are actually artifacts of poor supply-and-demand matching—a market response to inefficient distribution. The main problem, if that's the word, is that we live in the physical world and, until recently, most of our entertainment media did, too. But that world puts two dramatic limitations on our entertainment.

The first is the need to find local audiences. An average movie theater will not show a film unless it can attract at least fifteen hundred people over a two-week run; that's essentially the rent for a screen. An average record store needs to sell at least two copies of a CD per year to make it worth carrying; that's the rent for a half inch of shelf space. And so on for DVD rental shops, videogame stores, booksellers, and newsstands.

In each case, retailers will carry only content that can generates sufficient demand to earn its keep. But each can pull only from a limited local population—perhaps a ten-mile radius for a typical movie theater, less than that for music and bookstores, and even less (just a mile or two) for video-rental shops. It's not enough for a great documentary to have a potential national audience of half a million; what matters is how many it has in the northern part of Rockville, Maryland, and among the mall shoppers of Walnut Creek, California.

There is plenty of great entertainment with potentially large, even rapturous, national audiences that cannot clear that bar. For instance, *The Triplets of Belleville*, a critically acclaimed film that was nominated for the best-animated-feature Oscar this year, opened on just six screens nationwide. An even more striking example is the plight of Bollywood in America. Each year, India's film industry puts out more than eight hundred feature films. There are an estimated 1.7 million Indians in the United States. Yet the top-rated (according to Amazon's Internet Movie Database) Hindi-language

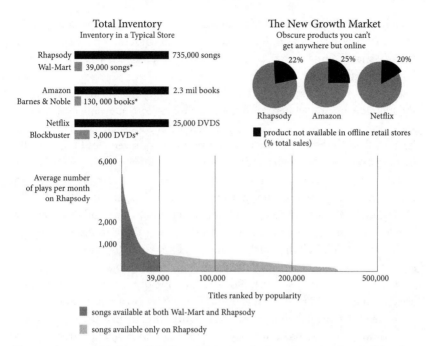

Fig. 10.1. *Anatomy of the long tail.* Online services carry far more inventory than traditional retailers. Rhapsody, for example, offers nineteen times as many songs as Wal-Mart's stock of thirty-nine thousand tunes. The appetite for Rhapsody's more obscure tunes (charted in light grey) makes up the so-called Long Tail. Meanwhile, even as consumers flock to mainstream books, music, and films (bottom), there is real demand for niche fare found only online.[1]

film, *Lagaan: Once Upon a Time in India*, opened on just two screens, and it was one of only a handful of Indian films to get any US distribution at all. In the tyranny of physical space, an audience too thinly spread is the same as no audience at all.

The other constraint of the physical world is physics itself. The radio spectrum can carry only so many stations, and a coaxial cable so many TV channels. And, of course, there are only twenty-four hours a day of programming. The curse of broadcast technologies is that they are profligate users of limited resources. The result is yet another instance of having to aggregate large audiences in one geographic area—another high bar, above which only a fraction of potential content rises.

The past century of entertainment has offered an easy solution to these constraints. Hits fill theaters, fly off shelves, and keep listeners and viewers from touching their dials and remotes. Nothing wrong with that; indeed, sociologists will tell you that hits are hardwired into human psychology, the combinatorial effect of conformity and word of mouth. And to be sure, a healthy share of hits earn their place: great songs, movies, and books attract big, broad audiences.

But most of us want more than just hits. Everyone's taste departs from the mainstream somewhere, and the more we explore alternatives, the more we're drawn to them. Unfortunately, in recent decades such alternatives have been pushed to the fringes by pumped-up marketing vehicles built to order by industries that desperately need them.

Hit-driven economics is a creation of an age without enough room to carry everything for everybody. Not enough shelf space for all the CDs, DVDs, and games produced. Not enough screens to show all the available movies. Not enough channels to broadcast all the TV programs, not enough radio waves to play all the music created, and not enough hours in the day to squeeze everything out through either of those sets of slots.

This is the world of scarcity. Now, with online distribution and retail, we are entering a world of abundance. And the differences are profound.

To see how, meet Robbie Vann-Adibé, the CEO of Ecast, a digital juke-box company whose barroom players offer more than 150,000 tracks—and some surprising usage statistics. He hints at them with a question that visitors invariably get wrong: "What percentage of the top ten thousand titles in any online media store (Netflix, iTunes, Amazon, or any other) will rent or sell at least once a month?"

Most people guess 20 percent, and for good reason: we've been trained to think that way. The 80-20 rule, also known as Pareto's principle (after Vilfredo Pareto, an Italian economist who devised the concept in 1906), is all around us. Only 20 percent of major studio films will be hits. Same for TV shows, games, and mass-market books—20 percent all. The odds are even worse for major-label CDs, of which fewer than 10 percent are profitable, according to the Recording Industry Association of America.

But the right answer, says Vann-Adibé, is 99 percent. There is demand for nearly every one of those top ten thousand tracks. He sees it in his own juke-box statistics; each month, thousands of people put in their dollars for songs that no traditional jukebox anywhere has ever carried.

People get Vann-Adibé's question wrong because the answer is counterintuitive in two ways. The first is we forget that the 20 percent rule in the entertainment industry is about hits, not sales of any sort. We're stuck in a hit-driven mind-set—we think that if something isn't a hit, it won't make money and so won't return the cost of its production. We assume, in other words, that only hits deserve to exist. But Vann-Adibé, like executives at iTunes, Amazon, and Netflix, has discovered that the "misses" usually make money, too. And because there are so many more of them, that money can add up quickly to a huge new market.

With no shelf space to pay for and, in the case of purely digital services like iTunes, no manufacturing costs and hardly any distribution fees, a miss sold is just another sale, with the same margins as a hit. A hit and a miss are on equal economic footing, both just entries in a database called up on demand, both equally worthy of being carried. Suddenly, popularity no longer has a monopoly on profitability.

The second reason for the wrong answer is that the industry has a poor sense of what people want. Indeed, we have a poor sense of what we want. We assume, for instance, that there is little demand for the stuff that isn't carried by Wal-Mart and other major retailers; if people wanted it, surely it would be sold. The rest, the bottom 80 percent, must be subcommercial at best.

But as egalitarian as Wal-Mart may seem, it is actually extraordinarily elitist. Wal-Mart must sell at least one hundred thousand copies of a CD to cover its retail overhead and make a sufficient profit; less than 1 percent of CDs do that kind of volume. What about the sixty thousand people who would like to buy the latest Fountains of Wayne or Crystal Method album or any other nonmainstream fare? They have to go somewhere else. Bookstores, the megaplex, radio, and network TV can be equally demanding. We equate mass market with quality and demand, when in fact it often just represents familiarity, savvy advertising, and broad, if somewhat shallow, appeal. What do we really want? We're only just discovering, but it clearly starts with more.

To get a sense of our true taste, unfiltered by the economics of scarcity, look at Rhapsody, a subscription-based streaming music service (owned by RealNetworks) that currently offers more than 735,000 tracks. Chart Rhapsody's monthly statistics and you get a "power law" demand curve that looks much like any record store's, with huge appeal for the top tracks, tailing off quickly for less popular ones. But a really interesting thing happens once you dig below the top forty thousand tracks, which is about the amount of the fluid inventory (the albums carried that will eventually be sold) of the average real-world record store. Here, the Wal-Marts of the world go to zero— either they don't carry any more CDs, or the few potential local takers for such fringy fare never find it or never even enter the store.

The Rhapsody demand, however, keeps going. Not only is every one of Rhapsody's top one hundred thousand tracks streamed at least once each month, but the same is true for its top two hundred thousand, top three hundred thousand, and top four hundred thousand. As fast as Rhapsody adds tracks to its library, those songs find an audience, even if it's just a few people a month, somewhere in the country.

This is the Long Tail.

You can find everything out there on the Long Tail. There's the back catalog, older albums still fondly remembered by longtime fans or rediscovered by new ones. There are live tracks, B-sides, remixes, even (gasp) covers. There are niches by the thousands, genre within genre within genre: imagine an entire Tower Records devoted to '80s hair bands or ambient dub. There are foreign bands, once priced out of reach in the Import aisle, and obscure bands on even more obscure labels, many of which don't have the distribution clout to get into Tower at all.

Oh, sure, there's also a lot of crap. But there's a lot of crap hiding between the radio tracks on hit albums, too. People have to skip over it on CDs, but they can more easily avoid it online, since the collaborative filters typically won't steer you to it. Unlike the CD, where each crap track costs perhaps one-twelfth of a fifteen-dollar album price, online it just sits harmlessly on some server, ignored in a market that sells by the song and evaluates tracks on their own merit.

What's really amazing about the Long Tail is the sheer size of it. Combine enough nonhits on the Long Tail and you've got a market potentially as big as the hits. Take books: The average Barnes & Noble carries 130,000 titles. Yet a quarter of Amazon's book sales already come from outside its top 130,000 titles. Consider the implication: if the Amazon statistics are any guide, the market for books that are not even sold in the average bookstore is at least a third as large as the market for those that are. And that's a growing fraction. The potential book market may be half again as big as it appears to be, if only we can get over the economics of scarcity. Venture capitalist and former music-industry consultant Kevin Laws puts it this way: "The biggest money is in the smallest sales."

The same is true for all other aspects of the entertainment business, to one degree or another. Just compare online and offline businesses: the average Blockbuster carries fewer than three thousand DVDs. Yet a fifth of Netflix rentals are outside its top three thousand titles. Rhapsody streams more songs each month beyond its top ten thousand than it does its top ten thousand. In each case, the market that lies outside the reach of the physical retailer is big and getting bigger.

When you think about it, most successful businesses on the Internet are about aggregating the Long Tail in one way or another. Google, for instance, makes most of its money off small advertisers (the long tail of advertising), and eBay is mostly tail as well—niche and one-off products. By overcoming the limitations of geography and scale, just as Rhapsody and Amazon have, Google and eBay have discovered new markets and expanded existing ones.

This is the power of the Long Tail. The companies at the vanguard of it are showing the way with three big lessons. Call them the new rules for the new entertainment economy.

Rule 1: Make Everything Available

If you love documentaries, Blockbuster is not for you. Nor is any other video store—there are too many documentaries, and they sell too poorly to justify stocking more than a few dozen of them on physical shelves. Instead, you'll want to join Netflix, which offers more than a thousand documentaries—because it can. Such profligacy is giving a boost to the documentary business; last year, Netflix accounted for half of all US rental revenue for *Capturing the Friedmans*, a documentary about a family destroyed by allegations of pedophilia.

Netflix CEO Reed Hastings, who's something of a documentary buff, took this newfound clout to PBS, which had produced *Daughter from Danang*, a documentary about the children of US soldiers and Vietnamese women. In 2002, the film was nominated for an Oscar and was named best documentary at Sundance, but PBS had no plans to release it on DVD. Hastings offered to handle the manufacturing and distribution if PBS would make it available as a Netflix exclusive. Now *Daughter from Danang* consistently ranks in the top fifteen on Netflix documentary charts. That amounts to a market of tens of thousands of documentary renters that did not otherwise exist.

There are any number of equally attractive genres and subgenres neglected by the traditional DVD channels: foreign films, anime, independent movies, British television dramas, old American TV sitcoms. These underserved markets make up a big chunk. The availability of offbeat content drives new customers to Netflix—and anything that cuts the cost of customer acquisition is gold for a subscription business. Thus the company's first lesson: embrace niches.

Netflix has made a good business out of what's unprofitable fare in movie theaters and video rental shops because it can aggregate dispersed audiences. It doesn't matter if the several thousand people who rent *Doctor Who* episodes each month are in one city or spread, one per town, across the country—the economics are the same to Netflix. It has, in short, broken the tyr-

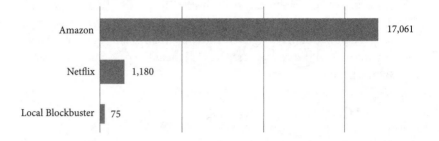

Documentaries Available

Amazon	17,061
Netflix	1,180
Local Blockbuster	75

Fig. 10.2. *The documentary niche gets richer.* More than forty thousand documentaries have been released, according to the Internet Movie Database. Of those, Amazon.com carries 40 percent, Netflix 3 percent, and the average Blockbuster just 0.2 percent.[2]

anny of physical space. What matters is not where customers are, or even how many of them are seeking a particular title, but only that some number of them exist, anywhere.

As a result, almost anything is worth offering on the off chance it will find a buyer. This is the opposite of the way the entertainment industry now thinks. Today, the decision about whether or when to release an old film on DVD is based on estimates of demand, availability of extras such as commentary and additional material, and marketing opportunities such as anniversaries, awards, and generational windows (Disney briefly rereleases its classics every ten years or so as a new wave of kids come of age). It's a high bar, which is why only a fraction of movies ever made are available on DVD.

That model may make sense for the true classics, but it's way too much fuss for everything else. The Long Tail approach, by contrast, is to simply dump huge chunks of the archive onto bare-bones DVDs, without any extras or marketing. Call it the "Silver Series" and charge half the price. Same for independent films. This year, nearly six thousand movies were submitted to the Sundance Film Festival. Of those, 255 were accepted, and just two dozen have been picked up for distribution; to see the others, you had to be there.

Why not release all 255 on DVD each year as part of a discount Sundance series? In a Long Tail economy, it's more expensive to evaluate than to release. Just do it! The same is true for the music industry. It should be securing the rights to release all the titles in all the back catalogs as quickly as it can—thoughtlessly, automatically, and at industrial scale. (This is one of those rare moments when the world needs more lawyers, not fewer.) So too for videogames. Retro gaming, including simulators of classic game consoles that run on modern PCs, is a growing phenomenon driven by the nostalgia of the first joystick generation. Game publishers could release every title as a ninety-nine-cent download three years after its release—no support, no guarantees, no packaging.

All this, of course, applies equally to books. Already, we're seeing a blurring of the line between in and out of print. Amazon and other networks of used booksellers have made it almost as easy to find and buy a secondhand book as it is a new one. By divorcing bookselling from geography, these networks create a liquid market at low volume, dramatically increasing both their own business and the overall demand for used books. Combine that with the rapidly dropping costs of print-on-demand technologies and it's clear why any book should always be available. Indeed, it is a fair bet that children today will grow up never knowing the meaning of "out of print."

Rule 2: Cut the Price in Half, Now Lower It

Thanks to the success of Apple's iTunes, we now have a standard price for a downloaded track: ninety-nine cents. But is it the right one? Ask the labels and they'll tell you it's too low: Even though ninety-nine cents per track works out to about the same price as a CD, most consumers just buy a track or two from an album online, rather than the full CD. In effect, online music has seen a return to the singles-driven business of the 1950s. So from a label perspective, consumers should pay more for the privilege of purchasing à la carte to compensate for the lost album revenue.

Ask consumers, on the other hand, and they'll tell you that ninety-nine cents is too high. It is, for starters, ninety-nine cents more than Kazaa. But piracy aside, ninety-nine cents violates our innate sense of economic justice: if it clearly costs less for a record label to deliver a song online, with no packaging, manufacturing, distribution, or shelf space overheads, why shouldn't the price be less, too?

Surprisingly enough, there's been little good economic analysis on what the right price for online music should be. The main reason for this is that pricing isn't set by the market today but by the record label demicartel. Record companies charge a wholesale price of around sixty-five cents per track, leaving little room for price experimentation by the retailers.

That wholesale price is set to roughly match the price of CDs, to avoid dreaded "channel conflict." The labels fear that if they price online music lower, their CD retailers (still the vast majority of the business) will revolt or, more likely, go out of business even more quickly than they already are. In either case, it would be a serious disruption of the status quo, which terrifies the already spooked record companies. No wonder they're doing price calculations with an eye on the downsides in their traditional CD business rather than the upside in their new online business.

But what if the record labels stopped playing defense? A brave new look at the economics of music would calculate what it really costs to simply put a song on an iTunes server and adjust pricing accordingly. The results are surprising.

Take away the unnecessary costs of the retail channel—CD manufacturing, distribution, and retail overheads. That leaves the costs of finding, making, and marketing music. Keep them as they are, to ensure that the people on the creative and label side of the business make as much as they currently do. For a popular album that sells three hundred thousand copies, the creative costs work out to about $7.50 per disc, or around sixty cents a track. Add to that the actual cost of delivering music online, which is mostly the cost of building and maintaining the online service rather than the negligible storage and bandwidth costs. Current price tag: around seventeen cents a track. By this calculation, hit music is overpriced by 25 percent online—it should cost just seventy-nine cents a track, reflecting the savings of digital delivery.

Putting channel conflict aside for the moment, if the incremental cost of making content that was originally produced for physical distribution available online is low, the price should be, too. Price according to digital costs, not physical ones.

All this good news for consumers doesn't have to hurt the industry. When you lower prices, people tend to buy more. Last year, Rhapsody did an experiment in elastic demand that suggested it could be a lot more. For a brief period, the service offered tracks at ninety-nine cents, seventy-nine cents, and forty-nine cents. Although the forty-nine-cent tracks were only half the price of the ninety-nine-cent tracks, Rhapsody sold three times as many of them.

Since the record companies still charged sixty-five cents a track—and Rhapsody paid another eight cents per track to the copyright-holding publishers—Rhapsody lost money on that experiment (but, as the old joke goes, made it up in volume). Yet much of the content on the Long Tail is older material that has already made back its money (or been written off for failing to do so): music from bands that had little record-company investment and was thus cheap to make, or live recordings, remixes, and other material that came at low cost.

```
Creation Costs
    Artist                  $1.50
    Marketing and Profit    $5.00
    Publishing              $0.96
                            _____
                            $7.46      ─→    Divided by 12 tracks
                                             =
              +                              $0.62/track
                                             +
Production Costs                             $.017 online delivery cost
    Packaging               $0.75
    Distribution            $2.00             ↓
    Retail markup           $5.00            $0.79/song
                            _____
                            $7.76


                             ↓

                        $15.21/CD
```

Fig. 10.3. *The real cost of music.* Online music services don't incur packaging, distribution, and retail fees—and they should charge accordingly.[3]

Such "misses" cost less to make available than hits, so why not charge even less for them? Imagine if prices declined the further you went down the Tail, with popularity (the market) effectively dictating pricing. All it would take is for the labels to lower the wholesale price for the vast majority of their content not in heavy rotation; even a two- or three-tiered pricing structure could work wonders. And because so much of that content is not available in record stores, the risk of channel conflict is greatly diminished. The lesson: pull consumers down the tail with lower prices.

How low should the labels go? The answer comes by examining the psychology of the music consumer. The choice facing fans is not how many songs to buy from iTunes and Rhapsody but how many songs to buy rather than download for free from Kazaa and other peer-to-peer networks. Intuitively, consumers know that free music is not really free: aside from any legal risks, it's a time-consuming hassle to build a collection that way. Labeling is inconsistent, quality varies, and an estimated 30 percent of tracks are defective in one way or another. As Steve Jobs put it at the iTunes Music Store launch, you may save a little money downloading from Kazaa, but "you're working for under minimum wage." And what's true for music is doubly true for movies and games, where the quality of pirated products can be even more dismal, viruses are a risk, and downloads take so much longer.

So free has a cost: the psychological value of convenience. This is the "not worth it" moment when the wallet opens. The exact amount is an impossible calculus involving the bank balance of the average college student multiplied by his or her available free time. But imagine that for music, at least, it's around twenty cents a track. That, in effect, is the dividing line between the commercial world of the Long Tail and the underground. Both worlds will continue to exist in parallel, but it's crucial for Long Tail thinkers to exploit the opportunities between twenty and ninety-nine cents to maximize their share. By offering fair pricing, ease of use, and consistent quality, you can compete with free.

Perhaps the best way to do that is to stop charging for individual tracks at all. Danny Stein, whose private equity firm owns eMusic, thinks the future of the business is to move away from the ownership model entirely. With ubiquitous broadband, both wired and wireless, more consumers will turn to the celestial jukebox of music services that offer every track ever made, playable on demand. Some of those tracks will be free to listeners and advertising supported, like radio. Others, like eMusic and Rhapsody, will be subscription services. Today, digital music economics are dominated by the iPod, with its notion of a paid-up library of personal tracks. But as the networks improve, the comparative economic advantages of unlimited streamed music, either financed by advertising or a flat fee (infinite choice for $9.99 a month), may shift the market that way. And drive another nail in the coffin of the retail music model.

Rule 3: Help Me Find It

In 1997, an entrepreneur named Michael Robertson started what looked like a classic Long Tail business. Called MP3.com, it let anyone upload music files that would be available to all. The idea was the service would bypass the record labels, allowing artists to connect directly to listeners. MP3.com would make its money in fees paid by bands to have their music promoted on the site. The tyranny of the labels would be broken, and a thousand flowers would bloom.

But it didn't work out that way. Struggling bands did not, as a rule, find new audiences, and independent music was not transformed. Indeed, MP3.com got a reputation for being exactly what it was: an undifferentiated mass of mostly bad music that deserved its obscurity.

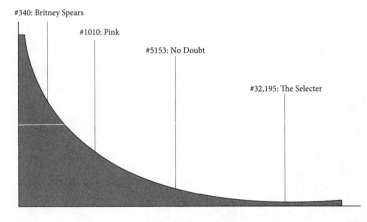

Fig. 10.4. *"If you like Britney, you'll love . . ."* Just as lower prices can entice consumers down the Long Tail, recommendation engines drive them to obscure content they might not find otherwise.[4]

The problem with MP3.com was that it was only Long Tail. It didn't have license agreements with the labels to offer mainstream fare or much popular commercial music at all. Therefore, there was no familiar point of entry for consumers, no known quantity from which further exploring could begin.

Offering only hits is no better. Think of the struggling video-on-demand services of the cable companies. Or think of Movielink, the feeble video-download service run by the studios. Due to overcontrolling providers and high costs, they suffer from limited content: in most cases just a few hundred recent releases. There's not enough choice to change consumer behavior, to become a real force in the entertainment economy.

By contrast, the success of Netflix, Amazon, and the commercial music services shows that you need both ends of the curve. Their huge libraries of less mainstream fare set them apart, but hits still matter in attracting consumers in the first place. Great Long Tail businesses can then guide consumers further afield by following the contours of their likes and dislikes, easing their exploration of the unknown.

For instance, the front screen of Rhapsody features Britney Spears, unsurprisingly. Next to the listings of her work is a box of "similar artists." Among them is Pink. If you click on that and are pleased with what you hear, you may do the same for Pink's similar artists, which include No Doubt. And on No Doubt's page, the list includes a few "followers" and "influencers," the last of which includes the Selecter, a 1980s ska band from Coventry, England. In

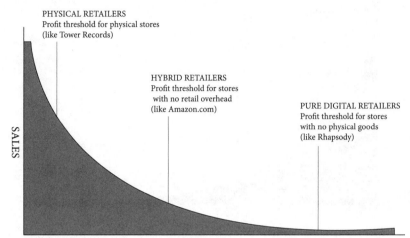

PHYSICAL RETAILERS
Profit threshold for physical stores
(like Tower Records)

HYBRID RETAILERS
Profit threshold for stores
with no retail overhead
(like Amazon.com)

PURE DIGITAL RETAILERS
Profit threshold for stores
with no physical goods
(like Rhapsody)

SALES

TITLES

Fig. 10.5. *The bit player advantage.* Beyond bricks and mortar, there are two main retail models—one that gets halfway down the Long Tail and another that goes all the way. The first is the familiar hybrid model of Amazon and Netflix, companies that sell physical goods online. Digital catalogs allow them to offer unlimited selection along with search, reviews, and recommendations, while the cost savings of massive warehouses and no walk-in customers greatly expands the number of products they can sell profitably. Pushing this even further are pure digital services, such as iTunes, which offer the additional savings of delivering their digital goods online at virtually no marginal cost. Since an extra database entry and a few megabytes of storage on a server cost effectively nothing, these retailers have no economic reason not to carry everything available.

three clicks, Rhapsody may have enticed a Britney Spears fan to try an album that can hardly be found in a record store.

Rhapsody does this with a combination of human editors and genre guides. But Netflix, where 60 percent of rentals come from recommendations, and Amazon do this with collaborative filtering, which uses the browsing and purchasing patterns of users to guide those who follow them ("Customers who bought this also bought . . ."). In each, the aim is the same: use recommendations to drive demand down the Long Tail.

This is the difference between push and pull, between broadcast and personalized taste. Long Tail business can treat consumers as individuals, offering mass customization as an alternative to mass-market fare.

The advantages are spread widely. For the entertainment industry itself, recommendations are a remarkably efficient form of marketing, allowing smaller films and less mainstream music to find an audience. For consumers, the improved signal-to-noise ratio that comes from following a good recommendation encourages exploration and can reawaken a passion for music and film, potentially creating a far larger entertainment market overall. (The average Netflix customer rents seven DVDs a month, three times the rate at brick-and-mortar stores.) And the cultural benefit of all of this is much more diversity, reversing the blanding effects of a century of distribution scarcity and ending the tyranny of the hit.

Such is the power of the Long Tail. Its time has come.

NOTES

This chapter was originally published in *Wired*, October 2004. This version is based on the updated version published on *Change This*, December 14, 2004, http://changethis. com/manifesto/show/10.LongTail (accessed July 20, 2010). This work is licensed under the Creative Commons Attribution-ShareAlike license.

1. Erik Brynjolfsson, Yu "Jeffrey" Hu, and Michael D. Smith, "Consumer Surplus in the Digital Economy: Estimating the Value of Increased Product Variety at Online Booksellers," *Management Science* 49, no. 11 [November 2003]: 1580–1596; Barnes & Noble, http:// www.barnesandnoble.com/; Netflix, Netflix.com; Rhapsody, http://www.rhapsody.com/.

2. "Movies & TV > Documentary," Amazon.com, http://www.amazon.com/ s/?node=2625373011&field-theme_browse-bin=2650367011; "Most Popular Documentaries," Internet Movie Database, http://www.imdb.com/search/title?genres=documentary; "Documentary," Netflix.com.

3. Jonathan Daniel and Joe Fleischer, Crush Music Media Management, interview, 2004.

4. "Best Sellers in Music," Amazon.com, http://www.amazon.com/gp/bestsellers/music.

Law

REMIX

How Creativity Is Being Strangled by the Law

LAWRENCE LESSIG

I've written five books. Four of these books are extraordinarily depressing. I like depressing, deep, dark stories about the inevitable destruction of great, fantastic ideas. After my first child was born, my thinking began to shift some, and I wrote *Remix*, which is quite new in the collection because it's a fundamentally happy book or, at least, mostly a happy book. It's optimistic. It's about how certain fantastic ideas will win in this cultural debate. Though the problem is that I'm not actually used to this optimism; I'm not used to living in a world without hopelessness. So I'm actually moving on from this field to focus on a completely hopeless topic, solving problems of corruption, actually. Completely hopeless. But I am happy to come here to talk about this most recent book.

I want to talk about it by telling you some stories, making an observation, and constructing an argument about what we need to do to protect the opportunity that technology holds for this society. There are three stories.

The first one is very short. A very long time ago, the elite spoke Latin, and the vulgar, the rest of the people, spoke other languages: English, French, and German. The elite ignored the masses. The masses ignored the elite. That's the first story. Very short, as I promised.

Here's number two: In 1906, John Philip Sousa traveled to the United States Congress to talk about phonographs, a technology he called the "talking machines." John Philip Sousa was not a fan of the talking machines. He was quoted as saying, "These talking machines are going to ruin the artistic development of music in this country. When I was a boy, in front of every house in the summer evenings, you would find young people together singing the songs of the day or the old songs. Today you hear these infernal machines going night and day. We will not have a vocal cord left. The vocal cords will be eliminated by a process of evolution, as was the tail of man when he came from the ape."[1]

I want you to focus on this picture of "young people together singing the songs of the day or even old songs." This is culture. You could call it a kind of read/write culture. It's a culture where people participate in the creation and re-creation of their culture. It is read/write, and Sousa's fear was that we would lose the capacity to engage in this read/write creativity because of these "infernal machines." They would take it away, displace it, and in its place, we'd have the opposite of read/write creativity: a kind of read-only culture. A culture where creativity is consumed, but the consumer is not a creator. A culture that is top down: a culture where the "vocal cords" of the millions of ordinary people have been lost.

Here is story three: In 1919, the United States voted itself dry as it launched an extraordinary war against an obvious evil—a war against the dependence on alcohol, a war inspired by the feminist movement, a war inspired by ideas of progressive reform, and a war that was inspired by the thought that government could make us a better society. Ten years into that war, it was pretty clear this war was failing. In places around the country, they asked how we could redouble our efforts to win the war. In Seattle, the police started to find ways to fight back against these criminals using new technology: the wiretap. Roy Olmstead and eleven others found themselves the target of a federal investigation into his illegal production and distribution of alcohol. His case, *Olmstead v. the United States* (1928), was heard by the Supreme Court to decide whether the wiretap was legal.[2] When the police tapped the phones of Olmsted and his colleagues, they didn't get a judge's permission, or a warrant, they just tapped the phones. The Supreme Court looked at the Fourth Amendment to the Constitution, which protects against "unreasonable searches and seizures." Chief Justice Taft concluded that the wiretap was not proscribed by this amendment. He said the Fourth Amendment was designed to protect against trespassing. But wiretapping doesn't involve any necessary trespass: they didn't enter Olmstead's home to attach anything to the wires; they attached the wiretap after the wires left Olmsted's home. There was no trespass, therefore no violation of the Fourth Amendment.

Louis Brandeis, in voicing his dissent, argued vigorously for a different principle. Brandeis said the objective of the Fourth Amendment was to protect against a certain form of invasion, so as to protect the privacy of people. He argued that how you protect privacy is a function of technology, and we need to translate the old protections from one era into a new context. He used the phrase "time works changes," citing *Weems v. United States* (1910). Brandeis lost in that case and the wiretap won, but the war that the wiretap was aiding was quickly recognized to be a failure. By 1933 people recognized this failure in increased costs they hadn't even anticipated when they first enacted this prohibition: the rise in organized crime and the fall in civil rights. They were also seeing a vanishing benefit from this war: everybody still drank. They realized that maybe the costs of this war were greater than the benefits. And so, in 1933 the Twenty-First Amendment repealed the Eighteenth Amendment, and Prohibition ended. Importantly, what was repealed was not the aim of fighting the dependence on alcohol but the idea of using war to fight this dependence.

Those are the stories, and here's the observation. In a sense that should be obvious, writing is an extraordinarily democratic activity. I don't mean that we vote to decide what people can write. I mean that everyone should have the capacity to write. Why do we teach everyone to write and measure education by the capacity people have to write? By "write," I mean more than just grade-school knowledge to make shopping lists and send text messages on cell phones. More specifically, between ninth grade and college, why do we waste time on essays on Shakespeare or Hemingway or Proust? What do we expect to gain? Because, as an academic, I can tell you the vast majority of this writing is just crap. So why do we force kids to suffer, and why do we force their professors to suffer this "creativity"?

The obvious answer is that we learn something. In the process of learning how to write, we at least learn respect for just how hard this kind of creativity is, and that respect is itself its own value. In this democratic practice of writing, which we teach everyone, we include quoting. I had a friend in college who wrote essays that were all exactly like this: strings of quotes from other people's writings that were pulled together in a way that was so convincing that he never got anything less than an A+ in all of his university writing classes. Now, he would take and use and build upon other people's words without permission of the other authors: *so long as you cite*. In my view, plagiarism is the only crime for which the death penalty is appropriate. So long as you cite, you can take whatever you want and use it for your purpose in creating. Imagine if the rule were different; imagine you went around and asked for permission to quote. Imagine how absurd it would be to write the Hemingway estate and ask for permission to include three lines in an essay about Hemingway for your English class. When you recognize how absurd it is, you've recognized how this is an essentially democratic form of expression; the freedom to take and use freely is built into our assumptions about how we create what we write.

Here's the argument. I want to think about writing or, more broadly, *creating* in a digital age. What should the freedom to write, the freedom to quote, the freedom to remix be? Notice the parallels that exist between this question and the stories that I've told. As with the war of Prohibition, we, in the United States, are in the middle of a war. Actually, of course, we're in the middle of many wars, but the one I want to talk about is the copyright war, those which my friend the late Jack Valenti used to refer to as his own "terrorist war."[3] Apparently the terrorists in this war are our children. As with the war Sousa launched, this war is inspired by artists and an industry terrified that changes in technology will effect a radical change in how culture gets made. As with the Twenty-First Amendment, these wars are raising an important new question: Are the costs of this war greater than its benefits? Or, alternatively, can we obtain the benefits without suffering much of the costs?

Now, to answer that question, we need to think first about the benefits of copyright. Copyright is, in my view, an essential solution to a particular unavoidable economic problem. It may seem like a paradox, but we would get less speech without copyright. Limiting the freedom of some people to copy creates incentives to create more speech. That's a perfect and happy story, and it should function in exactly this way. But, as with privacy, the proper regulation has to reflect changes in technology. As the technology changes, the architecture of the proper regulation is going to change. What made sense in one period might not make sense in another. We need to adjust, in order to achieve the same value in a different context. So with copyright, what would the right regulation be?

The first point of regulation would be to distinguish, as Sousa did, between the amateur and the professional. Copyright needs to encourage both. We need to have the incentives for the professional and the freedom for the amateur. We can see something about how to do this by watching the evolution of digital technologies in the Internet era. The first stage begins around 2000, which is a period of extraordinary innovation to extend read-only culture. Massively efficient technology enables people to consume culture created elsewhere. Apple's iTunes Music Store allows you to download culture for ninety-nine cents, though only to an iPod and, of course, only to *your* iPod (and a few other iPods whose owners you trust with your iTunes login). This is an extraordinarily important and valuable part of culture, which my colleague Paul Goldstein used to refer to as the "celestial jukebox."[4] This step is critically important, as it gives people access to extraordinary diversity for the first time in human history. That is one stage.

A second stage begins around 2004, a reviving of Sousa's read/write culture. The poster child for this culture is probably something like Wikipedia, but the version I want to focus on is something I call "remix." Think about remix in the context of music. Everybody knows the Beatles' *White Album*. It inspired Jay Z's *Black Album*, which inspired DJ Danger Mouse's *Grey Album*, which literally synthesizes the tracks so that the *White Album* and *Black Album* together produce something gray. That's 2004: two albums synthesized together in what came to be known as a mashup. The equivalent today is something like the work of Girl Talk, who synthesizes up to 280 different songs together into one particular song. Think in the same context about film: in 2004, with a budget of $218, Jonathan Caouette's *Tarnation* makes its debut in wowing Cannes and wining the 2004 Los Angeles International Film Festival.[5] Caouette took twenty years of Super-8 and VHS home movies and an iMac given to him by a friend to create an incredibly moving documentary about his life and relationship with his mentally ill mother. On a more modest but more prevalent level, YouTube is full of something called anime music videos. These videos are anime, the Japanese cartoons sweeping America today. It is not just kids making them, but we'll just pretend for a second that it is kids who take the original video and reedit it to a different sound track. It can be banal or interesting. And almost all of this read/write has emerged on YouTube.

Many people focus on the copyrighted TV shows that are digitized and posted onto YouTube overnight. I want you to think about the call-and-response pattern that YouTube inspires, where someone will create something and then someone else will create another version of the same thing. A hip-hop artist named Soulja Boy created a song called "Crank Dat," which featured a dance called "The Superman." The beat was catchy; the lyrics were literally a set of instructions on how to reproduce the dance. The original music video was a low-budget demonstration of the steps required to reproduce the dance.[6] And reproduce it did.[7] That how-to video has been viewed over forty million times as of June 2009. There are hundreds, if not thousands, of videos of the Soulja Boy Superman dance—each one building on the next: cartoon characters, people of all ethnicities, Internet celebrities, politicians.[8] The point is these are increasingly conversations between young people from around the world. YouTube has become a platform where people talk to each other. It's the modern equivalent of what Sousa spoke of when he spoke of "the young people together, singing the songs of the day or the old songs." But rather than gathering on the front lawn, they now do it with digital technologies, sharing creativity with others around the world.

Just today I discovered a remix of the presidential debates that emphasizes the prevalence of talking points through remix.[9] Many people saw the "Yes We Can" video featuring famous musicians singing along to one of Barack

Obama's speeches.[10] This kind of pastiche of songs, sounds, and words has become a natural way to express politics that maybe a decade ago would not have been understandable.[11] My favorite is Johan Soderberg's "Bush Blair Endless Love," which edits their speeches to a love song by Diana Ross and Lionel Ritchie.[12] I'm very sad, but this is one of the last times I get to share this one, as Bush's term is ending shortly.

Remix has nothing to do with technique, because the techniques this work employs have been available to filmmakers and videographers from the beginning of those forms of expression. What's important here is that the technique has been democratized for anyone who has access to a fifteen-hundred-dollar computer. Anyone can take images, sounds, video from the culture around us and remix them in ways that speak to a generation more powerfully than raw text ever could. That's the key. This is just *writing* for the twenty-first century. We who spend our lives writing have to recognize that nonmultimedia, plain alphanumeric text in the twenty-first century is the Latin from the Middle Ages. The words, images, sounds, and videos of the twenty-first century speak to the vulgar; they are the forms of expression that are understood by most people. The problem is that the laws governing quoting in these new forms of expression are radically different from the norms that govern quoting from text. In this new form of expression that has swept through online communities that use digital technology, permission is expected first. Why is there this difference?

It is a simple, technical clause in the law, a conflict between two architectures of control. One architecture, copyright, is triggered every time a copy is made. The other architecture, digital technology, produces a copy in every single use of culture. This is radical change in the way copyright law regulated culture.

Think, for example, about a book that is regulated in physical space by copyright law. An important set of uses of a book constitute *free* uses of a book, because to read a book is not to produce a copy. To give someone a book is not a fair use of a book; it's a *free* use of a book, because to give someone a book is not to *produce* a copy of a book. To sell a book requires no permission from the copyright owner, because to sell a book is not to produce a copy. To sleep on a book is an unregulated act in every jurisdiction around the world because sleeping on a book does not produce a copy. These unregulated uses are balanced with a set of regulated uses that create the incentives necessary to produce great new works. If you want to publish a book, you need permission from the copyright owner. In the American tradition, there is a thin sliver of "fair use," exceptions that would otherwise have been regulated by the law but which the law says ought to remain free to create the incentive for people to build upon or critique earlier work.

Enter the Internet, where every single use produces a copy: we go from this balance between unregulated, regulated, and fair uses to a presumptive rule of regulated uses merely because the platform through which we get access to our culture has changed, rendering this read/write activity presumptively illegal. DJ Danger Mouse knew he could never get permission from the Beatles to remix their work. Caouette discovered he could wow Cannes for $218, then discovered it would cost over $400,000 to clear the rights to the music in the background of the video that he had shot. Anime music videos are increasingly getting takedowns and notices from lawyers who are not happy about the one thousand hours of remixed video needed to create the anime music videos. And back to my favorite example of "Bush Blair Endless Love": I don't care what you think about Tony Blair, I don't care what you think about George Bush, and I don't care what you think about the war. The one thing that you cannot say about this video is what the lawyers said when they were asked for permission to synchronize those images with that soundtrack. The lawyers said no, you can't have our permission, because "it's not funny." So the point here is to recognize that no one in Congress ever thought about this. There was no ATM-RECA Act, the "Act to Massively Regulate Every Creative Act" Act. This is the unintended consequence of the interaction between two architectures of regulation, and, in my view, this is problem number one: the law is fundamentally out of sync with the technology. And, just as with the Fourth Amendment, this needs to be updated. Copyright law needs an update.

Problem number two is what those who live in Southern California typically think of as problem number one: piracy or, more specifically, peer-to-peer piracy. Piracy is the "terrorism" that Jack Valenti spoke of when he called kids terrorists. Now, I think this is a problem; I don't support people using technology to violate other people's rights. In my book *Free Culture* and in *Remix*, I repeatedly say you should not use peer-to-peer networks to copy without the permission of the copyright owner. But all of that acknowledged, we need to recognize that this war of prohibition has not worked; it has not changed the bad behavior. Here's a chart of peer-to-peer simultaneous users (see fig. 11.1). The one thing we learn from this chart is that peer-to-peer users don't seem to read the Supreme Court's briefs: the arrow marks the date that the Supreme Court declared completely, unambiguously, that this is presumptively illegal. After the ruling, the number of users did not decrease.

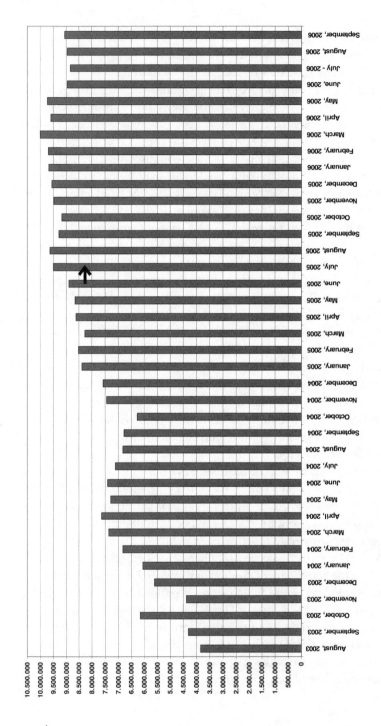

Fig. 11.1. Average simultaneous P2P users

All this war has done is produce a generation of "criminals." That part of the story is very ugly, unhappy, and sad. It is the sort of inspiration that I used for my last book, *Free Culture*. But times have changed, and the story in *Remix* is a story of change, a change that is inspired by what I think of as the third stage in this development: the development of hybrid economies.

To understand a hybrid economy, first think about what "economies" means. Economies are repeated practices of exchange, over time between at least two parties. I want to identify three such economies. First, there are commercial economies. At the grocery store it is a quid pro quo: you get a certain number of bananas for a certain number of dollars. Money is how we speak in this economy. Second, there are economies where money is not part of the exchange. For example, two kids playing on the playground is a sharing economy. Friends going out to lunch sharing their time with each other is a sharing economy. And romantic love is a sharing economy. They are economies, because they exist over time, but, for these economies, money is *not* how we speak. Indeed, if we introduced money into these economies, we would radically change them. Imagine if two friends were planning a lunch date, and one says, "How about next week?" and the other one says, "Nah, how about fifty dollars instead?" Or consider that when money is introduced into romantic relationships, it radically changes the meaning of that economy for both parties involved. These are both rich and important economies that coexist with the commercial economy. They don't necessarily compete, but we want lives where we have both.

Now the Internet, of course, has produced both commercial and sharing economies. The Internet has commercial economies where people leverage knowledge to produce financial value, and it has sharing economies like Wikipedia or free sound resources like FreeSound.org or SETI@home, where people make their resources available to discover information about the universe. The Internet also has hybrid economies, which I want to focus on.

A hybrid economy is one where a commercial entity leverages a sharing economy or a sharing entity leverages a commercial economy. I'm not going to talk about the second case. I want to focus on the first case, where commercial economies leverage sharing economies. So here are some examples, obvious examples. Flickr, from its very birth, was a photo-sharing site that built sharing into its DNA. Indeed, it facilitated sharing by setting "public" as the default viewing state for all uploaded images and giving people the option to license their photos explicitly under a Creative Commons license. This sharing enabled community creation. Yahoo bought Flickr with the goal of leveraging value out of this sharing economy. Likewise, Yelp has exploded, as thousands of people around the world share reviews of hotels or restaurants. These shared reviews, which people do for free, produce value for Yelp. Second Life began as a virtual world filled with big blue oceans and beautiful green fields, but through literally hundreds and thousands of hours of volunteer labor by people from around the world creating objects, places, and buildings, they have produced an extraordinarily rich environment that attracts people to Second Life and which profits the company, Linden Labs.[13]

These are examples of what I think of as a hybrid. Once you see these examples, you will begin to see hybrids everywhere. Is Amazon really a commercial economy in this sense? Because, though it is selling books, much of the value of Amazon comes from the enormous amount of activity that people devote toward helping other people navigate the products which Amazon tries to sell. Apple is doing this. Even Microsoft gets this deep down in its DNA. Of course, Microsoft builds much of its support through volunteers who spend an enormous amount of their time not helping their local church but helping other people run Microsoft products more simply. Now this is not an accident. Mark Smith, a very bright former academic, works in something called the Community Technologies Group at Microsoft. This group develops all sorts of technologies to gauge the health of these communities, to encourage these communities to be more healthy so that other people want to spend more unpaid time helping Microsoft get richer. This dynamic is extraordinary. And it's no surprise, then, that at a conference about a year and one-half ago, I heard Steve Ballmer declare that every single successful Internet business will be a hybrid business. I think there is enormous promise in these hybrid combinations of free culture and free markets. This presents an enormous potential for the Internet economy to drive value back into these creative industries. That is the argument for what I think can happen, but this takes us doing something to produce it.

I want to identify two kinds of changes. The first change is a very technical legal change: the law needs to give up the obsession with the copy. As discussed earlier, copyright law is triggered on the production of every copy. This is, to use a technical and legal term, insane. I believe the law needs to focus on meaningful activity; in a digital world, the copy is not a meaningful activity. Meaningful activity, instead, is a function of the context of the copy's use. Context will help us distinguish between copies and remixes. We need to distinguish between taking someone's work and just duplicating it versus doing something with the work that creates something new. Context will help us distinguish between the professional and amateur. The copyright law, as it exists right now, presumptively regulates all this in the same way.

Never before in the history of copyright law has it regulated so broadly. In my view, it makes no sense to regulate this broadly right now. Instead, copyright law needs to focus on professional work being copied without being remixed. It needs to effectively guarantee professionals can control copies of their works that are made available commercially. Amateurs making remixes need to have free use, not fair use; they need to be exempted from the law of copyright. Amateurs need to be able to remix work without worrying about whether a lawyer would approve their remix or not. And between these two very easy cases, there are two very hard cases, professional remixes and amateur copying, cases where the law of fair use needs to continue to negotiate to make sure that sufficient incentives are created while leaving important creativity free. Now, if you look at this and you have any conservative instincts inside you, you might recognize this as a kind of conservative argument. I am arguing in favor of deregulating a significant space of culture and focusing regulation where the regulators can convince us that it will be doing some good. That's change number one.

Change number two is about peer-to-peer piracy. As discussed earlier, we have to recognize we're a decade into a war on piracy that has totally failed. In response to totally failed wars, some continue to wage that same war against the enemy. That was Jack Valenti's instinct. My instinct is the opposite. It's to stop suing kids and to start suing for peace. For the past decade, the very best scholars around the country have created an enormous number of proposals for ways to facilitate compensation to artists without breaking the Internet, proposals like compulsory licenses or the voluntary collective license.[14] But as you look at all of these proposals, what we should recognize is what the world would have been like if we had had these proposals a decade ago. Number one, artists would have more money; of course, artists get nothing from peer-to-peer file sharing, and they don't get anything when lawyers sue to stop peer-to-peer file sharing (because any money collected goes to the lawyers, not the artists). Number two, we would have more competition in businesses; the rules would be clearer, so there would be more businesses that could get venture capital to support them as they innovate around ways to make content more easily accessible. Number three, and the point that is most important to me, is that we would not have a generation of criminals surrounding us. We need to consider these proposals now. We need this legal change.

The law needs to change, but so do we. We need to find ways to chill control-obsessed individuals and corporations that believe the single objective of copyright law is to control use, rather than thinking about the objective of copyright law as to create incentives for creation. We need to practice respect for this new generation of creators. For example, there is a kind of hybrid which I unfairly refer to as a Darth Vader hybrid. This name was inspired by the Star Wars MashUps site that enables users to remix this thirty-year-old franchise through access to video footage from the films, into which you can upload and insert your own material. You can integrate your own music and pictures into the *Star Wars* series. But if you read the terms of service for this site, the mashups are all owned by Lucas Film.[15] Indeed, Lucas Film has a worldwide perpetual license to exploit all content you upload for free, without any recognition back to the original creator. Yes, this is a hybrid economy, but an economy where the creator doesn't have any rights. Instead, it's a sharecropping economy in the digital age. This is an important understanding to track because people are increasingly taking notice of the way hybrid economies work and wondering whether there is justice in it. Om Malik asks, does "this culture of participation . . . build businesses on our collective backs? . . . Whatever 'the collective efforts' are, they are going to boost the economic value of those entities. Will they share in their upside? Not likely!"[16]

We increasingly arrive at this question: what is a *just* hybrid? I don't think we know the answer to that question completely. I do think we have some clues. Neither historical nor digital sharecropping is a just hybrid. So how, then, can we express this respect? One way to express this respect is to practice it. Companies can practice it, and you can practice it by doing as Radiohead, Nine Inch Nails, Girl Talk, Beastie Boys, David Byrne, Spoon, Fort Minor, Danger Mouse, Gilberto Gil, Thievery Corporation, Matmos, Cee-Lo, Le Tigre, and My Morning Jacket have done, making your works available in ways that expressly permit people to share and build upon your works. Many companies are already doing this, companies like Flickr, Blip TV, Picasa, Fotonaut, Yahoo, and, I promise, before the end of next year, Wikipedia.[17] All of these entities build encouragement on top of Creative Commons licenses—licenses which we launched in 2003 and which over the past six years have exploded in numbers so that there are probably more than 150 million digital objects out there that are licensed under Creative Commons licenses. This is a way to say to creators, "We respect the creativity you have produced. We give you a freedom to express that respect to others." And it's an opportunity for us to say "happy birthday" to Creative Commons because it turns six today. And you can say "happy birthday" by giving money at https://support.creativecommons.org/. But of course you can't sing "Happy Birthday," because it is still under copyright, and we haven't cleared those rights. That's what we need to do, and your support is really critical.

I want to end with just one more story. I was asked to go the Association of the Bar of the City of New York and speak in a beautiful room with red velvet curtains and red carpet. The event had many different aspects. The room was packed with artists and creators and at least some lawyers. All of these people were there because they were eager to learn how they could create using digital technologies, while respecting the law of fair use. The people who organized this conference had a lawyer speak on each of the four factors in fair use for fifteen minutes, with the thought that, by the end of the hour, we'd have an audience filled with people who understood the law of fair use. As I sat there and watched in the audience, I was led to a certain kind of daydreaming. I was trying to remember what this room reminded me of. And then I recalled when I was a kid in my early twenties, I spent a lot of time traveling the Soviet system, seeing great halls where the annual conventions took place. I recognized that the room had reminded me of the Soviet system's extraordinary tribunals. I began to wonder, when was it in the history of the Soviet system that the system had failed, and what could you have said to convince people of that? 1976 was way too early: it was still puttering along at that point. And 1989 was too late: if you didn't get it by then, you weren't going to get it. So when was it? Between 1976 and 1988, if you could have convinced members of the Politburo that the system had failed, what could you have said to them to convince them? For them to know that this romantic ideal that they grew up with had crashed and burned and yet to continue with the Soviet system was to reveal a certain kind of insanity. Because, as I sat in that room and listened to lawyers insisting, "Nothing has changed. The same rules apply. It's the pirates who are the deviants," I increasingly recognize that it is we who are insane, that the existing system of copyright simply could never work in the digital age. Either we will force our kids to stop creating, or they will force on us a revolution around copyright law. In my view, both options are not acceptable.

Copyright extremists need to recognize that there is a growing movement of abolitionism out there. Kids were convinced that copyright was for another century and that in the twenty-first century it is just not needed. Now, I am not an abolitionist. I believe copyright is an essential part of a creative economy. It makes a creative economy rich in both the monetary and cultural sense. In this sense, I'm more like Gorbachev in this debate than Yeltsin. I'm just an old Communist trying to preserve copyright against these extremisms—extremisms that will, in my view, destroy copyright as an important part of creative culture and industries.

Now, you may not be concerned about the survival of copyright. You may say, "Whatever. If it disappears, my machines will still run." If that's not enough to get you into this battle, let me try one last effort. What you know is that there is no way for us to kill this form of creativity. We can only criminalize it. We can't stop our kids from creating in these new ways; we can only drive that creativity underground. We can't make our kids passive the way I, at least, was. We can only make them "pirates." The question is, is that any good? Our kids live in an age of prohibition. All sorts of aspects of their life are against the law. They live their life against the law. That way of living is extraordinarily corrosive. It is extraordinarily corrupting of the rule of law and ultimately corrupting to the premise of a democracy. If you do nothing else, after you've supported Creative Commons, you need to support this movement to stop this war now.

NOTES

This chapter was transcribed and edited by Michael Mandiberg from a talk given at the Computer History Museum in Mountain View, California, December 16, 2008. Lessig gave versions of this stump-style speech to share his ideas on free culture and promote Creative Commons. He kept the basic structure of a series of stories, observations, and a call to arms but updated the examples in the later part to reflect the rapid changes in digital culture. I have tried to preserve Lessig's powerful didactic, spoken presentation style, while streamlining the transcript to be effective in print form. The video of this talk is available at http://lessig.blip.tv/file/1591892/ (accessed May 31, 2009). This chapter is licensed CC BY.

    1.   United States Congress, House Committee on Patents, *Arguments before the Committee on Patents of the House of Representatives, Conjointly with the Senate Committee on Patents, on H.R. 19853, to Amend and Consolidate the Acts Respecting Copyright: June 6, 7, 8, and 9, 1906* (Washington, DC: Government Printing Office, 1906), http://books.google.com/books?id=zmEoAAAAMAAJ&printsec=titlepage#PPA24,M1 (accessed May 31, 2009).

    2.   Olmstead v. United States, 277 U.S. 438 (1928).

    3.   Amy Harmon, "Black Hawk Download: Pirated Videos Thrive Online," *New York Times*, January 17, 2002, http://www.nytimes.com/2002/01/17/technology/circuits/17VIDE.html (accessed May 31, 2009).

    4.   Paul Goldstein, *Copyright's Highway: From Gutenberg to the Celestial Jukebox* (Stanford: Stanford University Press, 2003).

    5.   Patricia Aufderheide and Peter Jaszi, "Untold Stories: Collaborative Research on Documentary Filmmakers' Free Speech and Fair Use," *Cinema Journal* 46, no. 2 (2007): 133–139, http://www.acsil.org/resources/rights-clearances-1/nps240.tmp.pdf (accessed July 20, 2010).

    6.   Soulja Boy, "How to Crank That—instructional video!," YouTube, originally posted April 2007, reposted August 2, 2007, http://www.youtube.com/watch?v=sLGLum5SyKQ (accessed May 31, 2009). At this point, Soulja Boy is still a self-produced amateur, without a label. Interscope signed him and made an official music video for the song: Soulja Boy, "Crank That," YouTube, August 9, 2007, http://www.youtube.com/watch?v=8UFIYGkROII

(accessed July 20, 2010). The premise of the official video is to reenact the discovery of Soulja Boy on YouTube: the hip-hop producer Mr. Collipark, who signed him to Interscope, is trying to understand the Soulja Boy phenomenon, after watching his children dance and surfing YouTube and seeing all of the videos that build on each other. He instant messages with Soulja Boy, eventually signing him to a record deal.

7. Ironically, after Interscope signed the artist, some of these fan videos have been subject to DMCA takedowns: see Kevin Driscoll, "Soulja Boy, Why Take My Crank Dat Video Down?," response video posted on YouTube, May 31, 2009, http://www.youtube.com/watch?v=wkeaxXLIjhs.

8. A tiny sampling of the Soulja Boy meme includes BEA5TED, "Soulja Boy—Crank Dat Pinocchio," YouTube, January 5, 2008, http://www.youtube.com/watch?v=aUM6NLeWQDc (accessed July 20, 2010); djtj1216, "Dora the Explorer (Crank Dat Soulja Boy)," YouTube, July 13, 2007, http://www.youtube.com/watch?v=vgMgLjMghuk (accessed July 20, 2010); Eric Schwartz, aka Smooth-E, "Crank That Kosha Boy," YouTube, December 5, 2007, http://www.youtube.com/watch?v=90YDBtCN-hk (accessed July 20, 2010); Barelypolitical, "Obama Girl . . . Does Soulja Boy . . . with Mike Gravel," YouTube, May 9, 2008, http://www.youtube.com/watch?v=RkZwF96IOyA (accessed July 20, 2010); Jordan Ross, "Crank That Soldier Boy," YouTube, July 21, 2007, http://www.youtube.com/watch?v=7ZE2OzguWHo (accessed July 20, 2010).

9. 236.com, "Synchronized Presidential Debating," YouTube, October 28, 2008, http://www.youtube.com/watch?v=wfd5g8Y_Jqo (accessed May 31, 2009).

10. will.i.am et al., "Yes We Can," YouTube, February 2, 2008, http://www.youtube.com/watch?v=jjXyqcx-mYY (accessed May 31, 2009).

11. For example, think about how differently this video treats editing and remix than the famous "We Are the World" video of the previous generation.

12. Johan Soderberg, "Read My Lips: Eternal Love," 2001–2004, http://www.soderberg.tv (accessed July 20, 2010).

13. *Editor's Note*: Not only is this labor unpaid, but it is done by customers who pay for the privilege to do this unpaid work; customers are charged a fee for monthly virtual land use, which we might call rent.

14. For more on the Electronic Frontier Foundation's alternate schema, see http://www.eff.org/wp/better-way-forward-voluntary-collective-licensing-music-file-sharing (accessed May 31, 2009).

15. See http://www.starwars.com/welcome/about/mashup-copyright (accessed May 31, 2009).

16. Om Malik, "Web 2.0, Community & the Commerce Conundrum," GigaOM.com, October 18, 2005, http://gigaom.com/2005/10/18/web-20-the-community-the-commerce-conundrum/ (accessed May 31, 2009).

17. In May 2009, the Wikipedia Community voted to switch from the GFDL license to a Creative Commons license: http://meta.wikimedia.org/wiki/Licensing_update/Result (accessed May 31, 2009).

Your Intermediary Is Your Destiny

FRED VON LOHMANN

Of Bouncers and Doormen

Although digital technologies are famous for "disintermediating" creators and audiences, the vast majority of video creators still depend on intermediaries to reach their audiences. Whether creators are making a film for theatrical distribution, a documentary for public broadcasters, or a humorous short for YouTube, they will be dependent on one or more commercial entities to carry their video to its intended audience. Consequently, it can be valuable for creative artists in the video arena to understand how the intermediaries on whom they intend to depend see the world.

Copyright is one critical issue that constrains intermediaries that carry video content. As any video creator who has struggled with "clearances" can attest, copyright is an omnipresent issue for video, arising whenever music is used in a production, a clip is taken from an existing film or television program, or a TV show appears in the background of a shot. The reality is that virtually all modern video creativity involves the use of some preexisting copyrighted work.

Because copyright is so often an issue of concern to intermediaries, it behooves video creators to understand how their intended intermediaries view copyright. In particular, it can be useful to understand that, thanks to the vagaries of copyright law, very different rules apply to traditional offline and newer online video distributors.

Traditional offline intermediaries, like television networks, theatrical distributors, and DVD distributors, often face very strict copyright rules, as is described in more detail later in this chapter. As a result, they have developed what has been called a "clearance culture"—the expectation that express permission will have been obtained for every copyrighted work that appears in a video.[1] This focus on clearances often goes hand in hand with an insistence on "errors and omissions" (often referred to as "E and O") insurance to cover them if any mistakes in clearances leads to a copyright-infringement lawsuit. In other words, the legal staffs of traditional offline intermediaries are like doormen, minding the velvet rope—they have to be satisfied before your video will be put on the air, in theaters, or sold on DVD.

Internet intermediaries like YouTube, in contrast, face a different set of copyright rules, rules that make them far more willing to adopt an "upload first, ask questions later" approach to video creators. This does not mean "anything goes"—if a copyright owner complains about an unauthorized use of material, the intermediary may have to take steps to remove the allegedly infringing content. And, of course, the video creator can be sued directly for copyright infringement. But, as a general matter, the legal departments of online video-hosting platforms are more like bouncers than doormen—they do not have to be consulted before the video is uploaded but, rather, get involved only if someone complains.

This nevertheless is a critical distinction: in the online context, video creators who have educated themselves on principles of copyright and believe that they are on the right side of the law (or willing to take the risk of being on the wrong side) are able to reach an audience of millions. This "lawyer-free" level of access to a mass-media platform has not previously been available in the offline world.

This represents a huge opportunity for video creators and a boon for audiences. For most of the modern media age, creators and audiences have only been entitled to see the material that risk-averse lawyers have been willing to put on the air. Thanks to the Internet and its different copyright rules for intermediaries, for the first time, we are all getting the opportunity to see the full scope of creativity in video. And, as a result of the different level of access for creators, the resulting creativity online often looks different from the material shown on prime-time TV or in theaters.

Traditional Media Intermediaries: Doormen Minding the Velvet Rope

Why are traditional media distributors, whether TV networks or theatrical and DVD distributors, so obsessed with "clearing" all the rights to every little thing before they will broadcast or distribute it?

The reason so many network lawyers seem so flint-hearted about copyright clearances arises directly from the copyright law rules they live under. Copyright law gives to copyright owners a number of exclusive rights, including the right to make reproductions, public performances, public displays, distributions, and derivative works.[2] Copyright law is what lawyers call a "strict liability" offense—people can be held liable even if they did not intend or know that they were infringing a copyright. So, for example, if the song that plays over the end credits of a film turns out not to have been cleared with the copyright owner, every theater that shows the film can be liable for copyright infringement (for publicly performing the song as part of the film), even if the theaters' owners had no idea that the song was not properly cleared. This strongly influences how an intermediary views copyright: if any copyright was infringed in a production, the intermediaries can be held legally responsible, even if they had no reason to suspect and even if they were (erroneously) assured that all the rights were cleared.

The penalties for copyright infringement are also potentially severe. If copyright owners have registered their works, they are generally entitled to a "statutory damages" award of between $750 and $30,000 for each work infringed, even if the infringement actually caused no harm at all.[3] In the preceding example, perhaps the owner of the copyright in the song that played over the end credits would have licensed the song for $500. Or perhaps the use of the song actually helped sell more copies of the song. The copyright owner would nevertheless be entitled to statutory damages from every theater that showed the film.

And it can get even worse. Unlike most other areas of commercial law, in copyright cases, copyright owners can often "pierce the corporate veil." That means that the copyright owner can not only sue the theater but can also go after the personal assets (e.g., houses and personal bank accounts) of the theater executives. Moreover, copyright lawsuits are expensive, irrespective of the outcome, and can result in legal fees reaching into the hundreds of thousands of dollars.

One of the reasons for these draconian rules is to put intermediaries in the hot seat and thereby to help copyright owners stop copyright infringement. But these same features in copyright law also have a chilling effect on intermediaries, leaving them unwilling to accept any risk at all, even for activities that do not infringe copyright. This leaves video creators facing a "clearance culture": intermediaries who insist on documented clearances for every scrap of copyrighted material that appears in any film or video that lands at their door and an insurance policy to stand behind any promises made by a shallow-pocketed production company. After all, if anything goes wrong, the copyright owner will probably sue the intermediary, as the entity with the deeper pockets to pay any judgments and attorneys' fees.

Internet Intermediaries: Bouncers at the Bar

Online intermediaries live by a very different set of copyright rules, by necessity. If the same sorts of rules described in the preceding section applied to the online intermediaries that provide digital storage and telecommunications services for every bit of data on the Internet, there simply would be no Internet.[4] No company could hope to vet every e-mail message, website, file transfer, and instant message for copyright infringement. The same is true for online video-hosting sites. If every video on YouTube had to first be vetted by a lawyer and insured by an errors-and-omissions policy, the videos on YouTube would be measured in the thousands, not the tens of millions.

Fortunately, as part of the Digital Millennium Copyright Act (DMCA) of 1998, Congress enacted a copyright "safe harbor" for many kinds of online intermediaries.[5] Thanks to these safe-harbor provisions, online video-hosting providers (like YouTube) can store and transmit video on behalf of their users without suffering the kind of "strict liability" that offline video distributors face. In order to qualify for the safe harbor, however, these online intermediaries have to establish a "notice-and-takedown" system—in other words, they have to establish a procedure whereby a copyright owner can notify them when an infringing video appears on the site.[6] After being notified, the online service provider must promptly disable access to the video.

The same law also provides that users whose videos have been removed may file a "counter-notice" if they believe that the "takedown" notice was incorrectly sent.[7] Once a counter-notice is sent, the copyright owner has approximately two weeks to sue, or else the video can be restored by the intermediary without fear of further copyright liability. Online service providers like YouTube also must establish a policy of terminating the accounts of "repeat infringers." For example, if a YouTube user receives multiple "takedown" notices for videos posted in her account, her account may be suspended or canceled.[8]

These two mechanisms—the "notice-and-takedown" system and "repeat infringer" policies—give copyright owners considerable power to police their content online. Many entertainment companies know how to use this power—Viacom, for example, once sent more than one hundred thousand takedown notices to YouTube on a single day.[9] Sometimes the power to remove content has been abused as a mechanism for censorship.[10]

But this "safe harbor" approach is nevertheless very different from the one that faces traditional offline video distributors. Thanks to the "safe harbors," intermediaries no longer have to rely on lawyers to be the "doormen," demanding clearances and insurance before accepting a video for distribution. Instead, where online intermediaries like YouTube are concerned, they can let their lawyers act as "bouncers"—let users post the videos first and only remove those that attract complaints under the "notice-and-takedown" system. So long as they abide by the requirements of the DMCA's safe harbors, online intermediaries will be sheltered from monetary liability arising from the infringing videos uploaded by users.

New Opportunities to Find an Audience

Where video creators are concerned, the different copyright rules for online intermediaries have opened up an incredible new set of opportunities to find an audience. Consider many of the new forms of "mashup" creativity that have flowered online. The "Vote Different" video, for example, recut and repurposed Apple's iconic "1984" television commercial as a campaign commercial critical of then-senator Hilary Clinton.[11] The video has been viewed more than six million times on YouTube. Given the unlikelihood that clearance could have been obtained from Apple for this use of its commercial, it is unlikely that any television station would have accepted the ad for broadcast, even if the creator could have found the money to buy air time. Similarly, entire genres of "remix" creativity have flourished on YouTube, genres that would have been barred from DVD, TV, and theatrical release due to rights-clearance complexities.

Another example is "The Hunt for Gollum," an entirely original fan-created "prequel" to Peter Jackson's film version of *The Lord of the Rings*.[12] A two-year effort that involved more than 150 people, this forty-minute short film was done without obtaining clearances from either the Tolkien estate or New Line Cinema. As a result, it would have been almost impossible to distribute the resulting short film through traditional offline channels. Nevertheless, thanks to the very different set of copyright rules that apply to online intermediaries, the fan-creators of "The Hunt for Gollum" were able to find a home on the Internet for their film. In the end, the copyright owners chose not to complain about the film, creating an object lesson in the benefits of asking forgiveness after the fact, rather than permission beforehand. To date, the film has been viewed more than three million times. The film has even been accepted for screening at a number of film festivals, presumably because the lawyers were reassured by the lack of legal action by the copyright owners of *The Lord of the Rings*.

This is not to say that copyright can be ignored online. Just because an *intermediary* may be protected by the DMCA's "safe harbors" does not mean that the creator of a video is immune from copyright-infringement liability. It just means that the *creator* is not putting the intermediary in the position of having to put its own assets on the line for every video it hosts. In other words, if video creators are willing to stand behind their videos, they can now find an audience without first having to satisfy a scrum of lawyers and insurance adjusters. But as the creators, they are still answerable for the use any copyrighted material that appears in their productions.

There are two principal ways to deal with uncleared copyrighted materials that might appear in a video production. The first is to consider whether the use might be excused under an exception or limitation to copyright. Although copyright law contains a number of exceptions and limitations, the one that is most often relevant when recognizable copyrighted materials are at issue is "fair use." The fair-use doctrine allows a court to evaluate an otherwise unauthorized use against four nonexclusive factors:

1. The nature and character of the use (transformative uses and noncommercial uses are favored)
2. The nature and character of the work used (news reports and other factual works are given less protection than are more creative works)
3. The amount and substantiality of the portion used
4. The effect of the use on the market for the work used

Although there is an increasing number of free resources available online to help explain how fair use applies to different video creators, it remains a complicated subject, and you should consult a qualified copyright lawyer for advice before jumping to conclusions about whether your use might be a fair use.[13]

A second way to deal with uncleared materials is to find out who the copyright owner in question might be and how that copyright owner has dealt with productions similar to yours in the past. Some copyright owners will have no objection to certain kinds of uses of their content, particularly noncommercial uses. For example, several major video-game companies have published "licenses" or guidelines for "machinima"—the emerging genre of films created inside video games.[14] Similarly, Warner Brothers and J. K. Rowling have been supportive of many kinds of noncommercial fan-created works building on the Harry Potter franchise.[15] And, as described earlier, "The Hunt for Gollum" has not been targeted for legal action by New Line Cinema or the Tolkien estate. Often fan communities will have an understanding of what kinds of activities a copyright owner will find "unobjection-able," even if they will not go so far as granting a written clearance.

The "notice-and-takedown" procedure also provides copyright owners a mechanism to express their objection to a video without resorting immediately to litigation in court. This can give creators a bit of a buffer in which to experiment. A copyright owner does not have to send a takedown notice before suing in court, but often a takedown notice sent to an online intermediary is a faster, cheaper way for copyright owners to achieve their goals. This is particularly true when the putative infringer has shallow pockets and is unlikely to be able to cough up an amount of money that would make a court fight economically sensible. As a result, posting a video and waiting to see whether it attracts a takedown notice from the copyright owner can be an inexpensive way to test a copyright owner's preferences.

Conclusion

The nice thing about the "clearance culture" that dominates offline media is its simplicity: if a video creator lacks clearances for everything, he or she is not going to get distribution for the video. The new opportunities in online distribution are exciting but more complicated, requiring that a video creator learn the basics of copyright law, fair use, and enforcement habits of particular copyright owners. Careful creators will want to consult with a qualified lawyer, as well as carefully researching whether the copyright owners in question are likely to object and, if so, how strenuously. While all of this can be time-consuming, it can also let video creators reach global audiences in ways that were never before possible.

NOTES

This work is licensed under the Creative Commons Attribution-ShareAlike license.

1. *See* Patricia Aufderheide & Peter Jaszi, *Untold Stories: Creative Consequences of the Rights Clearance Culture for Documentary Filmmakers* (Center for Social Media 2004), available at http://www.centerforsocialmedia.org/sites/default/files/UNTOLDSTORIES_Report.pdf (accessed July 17, 2010)

2. The U.S. Copyright Act is contained in Title 17 of the U.S. Code, available at http://www.copyright.gov/title17/ (accessed July 17, 2010). The exclusive rights are set forth in 17 U.S.C. § 106.

3. See 17 U.S.C. § 504(c).

4. *See generally* Center for Democracy and Technology, *Intermediary Liability: Protecting Internet Platforms for Expression and Innovation* (2010), available at http://www.cdt.org/paper/intermediary-liability-protecting-internet-platforms-expression-and-innovation (accessed July 17, 2010).

5. *See* 17 U.S.C. § 512.

6. *See* 17 U.S.C. § 512(c)(3); *see generally* Citizen Media Law Project, *Copyright Claims Based on User Content* (last modified Oct. 29, 2009), available at http://www.citmedialaw. org/legal-guide/copyright-claims-based-user-content (accessed July 17, 2010).

7. *See* 17 U.S.C. § 512(g); *see generally* Citizen Media Law Project, *Responding to a DMCA Takedown Notice Targeting Your Content* (last modified May 8, 2008), available at http://www.citmedialaw.org/legal-guide/responding-dmca-takedown-notice-targeting-your-content (accessed July 17, 2010).

8. *See* YouTube, *What Will Happen If You Upload Infringing Content* (last modified Oct. 9, 2010), available at http://www.google.com/support/youtube/bin/answer. py?hl=en&answer=143456 (accessed July 17, 2010).

9. *See* Candace Lombardi, *Viacom to YouTube: Take Down Pirated Clips*, CNET News, Feb. 2, 2007, available at http://news.cnet.com/Viacom-to-YouTube-Take-down-pirated-clips/2100-1026_3-6155771.html (accessed July 17, 2010).

10. *See* Wendy Seltzer, *Free Speech Unmoored in Copyright's Safe Harbor: Chilling Effects of the DMCA on the First Amendment*, 24 Harv. J.L. & Tech. 171 (2010), available at http:// papers.ssrn.com/sol3/papers.cfm?abstract_id=1577785 (accessed July 17, 2010).

11. Available at http://www.youtube.com/watch?v=6h3G-lMZxjo (accessed July 17, 2010).

12. Available at http://www.thehuntforgollum.com/ (accessed July 17, 2010).

13. The American University's Center for Social Media maintains an excellent collection of documents that describe "best practices" for fair use for a variety of different genres of video creators. *See* http://www.centerforsocialmedia.org/resources/fair_use/ (accessed July 17, 2010).

14. *See, e.g.*, Microsoft, *Game Content Usage Rules*, available at http://www.xbox.com/ en-US/community/developer/rules.htm (accessed July 17, 2010); World of Warcraft, *Letter to the Machinimators of the World*, available at http://web.archive.org/web/20101107211345/ http://www.worldofwarcraft.com/community/machinima/letter.html (accessed July 1, 2011).

15. *See* Comments of Jeremy Williams, Warner Brothers Senior Vice President, in the Intellectual Property Colloquium, *Derivative Work*, available at http://ipcolloquium.com/ mobile/2009/09/derivative-work/ (accessed July 17, 2010).

13

On the Fungibility and Necessity of Cultural Freedom

FRED BENENSON

For these Utopians, free culture is a glimpse of ideal world
where knowledge can be used, studied, modified, built upon,
distributed, and shared without restriction.
                              —Benjamin Mako Hill, "Wikimedia and
                                  the Free Culture Movement," 2007[1]

I've been involved in the copyright-reform and free-culture space
for almost a decade. I've protested record companies, organized free-culture
art shows, and released thousands of my own photos under various Creative
Commons licenses. Throughout my time as a free-culture creator and activist, I was consistently confronted with a difficult question to answer: how
free, exactly, should I make my work? Moreover, how free should I encourage others to make their work? Many other people have been thinking
hard about this question, and while some have offered definitions, I remain
unconvinced that there is one prescriptive solution for the future of cultural
production, online or off. I'm most interested in attempting to answer these
questions in light of what could be considered party lines in the free-culture
space. On one side there are the free-software advocates whose deep dedication to the principles established by Richard Stallman and the Free Software
Foundation in the late 1980s continues to nurture an unprecedented ecosystem of free and open-source software. On the other side is a newer generation of creators who casually share and remix their creations using Creative
Commons licenses. This essay is not meant to pit these two perspectives
against each other (in fact, relations between the two organizations are and
have always been excellent) but, rather, to offer an explanation of why they
appear to be so oppositional. I hope to demonstrate that there's a core confusion occurring when we attempt to reconcile answers to these questions.
Ultimately I believe this confusion can be mitigated if we acknowledge the
fundamental differences between cultural and utilitarian works.

To begin with, let's take a look at an example of where these two perspectives collided. On December 8, 2007, Michael David Crawford sent an e-mail to the Creative Commons Community list asking for advice on how to decide on a license for his "magnum opus."[2] Crawford was deliberating between the Attribution-NoDerivatives license and the Attribution-Non-Commercial-NoDerivatives license. As public licenses go, the Creative Commons community considers these two choices as being the most restrictive. In the first instance, Crawford would have allowed only whole duplication of his work without modification; in the second, he would have allowed only whole duplication of his work so long as it was noncommercial. The only freedoms Crawford was interested in granting his audience would be those of sharing and, possibly, commercial use.

The cc-community list that Crawford posted to is a large e-mail list with a membership consisting of dozens of creators, lawyers, authors, programmers, and cultural advocates who are interested in discussing Creative Commons and their licenses. Creators interested in releasing their work under CC often pose questions to the list in order to facilitate their decision-making process.

Crawford had titled his self-designated "magnum opus" "Living with Schizoaffective Disorder." His e-mail linked to the work inside a subdirectory named "Madness/" on his personal web server, where it was rendered with simple HTML formatting.[3] Crawford's intention was eventually to release the work as a fifty-page PDF. In Crawford's initial e-mail to the Creative Commons list, he emphasized that since "the piece is a very personal story, and expresses some very deeply-held personal opinions," he was not interested in allowing others to remix it.

Crawford went on to summarize his illness and his motivations for writing "Living": "I have a lot of reason to believe that writing Living . . . was the best thing I have done in my entire life, and may well in the end be the best thing I will have ever done."[4]

He was interested in having others benefit and share his work and was looking toward Creative Commons as the legal structure that would enable him to do so. Crawford clearly wanted his work to be shared so that it could benefit others like him. But he was wary of allowing the work to be commercially exploited as well. He stated that he feared traditional book publishers might release his work as "a best-seller" and not give him "a cut of the profits."[5] Crawford concluded his message by noting that he regularly receives many encouraging missives from others with similar diagnoses and believes there to be a strong demand for a work exploring his disease from a personal perspective.

Our culture depends on original work being shared, reused, and remixed. Without public licensing schemes that standardize these terms and mores, copyright law necessarily silos every new creative work. By merely fixing a minimally original work in a medium (for example, typing a manuscript and saving it) authors are automatically availed of the full strength of "All Rights Reserved" copyright until seventy years after their death. Moreover, anyone who infringes on the copyright of another can be held liable for fines up to $150,000 per infringement.[6]

There are countless stories of naive Internet remixers and sharers accidentally stumbling into a thicket of copyright litigation. And while the Digital Millennium Copyright Act's Section 512 has mitigated this risk on behalf of service providers like YouTube, individual creators still face an uncertain landscape when noncommercially sharing and remixing others' work online.[7] But this essay is not about those stories or those lawsuits. This essay is about the efforts aimed at maneuvering new modes of cultural production out of those waters. Creative Commons licenses represent one of the most substantial efforts in that respect.

At the end of Crawford's message he solicits arguments for or against his potential license choices. Crawford's criteria for licensing the work may seem intuitive and uncontroversial to the lay reader, but only seven hours after posting, a response from a list member named Drew Roberts encouraged him, unsuccessfully, to abandon consideration of both the NoDerivatives stipulation and the NonCommercial stipulation.[8] Roberts encouraged Crawford to pick either one of the two most "liberal" CC licenses—either Attribution or Attribution-ShareAlike. If Crawford were to have chosen the CC Attribution (abbreviated as CC BY), then his work would be closest to the uncontrollable public domain, and the only requirement for reusing it, or portions of it, would be to credit Crawford as the original author and note that the original work was under a Creative Commons license. Doing this would explicitly invite modified and derivative versions of Crawford's work.

Similarly, if Crawford chose Roberts's other suggestion, the Creative Commons copyleft license, Attribution-ShareAlike (abbreviated CC BY-SA), then others could use "Living" so long as they redistributed modified versions of the work under the same license. Some people identify the act of securing the freedom of downstream copies or derivatives under the same terms as the original as "copyleft" or "viral licensing." Roberts went on to detail ways in which Crawford could leverage his copyleft in order to prevent his work from being commercially exploited in the ways he feared. After one response from another list member commending Crawford on his courage to release his deeply personal work in order to help others, but not weighing in on the licensing question, activity on the thread petered out. To this date, Crawford has made no indication as to how he intends on licensing "Living," and the page where the essay resides still indicates that the work is under an "All Rights Reserved" copyright.

The exchange between Drew Roberts and Michael Crawford on the cc-community list represented an ongoing rift in the Creative Commons and free-culture community between those who believe in "free licenses" to the exclusion of "nonfree licenses" (those including NonCommercial and NoDerivatives terms) and those who believe that these options allow for greater flexibility in cultural productions.

This conflict represents a larger schism dogging user-generated content: what are the ethical and just ways that users should share work? Is there a "right" way to release or license a work? Are non-commercially-licensed works necessarily unethical?

A very vocal minority of those using Creative Commons licenses and engaged in the community believe that Creative Commons should offer only the Attribution and Attribution-ShareAlike options for its licenses. All culture, they believe, should be able to be peer produced and should be licensed, released, and distributed in ways that facilitate derivatives and sharing. For the purpose of this essay, I'll call this the fundamentalist perspective of user-generated utopianism. My interest is in exploring the viability of user-generated utopianism and answering the question of whether *all* culture should be available to be remixed and reused unconditionally. Should we license it as such? Specifically, what are the ethical and practical considerations we should take into account when trying to convince creators like Michael Crawford to allow their work to be peer produced?

To understand user-generated utopianism, it is first important to understand that Creative Commons is a single legal project created to facilitate sharing of cultural artifacts, and it is not the first. Richard Stallman's Free Software Foundation created the General Public License (GPL) in 1989 in order to codify Stallman's belief that there should be four basic freedoms of software.[9] Linus Torvalds chose the Free Software Foundation's GPL for his fledgling software kernel, called Linux, in order to encourage others to help him work on it.[10] If Torvalds had not licensed his work under the GPL, or any other free license, he would have risked the potential of a future copyright lawsuit by anyone developing the code with him. Without the GPL, a rogue developer could have claimed exclusive rights over his or her additions to the kernel, and the integrity of the project would have been jeopardized. The

GPL also enabled Torvalds to make an implicit guarantee to his codevelopers because it legally prevented him from co-opting their work and restricting the kernel's distribution. The GPL ensures that Torvalds's kernel remains open and available for anyone to build on its code and release his or her own versions of it, so long as his or her code is distributed alongside as well.

The GPL was a precondition for the success of the Linux ecology in that it provided a legal and social tool that could enforce a community of practice within a specific field of developers and hobbyists. First launched in 2002, the Creative Commons license suite attempted to provide a similar set of legal tools and licenses for cultural producers. Whereas the GPL shouldn't be used for nonsoftware media, the CC licenses were not intended for software distribution.

For the most part, those who call for a definition of free culture, or for Creative Commons to rescind its NonCommercial and NoDerivatives licenses, are current or past members of the free-software community. The majority are software programmers who acutely understand the benefits of the GPL for peer-produced free software and who are keen to port the model to other cultural productions. The only licenses that persevered over the years were those that preserved the freedoms established by the FSF, with the GPL being the most notable and popular example, but noncopyleft licenses like Berkeley Software Distribution (BSD) are also included. These free-software advocates criticize Creative Commons for not articulating a specific social movement like Stallman did for free software (i.e., the free-software definition) and worry that CC will jeopardize the future of free culture by offering licenses that enable creators to release work gratis but not freely. So is a utopia like they envision possible? What would happen if all work necessarily allowed peer production like all free software does? To answer this question, it is useful to consider the concept of a fungible object.

A fungible object has individual units that are capable of mutual substitution. A hammer is an example of a physical object that is explicitly fungible. If one hammer is more or less the same as another hammer, the two are substitutable and therefore fungible (especially if the same company manufactures both hammers). Functional software applications are also largely fungible; this is especially true of lower-level applications such as drivers or operating-system tools such as compilers. The general fungibility of software reflects how software objects are largely defined by their utility. The first set of applications Richard Stallman wrote for the GNU project were, by definition, fungible because they replaced the proprietary UNIX versions of the C compilers and shell utilities that MIT's media lab had become dependent on.

Consequently, we can exchange software applications for one another (e.g., one application that is fungible for another), so long as their core functionality remains the same. Linux's growth can be attributed to its fungibility, because the kernels of operating systems are fungible. By 2006, dozens of different kernels (from Microsoft Windows to Apple OS X to Ubuntu GNU/Linux) had been developed for various hardware configurations, but all continue to serve essentially the same purpose.

If hammers, operating systems, and other tools are prime examples of fungible objects, art provides us with some interesting examples of nonfungible objects. A work of art's ostensible purpose is to cover a bare wall, and as such, an anonymous store-bought painting or photograph is effectively exchangeable for another. This easy replaceability disappears when you consider famous works of art: the Louvre would certainly not accept any kind of replacement for the "Mona Lisa," despite the availability of any other works that might cover the wall in a similar way. We aren't interested in using these types of objects for any particular use. We want to enjoy them. We want to admire them for their perfection, their history, or their uniqueness but not for their utility. A work of art does not have to be useful in order to be successful.

It is essential, then, that we're not interested in using an artwork in the utilitarian sense in order to properly appreciate it. We don't hang pictures to obscure blemishes on the wall; we hang them to appreciate them for their own sake. Along with famous works of art, we should also understand that personal works are nonfungible. Michael Crawford's "Living with Schizoaffective Disorder" is a perfect example of a nonfungible work because, while it may be a useful guide for those who have this disorder, it is particular to Crawford and his views, so much so that he believes that it cannot be substituted or modified.

It stands to reason that Crawford chose to prohibit derivatives of his work because he believed it was a nonfungible work. Crawford did not want others to modify the work to a point where a derivative could be substituted for the original. The effort and meaning Crawford had poured into his writing would need to remain coupled to his identity as its author, because the work was *about* him, much like all artistic work is to some extent *about* its creator. "Living" was meant to stand on its own as a finished product representing its author and his life, so it would be wrong to think of it as being capable of being revisable by others. This starkly contrasts with Torvalds's intentions when he released his work, the Linux kernel, under the GPL. Whatever future versions might be derived from his initial version, he was only too happy to see the work modified and improved. Similarly, Torvalds's work, while superficially tied to his identity (the name "Linux" derives from his given name), wasn't so much about Torvalds as it was about a specific tool that needed to exist.

Wikipedia provides another example, as the peer-produced encyclopedia is, despite its depth and unique character, composed of fungible articles. There are many other encyclopedias that not only predate its existence but also continue to compete with it. Peer production on Wikipedia is made possible not only by its particularly liberal copyright license (which happens to be the Creative Commons Attribution-ShareAlike license) but also by the nature of its content. For example, an article on bitumen can be substituted by any other article on bitumen, so long as it properly describes the subject in an encyclopedic way. Direct knowledge is another fungible entity: a fact is a fact is a fact, and it is void of any nonfungible uniqueness. Both copyright and, to some extent, patent law acknowledge this reality, as they both have substantial precedent for preventing ownership of facts, obvious ideas, short phrases, or even databases.

User-generated utopianism challenges us to believe that all cultural objects are effectively fungible. This conclusion feels problematic mainly because it requires us to tell creators like Michael Crawford that they must release their work freely for others to build on and that they are essentially wrong and misguided in their intentions to protect their work in the ways they choose. Dictating to authors and creators what they can and can't do with their work is a remarkably unpopular challenge and is one reason why a licensing regime like Creative Commons has made its mission about the creator's choice, not adhesion to an ideological purity.

User-generated utopians will defend their position by pointing out that authors can produce "authorized" versions of their work, thereby attenuating the risk of others' misinterpreting the meaning and purpose of their work. The strategy that free-software advocates argue for is to distribute "authorized" versions of work so that they are omnipresent and free. The argument is that this authorized version defeats any commercial advantage of potential freeriders who might download the work and try to resell it. By making free-software projects ubiquitous and freely distributable, software developers have neutralized the potential commercial market for exploitation. In other words, it's impossible to pirate a work if it's already available on GitHub for download. But this approach has less appeal for cultural producers. If Pfizer were to use a freely licensed version of Crawford's personal essay in an advertising pamphlet for antidepressants, Crawford would probably have felt that the integrity of his work had been compromised, despite having offered the work for free and authorizing his own version of it. For some creators, like Crawford, neutralizing potential commercial competition is not enough of an incentive to release their work freely. They need to know that the integrity of their work will be preserved in some capacity in future generations. It's unclear whether free-software principles applied to cultural works have anything to offer in this regard.

So there's a strong moral case to be made that fungible works should always be free to be built on and remixed. They can be swapped out for better, more efficient versions. They can be modified, they can break, they can be fixed, and most importantly, they can be collaborated on. But can the same be said for artistic works? Must creators necessarily confront and accept all of these potentialities when releasing their work? We loosely use the term "successful" when speaking about creative works, but we don't mean it in the same way that a new kernel module is successful at fixing a longstanding hardware incompatibility. Kernel modules either work or they don't, but it is hard to make this argument for art, especially in light of a multipolar culture which is constantly reevaluating and interpreting itself.

The hard-line argument for the freedom of fungible works (i.e., tools) makes a lot of sense in this light, but it makes less sense when applied to cultural works. To argue that all cultural works are, or should be, fungible, we risk denigrating and confusing a work with the tools required to create it. This argument shouldn't be confused as one against remixing or pastiche. I hold the remix in the highest possible cultural esteem, and I truly believe that all culture is a conversation requiring generations of experimentation and revolution. And it's clear that copyright law needs to be reformed and that its terms must be reduced. Despite this, I remain unconvinced that all culture must necessarily be regarded as replaceable and modifiable, like all of our tools effectively are.

To put it another way, I do not see it as a valuable or interesting strategy to disintegrate the notion of authorship completely when encouraging creators to share their works. Copyright law may have created perverse incentives (for example, encouraging creators to invest in lawyers and lawsuits rather than in future creation) and may remain unenforceable in light of technological innovation, but it was created with the understanding that recognizing authors as unique creators helped them conceive and produce new work.

In the end, I'm most worried that if we succeed in convincing creators that their works are no different from their tools, we might end up disincentivizing them to create in the first place. So while it is unclear whether copyright law will ever be reformed in a meaningful manner, I hope I've presented some compelling reasons that demonstrate that there are still plenty of opportunities for authors and publishers to continue experimenting with the rights they offer to the public.

NOTES

This work is licensed under the Creative Commons Attribution-ShareAlike license.

1. Benjamin Mako Hill, "Wikipedia and the Free Culture Movement," *Why Give Blog* (last modified November 8, 2008), Wikimedia Foundation, http://meta.wikimedia.org/wiki/Fundraising_2007/Why_Give_blog/Wikipedia_and_the_Movement_for_Free_Culture (accessed July 20, 2010).

2. Michael D. Crawford, "[cc-community] Help me decide on a license," message to the Creative Commons Community list, December 8, 2007, http://lists.ibiblio.org/pipermail/cc-community/2007-December/002778.html (accessed July 20, 2010).

3. Michael D. Crawford, "Living with Schizoaffective Disorder," http://www.geometricvisions.com/schizoaffective-disorder/ (accessed June 29, 2011).

4. Ibid.

5. Ibid.

6. United States Copyright Office, "Highlights of Copyright Amendments in URAA," 2010, http://www.copyright.gov/circs/circ38b.pdf (accessed July 20, 2010).

7. 17 U.S.C. §§ 512, 1201–1205.

8. Drew Roberts, "Re: [cc-community] Help me decide on a license," message to the Creative Commons Community list, December 8, 2007, http://lists.ibiblio.org/pipermail/cc-community/2007-December/002781.html (accessed July 20, 2010).

9. The four essential freedoms according to the Free Software Foundation are (1) "the freedom to run the program, for any purpose," (2) "the freedom to study how the program works, and change it to make it do what you wish," (3) "the freedom to redistribute copies so you can help your neighbor," and (4) "the freedom to distribute copies of your modified versions to others." Free Software Foundation, "The Free Software Definition," 1996, http://www.gnu.org/philosophy/free-sw.html (accessed July 20, 2010).

10. Linus Torvalds, "Free minix-like kernel sources for 386-AT," message to the comp.os.minix Usenet group, October 5, 1991, http://groups.google.com/group/comp.os.minix/msg/2194d253268b0a1b (accessed July 20, 2010).

14

Giving Things Away Is Hard Work

Three Creative Commons Case Studies

MICHAEL MANDIBERG

Open-source software and the free-culture movement have created vibrant and thriving sharing-based online communities. These communities and individuals have created an enormous quantity of open-source and free-culture projects. Many examples of these are well-known and much heralded: Wikipedia, Linux, WordPress, and the like. These success stories primarily revolve around code- and/or text-focused projects and are much less common among other work whose medium is not code or text. While one could disagree from a semiotic or a materialist perspective, code and text are effectively immaterial in relationship to other forms of physical creation. A copy of the original is merely a keystroke's effort, and the basic tools to create or modify the original are so commonplace as to be universal: a keyboard and a mouse. Obviously one also needs fluency in the human or computer language of the project, but one does not need access to expensive or specialized materials or tools; nor does one need the physical skills of a craftsperson in the medium.

Unlike code- or text-based practices, art, design, and other creations that are manifest in nondigital forms require production outside of the keyboard-mouse-language toolset. While there may be a code- or text-based set of instructions, the final form of the project usually must be transformed into a physical object, either through a machine like a printer or laser cutter, a physical technology like a circuit board or paint, or an offline social process like agreements and collaborations with people or business entities that have the tools or knowledge to realize a project. It seems that this additional step often makes it more difficult to realize a physical project. Despite this difficulty, or maybe *because* of this challenge, there are examples of artists, designers, and engineers working in this model, myself included. After producing three years of art/design work with open licenses, I want to look back and consider the results.[1] The central question I seek to answer is if and how an art or design idea/project/product is helped, hindered, or not affected at all by its open licensing model. I have chosen three key examples from my creative practice and explore their successes and failures as a way of assessing this question.

A Genealogy

"Open source" is a term used to refer to computer software for which the source code can be viewed, modified, and used by anyone. As the story goes, once upon a time all software was open source. In 1980, MIT researcher Richard Stallman was using one of the first laser printers. It took so long to print documents that he decided he would modify the printer driver so that it sent a notice to the user when the print job was finished. Unlike previous printer drivers, this software only came in its compiled version. Stallman asked Xerox for the source code. Xerox would not let him have the source code. Stallman got upset and wrote a manifesto, and the Free Software movement began.[2] Later, Eric Raymond, a fellow computer programmer, published *The Cathedral and the Bazaar*, which popularized the term "open source."[3] The two terms are frequently referred to by the acronym I use in this essay: FLOSS, which stands for "free/libre/open-source software."[4]

More recently this concept has been extended from code to other forms of cultural production via Creative Commons licenses and what has become known as the free-culture movement.[5] The Creative Commons licenses provide a legal tool for applying FLOSS licensing to media other than computer code: text, image, sound, video, design, and so on. Many websites that are focused on fostering creative communities, like Flickr or Vimeo, incorporate this license into their content-upload process. Creative Commons estimates that there are 135 million Creative Commons–licensed works on Flickr alone.[6] While this has been a very successful initiative, most of these millions of works are digital. They are infinitely copyable, quickly transferable, and easily distributable. What I seek to answer is what happens when this license is applied to works that are not exclusively digital. What happens when the license is applied to cultural objects whose materiality prevents them from being effortlessly copyable.

Inside this larger free-culture community, there are groups of engineers, artists, and designers using open licenses for physical objects which are not as easily reproduced.[7] The genealogy of the move to license physical works with Creative Commons licenses that I trace here comes out of Limor Fried's work as an R&D fellow at the Eyebeam Center for Art and Technology's OpenLab. Located in New York City, Eyebeam is like a think tank, where artists, engineers, designers, and programmers work together on projects dedicated to public-domain research and development. In a sense, it is not so much a think tank as a *make* tank. I was a resident, fellow, and senior fellow at Eyebeam from 2006 to 2010, and my time at Eyebeam has strongly influenced my work and, thus, this essay.

One of the requirements for working in the Eyebeam OpenLab is that all work is published with an open license; this stipulation is written into the contract that all R&D fellows sign.[8] This is easy to comply with as a programmer, but Fried primarily worked in what is known as physical computing, which is the intersection between computer and electrical engineering, and experimental art and design. Fried and Jonah Peretti, the director of R&D at the time, spent some time trying to figure out the right way to comply with the contract. In the end, the decision was made to publish a full instruction set and to make available DIY kits with the circuit board and all components.

At Eyebeam, one of the central goals is to be copied. At my orientation in 2006, then senior fellows James Powderly and Evan Roth of the Graffiti Research Lab gave a presentation of their work, tracing their LED Throwies project from its original form, a simple LED with a magnet and a battery, through the modifications made by hackers and aficionados across the world (one had a timed blinker, another used a photosensor to turn on only at night to conserve battery, someone offered LED Throwies for sale).[9] They noted that the form of distribution that generated the most views of the project was not their blog or their video on YouTube but their instruction set at Instructables.com, a site that allows creators to give instructions on how to make things. The point of their presentation was that the life of a project as a social phenomenon is its most important form and is often the primary form to be evaluated for success. The sharing of the project creates participation. And participation is at the edge of the beginnings of community.[10] It is not quite community, but it is one of the preconditions for community.

One of the most important points about this example, and a point that Powderly and Roth emphasized, is that these were ideas they would not have come up with by themselves, or if they had come up with the idea, they would not have had the time to execute it. They had one idea, which they shared with the world. People thought the original idea was interesting, but these people had their own ideas to contribute. The end result is something that is much greater than the original idea and something that could not have been created without the contribution of others.

That is the optimistic side of the Eyebeam model, a model influenced by Peretti and R&D technical director Michael Frumin. The flip side is that success is also measured in pure numbers: YouTube, Vimeo, and Flickr views, incoming links ritualistically tracked via analytics software, Diggs, blog posts, and overall hits. This became known as "The Famo."[11] Powderly, Roth, and Jamie Wilkinson coined the phrase, and by the time I arrived at Eyebeam, there were plans to create a complete Famo-meter, which would pull all the statistics from every possible source of views, hits, referrals, and rankings and crown a king of Famo. They even created and taught a class at Parsons (The New School for Design) in which the final grade was entirely determined by Famo.[12]

Famo is relevant here because in order to be copied, a project has to be viewed many, many times. As codified in the 1% rule (or the 90-9-1 principle), a very small number of people are committed enough to take up a project and modify it.[13] If you have lots of eyes on a project, it is much more likely that someone will also put his or her hands on it. In the process of being copied, a change is made. No copy is a direct copy: every copy is a mutation in some form.[14] When the ultimate goal is to change culture, the intermediary goal is to get copied.

One Example

Limor Fried was one of the first people to laser-etch the top of a laptop and publicly share the results.[15] She and her partner and collaborator Phil Torrone figured out the process for etching laptops (specifically Apple's Powerbooks), and then she did something really crucial: she published the instructions on her website with an open license. As a result, she created an industry. There is now a growing number of commercial engravers who focus on using the laser cutter as an artistic tool to engrave laptops, cell phones, Moleskine notebooks, leather accessories, fingernails, and so on. For example, etchstar was built off Fried and Torrone's published materials;[16] the business was purchased for an undisclosed sum by the Microsoft-funded Wallop and is now known as Coveroo.[17]

When I was in Portland, Oregon, in 2008, I was introduced to Joe Mansfield, who runs an engraving business called Engrave Your Tech. I met him right as he was scaling up from individual projects to larger runs and big architectural projects. He had just broken the news to the rest of the Moleskine-notebook fan community that despite initial disavowals, the Chinese manufacturer of the notebooks includes PVC in the covers, and they therefore could not be lasercut.[18] It was clear when I met Mansfield that he was pretty well established in the scene. When I told him I was working out of

Eyebeam, he looked at me blankly. I said, "You know, Eyebeam, where Limor Fried, a.k.a. Lady Ada, came up with the idea to use the laser cutter to do what you make a living doing?" And he said that the name seemed familiar somehow. You could argue that this is a failure, because people using this technology do not know who created this use, but I would argue that this is a success: the practice has become so pervasive that the origins are no longer important.

Three Case Studies

I'm going to talk about three projects and try to evaluate their success in the terms I have laid out thus far. Notably, these three projects are design projects, not artworks; artworks would activate a different set of terms for success. I want to view all of these through the cycle of taking things and making them better I have laid out earlier in this chapter: participation breeds creative mutation, and creative mutation leads to better ideas through this collaborative process.

Steve Lambert and I made a laser-cut lampshade for compact fluorescent bulbs (CFLs) that we called the Bright Idea Shade. We identified a problem and tried to come up with a solution for it. The Eyebeam space is two dark converted industrial buildings; most recently one side was an S&M club, and the other was a taxi garage. When Eyebeam first moved in, it was only one floor with twenty-five-foot ceilings. When it was built out for office and work space, the architects lit the space with bare silver-tipped incandescent light bulbs in raw porcelain fixtures. This was very much in vogue during the 1995–2005 loft conversions in New York and San Francisco. It looks great in photographs and is an inexpensive solution, but it became a problem when we started to switch out our incandescent bulbs for CFLs. The bulbs were now *really* just bare bulbs. We needed a solution that made it possible to use CFLs without blinding ourselves.

After some initial tests, we settled on a polygon solution, based on an Instructable, which was based on a *ReadyMade* magazine project, which was based on the work of several designers from the '60s and '70s who each claim authorship of the original shape.[19] We consulted with an intellectual-property lawyer, who of course would not actually give us an answer as to any potential legal liability. But from our discussion with him and the transformative changes we made, we felt comfortable making the project public.

To recap an earlier point: in order to get hands on a project, you have to get a lot of eyes on it first. We followed the internal Eyebeam model identified by Peretti, Powderly, and Roth and created an interrelated video and Instructable.com instruction set.[20] This video showed how exciting the project was and then explicitly stated that the whole purpose of the video was to give the idea away. The video clearly said that we wanted someone to take the idea and manufacture it and encouraged people to make money off the idea in the process. Through our Attribution-ShareAlike license (CC BY-SA) and our text in the video, we made it clear that we expected no money. We just wanted someone to make it.

Steve Lambert and I are artists, designers, educators, and activists, but we are not business people. When we design things, we generally make prototypes and give them away. It's great for code, but maybe it's not so great for objects. Many, many people who saw this video wanted to buy a Bright Idea Shade. But it isn't for sale. It is free, but not as in beer. All the patterns and instructions are there, but you have to do it yourself. A manufacturer could do it and then sell the kits, but manufacturers aren't used to this idea of taking someone's ideas, prototypes, and intellectual property for free.

There are business questions and problems with fabricating and marketing a free-culture product. Despite the fact that this project generated several million impressions in video, image, and blog views, there was only one failed lead, and that was from Urban Outfitters. When I tell people that Urban Outfitters was our only lead, they often laugh, as Urban Outfitters' business model is perceived to be focused on copying artists and designers and selling the infringing derivative work on the cheap. I had a direct connection to someone at the top of the company's design team. We offered the project to them, and they wouldn't copy us when we handed it to them.

There is a lot of fear built into this process by the law and capitalism. Intellectual-property law creates fear that companies *do* have some unknowable liability because there are competing claims on the original shape, and we may not have done enough to modify the original shape to make the new work outside the original copyright. It does not help that no lawyer can give an authoritative answer on this question, so the large company with highly suable assets shies away. Companies also fear that if they invest to streamline the production process, brand the product, and create a market, their competitor will jump in and produce it cheaper, and their effort will be for naught. If this did happen, it would be great for the end user/consumer/citizen who wants to use CFLs, but it is not so great for the bottom line of the profit-driven company that invested the time and money into producing the first version.

Part of me wonders about Urban Outfitters and the rest of the corporate design community that perpetually poaches art for their own uses. I jokingly think that they can't even do anything legitimately. They actually have to rip off someone's art. Playfully, I think that maybe if we said, "Don't touch this. This is our artwork!" maybe they would have copied it. But I know this is a simple and incomplete response. There are larger problems that this example highlights. I came to realize that there were better ways of getting this kind of project scaled up and distributed, and to accept that we pitched the product and gave it away for free, and it didn't work. The lesson learned is that giving things away is hard work.

I took that lesson into my next major project, *Digital Foundations: An Intro to Media Design*, a textbook that integrates Bauhaus pedagogy and art-historical examples into a software-focused design primer.[21] I coauthored this book with xtine burrough. Though this project is closer to the code and text projects I referred to in the introduction, it involves so much design work that it is not copyable and translatable like software or wikis. This book teaches the formal principles and exercises of the Bauhaus Basic Course through the Adobe Creative Suite. One prime example of this strategy is the chapter on color theory. We teach color theory using Josef Albers's classic Bauhaus exercises, which defined the modern artistic use of color, showing the interrelationship of color's components: hue, value, and saturation. We point out the way these principles have been directly integrated into the computer interface used to select colors. This is a classic exercise from the traditional Studio Foundations course that introduces students to the basic techniques and formal characteristics of art and design. The classrooms where these studio classes used to take place have been converted into computer labs, and more and more curricula skip this traditional analog foundations course and instead go straight into a computer class. Students are not trained in the basic formal principles of visual composition: balance, harmony, symmetry, dynamism, negative space, and so on, nor do they learn color theory or basic drawing.

We made a number of strategic decisions at the beginning that attempted to avoid the problems Lambert and I encountered with the Bright Idea Shade. Instead of waiting for someone to find the book and publish it, we went through the traditional book-proposal process. Once we had the publisher excited about the book, we then started negotiating the Creative Commons license on the work. Before the work was even finished, we actively worked to give the work away by partnering with an organization called FLOSSmanuals to translate the book from the proprietary Adobe design applications like Photoshop and Illustrator to the FLOSS design applications like GIMP and Inkscape.

We wrote the book on a wiki, which at the time was rather unusual for textbook writing.[22] It was so unusual that we were concerned about the publisher's reaction. We decided to go ahead with it, as it was the most effective way for the two of us to collaborate, share the results with our peers who were providing feedback, and test the exercises from the book in our classes as we were writing them. When we did show the publisher, they were thrilled. They sent the site around to everyone in the company as an example of how they could start to adopt new peer production techniques for their books.

We wrote it on a wiki with the Creative Commons license we were in the process of negotiating with the publisher. We only used public-domain or Creative Commons–licensed images. After nine months of negotiating, during which time we wrote the majority of the book, we finally signed a Creative Commons–licensed contract with the publisher, AIGA Design Press/ New Riders, which is an imprint of Peachpit Press, which is a division of Pearson, one of the largest publishers in the world. Their legal department took nine months to churn its wheels and finally agreed to a Creative Commons license. We licensed this work with a Creative Commons license on principle and also because I was contractually obliged to do so by my contract with Eyebeam. Most importantly, we did it out of the hope that this time we would be able to succeed at giving the work away.

As I mentioned, we were building plans with FLOSSmanuals to translate the book into FLOSS software. Run by Adam Hyde, FLOSSmanuals' mission is to create free manuals for free software. For *Digital Foundations*, FLOSSmanuals assembled a team in New York and ported the whole book to open-source applications like Inkscape, GIMP, and Processing. In a three-day book sprint, eight to ten people per day, with a wide range of technical experience, "FLOSSified" the whole book.[23] I attended the sprint primarily to observe and advise but did almost no actual translation; burrough did not attend. Since then, Jennifer Dopazo, at the time a graduate student in NYU's Interactive Telecommunications Program, led a translation of the whole book into Spanish.[24] This book has been published and is going to be released in an extremely low-cost newsprint edition sponsored by Media Lab Prado in Madrid and distributed for free to design centers, schools, Internet cafes, co-working spaces, and community centers. In addition, there are active translations into French, Farsi, Mandarin Chinese, Finnish, and German.

We succeeded in giving the project away, and the project continues to evolve into new transformations and uses. We were able to achieve this because we were more strategic at an earlier stage than Lambert and I were with the Bright Idea Shade. We formed a partnership early and made sure that it was an open partnership that allowed us to make further partnerships with other individuals and organizations that were interested in the material we covered in the book and in the process by which we made the book.

The materiality of the two projects differentiates them in a way that may be instructive. *Digital Foundations* has taken multiple physical forms: a trade paperback technical book published in an initial 2008 run of eight thousand copies, with a 2009 reprint of four thousand copies; two print-on-demand books published by FLOSSmanuals; and in the future, as five thousand copies of a newsprint edition.[25] It has also taken multiple digital forms: the whole book is up on a wiki; the full FLOSS version is available in English and Spanish from the FLOSSmanuals.net website, where partially translated versions also live; and I put the entire master design file for the original book up as a torrent file on Clear Bits, a legal torrent site.[26] *Digital Foundations* was also closer in form to the more successful text/code-based examples discussed in the introduction, though the significant design work in the book differentiates it from these text/code examples. Conversely, the Bright Idea Shade was necessarily a physical object. It was effectively a prototype for a kit that could have been manufactured in large scale. Its digital form was a set of vector files that a laser cutter could use to cut copies and an instruction set on Instructables. com: these were not the product; they were procedural tools that would help get to the end product. The Bright Idea Shade was rooted in physical materiality, while *Digital Foundations* was whole both in physical and digital forms.

The demands of participation were very different between the two projects. For *Digital Foundations* we were able to make the process of sharing into a collaborative process, and one which accessed collaborators who had a range of experience, from expert to novice software users, to translators in multiple languages. Some of the most helpful participants in the translation book sprint were the people who had no experience with the FLOSS software into which we were translating the book; these contributors' responsibility was simply to work their way through the finished chapters, following the new instructions, and successfully completing each step along the way. When they got confused or encountered errors, the translators knew they had to rewrite that section. In the process they learned the software. With the translation process, contributions could be large or small. Though Dopazo translated the majority of the Spanish version, she did have collaborators translate and proofread. It is not all or nothing, and many small contributions led to a complete project. Conversely, the Bright Idea Shade was all or nothing. We were not trying to find a person to collaborate with but, rather, a company that had very specific capabilities. We were looking for a company to commit to the large-scale production of the design prototype we had created. This was not possible through collaboration; this did not access multiple skill levels; nor did it allow for incremental production. It was an all-or-nothing proposition, and as a result, it was not successful.

Some time after we made the Bright Idea Shade, I covered my bicycle in black retroreflective vinyl. "Retroreflective" is a technical term that means that the material reflects directly back in the direction of a light source. This is the same reflective material on the backs of running shoes and night safety vests. I called the project Bright Bike, made a video, and released it online.[27] By this time I was beginning to see the flaws with the plan for the Bright Idea Shade and to see the potential successes of the way we were planning the *Digital Foundations* project. I tried to include some of this knowledge in the plan for the Bright Bike.

The vinyl comes in sizes starting at thirty-foot-long, fifteen-inch-wide rolls, but the initial kit required only six feet of fifteen-inch-wide vinyl. Eyebeam sold six-foot sections of the vinyl out of the Eyebeam Bookstore, but that was only accessible to people who happened to stop by in person. In an effort to expand that range, we approached our vinyl supplier to see if they would be willing to sell six-foot lengths of vinyl cut for the Bright Bike project. The supplier was interested, as the company happened to be run by an avid cyclist. They sold the vinyl in six-foot lengths to correspond to the Instructable that had the directions on it.[28]

We achieved some success. Despite the kits' being buried deep in the vinyl supplier's website, people did order them. Somewhere along the way I also realized that, like it or not, I was going to have to become a businessman, if only a small-scale DIY one. In this, I turned to Limor Fried's practice as an example. During her time at Eyebeam, she and Torrone had started a business called Adafruit Industries, selling the DIY kits she was making.[29] I made revisions to the original design, creating two different DIY kits that take five and fifteen minutes to apply each.[30] I made a about one hundred of these kits on a friend's vinyl cutter, sent out one e-mail, and quickly sold out. I launched a fundraising campaign via the crowdfunding site Kickstarter.com which raised $2,500 from eighty-six different "project backers" who each received rewards in the form of DIY kits.[31] Their support allowed me to buy a bulk order of the expensive vinyl and to make dedicated jigs, so I could fabricate the kits quickly (hand cutting with jigs proved faster and more accurate than using a vinyl cutter).

Presently, I have shipped wholesale orders to a bicycle shop in Portland, Oregon, and to several design boutiques and bike shops in San Francisco and Amsterdam. I have an assistant who cuts and ships kits one day a week. The

revenue from the kits is paying the wages of the assistant and for new sup-
plies of the vinyl. The project is creating enough profit to sustain itself. By
sustaining the project, I am creating the possibility for more people to get it
in their hands, in the hope that one of them will use their hands and transform the project. It appears that this strategy is working: a number of Flickr
users have posted creative applications of the kits, and I recently discovered
that a bike shop to which I gave a sample has derived a modified version of
the kit which they are putting on all of the bikes they sell.[32]

I was at a family event, and a distant cousin came up to me to talk about
the Bright Bike kits. She thought it was a great idea, but she was very concerned that I patent the idea as soon as possible, lest "one of the big bike
manufacturers steal it from you and make a lot of money and leave you with
nothing." I told her that it would be wonderful if that happened, because I
was really interested in design for bike safety and that a major bike manufacturer could scale up the project much larger than an individual like me
could. I also told her that based on my past experience, it was pretty unlikely
that her fears would play out but that I still hoped they might.

NOTES

This work is licensed under the Creative Commons Attribution-ShareAlike license.

1. One of the potential pitfalls of this essay is trying to define the boundary between
the two categories I am setting up. I do not set up this binary for the sake of defining borders and establishing categories but, rather, to articulate different modes of production. In
reality, this is a continuum, with some interesting cases floating in the middle. A digitized
photograph is code, but the image itself has to be inputted and outputted from the computer. Additionally, it cannot be reworked quite as easily as code/text. While interesting,
the exploration of these boundary cases is not the focus of this essay.

2. Richard Stallman, "The GNU Manifesto," http://www.gnu.org/gnu/manifesto.html;
and Free Software Foundation, "The Free Software Definition," http://www.gnu.org/phi-
losophy/free-sw.html (accessed June 25, 2010). One of Richard Stallman's most creative
contributions to this movement was the General Public License or GPL, http://www.gnu.
org/licenses/gpl.html. Software licensed with the GPL is required to maintain that license
in all future incarnations; this means that code that starts out open has to stay open. You
cannot close the source code. This is known as a "copyleft" license.

3. Eric Raymond, *The Cathedral and the Bazaar* (Sebastopol, CA: O'Reilly, 2001).

4. There is much debate in the subcultures of the free-culture movement about what
terms to use. Some argue that the term "open source" is a neutered version of "free software" that caters to corporate entities like IBM that see the business potential in a software-
authoring model that is built around sharing and group work but cannot allow the word
"free" to enter into their business lexicon. While these disputes arise from time to time, the
term "FLOSS" (or "FOSS") is used as a catchall acronym to refer to both terms.

5. For more on the mechanics of Creative Commons licenses, please see http://creativecommons.org/about/licenses/.

6. Mike Linksvayer, "Creative Commons Licenses on Flickr: Many More Images, Slightly More Freedom," *Creative Commons Blog*, March 10, 2010, http://creativecommons.org/weblog/entry/20870 (accessed June 25, 2010).

7. There are even limitations beyond the materiality of the works: one group of leading artist-engineers is currently working with Creative Commons on making it possible to license an electronic circuit via an open license, as it is currently not possible to fully do so. For video documentation, see Eyebeam, "Opening Hardware," March 17, 2010, http://eyebeam.org/projects/opening-hardware (accessed April 11, 2010).

8. Eyebeam has changed its internal structure to adapt to changing needs of its fellows and resident artists: at the time of Fried's fellowship, there were multiple labs with different licensing requirements. Due to external factors like the growing importance of free culture and internal factors like the fellows' desire to all work in one shared lab, the organization collapsed the labs into one lab. Fellows are no longer designated "R&D fellow" or "production fellow" but are simply "fellows," and all contracts require open licenses.

9. Graffiti Research Lab, "LED Throwies," Instructables, 2006, http://www.instructables.com/id/LED-Throwies. For modifications, see projects tagged "Throwies" on Instructables.com: http://www.instructables.com/tag/throwies/ (accessed June 25, 2010). LED Throwies for sale: Hebei Ltd., http://www.hebeiltd.com.cn/?p=throwies (accessed June 25, 2010).

10. Lewis Hyde, *The Gift* (New York: Vintage, 1979); Adam Hyde et al., *Collaborative Futures*, FLOSSmanuals.net, 2010, http://www.booki.cc/collaborativefutures/ (accessed June 25, 2010).

11. The term "Famo" comes from the URL www.internetfamo.us; without the TLD (top-level domain ".us"), the word "famous" is cut to "famo."

12. James Powderly, Evan Roth, and Jamie Wilkinson, "Internet Famous Class, 2007–2008," http://internetfamo.us/class/ (accessed June 25, 2010).

13. Ben McConnell, "The 1% Rule: Charting Citizen Participation," *Church of the Customer Blog*, May 3, 2006, http://customerevangelists.typepad.com/blog/2006/05/charting_wiki_p.html (accessed June 29, 2011); Julia Angwin and Geoffrey A. Fowler, "Volunteers Log Off as Wikipedia Ages," *Wall Street Journal*, November 27, 2009, http://online.wsj.com/article/SB125893981183759969.html (accessed June 25, 2010).

14. For an edge case of this idea, see Michael Mandiberg, AfterSherrieLevine.com, 2001.

15. Limor Fried and Phil Torrone, "Adafruit Laser Information Wiki," LadyAda.net, first posted December 2005, last updated March 5, 2010, http://www.ladyada.net/wiki/laserinfo/start (accessed July 20, 2010).

16. Phil Torrone, personal interview, July 1, 2010.

17. Camille Ricketts, "Microsoft Social App Co. Wallop Rebrands as Coveroo," Deals & More, December 17, 2008, http://deals.venturebeat.com/2008/12/17/microsoft-social-app-co-wallop-rebrands-as-coveroo/ (accessed July 20, 2010).

18. Vaporized PVC releases deadly chlorine gas.

19. Dan Goldwater, "Universal Lamp Shade Polygon Building Kit," Instructables, http://www.instructables.com/id/Universal-lamp-shade-polygon-building-kit/ (accessed June 25, 2010). "RE-WIRE: Piece Together Pendant Lamps," *ReadyMade*, December–January

2007–2008. Antonio Carrillo, modular construction system, 1964; see, e.g., http://www.ylighting.com/brs-lj-col-drop.html (accessed June 25, 2010). Holger Strom, "IQ Light," 1972; see overview at http://www.sadiethepilot.com/iqweb/iqstory.htm (accessed June 25, 2010).

20. Steve Lambert and Michael Mandiberg, "Bright Idea Shade," Vimeo, 2008, http://vimeo.com/1553079 (accessed June 25, 2010).

21. xtine burrough and Michael Mandiberg, *Digital Foundations: An Intro to Media Design* (Berkeley, CA: Peachpit, 2008).

22. xtine burrough and Michael Mandiberg, "Digital Foundations Wiki," http://wiki.digital-foundations.net (accessed July 20, 2010).

23. FLOSSmanuals.net community, *Digital Foundations: Introduction to Media Design with FLOSS*, 2009, http://en.flossmanuals.net/DigitalFoundations (accessed June 25, 2010).

24. FLOSSmanuals.net community, *Fundamentos Digitales: Introducción al diseño de medios con FLOSS*, 2009, http://translate.flossmanuals.net/DigitalFoundations_es (accessed June 25, 2010).

25. burrough and Mandiberg, *Digital Foundations*; FLOSSmanuals.net community, *Digital Foundations*; FLOSSmanuals.net community, *Fundamentos Digitales*.

26. burrough and Mandiberg, "Digital Foundations Wiki"; xtine burrough and Michael Mandiberg, "Digital Foundations Master File," Clear Bits, 2009, http://www.clearbits.net/torrents/597-digital-foundations-textbook-master-file-including-all-files-links-images (accessed June 25, 2010).

27. Steve Lambert and Michael Mandiberg, "Bright Bike," Vimeo, 2008, http://vimeo.com/2409360 (accessed June 25, 2010).

28. Beacon Graphics, http://www.beacongraphics.com/brightbike.html (accessed June 25, 2010); Michael Mandiberg, "Bright Bike," Instructables, http://www.instructables.com/id/Bright-Bike/ (accessed June 25, 2010).

29. The business, Adafruit Industries (http://adafruit.com/), is the creative outlet for Fried's physical computing projects and distributes her work into the hands and soldering irons of those who want to use the tools she is making.

30. All of the images and blog posts about the first version that appeared online emphasized how *hard* it was to actually complete the project and how long it took those who tried. Michael Mandiberg, "Bright Bike v2.0," Vimeo, 2009, http://vimeo.com/8159498 (accessed June 25, 2010).

31. Michael Mandiberg, "Bright Bike DIY Kits: Night Visibility for Safer Riding," Kickstarter, 2010, http://www.kickstarter.com/projects/mandiberg/bright-bike-diy-kits-night-visibility-for-safer-r (accessed June 25, 2010).

32. Michael Mandiberg, "Bright Bike Mod in Brooklyn," Michael Mandiberg's website, August 31, 2010, http://www.mandiberg.com/2010/08/31/bright-bike-mod-in-brooklyn/ (accessed August 31, 2010).

PART VI

Labor

15

Quentin Tarantino's *Star Wars?*

Grassroots Creativity Meets the Media Industry

HENRY JENKINS

Shooting in garages and basement rec rooms, rendering F/X on home computers, and ripping music from CDs and MP3 files, fans have created new versions of the *Star Wars* (1977) mythology. In the words of *Star Wars or Bust* director Jason Wishnow, "This is the future of cinema—*Star Wars* is the catalyst."[1]

The widespread circulation of *Star Wars*–related commodities has placed resources into the hands of a generation of emerging filmmakers in their teens or early twenties. They grew up dressing as Darth Vader for Halloween, sleeping on Princess Leia sheets, battling with plastic light sabers, and playing with Boba Fett action figures. *Star Wars* has become their "legend," and now they are determined to remake it on their own terms.

When AtomFilms launched an official *Star Wars* fan film contest in 2003, they received more than 250 submissions. Although the ardor has died down somewhat, the 2005 competition received more than 150 submissions.[2] And many more are springing up on the web via unofficial sites such as TheForce.net, which would fall outside the rules for the official contest. Many of these films come complete with their own posters or advertising campaigns. Some websites provide updated information about amateur films still in production.

Fans have always been early adapters of new media technologies; their fascination with fictional universes often inspires new forms of cultural production, ranging from costumes to fanzines and, now, digital cinema. Fans are the most active segment of the media audience, one that refuses to simply accept what they are given but, rather, insists on the right to become full participants.[3] None of this is new. What has shifted is the visibility of fan culture. The web provides a powerful new distribution channel for amateur cultural production. Amateurs have been making home movies for decades; these movies are going public.

When Amazon introduced DVDs of *George Lucas in Love* (1999), perhaps the best known of the *Star Wars* parodies, it outsold the DVD of *Star Wars Episode I: The Phantom Menace* (1999) in its opening week.[4] Fan filmmakers, with some legitimacy, see their works as "calling cards" that may help them break into the commercial industry. In spring 1998, a two-page color spread in *Entertainment Weekly* profiled aspiring digital filmmaker Kevin Rubio, whose ten-minute, $1,200 film, *Troops* (1998), had attracted the interests of Hollywood insiders.[5] *Troops* spoofs *Star Wars* by offering a *Cops*-like profile of the stormtroopers who do the day-in, day-out work of policing Tatooine, settling domestic disputes, rounding up space hustlers, and trying to crush the Jedi Knights. As a result, the story reported, Rubio was fielding offers from several studios interested in financing his next project. Lucas admired the film so much that he gave Rubio a job writing for the *Star Wars* comic books. Rubio surfaced again in 2004 as a writer and producer for *Duel Masters* (2004), a little-known series on the Cartoon Network.

Fan digital film is to cinema what the punk DIY culture was to music. There, grassroots experimentation generated new sounds, new artists, new techniques, and new relations to consumers which have been pulled more and more into mainstream practice. Here, fan filmmakers are starting to make their way into the mainstream industry, and we are starting to see ideas—such as the use of game engines as animation tools—bubbling up from the amateurs and making their way into commercial media.

If, as some have argued, the emergence of modern mass media spelled the doom for the vital folk culture traditions that thrived in nineteenth-century America, the current moment of media change is reaffirming the right of everyday people to actively contribute to their culture. Like the older folk culture of quilting bees and barn dances, this new vernacular culture encourages broad participation, grassroots creativity, and a bartering or gift economy. This is what happens when consumers take media into their own hands. Of course, this may be altogether the wrong way to talk about it—since in a folk culture, there is no clear division between producers and consumers. Within convergence culture, everyone's a participant—although participants may have different degrees of status and influence.

It may be useful to draw a distinction between interactivity and participation, words that are often used interchangeably but which, in this essay, assume rather different meanings.[6] Interactivity refers to the ways that new technologies have been designed to be more responsive to consumer feedback. One can imagine differing degrees of interactivity enabled by different communication technologies, ranging from television, which allows us only to change the channel, to video games that can allow consumers to act upon the represented world. Such relationships are of course not fixed: the introduction of TiVo can fundamentally reshape our interactions with television. The constraints on interactivity are technological. In almost every case, what you can do in an interactive environment is prestructured by the designer.

Participation, on the other hand, is shaped by the cultural and social protocols. So, for example, the amount of conversation possible in a movie theater is determined more by the tolerance of audiences in different subcultures or national contexts than by any innate property of cinema itself. Participation is more open-ended, less under the control of media producers and more under the control of media consumers.

Initially, the computer offered expanded opportunities for interacting with media content, and as long as it operated on that level, it was relatively easy for media companies to commodify and control what took place. Increasingly, though, the web has become a site of consumer participation that includes many unauthorized and unanticipated ways of relating to media content. Though this new participatory culture has its roots in practices that have occurred just below the radar of the media industry throughout the twentieth century, the web has pushed that hidden layer of cultural activity into the foreground, forcing the media industries to confront its implications for their commercial interests. Allowing consumers to interact with media under controlled circumstances is one thing; allowing them to participate in the production and distribution of cultural goods—on their own terms—is something else altogether.

Grant McCracken, the cultural anthropologist and industry consultant, suggests that in the future, media producers must accommodate consumer demands to participate, or they will run the risk of losing the most active and passionate consumers to some other media interest that is more tolerant: "Corporations must decide whether they are, literally, in or out. Will they make themselves an island or will they enter the mix? Making themselves an island may have certain short-term financial benefits, but the long-term costs can be substantial."[7] As we have seen, the media industry is increasingly dependent on active and committed consumers to spread the word about valued properties in an overcrowded media marketplace, and in some cases they are seeking ways to channel the creative output of media fans to lower their production costs. At the same time, they are terrified of what happens if this consumer power gets out of control, as they claim occurred following the introduction of Napster and other file-sharing services. As fan productivity goes public, it can no longer be ignored by the media industries, but it cannot be fully contained or channeled by them, either.

One can trace two characteristic responses of media industries to this grassroots expression: starting with the legal battles over Napster, the media industries have increasingly adopted a scorched-earth policy toward their consumers, seeking to regulate and criminalize many forms of fan participation that once fell below their radar. Let's call them the prohibitionists. To date, the prohibitionist stance has been dominant within old media companies (film, television, the recording industry), though these groups are to varying degrees starting to reexamine some of these assumptions. So far, the prohibitionists get most of the press—with lawsuits directed against teens who download music or against fan webmasters getting more and more coverage in the popular media. At the same time, on the fringes, new media companies (Internet, games, and to a lesser degree, the mobile phone companies) are experimenting with new approaches that see fans as important collaborators in the production of content and as grassroots intermediaries helping to promote the franchise. We will call them the collaborationists.

The *Star Wars* franchise has been pulled between these two extremes both over time (as it responds to shifting consumer tactics and technological resources) and across media (as its content straddles between old and new media). Within the *Star Wars* franchise, Hollywood has sought to shut down fan fiction, later to assert ownership over it, and finally to ignore its existence; they have promoted the works of fan video makers but also limited what kinds of movies they can make; and they have sought to collaborate with gamers to shape a massively multiplayer game so that it better satisfies player fantasies.

Folk Culture, Mass Culture, Convergence Culture

At the risk of painting with broad strokes, the story of American arts in the nineteenth century might be told in terms of the mixing, matching, and merging of folk traditions taken from various indigenous and immigrant populations. Cultural production occurred mostly on the grassroots level; creative skills and artistic traditions were passed down mother to daughter, father to son. Stories and songs circulated broadly, well beyond their points of origin, with little or no expectation of economic compensation; many of the best ballads or folktales come to us today with no clear marks of individual authorship. While new commercialized forms of entertainment—the minstrel shows, the circuses, the showboats—emerged in the mid- to late nineteenth century, these professional entertainments competed with thriving local traditions of barn dances, church sings, quilting bees, and campfire stories. There was no pure boundary between the emergent commercial culture and the residual folk culture: the commercial culture raided folk culture, and folk culture raided commercial culture.

The story of American arts in the twentieth century might be told in terms of the displacement of folk culture by mass media. Initially, the emerging entertainment industry made its peace with folk practices, seeing the availability of grassroots singers and musicians as a potential talent pool, incorporating community sing-alongs into film exhibition practices, and broadcasting amateur-hour talent competitions. The new industrialized arts required huge investments and thus demanded a mass audience. The commercial entertainment industry set standards of technical perfection and professional accomplishment few grassroots performers could match. The commercial industries developed powerful infrastructures that ensured that their messages reached everyone in America who wasn't living under a rock. Increasingly, the commercial culture generated the stories, images, and sounds that mattered most to the public.

Folk culture practices were pushed underground—people still composed and sang songs, amateur writers still scribbled verse, weekend painters still dabbled, people still told stories, and some local communities still held square dances. At the same time, grassroots fan communities emerged in response to mass media content. Some media scholars hold on to the useful distinction between mass culture (a category of production) and popular culture (a category of consumption), arguing that popular culture is what happens to the materials of mass culture when they get into the hands of consumers—when a song played on the radio becomes so associated with a particularly romantic evening that two young lovers decide to call it "our song," or when a fan becomes so fascinated with a particular television series that it inspires her to write original stories about its characters. In other words, popular culture is what happens as mass culture gets pulled back into folk culture. The culture industries never really had to confront the existence of this alternative cultural economy because, for the most part, it existed behind closed doors and its products circulated only among a small circle of friends and neighbors. Home movies never threatened Hollywood, as long as they remained in the home.

The story of American arts in the twenty-first century might be told in terms of the public reemergence of grassroots creativity as everyday people take advantage of new technologies that enable them to archive, annotate, appropriate, and recirculate media content. It probably started with the photocopier and desktop publishing; perhaps it started with the videocassette revolution, which gave the public access to moviemaking tools and enabled every home to have its own film library. But this creative revolution has so far culminated with the web. To create is much more fun and meaningful if you can share what you can create with others, and the web, built for collaboration within the scientific community, provides an infrastructure for sharing the things average Americans are making in their rec rooms. Once you have a reliable system of distribution, folk culture production begins to flourish again overnight. Most of what the amateurs create is gosh-awful bad, yet a thriving culture needs spaces where people can do bad art, get feedback, and get better. After all, much of what circulates through mass media is also bad by almost any criteria, but the expectations of professional polish make it a less hospitable environment for newcomers to learn and grow. Some of what amateurs create will be surprisingly good, and some artists will be recruited into commercial entertainment or the art world. Much of it will be good enough to engage the interest of some modest public, to inspire someone else to create, to provide new content which, when polished through many hands, may turn into something more valuable down the line. That's the way the folk process works, and grassroots convergence represents the folk process accelerated and expanded for the digital age.

Given this history, it should be no surprise that much of what the public creates models itself after, exists in dialogue with, reacts to or against, and/or otherwise repurposes materials drawn from commercial culture. Grassroots convergence is embodied, for example, in the work of the game modders, who build on code and design tools created for commercial games as a foundation for amateur game production, or in digital filmmaking, which often directly samples material from commercial media, or adbusting, which borrows iconography from Madison Avenue to deliver an anticorporate or anticonsumerist message. Having buried the old folk culture, this commercial culture becomes the common culture. The older American folk culture was built on borrowings from various mother countries; the modern mass media builds upon borrowings from folk culture; the new convergence culture will be built on borrowings from various media conglomerates.

The web has made visible the hidden compromises that enabled participatory culture and commercial culture to coexist throughout much of the twentieth century. Nobody minded, really, if you photocopied a few stories and circulated them within your fan club. Nobody minded, really, if you copied a few songs and shared the dub tape with a friend. Corporations might know, abstractly, that such transactions were occurring all around them, every day, but they didn't know, concretely, who was doing it. And even if they did, they weren't going to come bursting into people's homes at night. But, as those transactions came out from behind closed doors, they represented a visible, public threat to the absolute control the culture industries asserted over their intellectual property.

With the consolidation of power represented by the Digital Millennium Copyright Act of 1998, American intellectual property law has been rewritten to reflect the demands of mass media producers—away from providing economic incentives for individual artists and toward protecting the enormous economic investments media companies made in branded entertainment; away from a limited-duration protection that allows ideas to enter general circulation while they still benefit the common good and toward the notion that copyright should last forever; away from the ideal of a cultural commons and toward the ideal of intellectual property. As Lawrence Lessig notes, the law has been rewritten so that "no one can do to the Disney Corporation what Walt Disney did to the Brothers Grimm."[8] One of the ways that the studios have propped up these expanded claims of copyright protection is through the issuing of cease-and-desist letters intended to intimidate amateur cultural creators into removing their works from the web. In such situations, the studios often assert much broader control than they could legally defend: someone who stands to lose their home or their kid's college funds by going head-to-head with studio attorneys is apt to fold. After three decades of such disputes, there is still no case law that would help determine to what degree fan fiction is protected under fair-use law.

Efforts to shut down fan communities run in the face of what we have learned so far about the new kinds of affective relationships advertisers and entertainment companies want to form with their consumers. Over the past several decades, corporations have sought to market branded content so that consumers become the bearers of their marketing messages. Marketers have turned our children into walking, talking billboards who wear logos on their T-shirts, sew patches on their backpacks, plaster stickers on their lockers, hang posters on their walls, but they must not, under penalty of law, post them on their home pages. Somehow, once consumers choose when and where to display those images, their active participation in the circulation of brands suddenly becomes a moral outrage and a threat to the industry's economic well-being.

Today's teens—the so-called Napster generation—aren't the only ones who are confused about where to draw the lines here; media companies are giving out profoundly mixed signals because they really can't decide what kind of relationships they want to have with this new kind of consumer. They want us to look at but *not* touch, buy but *not* use, media content. This contradiction is felt perhaps most acutely when it comes to cult media content. A cult media success depends on courting fan constituencies and niche markets; a mainstream success is seen by the media producers as depending on distancing themselves from them. The system depends on covert relationships between producers and consumers. The fans' labor in enhancing the value of an intellectual property can never be publicly recognized if the studio is going to maintain that the studio alone is the source of all value in that property. The Internet, though, has blown their cover, since those fan sites are now visible to anyone who knows how to Google.

Some industry insiders—for example, Chris Albrecht, who runs the official *Star Wars* film competition at AtomFilms, or Raph Koster, the former MUDder who has helped shape the *Star Wars Galaxies* (2002) game—come out of these grassroots communities and have a healthy respect for their value. They see fans as potentially revitalizing stagnant franchises and providing a low-cost means of generating new media content. Often, such people are locked into power struggles within their own companies with others who would prohibit grassroots creativity.

"Dude, We're Gonna Be Jedi!"

George Lucas in Love depicts the future media mastermind as a singularly clueless USC film student who can't quite come up with a good idea for his production assignment, despite the fact that he inhabits a realm rich with narrative possibilities. His stoner roommate emerges from behind the hood of his dressing gown and lectures Lucas on "this giant cosmic force, an energy field created by all living things." His sinister next-door neighbor, an archrival, dresses all in black and breathes with an asthmatic wheeze as he proclaims, "My script is complete. Soon I will rule the entertainment universe." As Lucas races to class, he encounters a brash young friend who brags about his souped-up sports car and his furry-faced sidekick who growls when he hits his head on the hood while trying to do some basic repairs. His professor, a smallish man, babbles cryptic advice, but all of this adds up to little until Lucas meets and falls madly for a beautiful young woman with buns on both sides of her head. Alas, the romance leads to naught as he eventually discovers that she is his long-lost sister.

George Lucas in Love is, of course, a spoof of *Shakespeare in Love* (1998) and of *Star Wars* itself. It is also a tribute from one generation of USC film students to another. As co-creator Joseph Levy, a twenty-four-year-old recent graduate from Lucas's alma mater, explained, "Lucas is definitely the god of USC. . . . We shot our screening-room scene in the George Lucas Instructional Building. Lucas is incredibly supportive of student filmmakers and developing their careers and providing facilities for them to be caught up to technology."[9] Yet what makes this film so endearing is the way it pulls Lucas down to the same level as countless other amateur filmmakers and, in so doing, helps to blur the line between the fantastical realm of space opera ("A long, long time ago in a galaxy far, far away") and the familiar realm of everyday life (the world of stoner roommates, snotty neighbors, and incomprehensible professors). Its protagonist is hapless in love, clueless at filmmaking, yet somehow he manages to pull it all together and produce one of the top-grossing motion pictures of all time. *George Lucas in Love* offers us a portrait of the artist as a young geek.

One might contrast this rather down-to-earth representation of Lucas—the auteur as amateur—with the way fan filmmaker Evan Mather's website (http://www.evanmather.com/) constructs the amateur as an emergent auteur.[10] Along one column of the site can be found a filmography, listing all of Mather's productions going back to high school, as well as a listing of the various newspapers, magazines, websites, and television and radio stations that have covered his work—*La Republica*, *Le Monde*, the *New York Times*, *Wired*, *Entertainment Weekly*, CNN, NPR, and so forth. Another sidebar provides up-to-the-moment information about his works in progress. Elsewhere, you can see news of the various film-festival screenings of his films and whatever awards they have won. More than nineteen digital films are featured with photographs, descriptions, and links for downloading them in multiple formats.

Another link allows you to call up a glossy, full-color, professionally designed brochure documenting the making of *Les Pantless Menace* (1999), which includes close-ups of various props and settings, reproductions of stills, score sheets, and storyboards, and detailed explanations of how he was able to do the special effects, soundtrack, and editing for the film (fig. 15.1). We learn, for example, that some of the dialogue was taken directly from Commtech chips that were embedded within Hasbro *Star Wars* toys. A biography provides some background:

> Evan Mather spent much of his childhood running around south Louisiana with an eight-millimeter silent camera staging hitchhikings and assorted buggery. . . . As a landscape architect, Mr. Mather spends his days designing a variety of urban and park environments in the Seattle

area. By night, Mr. Mather explores the realm of digital cinema and is the renowned creator of short films which fuse traditional hand drawn and stop motion animation techniques with the flexibility and realism of computer generated special effects.

Though his background and production techniques are fairly ordinary, the incredibly elaborate, self-conscious, and determinedly professional design of his website is anything but. His website illustrates what happens as this new amateur culture gets directed toward larger and larger publics.

TheForce.net's Fan Theater, for example, allows amateur directors to offer their own commentary. The creators of *When Senators Attack IV* (1999), for example, give "comprehensive scene-by-scene commentary" on their film: "Over the next 90 pages or so, you'll receive an insight into what we were thinking when we made a particular shot, what methods we used, explanations to some of the more puzzling scenes, and anything else that comes to mind."[11] Such materials mirror the tendency of recent DVD releases to include alternative scenes, cut footage, storyboards, and director's commentary. Many of the websites provide information about fan films under production, including preliminary footage, storyboards, and trailers for films that may never be completed. Almost all of the amateur filmmakers create posters and advertising images, taking advantage of Adobe PageMaker and Adobe Photoshop. In many cases, the fan filmmakers produce elaborate trailers. These materials facilitate amateur film culture. The making-of articles share technical advice; such information helps to improve the overall quality of work within the community. The trailers also respond to the specific challenges of the web as a distribution channel: it can take minutes to download relatively long digital movies, and the shorter, lower-resolution trailers (often distributed in a streaming video format) allow would-be viewers to sample the work.

All of this publicity surrounding the *Star Wars* parodies serves as a reminder of what is the most distinctive quality of these amateur films—the fact that they are so public. The idea that amateur filmmakers could develop such a global following runs counter to the historical marginalization of grassroots media production. In the book *Reel Families: A Social History of Amateur Film* (1995), film historian Patricia R. Zimmermann offers a compelling history of amateur filmmaking in the United States, examining the intersection between nonprofessional film production and the Hollywood entertainment system. While amateur filmmaking has existed since the advent of cinema, and while periodically critics have promoted it as a grass-

Fig. 15.1. Fan filmmaker Evan Mather's *Les Pantless Menace*
creates anarchic comedy through creative use of *Star Wars*
action figures. (Reprinted with the permission of the artist)

roots alternative to commercial production, the amateur film has remained,
first and foremost, the "home movie" in several senses of the term: first,
amateur films were exhibited primarily in private (and most often, domestic) spaces lacking any viable channel of public distribution; second, amateur
films were most often documentaries of domestic and family life; and third,
amateur films were perceived to be technically flawed and of marginal interest beyond the immediate family. Critics stressed the artlessness and spontaneity of amateur film in contrast with the technical polish and aesthetic
sophistication of commercial films. Zimmermann concludes, "[Amateur
film] was gradually squeezed into the nuclear family. Technical standards,
aesthetic norms, socialization pressures and political goals derailed its cultural construction into a privatized, almost silly, hobby."[12] Writing in the early
1990s, Zimmermann saw little reason to believe that the camcorder and the
VCR would significantly alter this situation. The medium's technical limitations made it difficult for amateurs to edit their films, and the only public
means of exhibition were controlled by commercial media makers (as in programs such as *America's Funniest Home Videos*, 1990).

Digital filmmaking alters many of the conditions that led to the marginalization of previous amateur filmmaking efforts—the web provides an exhibition outlet moving amateur filmmaking from private into public space;
digital editing is far simpler than editing Super-8 or video and thus opens
up a space for amateur artists to reshape their material more directly; the
home PC has even enabled the amateur filmmaker to mimic the special
effects associated with Hollywood blockbusters like *Star Wars*. Digital cinema is a new chapter in the complex history of interactions between amateur

filmmakers and the commercial media. These films remain amateur, in the sense that they are made on low budgets, produced and distributed in non-commercial contexts, and generated by nonprofessional filmmakers (albeit often by people who want entry into the professional sphere). Yet many of the other classic markers of amateur film production have disappeared. No longer home movies, these films are public movies—public in that, from the start, they are intended for audiences beyond the filmmaker's immediate circle of friends and acquaintances; public in their content, which involves the reworking of popular mythologies; and public in their dialogue with the commercial cinema.

Digital filmmakers tackled the challenge of making *Star Wars* movies for many different reasons. As *George Lucas in Love* co-creator Joseph Levy has explained, "Our only intention . . . was to do something that would get the agents and producers to put the tapes into their VCRs instead of throwing them away."[13] *Kid Wars* (2000) director Dana Smith is a fourteen-year-old who had recently acquired a camcorder and decided to stage scenes from *Star Wars* involving his younger brother and his friends, who armed themselves for battle with squirt guns and Nerf weapons. *The Jedi Who Loved Me* (2000) was shot by the members of a wedding party and intended as a tribute to the bride and groom, who were *Star Wars* fans. Some films—such as *Macbeth* (1998)—were school projects. Two high school students—Bienvenido Concepcion and Don Fitz-Roy—shot the film, which creatively blurred the lines between Lucas and Shakespeare, for their high school advanced-placement English class. They staged light-saber battles down the school hallway, though the principal was concerned about potential damage to lockers; the Millennium Falcon lifted off from the gym, though they had to composite it over the cheerleaders who were rehearsing the day they shot that particular sequence. Still other films emerged as collective projects for various *Star Wars* fan clubs. *Boba Fett: Bounty Trail* (2002), for example, was filmed for a competition hosted by a Melbourne, Australia, Lucasfilm convention. Each cast member made his or her own costumes, building on previous experience with science-fiction masquerades and costume contests. Their personal motives for making such films are of secondary interest, however, once they are distributed on the web. If such films are attracting worldwide interest, it is not because we all care whether Bienvenido Concepcion and Don Fitz-Roy got a good grade on their Shakespeare assignment. Rather, what motivated faraway viewers to watch such films is their shared investment in the *Star Wars* universe.

Amateur filmmakers are producing commercial- or near-commercial-quality content on minuscule budgets. They remain amateur in the sense that they do not earn their revenue through their work (much the way we might call Olympic athletes amateur), but they are duplicating special effects that had cost a small fortune to generate only a decade earlier. Amateur filmmakers can make pod racers skim along the surface of the ocean or land speeders scatter dust as they zoom across the desert. They can make laser beams shoot out of ships and explode things before our eyes. Several fans tried their hands at duplicating Jar Jar's character animation and inserting him into their own movies, with varying degrees of success. The light-saber battle, however, has become the gold standard of amateur filmmaking, with almost every filmmaker compelled to demonstrate his or her ability to achieve this particular effect. Many of the *Star Wars* shorts, in fact, consist of little more than light-saber battles staged in suburban dens and basements, in empty lots, in the hallways of local schools, inside shopping malls, or more exotically against the backdrop of medieval ruins (shot during vacations). Shane Faleux used an open-source approach to completing his forty-minute opus, *Star Wars: Revelations* (2005), one of the most acclaimed recent works in the movement (fig. 15.2). As Faleux explained, "*Revelations* was created to give artisans and craftsmen the chance to showcase their work, allow all those involved a chance to live the dream, and maybe—just maybe—open the eyes in the industry as to what can be done with a small budget, dedicated people, and undiscovered talent."[14] Hundreds of people around the world contributed to the project, including more than thirty different computer-graphics artists, ranging from folks within special-effects companies to talented teenagers. When the film was released via the web, more than a million people downloaded it.

As amateur filmmakers are quick to note, Lucas and Steven Spielberg both made Super-8 fiction films as teenagers and saw this experience as a major influence on their subsequent work. Although these films are not publicly available, some of them have been discussed in detail in various biographies and magazine profiles. These "movie brat" filmmakers have been quick to embrace the potentials of digital filmmaking, not simply as a means of lowering production costs for their own films but also as a training ground for new talent. Lucas, for example, told *Wired* magazine, "Some of the special effects that we redid for *Star Wars* were done on a Macintosh, on a laptop, in a couple of hours. . . . I could have very easily shot the Young Indy TV series on Hi-8. . . . So you can get a Hi-8 camera for a few thousand bucks, more for the software and the computer for less than $10,000 you have a movie studio. There's nothing to stop you from doing something provocative and significant in that medium."[15] Lucas's rhetoric about the potentials of digital

Fig. 15.2. Publicity materials created for *Star Wars: Revelations*,
a forty-minute opus made through the combined efforts of
hundreds of fan filmmakers worldwide.

filmmaking has captured the imagination of amateur filmmakers, and they
are taking on the master on his own ground.

As Clay Kronke, a Texas A&M University undergraduate who made *The
New World* (1999), explained, "This film has been a labor of love. A venture
into a new medium. . . . I've always loved light sabers and the mythos of the
Jedi and after getting my hands on some software that would allow me to
actually become what I had once only admired at a distance, a vague idea
soon started becoming a reality. . . . Dude, we're gonna be Jedi."[16] Kronke
openly celebrates the fact that he made the film on a $26.79 budget, with
most of the props and costumes part of their preexisting collections of *Star
Wars* paraphernalia, that the biggest problem they faced on the set was that
their plastic light sabers kept shattering, and that its sound effects included
"the sound of a coat hanger against a metal flashlight, my microwave door,
and myself falling on the floor several times."

The mass marketing of *Star Wars* inadvertently provided many of the
resources needed to support these productions. *Star Wars* is, in many ways, the
prime example of media convergence at work. Lucas's decision to defer salary
for the first *Star Wars* film in favor of maintaining a share of ancillary profits
has been widely cited as a turning point in the emergence of this new strategy
of media production and distribution. Lucas made a ton of money, and Twentieth Century Fox Film Corporation learned a valuable lesson. Kenner's *Star
Wars* action figures are thought to have been the key in reestablishing the value
of media tie-in products in the toy industry, and John Williams's score helped

to revitalize the market for soundtrack albums. The rich narrative universe of the *Star Wars* saga provided countless images, icons, and artifacts that could be reproduced in a wide variety of forms. Despite the lengthy gap between the release dates for *Return of the Jedi* (1983) and *The Phantom Menace* (1999), Lucasfilm continued to generate profits from its *Star Wars* franchise through the production of original novels and comic books, the distribution of video tapes and audio tapes, the continued marketing of *Star Wars* toys and merchandise, and the maintenance of an elaborate publicity apparatus, including a monthly glossy newsletter for *Star Wars* fans.

Many of these toys and trinkets were trivial when read in relation to other kinds of transmedia storytelling: they add little new information to the expanding franchise. Yet they took on deeper meanings as they became resources for children's play or for digital filmmaking. The amateur filmmakers often make use of commercially available costumes and props, sample music from the soundtrack album and sounds of *Star Wars* videos or computer games, and draw advice on special-effects techniques from television documentaries and mass-market magazines. For example, the makers of *Duel* described the sources for their soundtrack: "We sampled most of the light saber sounds from *The Empire Strikes Back* Special Edition laserdisc, and a few from *A New Hope*. *Jedi* was mostly useless to us, as the light saber battles in the film are always accompanied by music. The kicking sounds are really punch sounds from *Raiders of the Lost Ark*, and there's one sound—Hideous running across the sand—that we got from *Lawrence of Arabia*. Music, of course, comes from *The Phantom Menace* soundtrack."[17] The availability of these various ancillary products has encouraged these filmmakers, since childhood, to construct their own fantasies within the *Star Wars* universe. One fan critic explained, "Odds are if you were a kid in the seventies, you probably fought in schoolyards over who would play Han, lost a Wookiee action figure in your backyard and dreamed of firing that last shot on the Death Star. And probably your daydreams and conversations weren't about William Wallace, Robin Hood or Odysseus, but, instead, light saber battles, frozen men and forgotten fathers. In other words, we talked about our legend."[18] The action figures provided this generation with some of their earliest avatars, encouraging them to assume the role of a Jedi Knight or an intergalactic bounty hunter, enabling them to physically manipulate the characters to construct their own stories.

Not surprisingly, a significant number of filmmakers in their late teens and early twenties have turned toward those action figures as resources for their first production efforts. *Toy Wars* (2002) producers Aaron Halon and Jason VandenBerghe launched an ambitious plan to produce a shot-by-shot remake of *Star Wars: A New Hope*, cast entirely with action figures. These action-figure movies require constant resourcefulness on the part of the amateur filmmakers. Damon Wellner and Sebastian O'Brien, two self-proclaimed "action-figure nerds" from Cambridge, Massachusetts, formed Probot Productions with the goal of "making toys as alive as they seemed in childhood." The Probot website (www.probotproductions.com) offers this explanation of their production process:

> The first thing you need to know about Probot Productions is that we're broke. We spend all our $$$ on toys. This leaves a very small budget for special effects, so we literally have to work with what we can find in the garbage. . . . For sets we used a breadbox, a ventilation tube from a dryer, cardboard boxes, a discarded piece from a vending machine, and milk crates. Large Styrofoam pieces from stereo component boxes work very well to create spaceship-like environments![19]

No digital filmmaker has pushed the aesthetics of action-figure cinema as far as Evan Mather. Mather's films, such as *Godzilla versus Disco Lando*, *Kung Fu Kenobi's Big Adventure*, and *Quentin Tarantino's Star Wars*, represent a no-holds-barred romp through contemporary popular culture. The rock-'em, sock-'em action of *Kung Fu Kenobi's Big Adventure* takes place against the backdrop of settings sampled from the film, drawn by hand, or built from LEGO blocks, with the eclectic and evocative soundtrack borrowed from Neil Diamond, *Mission Impossible* (1996), *Pee-Wee's Big Adventure* (1985), and *A Charlie Brown Christmas* (1965). Disco Lando puts the moves on everyone from Admiral Ackbar to Jabba's blue-skinned dancing girl, and all of his pickup lines come from the soundtrack of *The Empire Strikes Back*. Mace Windu "gets medieval" on the Jedi Council, delivering Samuel L. Jackson's lines from *Pulp Fiction* (1994) before shooting up the place. The camera focuses on the bald head of a dying Darth Vader as he gasps, "Rosebud." Apart from the anarchic humor and rapid-fire pace, Mather's films stand out because of their visual sophistication. Mather's own frenetic style has become increasingly distinguished across the body of his works, constantly experimenting with different forms of animation, flashing or masked images, and dynamic camera movements.

Yet, if the action-figure filmmakers have developed an aesthetic based on their appropriation of materials from the mainstream media, then the mainstream media has been quick to imitate that aesthetic. Nickelodeon's short-lived *Action League Now!!!* (1994), for example, had a regular cast of characters consisting of mismatched dolls and mutilated action figures. In some cases, their faces had been melted or mangled through inappropriate play. One protagonist had no clothes. They came in various size scales, suggesting the collision of different narrative universes that characterizes children's action-figure play. MTV's *Celebrity Deathmatch* (1998) created its action figures using claymation, staging World Wrestling Federation–style bouts between various celebrities, some likely (Monica Lewinsky against Hillary Clinton), some simply bizarre (the rock star formerly known as Prince against Prince Charles).

Or consider the case of the Cartoon Network's *Robot Chicken* (a stop-motion animation series) produced by Seth Green (formerly of *Buffy the Vampire Slayer* and *Austin Powers*) and Matthew Senreich: think of it as a sketch-comedy series where all of the parts are played by action figures. The show spoofs popular culture, mixing and matching characters with the same reckless abandon as a kid playing on the floor with his favorite collectibles. In its rendition of MTV's *The Real World*, Superman, Aquaman, Batman, Wonder Woman, Cat Woman, the Hulk, and other superheroes share an apartment and deal with real-life issues, such as struggles for access to the bathroom or conflicts about who is going to do household chores. Or, in its take on *American Idol*, the contestants are zombies of dead rock stars, and the judges are breakfast-cereal icons—Frankenberry (as Randy), Booberry (as Paula), and Count Chocula (as Simon).

The series originated as part of a regular feature in *Toy Fare*, a niche magazine which targets action-figure collectors and model builders. Seth Green, a fan of the publication, asked the magazine's contributors to help him put together a special animated segment for Green's forthcoming appearance on *The Conan O'Brien Show*, which in turn led to an invitation to produce a series of web toons for Sony's short-lived but highly influential Screenblast, which in turn led to an invitation to produce a television series as part of the Cartoon Network's "Adult Swim" lineup. We can thus trace step by step how this concept moves from the fan subculture across a range of sites noted for cult media content.[20] News coverage of the series stresses Seth Green's own status as a toy collector and often describes the challenges faced by the program's "toy wrangler," who goes onto eBay or searches retro shops for the specific toys needed to cast segments, blurring the line between amateur and commercial media-making practices.[21]

The web represents a site of experimentation and innovation, where amateurs test the waters, developing new practices and themes and generating materials that may well attract cult followings on their own terms. The most commercially viable of those practices are then absorbed into the mainstream media, either directly through the hiring of new talent or the development of television, video, or big-screen works based on those materials, or indirectly, through a second-order imitation of the same aesthetic and thematic qualities. In return, the mainstream media materials may provide inspiration for subsequent amateur efforts, which push popular culture in new directions. In such a world, fan works can no longer be understood as simply derivative of mainstream materials but must be understood as themselves open to appropriation and reworking by the media industries.

"The 500-Pound Wookiee"

Fans take reassurance that Lucas and his cronies, at least sometimes, take a look at what fans have made and send them his blessing. In fact, part of the allure of participating in the official *Star Wars* fan cinema competition is the fact that Lucas personally selects the winner from finalists identified by AtomFilms' Chris Albrecht and vetted by staffers at LucasArts. There is no doubt that Lucas personally likes at least some form of fan creativity. As Albrecht explains, "Hats off to Lucas for recognizing that this is happening and giving the public a chance to participate in a universe they know and love. There's nothing else like this out there. No other producer has gone this far."[22] On other levels, the company—and perhaps Lucas himself—has wanted to control what fans produced and circulated. Jim Ward, vice president of marketing for Lucasfilm, told *New York Times* reporter Amy Harmon in 2002, "We've been very clear all along on where we draw the line. We love our fans. We want them to have fun. But if in fact somebody is using our characters to create a story unto itself, that's not in the spirit of what we think fandom is about. Fandom is about celebrating the story the way it is."[23] Lucas wants to be "celebrated" but not appropriated.

Lucas has opened up a space for fans to create and share what they create with others but only on his terms. The franchise has struggled with these issues from the 1970s to the present, desiring some zone of tolerance within which fans can operate while asserting some control over what happens to his story. In that history, there have been some periods when the company was highly tolerant and others when it was pretty aggressive about trying to close off all or some forms of fan fiction. At the same time, the different divisions of the same company have developed different approaches to dealing with fans: the games division has thought of fans in ways consistent with how other game companies think about fans (and is probably on the more permissive end of the spectrum), and the film division has tended to think like a motion-picture company and has been a bit less comfortable with fan participation. I make this point not to say LucasArts is bad to fans—in many ways, the company seems more forward thinking and responsive to the fan community than most Hollywood companies—but to illustrate the ways the media industry is trying to figure out its response to fan creativity.

In the beginning, Lucasfilm actively encouraged fan fiction, establishing a no-fee licensing bureau in 1977 that would review material and offer advice about potential copyright infringement.[24] By the early 1980s, these arrangements broke down, allegedly because Lucas had stumbled onto some examples of fan erotica that shocked his sensibilities. By 1981, Lucasfilm was issuing warnings to fans who published zines containing sexually explicit stories, while implicitly giving permission to publish nonerotic stories about the characters as long as they were not sold for profit: "Since all of the *Star Wars* saga is PG-rated, any story those publishers print should also be PG. Lucasfilm does not produce any X-rated *Star Wars* episodes, so why should we be placed in a light where people think we do?"[25] Most fan erotica was pushed underground by this policy, though it continued to circulate informally. The issue resurfaced in the 1990s: fan fiction of every variety thrived on the "electronic frontier." One website, for example, provided regularly updated links to fan and fan-fiction websites for more than 153 films, books, and television shows, ranging from *Airwolf* (1984) to *Zorro* (1975).[26] *Star Wars* zine editors poked their heads above ground, cautiously testing the waters. Jeanne Cole, a spokesperson for Lucasfilm, explained, "What can you do? How can you control it? As we look at it, we appreciate the fans, and what would we do without them? If we anger them, what's the point?"[27]

Media scholar Will Brooker cites a 1996 corporate notice that explains, "Since the internet is growing so fast, we are in the process of developing guidelines for how we can enhance the ability of *Star Wars* fans to communicate with each other without infringing on *Star Wars* copyrights and trademarks."[28] The early lawless days of the Internet were giving way to a period of heightened corporate scrutiny and expanding control. Even during what might be seen as a "honeymoon" period, some fans felt that Lucasfilm was acting like a "500-pound Wookiee," throwing its weight around and making threatening noises.[29]

Lucasfilm's perspective seemed relatively enlightened, even welcoming, when compared with how other media producers responded to their fans. In the late 1990s, Viacom experimented with a strong-arm approach to fan culture—starting in Australia. A representative of the corporation called together leaders of fan clubs from across the country and laid down new guidelines for their activities.[30] These guidelines prohibited the showing of series episodes at club meetings unless those episodes had previously been made commercially available in that market. (This policy has serious consequences for Australian fans because they often get series episodes a year or two after they air in the United States, and the underground circulation and exhibition of video tapes had enabled them to participate actively in online discussions.) Similarly, Viacom cracked down on the publication and distribution of fanzines and prohibited the use of *Star Trek* (1966) trademarked names in convention publicity. Their explicitly stated goal was to push fans toward participation in a corporately controlled fan club.

In 2000, Lucasfilm offered *Star Wars* fans free web space (www.starwars. com) and unique content for their sites, but only under the condition that whatever they created would become the studio's intellectual property. As the official notice launching this new "Homestead" explained, "To encourage the on-going excitement, creativity, and interaction of our dedicated fans in the online *Star Wars* community, Lucas Online (http://www.lucasfilm.com/divi-sions/online/) is pleased to offer for the first time an official home for fans to celebrate their love of *Star Wars* on the World Wide Web."[31] Historically, fan fiction had proven to be a point of entry into commercial publication for at least some amateurs, who were able to sell their novels to the professional book series centering on the various franchises. If Lucasfilm Ltd. claimed to own such rights, they could publish them without compensation, and they could also remove them without permission or warning.

Elizabeth Durack was one of the more outspoken leaders of a campaign urging her fellow *Star Wars* fans not to participate in these new arrangements: "That's the genius of Lucasfilm's offering fans web space—it lets them both look amazingly generous *and* be even more controlling than before. . . . Lucasfilm doesn't hate fans, and they don't hate fan websites. They can indeed see how they benefit from the free publicity they represent—and who doesn't like being adored? This move underscores that as much as anything. But they're also scared, and that makes them hurt the people who love them."[32] Durack argued that fan fiction does indeed pay respect to Lucas as the creator of *Star Wars*, yet the fans also wanted to hold on to their right to participate in the production and circulation of the *Star Wars* saga that had become so much a part of their lives: "It has been observed by many writers that *Star Wars* (based purposely on the recurring themes of mythology by creator George Lucas) and other popular media creations take the place in modern America that culture myths like those of the Greeks or Native

Americans did for earlier peoples. Holding modern myths hostage by way of corporate legal wrangling seems somehow contrary to nature."

Today, relations between LucasArts and the fan-fiction community have thawed somewhat. Though I haven't been able to find any official statement signaling a shift in policy, *Star Wars* fan fiction is all over the web, including on several of the most visible and mainstream fan sites. The webmasters of those sites say that they deal with the official production company all the time on a range of different matters, but they have never been asked to remove what once might have been read as infringing materials. Yet what Lucas giveth, he can also taketh away. Many fan writers have told me that they remain nervous about how the "Powers That Be" are apt to respond to particularly controversial stories.

Lucas and his movie-brat cronies clearly identified more closely with the young digital filmmakers who were making "calling card" movies to try to break into the film industry than they did with female fan writers sharing their erotic fantasies. By the end of the 1990s, however, Lucas's tolerance of fan filmmaking had given way to a similar strategy of incorporation and containment. In November 2000, Lucasfilm designated the commercial digital-cinema site AtomFilms.com as the official host for *Star Wars* fan films. The site would provide a library of official sound effects and run periodic contests to recognize outstanding amateur accomplishment. In return, participating filmmakers would agree to certain constraints on content: "Films must parody the existing *Star Wars* universe, or be a documentary of the *Star Wars* fan experience. No 'fan fiction'—which attempts to expand on the *Star Wars* universe—will be accepted. Films must not make use of copyrighted *Star Wars* music or video, but may use action figures and the audio clips provided in the production kit section of this site. Films must not make unauthorized use of copyrighted property from any other film, song, or composition."[33] Here, we see the copyright regimes of mass culture being applied to the folk culture process.

A work like *Star Wars: Revelations* would be prohibited from entering the official *Star Wars* competition because it sets its own original dramatic story in the interstices between the third and fourth *Star Wars* films and thus constitutes "fan fiction." Albrecht, the man who oversees the competition, offered several explanations for the prohibition. For one thing, Lucas saw himself and his company as being at risk for being sued for plagiarism if he allowed himself to come into contact with fan-produced materials that mimicked the dramatic structure of the film franchise should anything in any official *Star Wars* material make use of similar characters or situations.

For another, Albrecht suggested, there was a growing risk of consumer con-fusion about what constituted an official *Star Wars* product. Speaking about *Revelations*, Albrecht suggested, "Up until the moment the actors spoke, you wouldn't be able to tell whether that was a real *Star Wars* film or a fan creation because the special effects are so good. . . . As the tools get better, there is bound to be confusion in the marketplace." In any case, Lucasfilm would have had much less legal standing in shutting down parody, which enjoys broad protections under current case law, or documentaries about the phenomenon itself, which would fall clearly into the category of journalistic and critical commentary. Lucasfilm was, in effect, tolerating what it legally must accept in return for shutting down what it might otherwise be unable to control.

These rules are anything but gender neutral: though the gender lines are starting to blur in recent years, the overwhelming majority of fan parody is produced by men, while "fan fiction" is almost entirely produced by women. In the female fan community, fans have long produced "song videos" that are edited together from found footage drawn from film or television shows and set to pop music. These fan vids often function as a form of fan fiction to draw out aspects of the emotional lives of the characters or otherwise get inside their heads. They sometimes explore underdeveloped subtexts of the original film, offer original interpretations of the story, or suggest plotlines that go beyond the work itself. The emotional tone of these works could not be more different from the tone of the parodies featured in the official contests—films such as *Sith Apprentice*, where the Emperor takes some would-be stormtroopers back to the board room; *Anakin Dynamite*, where a young Jedi must confront "idiots" much like his counterpart in the cult success *Napoleon Dynamite* (2004); or *Intergalactic Idol* (2003), where audi-ences get to decide which contestant really has the force. By contrast, Diane Williams's *Come What May* (2001), a typical song vid, uses images from *The Phantom Menace* to explore the relationship between Obi-Wan Kenobi and his mentor, Qui-Gon Jinn. The images show the passionate friendship between the two men and culminate in the repeated images of Obi-Wan cra-dling the crumbled body of his murdered comrade following his battle with Darth Maul. The images are accompanied by the song "Come What May," taken from the soundtrack of Baz Luhrmann's *Moulin Rouge!* (2001) and per-formed by Ewan McGregor, the actor who also plays the part of Obi-Wan Kenobi in *Phantom Menace*.

Whether AtomFilms would define such a work to be a parody would be a matter of interpretation: while playful at places, it lacks the broad comedy of

most of the male-produced *Star Wars* movies, involves a much closer identification with the characters, and hints at aspects of their relationship that
have not explicitly been represented on screen. *Come What May* would be
read by most fans as falling within the slash subgenre, constructing erotic
relations between same-sex characters, and would be read melodramatically
rather than satirically. Of course, from a legal standpoint, *Come What May*
may represent parody, which doesn't require that the work be comical but
simply that it be appropriate and transform the original for the purposes of
critical commentary. It would be hard to argue that a video that depicts Obi-
Wan and Qui-Gon as lovers does not transform the original in a way that
expands its potential meanings. Most likely, this and other female-produced
song videos would be regarded as fan fiction; *Come What May* would also
run afoul of AtomFilms' rules against appropriating content from the films
or from other media properties.

These rules create a two-tier system: some works can be rendered more
public because they conform to what the rights holder sees as an acceptable
appropriation of their intellectual property, while others remain hidden from
view (or at least distributed through less official channels). In this case, these
works have been so cut off from public visibility that when I ask *Star Wars*
digital filmmakers about the invisibility of these mostly female-produced
works, most of them have no idea that women were even making *Star Wars*
movies.

Anthropologist and marketing consultant Grant McCracken has expressed
some skepticism about the parallels fans draw between their grassroots cultural production and traditional folk culture: "Ancient heroes did not belong
to everyone, they did not serve everyone, they were not for everyone to do
with what they would. These commons were never very common."[34] For the
record, my claims here are altogether more particularized than the sweeping
analogies to Greek myths that provoked McCracken's ire. He is almost certainly right that who could tell those stories, under what circumstances, and
for what purposes reflected hierarchies operating within classical culture. My
analogy, on the other hand, refers to a specific moment in the emergence
of American popular culture, when songs often circulated well beyond their
points of origin, lost any acknowledgment of their original authorship, were
repurposed and reused to serve a range of different interests, and were very
much part of the texture of everyday life for a wide array of nonprofessional
participants. This is how folk culture operated in an emergent democracy.

I don't want to turn back the clock to some mythic golden age. Rather, I
want us to recognize the challenges posed by the coexistence of these two

kinds of cultural logic. The kinds of production practices we are discussing here were a normal part of American life over this period. They are simply more visible now because of the shift in distribution channels for amateur cultural productions. If the corporate media couldn't crush this vernacular culture during the age when mass media power went largely unchallenged, it is hard to believe that legal threats are going to be an adequate response to a moment when new digital tools and new networks of distribution have expanded the power of ordinary people to participate in their culture. Having felt that power, fans and other subcultural groups are not going to return to docility and invisibility. They will go farther underground *if they have to*—they've been there before—but they aren't going to stop creating.

This is where McCracken's argument rejoins my own. McCracken argues that there is ultimately no schism between the public interest in expanding opportunities for grassroots creativity and the corporate interest in protecting its intellectual property: "Corporations will allow the public to participate in the construction and representation of its creations or they will, eventually, compromise the commercial value of their properties. The new consumer will help create value or they will refuse it. . . . Corporations have a right to keep copyright but they have an interest in releasing it. The economics of scarcity may dictate the first. The economics of plenitude dictate the second."[35] The expanding range of media options, what McCracken calls the "economics of plenitude," will push companies to open more space for grassroots participation and affiliation—starting perhaps with niche companies and fringe audiences but eventually moving toward the commercial and cultural mainstream. McCracken argues that those companies that loosen their copyright control will attract the most active and committed consumers, and those that ruthlessly set limits will find themselves with a dwindling share of the media marketplace.[36] Of course, this model depends on fans and audience members acting collectively in their own interest against companies that may tempt them with entertainment that is otherwise tailored to their needs. The production companies are centralized and can act in a unified manner; fans are decentralized and have no ability to ensure conformity within their rights. And so far, the media companies have shown a remarkable willingness to antagonize their consumers by taking legal actions against them in the face of all economic rationality. This is going to be an uphill fight under the best of circumstances. The most likely way for it to come about, however, may be to create some successes that demonstrate the economic value of engaging the participatory audience.

Design Your Own Galaxy

Adopting a collaborationist logic, the creators of massively multiplayer online role-playing games (MMORPGs) have already built a more open-ended and collaborative relationship with their consumer base. Game designers acknowledge that their craft has less to do with prestructured stories than with creating the preconditions for spontaneous community activities. Raph Koster, the man LucasArts placed in charge of developing *Star Wars Galaxies*, built his professional reputation as one of the prime architects of *Ultima Online* (1997). He was the author of an important statement of players' rights before he entered the games industry, and he has developed a strong design philosophy focused on empowering players to shape their own experiences and build their own communities. Asked to describe the nature of the MMORPG, Koster famously explained, "It's not just a game. It's a service, it's a world, it's a community."[37] Koster also refers to managing an online community, whether a noncommercial MUD or a commercial MMORPG, as an act of governance: "Just like it is not a good idea for a government to make radical legal changes without a period of public comment, it is often not wise for an operator of an online world to do the same."[38]

Players, he argues, must feel a sense of "ownership" over the imaginary world if they are going to put in the time and effort needed to make it come alive for themselves and for other players. Koster argues, "You can't possibly mandate a fictionally involving universe with thousands of other people. The best you can hope for is a world that is vibrant enough that people act in manners consistent with the fictional tenets."[39] For players to participate, they must feel that what they bring to the game makes a difference, not only in terms of their own experiences but also the experiences of other players. Writing about the challenges of meeting community expectations on *Ultima Online*, Koster explains, "They want to shape their space, and leave a lasting mark. You must provide some means for them to do so."[40] Richard Bartle, another game designer and theorist, agrees: "Self expression is another way to promote immersion. By giving players free-form ways to communicate themselves, designers can draw them more deeply into the world—they feel more of a part of it."[41]

Koster is known as a strong advocate of the idea of giving players room to express themselves within the game world:

> Making things of any sort does generally require training. It is rare in any medium that the naïf succeeds in making something really awesome or

popular. By and large it is people who have taught themselves the craft and are making conscious choices. But I absolutely favor empowering people to engage in these acts of creation, because not only does talent bubble up but also economies of scale apply. If you get a large enough sample size, you will eventually create something good.

As Koster turned his attention to developing *Star Wars Galaxies*, he realized that he was working with a franchise known in all of its details by hardcore fans who had grown up playing these characters with action figures or in their backyard and who wanted to see those same fantasies rendered in the digital realm. In an open letter to the *Star Wars* fan community, Koster described what he hoped to bring to the project:

> *Star Wars* is a universe beloved by many. And I think many of you are like me. You want to be there. You want to feel what it is like. Even before we think about skill trees and about Jedi advancement, before we consider the stats on a weapon or the distance to Mos Eisley and where you have to go to pick up power converters—you want to just *be* there. Inhale the sharp air off the desert. Watch a few Jawas haggle over a droid. Feel the sun beat down on a body that isn't your own, in a world that is strange to you. You don't want to know about the stagecraft in those first few moments. You want to feel like you are offered a passport to a universe of limitless possibility. . . . My job is to try to capture that magic for you, so you have that experience."[42]

Satisfying fan interests in the franchise proved challenging. Koster told me, "There's no denying it—the fans know *Star Wars* better than the developers do. They live and breathe it. They know it in an intimate way. On the other hand, with something as large and broad as the *Star Wars* universe, there's ample scope for divergent opinions about things. These are the things that lead to religious wars among fans, and all of a sudden you have to take a side because you are going to be establishing how it works in this game."

To ensure that fans bought into his version of the *Star Wars* universe, Koster essentially treated the fan community as his client team, posting regular reports on the web about many different elements of the game's design, creating an online forum where potential players could respond and make suggestions, ensuring that his staff regularly monitored the online discussion and posted back their own reactions to the community's recommendations. By comparison, the production of a *Star Wars* film is shrouded by secrecy.

Koster compares what he did with the test-screening or focus-group process many Hollywood films endure, but the difference is that much of that testing goes on behind closed doors, among select groups of consumers, and is not open to participation by anyone who wants to join the conversation. It is hard to imagine Lucas setting up a forum site to preview plot twists and character designs with his audience. If he had done so, he would never have included Jar Jar Binks or devoted so much screen time to the childhood and adolescence of Anakin Skywalker, decisions that alienated his core audience. Koster wanted *Star Wars* fans to feel that they had, in effect, designed their own galaxy.

Games scholars Kurt Squire and Constance Steinkuehler have studied the interactions between Koster and his fan community. Koster allowed fans to act as "content generators creating quests, missions, and social relationships that constitute the *Star Wars* world," but more importantly, fan feedback "set the tone" for the *Star Wars* culture:

> These players would establish community norms for civility and role playing, giving the designers an opportunity to effectively *create* the seeds of the *Star Wars Galaxies* world months before the game ever hit the shelves. . . . The game that the designers promised and the community expected was largely player-driven. The in-game economy would consist of items (e.g., clothing, armor, houses, weapons) created by players with its prices also set by players through auctions and player-run shops. Cities and towns would be designed by players, and cities' mayors and council leaders would devise missions and quests for other players. The Galactic Civil War (the struggle between rebels and imperials) would frame the game play, but players would create their own missions as they enacted the *Star Wars* saga. In short, the system was to be driven by *player interaction*, with the world being created less by designers and more by players themselves.[43]

Players can adopt the identities of many different alien races, from Jawas to Wookiees, represented in the *Star Wars* universe, assume many different professional classes—from pod racers to bounty hunters—and play out many different individual and shared fantasies. What they cannot do is adopt the identity of any of the primary characters of the *Star Wars* movies, and they have to earn the status of Jedi Knight by completing a series of different ingame missions. Otherwise, the fiction of the game world would break down as thousands of Han Solos tried to avoid capture by thousands of Boba Fetts. For the world to feel coherent, players had to give up their childhood fantasies of being the star and instead become a bit player, interacting with countless other bit players, within a mutually constructed fantasy. What made it possible for such negotiations and collaborations to occur was the fact that they shared a common background in the already well-established *Star Wars* mythology. As Squire and Steinkuehler note, "Designers cannot require Jedis to behave consistently within the *Star Wars* universe, but they *can* design game structures (such as bounties) that elicit Jedi-like behavior (such as placing a high reward on capturing a Jedi which might produce covert action on the part of Jedis)."[44]

Coming full circle, a growing number of gamers are using the sets, props, and characters generated for the *Star Wars Galaxies* game as resources to produce their own fan films. In some cases, they are using them to do their own dramatic reenactments of scenes from the movie or to create, gasp, their own "fan fiction." Perhaps the most intriguing new form of fan cinema to emerge from the game world is the so-called Cantina Crawl.[45] In the spirit of the cantina sequence in the original *Star Wars* feature film, the game created a class of characters whose function in the game world is to entertain the other players. They were given special moves that allow them to dance and writhe erotically if the players hit complex combinations of keys. Teams of more than three-dozen dancers and musicians plan, rehearse, and execute elaborate synchronized musical numbers: for example, The Gypsies' *Christmas Crawl 1* featured such numbers as "Santa Claus Is Coming to Town" and "Have Yourself a Merry Little Christmas"; blue-skinned and tentacle-haired dance girls shake their bootie, lizard-like aliens in Santa caps play the sax, and guys with gills do boy-band moves while twinkly snowflakes fall all around them (fig. 15.3). Imagine what *Star Wars* would have looked like if it had been directed by Lawrence Welk! Whatever aesthetic abuse is taking place here, one has to admire the technical accomplishment and social coordination that goes into producing these films. Once you put creative tools in the hands of everyday people, there's no telling what they are going to make with them—and that's a large part of the fun.

Xavier, one of the gamers involved in producing the Cantina Crawl videos, would turn the form against the production company, creating a series of videos protesting corporate decisions which he felt undermined his engagement with the game. Ultimately, Xavier produced a farewell video announcing the mass departure of many loyal fans. The fan-friendly policies Koster created had eroded over time, leading to increased player frustration and distrust. Some casual players felt the game was too dependent on player-generated content, while the more creative players felt that upgrades actually restricted their ability to express themselves and marginalized the

Fig. 15.3. Each character in this musical number from
The Gypsies' *Christmas Crawl 1*, made using the *Star
Wars Galaxies* game, is controlled by a separate player.

Entertainer class from the overall experience. At the same time, the game
failed to meet the company's own revenue expectations, especially in the face
of competition from the enormously successful *World of Warcraft*.

In December 2005, the company announced plans to radically revamp
the game's rules and content, a decision that resulted in massive defections
without bringing in many new customers. A statement made by Nancy
MacIntyre, the game's senior director at LucasArts, to the *New York Times*
illustrates the huge shift in thinking from Koster's original philosophy to this
"retooled" franchise:

> We really just needed to make the game a lot more accessible to a much
> broader player base. There was lots of reading, much too much, in the
> game. There was a lot of wandering around learning about different abili-
> ties. We really needed to give people the experience of being Han Solo or
> Luke Skywalker rather than being Uncle Owen, the moisture farmer. We
> wanted more instant gratification: kill, get treasure, repeat. We needed to
> give people more of an opportunity to be a part of what they have seen in
> the movies rather than something they had created themselves.[46]

Over a concise few sentences, MacIntyre had stressed the need to simplify
the content, had indicated plans to recenter the game around central characters from the films rather than a more diverse range of protagonists, had
dismissed the creative contributions of fans, and had suggested that *Star Wars
Galaxies* would be returning to more conventional game mechanics. This
"retooling" was the kind of shift in policy without player input that Koster had
warned might prove fatal to these efforts. Thanks to the social networks that

fans have constructed around the game, soon every gamer on the planet knew that MacIntyre had called her players idiots in the *New York Times*, and many of them departed for other virtual worlds which had more respect for their participation—helping, for example, to fuel the early growth of *Second Life*.

Where Do We Go from Here?

It is too soon to tell whether these experiments in consumer-generated content will have an influence on the mass media companies. In the end, it depends on how seriously, if at all, we should take their rhetoric about enfranchising and empowering consumers as a means of building strong brand loyalties. For the moment, the evidence is contradictory: for every franchise which has reached out to court its fan base, there are others that have fired out cease-and-desist letters. As we confront the intersection between corporate and grassroots modes of convergence, we shouldn't be surprised that neither producers nor consumers are certain what rules should govern their interactions, yet both sides seem determined to hold the other accountable for their choices. The difference is that the fan community must negotiate from a position of relative powerlessness and must rely solely on its collective moral authority, while the corporations, for the moment, act as if they had the force of law on their side.

Ultimately, the prohibitionist position is not going to be effective on anything other than the most local level unless the media companies can win back popular consent; whatever lines they draw are going to have to respect the growing public consensus about what constitutes fair use of media content and must allow the public to participate meaningfully in their own culture. To achieve this balance, the studios are going to have to accept (and actively promote) some basic distinctions: between commercial competition and amateur appropriation, between for-profit use and the barter economy of the web, between creative repurposing and piracy.

Each of these concessions will be hard for the studios to swallow but necessary if they are going to exert sufficient moral authority to rein in the kinds of piracy that threaten their economic livelihood. On bad days, I don't believe the studios will voluntarily give up their stranglehold on intellectual property. What gives me some hope, however, is the degree to which a collaborationist approach is beginning to gain some toehold within the media industries. These experiments suggest that media producers can garner greater loyalty and more compliance to legitimate concerns if they court the allegiance of fans; the best way to do this turns out to be giving them some stake in the survival of the franchise, ensuring that the provided content more fully reflects their interests, creating a space where they can make their own creative contributions, and recognizing the best work that emerges. In a world of ever-expanding media options, there is going to be a struggle for viewers the likes of which corporate media has never seen before. Many of the smartest folks in the media industry know this: some are trembling, and others are scrambling to renegotiate their relationships with consumers. In the end, the media producers need fans just as much as fans need them.

NOTES

1. AtomFilms, "Internet Users Are Makin' Wookiee!," press release, April 23, 1999.

2. Chris Albrecht, personal interview, July 2005.

3. For more discussion of fans and new media, see Henry Jenkins, "The Poachers and the Stormtroopers: Cultural Convergence in the Digital Age," in Philippe Le Guern, ed., *Les cultes mediatiques: Culture fan et oeuvres cultes* (Rennes: Presses Universitaires de Rennes, 2002).

4. Paul Clinton, "Filmmakers Score with *Lucas in Love*," CNN.com, June 24, 1999, http://www.cnn.com/SHOWBIZ/Movies/9906/24/movies.lucas.love.

5. Josh Wolk, "Troop Dreams," *Entertainment Weekly*, March 20, 1998, pp. 8–9.

6. Manuel Castells, on p. 201 of *The Internet Galaxy: Reflections on the Internet, Business, and Society* (Oxford: Oxford University Press, 2003), defines "interactivity" as "the ability of the user to manipulate and affect his experience of media directly and to communicate with others through media." I prefer to separate out the two parts of this definition—so that "interactivity" refers to the direct manipulation of media within the technology, and "participation" refers to the social and cultural interactions that occur around media.

7. Grant McCracken, "The Disney TM Danger," in *Plenitude* (self-published, 1998), p. 5.

8. Lawrence Lessig, "Keynote from OSCON 2002," August 15, 2002, accessed at http://www.oreillynet.com/pub/a/policy/2002/08/15/lessig.html.

9. Clinton, "Filmmakers Score with *Lucas in Love*."

10. The site is described here as it existed in 2000, at the time this essay was first written. As of 2004, Mather continued to be productive, and the site hosted more than forty-eight digital films. Much of his recent work has taken him far afield from *Star Wars*, showing how his early fan work has paved the way for a much more varied career.

11. "When Senators Attack IV" (Ryan Mannion and Daniel Hawley), TheForce.net, http://www.theforce.net/latestnews/story/tfn_theater_when_senators_attack_iv_77653.asp (accessed July 1, 2011).

12. Patricia R. Zimmermann, *Reel Families: A Social History of Amateur Film* (Bloomington: Indiana University Press, 1995), p. 157.

13. Clinton, "Filmmakers Score with *Lucas in Love*."

14. "A Word from Shane Felux," TheForce.Net, http://www.theforce.net/fanfilms/comingsoon/revelations/director.asp; Clive Thompson, "May the Force Be with You, and You, and You . . . : Why Fans Make Better *Star Wars* Movies Than George Lucas," *Slate*, April 29, 2005, http://slate.msn.com/id/2117760/.

15. Kevin Kelly and Paula Parisi, "Beyond Star Wars," *Wired*, February 1997, http://www.wired.com/wired/archive/5.02/fflucas.html (accessed July 1, 2011).

16. Clay Kronke, Director's Note, *The New World*, TheForce.net, February 2000, http://web.archive.org/web/20000816150019/http://www.theforce.net/theater/shortfilms/new-world/director_newworld.shtml (accessed July 1, 2011).

17. *Duel* (Mark Thomas and Dave Macomber), no longer online.

18. Mark Magee, "Every Generation Has a Legend," Shift.com, June 15, 2005, http://web.archive.org/web/20050615082451/http://www.shift.com/content/web/259/1.html (accessed July 1, 2011).

19. Probot Productions, no longer online.

20. Coury Turczyn, "Ten Minutes with the *Robot Chicken* Guys," G4, February 17, 2005, http://www.g4tv.com/screensavers/features/51086/Ten_Minutes_with_the_Robot_Chicken_Guys.html. See also Henry Jenkins, "Ode to *Robot Chicken*," *Confessions of an Aca-Fan* (blog), June 20, 2006, http://www.henryjenkins.org/2006/06/ode_to_robot_chicken.html.

21. Henry Jenkins, "So What Happened to *Star Wars Galaxies?*," *Confessions of an Aca-Fan* (blog), July 21, 2006, http://www.henryjenkins.org/2006/07/so_what_happened_to_star_wars.html.

22. Chris Albrecht, personal interview, July 2005.

23. Amy Harmon, "*Star Wars* Fan Films Come Tumbling Back to Earth," *New York Times*, April 28, 2002.

24. Will Brooker, *Using the Force: Creativity, Community and Star Wars Fans* (New York: Continuum, 2002), pp. 164–171.

25. For a fuller discussion, see Henry Jenkins, *Textual Poachers: Television Fans and Participatory Culture* (New York: Routledge, 1992), pp. 30–32.

26. Fan Fiction on the Net, http://members.aol.com:80/ksnicholas/fanfic/index.html.

27. Janelle Brown, "Fan Fiction on the Line," Wired.com, August 11, 1997, http://web.archive.org/web/19991117055842/http://www.wired.com/news/news/wiredview/story/5934.html (accessed July 1, 2011).

28. Brooker, *Using the Force*, p. 167.

29. David R. Phillips, "The 500-Pound Wookiee," Echo Station, August 1, 1999, http://www.echostation.com/features/lfl_wookiee.htm.

30. Richard Jinman, "Star Wars," *Australian Magazine*, June 17, 1995, pp. 30–39.

31. Homestead statement, official *Star Wars* home page, as quoted by Elizabeth Durack, "fans.starwars.con," Echo Station, March 12, 2000, http://www.echostation.com/editorials/confans.htm.

32. Durack, "fans.starwars.con."

33. AtomFilms, "The Official *Star Wars* Fan Film Awards," no longer online.

34. McCracken, *Plenitude*, p. 84.

35. Ibid., p. 85.

36. For an interesting essay that contrasts Peter Jackson's efforts to court *Lord of the Rings* fans with the more commercially oriented approach to fandom surrounding *Star Wars*, see Elana Shefrin, "*Lord of the Rings*, *Star Wars*, and Participatory Fandom: Mapping New Congruencies between the Internet and Media Entertainment Culture," *Critical Studies in Media Communication*, September 2004, pp. 261–281.

37. Raph Koster, "CGDC Presentation: The Rules of Online World Design," 1999, http://www.raphkoster.com/gaming/gdc.html.

38. Unless otherwise noted, quotations from Raph Koster come from a personal interview with the author conducted in October 2004.

39. Kurt Squire, "Interview with Raph Koster," *Joystick101*, November 25, 2000, http://www.raphkoster.com/gaming/joystick101.html.

40. Koster, "CGDC Presentation."

41. Richard A. Bartle, *Designing Virtual Worlds* (Indianapolis: New Riders, 2004), p. 244.

42. Raph Koster, "Letter to the Community," January 8, 2001, http://www.raphkoster.com/gaming/swgteamcomment.shtml.

43. Kurt Squire and Constance Steinkuehler, "The Genesis of 'Cyberculture': The Case of *Star Wars Galaxies*," in Donna Gibbs and Kerri-Lee Krause, eds., *Cyberlines: Languages and Cultures of the Internet* (Albert Park, Australia: James Nicholas, 2000). See also Kurt Squire, "*Star Wars Galaxies*: A Case Study in Participatory Design," Joystick101, July 20, 2001, http://web.archive.org/web/20020201194951/http://www.joystick101.org/?op=display story&sid=2001/7/14/18208/3248 (accessed July 1, 2011).

44. Squire and Steinkuehler, "The Genesis of 'Cyberculture.'" For another interesting account of fan creativity within *Star Wars Galaxies*, see Douglas Thomas, "Before the Jump to Lightspeed: Negotiating Permanence and Change in *Star Wars Galaxies*," presented at the Creative Gamers Conference, University of Tampiere, Tampiere, Finland, January 2005.

45. I am indebted to Doug Thomas for calling this phenomenon to my attention. Thomas writes about cantina musicals and other forms of grassroots creativity in "Before the Jump to Lightspeed."

46. Seth Schiesel, "For Online Star Wars Game, It's Revenge of the Fans," *New York Times*, December 10, 2005.

16

Gin, Television, and Social Surplus

CLAY SHIRKY

I was recently reminded of something I read in college, way back in the last century, by a British historian who argued that the critical technology for the early phase of the Industrial Revolution was gin. The transformation from rural to urban life was so sudden, and so wrenching, that the only thing society could do to cope was to drink itself into a stupor for a generation. The stories from that era are amazing: there were gin pushcarts working their way through the streets of London. And it wasn't until society woke up from that collective bender that we actually started to create the institutional structures that we associate with the Industrial Revolution today. Things such as public libraries and museums, increasingly broad education for children, elected leaders didn't happen until the presence all of those people together stopped being perceived as a crisis and started seeming like an asset. It wasn't until people started thinking of this as a vast civic surplus that they could design for, rather than just dissipate, that we started to get what we now think of as an industrial society.

If I had to pick the critical technology for the twentieth century, the bit of social lubricant without which the wheels would have come off the whole enterprise, I would say it was the sitcom. Starting with the Second World War, a whole series of things happened, including rising GDP per capita, rising educational attainment, rising life expectancy, and, critically, a rising number of people who were working five-day work weeks. For the first time, society forced an enormous number of its citizens to manage something they had never had to manage before—free time. What did we do with that free time? Well, mostly we spent it watching TV.

We did that for decades. We watched *I Love Lucy*. We watched *Gilligan's Island*. We watch *Malcolm in the Middle*. We watch *Desperate Housewives*. *Desperate Housewives* essentially functioned as a kind of cognitive heat sink, dissipating thinking that might otherwise have built up and caused society to overheat. And it's only now, as we're waking up from that collective bender, that we're starting to see the cognitive surplus as an asset rather than as a crisis. We're seeing things being designed to take advantage of that surplus, to deploy it in ways more engaging than just having a TV in everybody's basement.

This hit me in a conversation I had about two months ago. I was being interviewed by a TV producer to see whether I should be on their show, and she asked me, "What are you seeing out there that's interesting?" I started telling her about the Wikipedia article on Pluto. You may remember that Pluto got kicked out of the planet club a couple of years ago, so all of a sudden there was a lot of activity on Wikipedia. The talk pages light up, people are editing the article like mad, and the whole community is in a ruckus, asking, "How should we characterize this change in Pluto's status?" A little bit at a time they move the article—fighting offstage all the while—from stating that "Pluto is the ninth planet" to "Pluto is an odd-shaped rock with an odd-shaped orbit at the edge of the solar system."[1]

So I tell her all this stuff, and I think, "Okay, we're going to have a conversation about authority or social construction or whatever." That wasn't her question. She heard this story, and she shook her head and said, "Where do people find the time?" That was her question. And I just kind of snapped. And I said, "No one who works in TV gets to ask that question. You know where the time comes from. It comes from the cognitive surplus you've been masking for fifty years." How big is that surplus? If you take Wikipedia as a kind of unit, all of Wikipedia, the whole project—every page, every edit, every talk page, every line of code, in every language that Wikipedia exists in—that represents something like the cumulation of one hundred million hours of human thought. I worked this out with Martin Wattenberg at IBM; it's a back-of-the-envelope calculation, but it's the right order of magnitude, about one hundred million hours of thought.

And television watching? Two hundred billion hours, in the United States alone, every year. Put another way, now that we have a unit, that's two thousand Wikipedia projects a year spent watching television. Or put still another way, in the United States, we spend one hundred million hours every weekend just watching the ads. This is a pretty big surplus. People who ask, "Where do they find the time?" when they look at things like Wikipedia don't understand how tiny that entire project is, as a carve-out of this collective asset that's finally being dragged into what Tim O'Reilly calls an architecture of participation.[2]

Now, the interesting thing about this kind of surplus is that society doesn't know what to do with it at first—hence the gin, hence the sitcoms. If people knew what to do with a surplus with reference to the existing social institutions, then it wouldn't be a surplus, would it? It's precisely when no one has any idea how to deploy something that people have to start experimenting with it, in order for the surplus to get integrated, and the course of that integration can transform society.

The early phase for taking advantage of this cognitive surplus, the phase I think we're still in, is all special cases. The physics of participation is much more like the physics of weather than it is like the physics of gravity. We know all the forces that combine to make these kinds of things work: there's an interesting community over here, there's an interesting sharing model over there, those people are collaborating on open-source software. But despite knowing the inputs, we can't predict the outputs yet because there's so much complexity.

The way you explore complex ecosystems is you just try lots and lots and lots of things, and you hope that everybody who fails, fails informatively so that you can at least find a skull on a pikestaff near where you're going. That's the phase we're in now.

I will just pick one small example, one I'm in love with. A couple of weeks ago one of my students at New York University's Interactive Telecommunications Program forwarded me a project started by a professor in Brazil, in Fortaleza, named Vasco Furtado. It's a Wiki map for crime in Brazil.[3] If there's an assault, burglary, mugging, robbery, rape, or murder, you can go and put a push-pin on a Google map; you can characterize the assault, and you start to see a map of where these crimes are occurring.

This already exists as tacit information. Anybody who knows a town has some sense of this street knowledge: "Don't go there. That street corner is dangerous. Don't go in this neighborhood. Be careful there after dark." It's something society knows without society really knowing it, which is to say there's no public source where you can take advantage of it. And if the cops have that information, they are certainly not sharing. In fact, one of the things Furtado says in starting the Wiki crime map is, "This information may or may not exist someplace in society, but it's actually easier for me to try to rebuild it from scratch than to try and get it from the authorities who might have it now."

Maybe this will succeed or maybe it will fail. The normal case of social software is still failure; most of these experiments don't pan out. But the ones that do are quite incredible, and I hope that this one succeeds. Even if it doesn't, it's illustrated the point already, which is that someone working alone, with really cheap tools, has a reasonable hope of carving out enough of the cognitive surplus, the desire to participate, and the collective goodwill of the citizens to create a resource you couldn't have imagined existing even five years ago.

That's the answer to the question, "Where do they find the time?" Or, rather, that's the numerical answer. Beneath that question was another thought, this one not a question but an observation. In this same conversation with the TV producer, I talked about *World of Warcraft* guilds. As I was talking, I could sort of see what she was thinking: "Losers. Grown men sitting in their basement pretending to be elves."

At least they're doing something.

Did you ever see that episode of *Gilligan's Island* where they almost get off the island, and then Gilligan messes up and then they don't? I saw that one. I saw that one a lot when I was growing up. Every half hour that I watched that was a half an hour I wasn't posting to my blog, editing Wikipedia, or contributing to a mailing list. Now I had an ironclad excuse for not doing those things, which is none of those things existed then. I was forced into the channel of media the way it was, because it was the only option. Now it's not, and that's the big surprise. However lousy it is to sit in your basement and pretend to be an elf, I can tell you from personal experience it is worse to sit in your basement and try to figure if Ginger or Mary Ann is cuter. I'm willing to raise that to a general principle: it's better to do something than to do nothing. Even LOLcats, even cute pictures of kittens made even cuter with the addition of cute captions, hold out an invitation to participation. One of the things a LOLcat says to the viewer is, "If you have some sans-serif fonts on your computer, you can play this game too." That message—"I can do that, too"—is a big change.

This is something that people in the media world don't understand. Media in the twentieth century was run as a single race of consumption. How much can we produce? How much can you consume? Can we produce more, and, if so, can you consume more? The answer to that question has generally been yes. In actuality, media is a triathlon; it's three different events. People like to consume, but they also like to produce, and they like to share.

What's astonished people who were committed to the structure of the previous society, prior to trying to take this surplus and do something interesting, is that they're discovering that when you offer people the opportunity to produce and to share, they'll take you up on that offer. It doesn't mean that we'll never sit around mindlessly watching *Scrubs* on the couch; it just means we'll do it less.

The cognitive surplus we're talking about is so large that even a small change could have huge ramifications. Let's say that everything stays 99 percent the same, that people watch 99 percent as much television as they used to, but 1 percent of that is carved out for producing and for sharing. The Internet-connected population watches roughly a trillion hours of TV a year. That's about five times the size of the annual U.S. TV consumption. One percent of that is one hundred Wikipedia projects per year worth of participation.

I think that's going to be a big deal. Don't you?

Well, the TV producer did not think this was going to be a big deal; she was not digging this line of thought. Her final question to me was essentially, "Isn't this all just a fad?" She more-or-less saw it alongside the flagpole-sitting of the early twenty-first century: it's fun to go out and produce and share a little bit, but then people are going to eventually realize, "This isn't as good as doing what I was doing before," and settle down. I made a spirited argument that, no, this wasn't the case, that this was in fact a big one-time shift, more analogous to the Industrial Revolution than to flagpole-sitting.

I argued that this isn't the sort of thing society grows out of. It's the sort of thing that society grows into. I'm not sure she believed me, in part because she didn't want to believe me but also in part because I didn't have the right story yet. Now I do.

I was having dinner with a group of friends about a month ago, and one of them was talking about sitting with his four-year-old daughter watching a DVD. In the middle of the movie, apropos of nothing, she jumps up off the couch and runs around behind the screen. It seems like a cute moment. Maybe she's going back there to see if Dora is really back there or whatever. That wasn't what she was doing. She started rooting around in the cables. Her dad asked her what she was doing, and she stuck her head out from behind the screen and said, "Looking for the mouse."

Here's something four-year-olds know: a screen that ships without a mouse ships broken. Here's something four-year-olds know: media that is targeted at you but doesn't include you may not be worth sitting still for. Those are things that make me believe that this is a one-way change. Four-year-olds, who are soaking most deeply in the current environment, who won't have to go through the trauma that I have to go through of trying to unlearn a childhood spent watching *Gilligan's Island*, just assume that media includes consuming, producing, and sharing.

This has also become my motto, when people ask me what we are doing— and when I say "we," I mean the larger society trying to figure out how to deploy this cognitive surplus, but I also mean we, the people who are working hammer and tongs at figuring out the next good idea—I'm going to tell them: We're looking for the mouse. We're going to look at every place that a reader or a listener or a viewer or a user has been locked out, has been served up passive or a fixed or a canned experience, and ask ourselves, "If we carve out a little bit of the cognitive surplus and deploy it here, could we make a good thing happen?" And I'm betting the answer is yes.

NOTES

This chapter was originally published on April 26, 2008 on HereComesEverybody.org, at http://www.herecomeseverybody.org/2008/04/looking-for-the-mouse.html (accessed July 17, 2010); based on a speech given at the Web 2.0 conference, April 23, 2008. This chapter is licensed under a Creative Commons Attribution-ShareAlike license.

1. See "Talk: Pluto/Archive 2," Wikipedia, http://en.wikipedia.org/wiki/Talk:Pluto/Archive_2#Requested_Move (accessed July 17, 2010); and "Talk: Pluto/Archive 5," Wikipedia, http://en.wikipedia.org/wiki/Talk:Pluto/Archive_5 (accessed July 17, 2010).

2. Tim O'Reilly, "The Architecture of Participation," O'Reilly About, June 2004, http://oreilly.com/pub/a/oreilly/tim/articles/architecture_of_participation.html (accessed July 17, 2010).

3. WikiCrimes, http://www.wikicrimes.org (accessed July 17, 2010). Site now includes worldwide statistics.

17

Between Democracy and Spectacle

The Front-End and Back-End of the Social Web

FELIX STALDER

As more of our data, and the programs to manipulate and communicate this data, move online, there is a growing tension between the dynamics on the front-end (where users interact) and on the back-end (to which the owners have access). If we look at the front-end, the social media of Web 2.0 may well advance semiotic democracy, that is, "the ability of users to produce and disseminate new creations and to take part in public cultural discourse."[1] However, if we consider the situation from the back-end, we can see the potential for Spectacle 2.0, where new forms of control and manipulation, masked by a mere simulation of involvement and participation, create the contemporary version of what Guy Debord called "the heart of the unrealism of the real society."[2] Both of these scenarios are currently being realized. How these relate to one another, and which is dominant in which situation and for which users, is not yet clear and is likely to remain highly flexible. The social meaning of the technologies is not determined by the technologies themselves; rather, it will be shaped and reshaped by how they are embedded into social life, advanced, and transformed by the myriad of individual actors, large institutions, practices, and projects that constitute contemporary reality.

Unfortunately, much of the current analysis focuses primarily on the front-end and thus paints an overly utopian and very one-sided picture. There are, of course, critical analyses that focus on the back-end, yet they also paint a very one-sided picture of technological dominance.[3] Both of these are characterized by extensive biases which are the result of two very common, if unacknowledged, assumptions. In a nutshell, the first one could be stated like this: all forms of social life involve communication; thus, changes in communication (technology) directly affect all forms of social life. This idea, first advanced by Marshall McLuhan in the early 1960s, has been a frequent theme in the techno-utopian (and dystopian) perspective ever since.

Rather than considering how social actors are able to appropriate new technologies to advance their existing, material agendas, the changes in the organization of the digital are taken to be so powerful that they simply impact on the material reality. Understanding the properties of the new modes of communication provides a privileged vantage point from which to understand a broad range of social transformations. Thus, the vectors of change are unidirectional. Such an analysis presents a simple dichotomy between the old and new, with the new replacing the old.[4]

The other very common assumption could be stated like this: conflicts are the result of miscommunication and a lack of information about the other side. Thus, improved communication leads to cooperation. This could well be the oldest utopian promise of communication technology. Just two years before the outbreak of World War I, Marconi famously predicted that his invention, radio, "will make war impossible, because it will make war ridiculous."[5] Today, building on the fact that it is individuals who have a vastly increased array of communication technologies at their disposal, this second assumption has inspired a new wave of communitarianism, envisioned as a blossoming of bottom-up, voluntary communities. This provides the current discourse with a particular populist character, different from earlier manifestations of techno-utopianism which focused on the technocratic elite's[6] influential vision of the postindustrial society. Yet, like these, it is the result of a rather linear extension of a technological property into the social. This time, the focus lies on the fact that in the realm of the digital, sharing means multiplying, rather than dividing as it does with respect to material goods. Since digital data is nonrivalrous, the social relationships mediated by the digital are assumed to exhibit a similar tendency.[7]

At its best, such a perspective is perceptive to early changes in the modes of social communication. Yet these two underlying assumptions limit our ability to understand the issues necessary to turn the semiotic possibilities into democratic ones. A case in point for the current, utopian discourse is Clay Shirky's *Here Comes Everybody*, widely lauded in the blogosphere as a "masterpiece,"[8] because it expresses elegantly the widely shared beliefs within this community. His central claim, memorably phrased, is that "we are used to a world where little things happen for love, and big things happen for money. . . . Now, though, we can do big things for love."[9] Before the massive adoption of digital social tools, the projects that could be realized without need for money were necessarily small, because only a small number of people could cooperate informally. Any bigger effort required a formal organization (business, government, NGO, or other), which created an overhead requiring funding, which, in turn, required an even more formal type of organization capable of raising and managing those funds. In other words, the act of organization itself, even of unpaid volunteers, was a complex and expensive task. It is supposed to have dramatically changed. Now, even large group efforts are no longer dependent on the existence of a formal organization, with its traditionally high overheads. Shirky argues that we can now organize a new class of interests, in a radically new way, that are "valuable to someone but too expensive to be taken on in any institutional way, because the basic and unsheddable costs of being an institution in the first place make those activities not worth pursuing."[10]

The technologies that allow love to scale are all easy to use by now: e-mail, web forums, blogs, wikis, and open publication platforms such as Blogger, Flickr, and YouTube. But that is precisely the point. Only now that they are well understood, and can be taken for granted, are they beginning to unfold their full social potential. For Shirky, what distinguishes Web 2.0 from Web 1.0 is less functionality than accessibility. What only geeks could do ten to fifteen years ago, everybody can do today (in Shirky's world, the digital divide has been closed, even though at the moment only 60 percent of US households have broadband).[11] The empowering potential of these tools is being felt now, precisely because they allow everyone—or, more precisely, every (latent) group to organize itself without running into limits of scale. These newly organizable groups create "postmanagerial organizations," based on ad hoc coordination of a potentially large number of volunteers with very low overheads.

For Shirky, organizing without organizations has become much easier for three reasons. First, failure is cheap. If all it takes is five minutes to start a new blog, there is little risk involved in setting one up. Indeed, it's often easier to try something out than to evaluate its chances beforehand. This invites experimentations which sometimes pay off. If a project gains traction, there is no ceiling to limit its growth. There is little structural difference between a blog read by ten or ten thousand people. Second, since everyone can publish their own material, it is comparatively easy for people with common interests to find each other. Trust is quickly established, based on everyone's published track record. Perhaps most importantly, it takes only a relatively small number of highly committed people to create a context where large numbers of people who care only a little can act efficiently, be it that they file a single bug report, do a small edit on a wiki, contribute a few images, or donate a small sum to the project. The result is an explosion of social cooperation, ranging from simple data sharing, or social cooperation within the domain of the digital, to full-blown collective action in the material world.

So far so good. Things get more complicated when the focus shifts beyond the digital. Despite correctly pointing out that "communication tools don't get socially interesting until they get technologically boring,"[12] Shirky remains squarely focused on them, linearly extending their properties into the social. Hence, he has no doubt that we are witnessing nothing short of a social revolution that "cannot be contained in the institutional structure of society."[13] The explosion of voluntary projects is taken to amount to the erosion of the power differentials between formally and informally organized interests or, more generally, between conventional organizations following strategic interests and people following authentic interests, a.k.a. love. "This is," as Shirky concludes, "leading to an epochal change."[14]

The characteristic limitations of this type of analysis are present in the four assertions that run through the book: First, voluntary user contributions are, indeed, expressions of authentic personal opinions ("love") with no connection to institutional agendas ("money"). Second, there is a free market of ad hoc communities where institutions play no role. Third, this is a world beyond economics. And, finally, (virtually) all forms of cooperation are beneficial.

Can Money Buy Love?

Over the last decades, trust in mass media has declined. It is widely seen as biased and in the hands of special interests. In January 2004, this trust dipped for good below 50 percent in the United States.[15] New modes of communication can be less institutional and commercial and are often perceived as more authentic (at least as far as one's preferred info-niche is concerned). After all, if someone is not making money or following orders, why should she publish anything other than her own opinion derived from a personal interest in the topic? However, it is clear by now that this is not always the case. What appears to be authentic, user-generated content often turns out to be part of a (viral) marketing campaign, a public-relations strategy, or other organized efforts by *hidden persuaders*. One of the first famous cases of a company hiding behind a fictional "user" in a social platform was the case of lonelygirl15. In June 2006, a teenage girl started to post intriguing entries about herself on YouTube, quickly building up enormous popularity. About three months later, it was revealed that the girl was a scripted character portrayed by a New Zealand actress, professionally produced by a young company trying to break into the entertainment industry.[16] Whether this should be understood as a hoax or interactive entertainment is beside the point.

More important is the fact that it is easy to pass off institutional contributions as personal ones. Editors of the "letters section" in newspapers have known this for a long time.

A similar problem occurs on Wikipedia, where many entries are modified by affected parties with strategic goals and no commitment to the "neutral point of view." The enormous popularity of the encyclopedia means that every PR campaign now pays attention to it. The same holds true in the blogosphere, where conflicts of interests, or direct sponsorship, often remain unacknowledged or willfully hidden. The strategies and effects of astroturfing (the faking of grassroots involvement by paid operatives) on the social web are different from case to case. Wikipedia, which has a very strong community dedicated to fighting such abuse (in part with help of custom-made tools such as WikiScanner), has an impressive track record of weeding out drastic and clumsy interventions, although the exact number of persistent, subtle interventions remains structurally unknowable. Extreme cases of blogola (pay for play on blogs) are uncovered through distributed, ad hoc coordinated research (like the one that revealed the real story of lonelygirl15), but there are many mundane cases that never attract enough eyeballs. Indeed, by focusing a lot of attention on one particular case, a large number of others will necessarily be ignored. The problem is endemic enough for the Federal Trade Commission (FTC) to propose an update of its 1980 guidelines "for editorials and testimonials in ads" to clarify how companies can court bloggers to write about their products.[17] Whether such regulation based on the old advertisement model can be effective is far from clear.

A more open practice of how business can reframe new forms of free cooperation is advanced as "crowdsourcing." In this context, "free" is understood as in "free beer," not "free speech" (to turn Richard Stallman's famous definition of "free software" on its head). In the *Wired* article which popularized the term, the very first example serves to illustrate how much cheaper user-generated (rather than professional) stock photography is for a large institutional client and how much money the founders of the mediating platform made by selling their service to the world's largest photo agency (created from the fortune of a very nondigital oil dynasty).[18] In refreshing clarity, it is celebrated that one side (business and institutions) can make or save lots of money, whereas the other side (the individual amateurs) do not, since for them, as Howe generously grants, "an extra $130 [per year] does just fine."[19] Continuing in this vein, he arrives at the logical conclusion:

For the last decade or so, companies have been looking overseas, to India or China, for cheap labor. But now it does not matter where the laborers are—they might be down the block, they might be in Indonesia—as long as they are connected to the network. . . . Hobbyists, part-timers, and dabblers suddenly have a market for their efforts, as smart companies in industries as disparate as pharmaceuticals and television discover ways to tap the latent talent of the crowd. The labor isn't always free, but it costs a lot less than paying traditional employees. It's not outsourcing; it's crowdsourcing.[20]

It's a bit of a confused statement since corporate outsourcing was already dependent on network connectivity (think of call centers in India), and the economic "market" for the crowd is admittedly minute. However, the main point is clear: there is now an even cheaper labor pool than China's, possibly right around the corner and highly educated. It is a strange economy in which one side is in it more for play, and the other only for money. Howe cannot explain how social and economic dimensions relate to one another, even when given the longer length of his follow-up book,[21] but he is very clear on how good this can be for corporations. Part of why this works so well for institutions is that the high turnover rate in the crowd masks the high burnout rate. This is one of the reasons why the size of the community matters, because with a larger community, any one individual matters less. Thus, what is sustainable on a systemic level (where the institutions operate) turns out to be unsustainable on the personal level (where the users operate).

But not all is bad. A constructive redrawing of the boundaries between community and commercial dynamics is taking place in the free and open-source software (FOSS) movement. Over the past decade, complex and mostly productive relationships between companies and FOSS projects have been created. Today, most of the major projects are supported by one or often multiple commercial companies. They directly and indirectly fund and staff foundations which serve the community of programmers; they donate resources or employ key developers. Today, up to 85 percent of Linux kernel developers are paid for their work.[22] This has led to a professionalization of these projects, with results ranging from better-quality management to more predictable release cycles and better-managed turnover of key staff. Thanks to legally binding software licenses—the GPLv2 in the case of the Linux kernel—and a growing understanding of the particulars of relationships between companies and communities, the overall effect of the influx of money into labors of love has been to strengthen, rather than weaken, the FOSS movement.

On the level of individual contributions to cooperative efforts, we are seeing complex and new ways in which the domain of "money" is enmeshed with the domain of "love." Positioning the two as mutually exclusive reminds one of the nineteenth-century conception of the private as the sphere of harmony independent of the competitive world of the economy. Rather, we need to develop an understanding of which forms of enmeshing are productive for the realization of semiotic democracy, and which social arrangements and institutional frameworks can promote them; at the same time, we need to take precautions against the negative forms of strategic interventions that are leading to the creation of Spectacle 2.0. This would also help to address the second major limitation of the Web 2.0 discourse.

The Institutional Side of Ad Hoc

The social web enables astonishingly effective yet very lightly organized cooperative efforts on scales previously unimaginable. However, this is only half of the story; this is the half of the story which plays out on the front-end. We cannot understand the full story if we do not take into account the other half, which play out on the back-end. New institutional arrangements make these ad hoc efforts possible in the first place. There is a shift in the location of the organizational intelligence away from the individual organization toward the provider of the infrastructure. It is precisely because so much organizational capacity resides now in the infrastructure that individual projects do not need to (re)produce this infrastructure and thus appear to be lightly organized. If we take the creation of voluntary communities and the provision of new infrastructures as the twin dimensions of the social web, we can see that the phenomenon as a whole is characterized by two contradictory dynamics. One is decentralized, ad hoc, cheap, easy to use, community oriented, and transparent. The other is centralized, based on long-term planning, very expensive, difficult to run, corporate, and opaque. If the personal blog symbolizes one side, the data center represents the other. All the trappings of conventional organizations, with their hierarchies, formal policies, and orientation toward money, which are supposed to be irrelevant on the front-end, are dominant on the back-end. Their interactions are complex, in flux, and hard to detect form the outside. Sometimes, though, a glitch reveals some aspects, like a déjà vu in the film *The Matrix*. One such revealing glitch was triggered by the Dutch photographer Maartin Dors. One day, one of his photos of Romanian street kids was deleted by the hosting platform Flickr. Why? Because it violated a pre-viously unknown, unpublished rule against depicting children smoking! What is the rationale of this rule? As a spokesperson explained, Flickr and its owner, Yahoo!, "must craft and enforce guidelines that go beyond legal requirements to protect their brands and foster safe, enjoyable communi-ties."[23] Every large Internet company has, and indeed must have, such gate-keepers that decide, on their own, if a contribution conflicts with the law, corporate policies and interests, and then proceed to remove or block it.[24] In other words, the ever-increasing usability of the social web and ever-decreasing user rights go hand in hand. But the specific balance is con-stantly changing, depending on laws and policies and on how much users push back to demand certain rights and features. There are many success stories. Maartin Dors managed to get his photo back online. But the odds are stacked against user vigilance. As Shirky points out well, the dynamics of stardom (disproportionate attention is concentrated on a few people or cases) operate also in the most distributed communication environments.[25] Thus, for every famous case of "censorship" that the public rallies against, there must be a vast number of cases that affect unskilled users or con-tent too unfashionable to ever make it to the limelight. This is a structural problem which cannot be solved by individual empowerment, since the very fact that attention focuses on one case implies that many others are ignored. Thus, there is a tension at the core of the social web created by the uneasy (mis)match of the commercial interests that rule the back-end and community interests advanced through the front-end. The communities are embedded within privately owned environments so that users, usually unaware of the problem, are faced with a take-it-or-leave-it decision. There is a structural imbalance between the service providers on the one side, who have strong incentives to carefully craft the infrastructures to serve their goals, and the users on the other side, who will barely notice what is going on, given the opacity of the back-end. To believe that competitive pressures will lead providers to offer more freedoms is like expecting the commercialization of news to improve the quality of reporting. If we are interested in realizing the empowering potential of new modes of collabo-ration, we need to focus on the relationship between back-end and front-end dynamics in order to understand if and where they are conflicting and to develop institutional frameworks that can balance the interest of ad hoc communities against those of the formally organized actors that support them.

The Surveillance Economy

If the dynamics on the front-end are a complex mix between community and commercial orientations, the dynamics of the back-end are purely business, reflecting the enormous costs of data centers. With a few exceptions, user access to this new infrastructure is free of direct costs. This leads to claims that in the new information economy everything is free (again, as in beer). Of course, there are costs to be offset and money to be made, so Chris Anderson points out four models of how this is possible: cross-subsidies (as in free phones to sell data and voice services), advertising (like TV and radio), "freemium" (basic version is free, advanced version is not), and user generation (like Wikipedia).[26] Right now, the dominant model is advertising. Google, for example, generates 98 percent of its revenue in this way.[27] In order to attract advertising customers, the platform providers need to know as much as possible about the users. In mass media, the weakness of a back-channel (the Nielsen box) limited the amount of data the provider could gather about the audience. Thus, only very large groups could be targeted (e.g., the twenty-five- to forty-four-year-old demographic in New York City). Online, this is entirely different. Even individuals can be tracked in great detail, and groups of any size and characteristics can be dynamically aggregated. Every activity online generates a trace that can be gathered and compiled, and companies go to great length making sure that traces are generated in a manner that they can gather. Google is probably the most aggressive in this area, providing a host of services on its own servers, as well as integrating its offers (mainly AdSense and Google Analytics) into independent sites on its users' servers, thus being able to gather user data in both locations.[28] Social platforms enable the gathering of highly detailed data about individual and group interests in real time, particularly when combined with other data sources (which is standard, since most Web 2.0 platforms are owned by or cooperate with large media conglomerates, e.g., via APIs, application programming interfaces). The extent, the precision, and the speed of this data gathering is unprecedented. In this framework, user profiles are the real economic asset, and an asset which Google exploits with great success (Google does not sell the profiles directly but, rather, sells the ability to customize advertisements based off these profiles). Because of the business model chosen, the back-end doubles as a surveillance infrastructure with the expressive aim of social sorting, that is, of differentiating the treatment of people according to criteria opaque to them.[29] Improvement of services and advertisement are the overt goals, but the knowledge which is thus created is not limited to such uses. In November 2008, Google launched a new application called Google Flu Trends. It is based on "a close relationship between how many people search for flu-related topics and how many people actually have flu symptoms. Some search queries tend to be popular exactly when flu season is happening, and are therefore good indicators of flu activity."[30] This allows Google to track the outbreak of the flu with only one-day lag time, roughly two weeks ahead of the US Centers for Disease Control and Prevention (CDC).[31] The laudable aim is to be able to detect early, and to be able to intervene in, the outbreak of epidemics. Yet there is no reason to assume that similar modeling techniques need be limited to public health issues. The range of emergent social phenomena that can be detected and intervened in early is wide, and the pressures to make use of this knowledge are significant. Yet the private and opaque character of the back-end makes this information accessible (and actionable) to only a very small number of very large institutions.

For commercial platforms, advertisement seems the only business model for now. Amassing very large amounts of data to improve services and advertiser relationships is the logical consequence of this. This data is the basis on which social work done by the users on the front-end—that is, the creation and maintenance of their social networks—is turned into financial value at the back-end.[32] Yet, beyond economics, there can be no doubt that real-time knowledge of group formation, of changing patterns of collective interests and desires, constitutes a new form of general power. Should this power only be privately owned and accountable to no more than fast-changing terms of service and a given corporation's need to maintain a positive public image? Current privacy legislation seems ill equipped to deal with these questions, focusing still on the data protection of individuals. If we do not find ways to address these issues, there is a real danger that the social web, and the enormous amounts of personal and community data generated, will empower the actors with access to the back-end considerably more than those at the front-end, thus tipping the balance not in favor of the lightly organized groups but, rather, the densely organized groups.

Cooperation and Conflicts

While voluntary cooperation appears to be a friendly form of organization, the actual experience may differ quite a bit. First, every community produces exclusion in the process of creating its identity. Second, the values of the different groups, created through authentic practice, can easily come in conflict with one another once they leave the fractured space of the digital and enter the unified space of law and politics. Because of the underlying assumption that communication leads to cooperation (and the lofty hopes attached to this process), current discourse is virtually silent on such issues. Shirky mentions only one problematic case of cooperation, namely, that of a group of young women using a social forum to celebrate anorexia and to offer each other mutual support to continue it. Here, it is easy to agree, the cause of the problem is less the community itself than the personal, psychological problems of individual contributors. Yet the case is atypical, because most conflicts emerging from cooperation cannot be remedied by psychological intervention.

On the contrary. The world of FOSS is often described as a meritocracy where the most able programmers rise to the top. While this is, indeed, the case, the definition of "capable" is not just a technical one but is also mediated through the codes of the community and its constitutive sociability. FOSS projects define "capable" in ways that manifestly exclude women. Whereas 15 percent of all PhDs in computer science are awarded to women,[33] the number of female contributors to FOSS projects is around 2 percent.[34] The reasons are complex, ranging from the gendering of leisure time to the lack of role models, but it is clear that more formal rules protect minorities (in this case women) while the informality of ad hoc communities allows for social biases to run unchecked. Thus, what appears as open, friendly cooperation to some may be experienced as a closed and hostile club by others.

It is not just that the modes of cooperation contain elements of hostility: the results of cooperation can fuel conflicts. In one way or the other, the back-end is the preferred place to address those systemically. Copyright law and criminal activity provide two illuminating examples of how these potential conflicts have been resolved on the back-end. In practice, the ease of cooperation and sharing often violates the exclusive rights of the owners of creations as defined by copyright law. The most radical example is peer-to-peer file sharing (strangely enough, the entire subject is ignored by most Web 2.0 discourse). Also, virtually every other activity that constitutes the social web at some point runs up against the problem of copyright regulations. The practice of Creative Commons licensing can mitigate some aspects but not all, since it covers only a fraction of the available material. Some of the resulting conflicts play out on the level of the front-end (where tens of thousands of users are being sued for everyday practices), but the real key lies in the architecture of the back-end. Software code, as Lessig pointed out, can be much more effective than legal code (though legal code is being strengthened, and often in favor of the well organized).[35] The surveillance infrastructure, created for business purposes, can easily be extended and transformed to discipline users and turn free as in free speech into free as in free beer, semiotic democracy into Spectacle 2.0. From 2007 onward, YouTube, for example, installed extensive back-end filtering to monitor content for copyright infringement. A sudden increase of content disappearing from the platform was detected in January 2009. As the Electronic Frontier Foundation (EFF) explained, "Thanks to a recent spat between YouTube and Warner Music Group, YouTube's Content ID tool is now being used to censor lots and lots of videos (previously, Warner just silently shared in the advertising revenue for the videos that included a "match" to its music)."[36] The scope of semiotic democracy was so significantly reduced that the EFF called it "YouTube's Fair Use Massacre." This conflict between social intentions of users and the commercial orientations of the owners (and their internal conflicts) was mediated through the back-end. Users could do nothing about it. The second case concerns the "hard question" to which Shirky devotes half a page. The cooperative infrastructure of the web is also used for full-rage criminal activity, including terrorism. The problem is that on the level of network analysis, these activities, people coming together and sharing information, are not different from what everyone else does. In order to detect such emergent criminal "organizations" and intervene in their activities, the same pattern-detection tools that detect flu outbreaks are being used for law-enforcement and national-security reasons. Thus, given the conflictive nature of social relationships, even if they incorporate some aspects of cooperation, and the increasing demands on law enforcement to prevent, rather than solve, crime, it is not difficult to see how the centralization of the back-end could contribute to the expansion of old-style, state-centered, big-brother surveillance capacities.

Conclusions

It would be too easy to contrast the light picture of semiotic democracy with a dark one of Spectacle 2.0: social relationships are becoming ever more distorted by hidden advertisement and other forms manipulation; the growing ranks of the creative-industry workers have to compete ever harder for work as potential clients learn to exploit free culture and drive down salaries through crowdsourcing; a gigantic surveillance machine is extending the reach of powerful institutions so that they can manipulate emerging social phenomena, either intervening before they can reach critical mass or else helping them to reach critical mass much sooner, depending on their goals and strategies.

But the world is not black or white, and neither is it an indiscriminate gray. Given the flexibility of the technology and its implementation, it is most likely to affect people in highly differentiated ways. These are decided by social actors and their conflicting agendas. Rather than placing our hope in some immanent quality of the technology, we need to ask urgent questions: how can we ensure that community spaces can develop according to their own needs and desires, even as strong external (commercial and law-enforcement) pressures are exerted on all levels? The FOSS movement, in large parts thanks to the ingenuity of the General Public License (GPL), has showed that this is possible in many respects. Wikipedia shows how much continued and organized effort this takes. How can we ensure that the power accumulated at the back-end is managed in a way so that it does not counteract the distribution of communicative power through the front-end? It seems clear that individual terms of service and market competition are not enough. A mixture of new legislation and granting public access to back-end data will be necessary.[37] If we simply ignore this, extending the ideology of the free market to communities (competing for sociability), as much of the discourse does, we are likely to see that the new infrastructure will enable only those whose interests are aligned, or at least do not conflict, with those who control the back-end. For others, it could be a future of reduced life chances and lost opportunities and connections systematically, yet undetectably, prevented from even occurring. As a result, we would not have a semiotic but a managed democracy.

NOTES

This chapter is based, in part, on my review of Clay Shirky's book *Here Comes Everybody*: Felix Stalder, "Analysis without Analysis," *Mute: Culture and Politics after the Net*, July 28, 2008, http://www.metamute.org/en/content/analysis_without_analysis.

1. Elisabeth Stark, "Free Culture and the Internet: A New Semiotic Democracy," openDemocracy.net, June 20, 2006, http://www.opendemocracy.net/arts-commons/semiotic_3662.js.

2. Guy Debord, *The Society of the Spectacle* (1967), trans. Ken Knabb (London: Rebel, 2006), § 6, http://www.bopsecrets.org/images/sos.pdf.

3. Among the first within this context was Lawrence Lessig, *Code and Other Laws of Cyberspace* (New York: Basic Books, 1999); the most prominent recent addition is Jonathan Zittrain, *The Future of the Internet—and How to Stop It* (New Haven: Yale University Press, 2008).

4. For a historical critique of such "McLuhanism," see Richard Barbrook, *Imaginary Futures: From Thinking Machines to the Global Village* (London: Pluto, 2007).

5. Ivan Narodny, "Marconi's Plans for the World," *Technical World Magazine*, October 1912, 145–150, available online at http://earlyradiohistory.us/1912mar.htm.

6. For example, Daniel Bell, *The Coming of Post-Industrial Society: A Venture in Social Forecasting* (New York: Basic Books, 1973).

7. For a critique of this extension, see Matteo Pasquinelli, *Animal Spirits: A Bestiary of the Commons* (Amsterdam: Institute of Network Cultures; NAi Publishers Matteo, 2008).

8. Cory Doctorow, "Clay Shirky's Masterpiece: Here Comes Everybody," BoingBoing, February 18, 2008, http://www.boingboing.net/2008/02/28/clay-shirkys-masterp.html.

9. Clay Shirky, *Here Comes Everybody: The Power of Organizing without Organizations* (New York: Penguin, 2008), 104.

10. Ibid., 11.

11. Nate Anderson, "US 20th in Broadband Penetration, Trails S. Korea, Estonia," ars technica, June 19, 2009, http://arstechnica.com/tech-policy/news/2009/06/us-20th-in-broadband-penetration-trails-s-korea-estonia.ars (accessed July 20, 2010).

12. Shirky, *Here Comes Everybody*, 105.

13. Ibid.

14. Ibid., 304.

15. Gallup, "Americans More Tuned In Than Ever to Political News: Record Interest in Political News Coincides with Record Distrust in Media," Gallup.com, September 22, 2008, http://www.gallup.com/poll/110590/americans-more-tuned-than-ever-political-news.aspx.

16. Virginia Heffernan and Tom Zeller, "'Lonely Girl' (and Friends) Just Wanted Movie Deal," *New York Times*, September 12, 2006, http://www.nytimes.com/2006/09/12/technology/12cnd-lonely.html.

17. Douglas McMillan, "Blogola: The FTC Takes On Paid Posts," *Business Week*, May 19, 2009, http://www.businessweek.com/technology/content/may2009/tc20090518_532031.htm.

18. Jeff Howe, "Rise of Crowdsourcing," *Wired* 14.06 (June 2006), http://www.wired.com/wired/archive/14.06/crowds.html.

19. Ibid.

20. Ibid.

21. Jeff Howe, *Crowdsourcing: Why the Power of the Crowd Is Driving the Future of Business* (New York: Crown Business, 2008).

22. Doc Searls, "Is Linux Now a Slave to Corporate Masters?" *Linux Journal*, April 30, 2008, http://www.linuxjournal.com/content/linux-now-slave-corporate-masters.

23. Anick Jesdanun, "'Public' Online Spaces Don't Carry Speech, Rights," MSNBC.com, July 7, 2008, http://www.msnbc.msn.com/id/25568534/ (accessed July 20, 2010).

24. See Jeffrey Rosen, "Google's Gatekeepers," *New York Times Magazine*, November 28, 2008, http://www.nytimes.com/2008/11/30/magazine/30google-t.html.

25. Shirky, *Here Comes Everybody*, 125–137.

26. Chris Anderson, *Free: The Future of a Radical Price: The Economics of Abundance and Why Zero Pricing Is Changing the Face of Business* (New York: Random House, 2009).

27. Eric Schmidt, interview with Charlie Rose, March 6, 2009, http://www.charlierose.com/view/interview/10131.

28. Felix Stalder and Christine Mayer, "The Second Index: Search Engines, Personalization and Surveillance," in *Deep Search: The Politics of Search Engines Beyond Google*, edited by Konrad Becker and Felix Stalder (New Brunswick, NJ: Transaction, 2009).

29. See David Lyon, ed., *Surveillance as Social Sorting: Privacy, Risk and Automated Discrimination* (London and New York: Routledge, 2002).

30. Google, "Google Flu Trends, Frequently Asked Questions," http://www.google.org/about/flutrends/faq.html (accessed July 20, 2010).

31. Jeremy Ginsberg et al., "Detecting Influenza Epidemics Using Search Engine Query Data," *Nature* 457 (February 19, 2009), http://research.google.com/archive/papers/detecting-influenza-epidemics.pdf.

32. Tiziana Terranova, "Free Labor: Producing Culture for the Global Economy," *Social Text* 18, no. 2 (2000): 33–57, http://www.electronicbookreview.com/thread/technocapitalism/voluntary; Trebor Scholz, "What the MySpace Generation Should Know about Working for Free," Re-public, 2007, http://www.re-public.gr/en/?p=138.

33. Ellen Spertus, "What We Can Learn from Computer Science's Differences from Other Sciences: Executive Summary: Women, Work and the Academy Conference," December 9–10, 2004, http://www.barnard.edu/bcrw/womenandwork/spertus.htm (accessed July 20, 2010).

34. Cheekay Cinco, "We Assume FOSS Benefits All Equally: But Does It Really?," genderIT.org, February 27, 2406, http://www.genderit.org/en/index.shtml?apc=—-e—1&x=93204 (accessed July 20, 2010).

35. Lessig, *Code and Other Laws of Cyberspace*.

36. Fred von Lohmann, "YouTube's January Fair Use Massacre," *Electronic Frontier Foundation Blog*, February 3, 2009, http://www.eff.org/deeplinks/2009/01/youtubes-january-fair-use-massacre (accessed July 20, 2010).

37. Bernhard Rieder, "Democratizing Search? From Critique to Society-Oriented Design," in *Deep Search: The Politics of Search Engines beyond Google*, edited by Konrad Becker and Felix Stalder (New Brunswick, NJ: Transaction, 2009).

18

DIY Academy?

Cognitive Capitalism, Humanist
Scholarship, and the Digital Transformation

ASHLEY DAWSON

The University of Michigan Press recently sent me (and other authors who have published with the press) an e-mail announcing the debut of a "transformative scholarly publishing model," the product of a cooperative agreement between the Press and the University of Michigan Libraries.[1] Starting in July 2009, the letter said, all future Michigan publications are to be made available "primarily in a range of digital formats," although high-quality print-on-demand versions of the e-books are also readily obtainable by bookstores, institutions, and individuals. The Press's long-term plans call for books to be "digitized and available to libraries and customers world-wide through an affordable site-license program," as most academic journals currently are. Moreover, these digital books, the communiqué informed me, will be "candidates for a wide range of audio and visual digital enhancements—including hot links, graphics, interactive tables, sound files, 3D animation, and video." This announcement by a major academic press is the harbinger of a seismic shift in the character of scholarly knowledge production and dissemination.

Over the past thirty years, the university presses have been pushed by academic administrators to act like for-profit publishing ventures rather than as facilitators of the professoriate's publishing ambitions in the erstwhile Fordist-era university.[2] As universities have cut back funding for both the presses and tenure-stream faculty appointments, turning increasingly to the precarious labor of graduate students and adjuncts to staff their core courses, the academic presses have become the de facto arbiters of tenure and promotion in the increasingly pinched world of the humanities and social sciences. The result, as a well-known letter published by Stephen Greenblatt during his tenure as president of the Modern Language Association attests, is a crisis in scholarly publishing.[3] It has become harder to publish in general and virtually impossible to publish books that do not ride the latest wave of theory.

At the same time, the remorseless creep toward informal labor has made it increasingly necessary to crank out books in order to survive in academia. The upshot is an increasingly Darwinian world of frenetic competition and commodification in which scholars illogically hand over their hard-won knowledge virtually for free to presses that then limit the circulation of that knowledge through various forms of copyright in order to maintain the precarious revenue stream that keeps them in business.

To what extent does digital publishing provide an exit from this dystopian world? As Michigan's announcement makes clear, digital publication clearly offers exciting possibilities for multimedia, interdisciplinary work. But this shift also opens broader vistas. Why should scholars not take publishing out of the hands of the academic presses and establish their own online publishing schemes? Within the sciences there is already a strong trend toward the publication of papers in open-access archives. Peer-reviewed, open-access journals are beginning to pop up in fields such as cultural studies. With support from their institutions or far-seeing not-for-profit foundations, scholars could publish and disseminate their own work freely. The potential for significantly democratizing knowledge represented by such developments cannot be gainsaid despite the enduring significant inequalities of access to digital information within the global North and South. We are, however, a long way from such developments becoming the norm. The danger is that the earthquake whose first tremors we are currently feeling will take us unawares and will make us passive victims rather than the architects of more egalitarian and socially just forms of learning and communication. There has, after all, been relatively little theorization of this tectonic shift in the modes of knowledge production and dissemination.[4] When not commandeered by progressive movements, technological innovations can all too easily be used to exacerbate existing forms of inequality.

In this essay, I situate discussion of the open-access movement within academia in the context of contemporary theories of the knowledge economy and immaterial labor. For theorists influenced by the Italian *operaismo* movement, shifts in the production process in advanced capitalist nations have produced a massification and commodification of intellectual work over the past several decades.[5] Today, the most strategically significant sector of the capitalist production process, the one that sets the terms for all other sectors, is what *operaismo* theorists term "immaterial labor"—the production of new software programs, novel social networking technologies, coding of genetic materials, and so forth.[6] This increasing commodification of knowledge has, however, generated a crippling contradiction: in almost all cases, immaterial labor is predicated on collaboration, and yet the continued accumulation of capital hinges on the privatization of intellectual-property rights. As Michael Hardt puts it, "There is emerging a powerful contradiction, in other words, at the heart of capitalist production between the need for the common in the interest of productivity and the need for the private in the interest of capitalist accumulation."[7]

This increasingly heated struggle over the commons reverberates strongly within academia since it is a crucial site of contemporary knowledge production. Despite the relative lack of theorization concerning the digital transformation of knowledge production and dissemination, my interviews with academic publishers and scholars working on issues of digitization and access reveal a keen sense of the nascent liberatory opportunities as well as the tensions that underlie current developments. Yet the movement for open access cannot, I argue, be seen outside broader institutional dynamics within academia and the knowledge economy in general. Given the unfolding collapse of print journalism and the for-profit publishing industry, Panglossian celebrations of academia as an incipient rhizomatic social network clearly will not do. In fact, as critics such as Michael Denning and Andrew Ross have argued, academia offers a vanguard example of the forms of ill-remunerated and insecure labor that are increasingly common in the knowledge economy in general. To what extent is the digital transformation likely to extend these dystopian trends rather than to enlarge the space for emancipatory practices? Drawing on the work of theorists such as the Edu-factory group, I situate my discussion of new forms of electronic knowledge production and dissemination within the broader terrain of the neoliberal university, thereby offering a hardboiled assessment of the possibilities as well as the limits of digital publishing and, more broadly, the DIY academy.

Digital Scholarship

Business as usual is over in scholarly publishing. The multifarious trend toward academic capitalism discussed in the previous section has also transformed the channels through which scholars disseminate their research. Once upon a time there was a virtuous circle that linked scholars who needed to publish their research to well-funded university publishing houses that communicated that research to university libraries, which in turn purchased the scholarly journals and monographs in which research was published. No more. Both private and public universities have cut funding for their publishing ventures, forcing them to bear considerations of marketability increasingly in mind when accepting projects for publication. Meanwhile, university libraries are being gouged by for-profit journal publishers, who have driven the cost of subscriptions to journals in the sciences and medicine through the roof. NYU's library, for example, spends 25 percent of its budget on journals from the European publisher Elsevier-North Holland and another 25 percent on journals from two or three additional for-profit publishers that realize libraries are unlikely to terminate a subscription.[8] Book acquisitions, the primary mode of publication for the humanities, are being squeezed out. The University of California system spends less than 20 percent of its budget on books, for instance, and now often recommends that only one copy of a book be purchased throughout the system rather than allowing each campus to purchase a copy.[9] Finally, the glut of precarious teachers discussed in the previous section has allowed administrators to up the ante for tenure and promotion at all colleges incessantly, whether or not their institutions host an academic press. As a result, the sheer number of scholars seeking to publish has multiplied many times over, while funding for presses and libraries has been axed.[10] It is increasingly hard for anyone except a small number of academic superstars to publish original work in book form.

The open-access (OA) movement is an emerging response to this crisis in academic publishing.[11] Inspired by conceptions of the digital commons evident among cognitarian insurgents such as the members of the FLOSS movement, scholarly proponents of OA argue that it makes little sense to give away hard-won research to publishers for free, only to have such publishers limit access to this work through exorbitant publication costs and subscription fees that exclude anyone lacking access to a university library in the developed world. Online publishing can in many instances be done nearly free of cost and very quickly, issues that are of immense concern to junior scholars.[12] OA proponents argue that academics want publicity, not fees, and that they therefore have little to lose and much to gain by disseminating their research online for free.[13] Although humanities scholars have, in comparison with those working in the "hard" sciences, been slow to embrace OA, protocols developed in the sciences that allow electronic publication of preprint copies of papers make it possible to avoid the restrictive copyright agreements imposed by both for-profit and university presses.[14] In addition to increasing publication outlets, the digitalization also offers notable resources for teaching. Rice University's Connexions project and MIT's OpenCourse-Ware program both make pedagogical materials available for free online, for example.[15] In the case of Connexions, faculty can remix and supplement materials available online to create their own unique course packets.

In addition to such innovations in distribution, digital media have begun to transform scholarly production in the humanities. Online publication promises to give more recondite subjects greater play, ending the tyranny of the market that prevents the publication of arcane scholarly work and that sees such work go out of print all too quickly. In addition, although the dominant trend remains to treat online publications simply as what Gary Hall calls "prosthetic" extensions of traditional print formats such as the journal article and the book chapter, the digital transformation is gradually catalyzing new forms of research.[16] Journals such as *Vectors* build articles from the ground up to include multiple different media, expanding the scholarly palette to include audio and visual as well as print media,[17] shifting the role of humanities scholars to include curatorial as well as exegetical functions, and auguring radically novel, hybrid disciplinary formations.[18] The possibilities for scholarly expression are exploding as academics experiment with not just the blog but also the video diary.[19] In addition, digital technologies also promise to extend the powerful data-analytical strategies pioneered by Franco Moretti in works such as *Graphs, Maps, and Trees*, which surveys the entire publication record in Britain during the nineteenth century to segment trends within the novel into microgeneric categories, generational patterns, and evolutionary literary tropes.[20] Emerging practices of data mining in journals such as the *Digital Humanities Quarterly* that push Moretti's structuralist approach further also promise to smash the model of the scholar as hermit or genius by encouraging truly collaborative, interdisciplinary research and publication.[21]

It is hard not to be intoxicated by the exciting possibilities proffered by the "digital revolution" in scholarly research and publication. In fact, I would argue strongly that this emerging movement constitutes a significant reclaiming of the networked commons on the part of humanities scholars. Nevertheless, I want to interrogate the institutional context within which such utopian movements gestate. This is because there is really no such thing as an academic gift economy. As is the case for other forms of user-generated culture, the extension of the networked commons is ultimately intertwined with and dependent on transformations in other sectors of the economy. After all, the Internet itself is a *public* creation (if one counts the Department of Defense as a public entity). Open-access protocols in the humanities will not forge ahead unless institutional structures are in place to support such initiatives. Certainly, digital research and publication offers exciting possibilities. But progress in this sphere as in other sectors of academic capitalism will come only through transformations on multiple levels, in struggle that is likely to be long and hard fought. Technology alone offers no magic bullet in fields beset with the kinds of structural challenges that confront the humanities today.

One of the primary issues to confront in this regard is the fact that the predominant use of computing power in contemporary culture is *not* for forms of self-organizing, autonomous culture. Instead, as David Golumbia points out at great length, computational power is used primarily to augment dominant institutions of corporate and state power, particularly through sophisticated forms of surveillance that segment and tabulate populations using remarkably conservative racial and gender paradigms.[22] Such bio-political manifestations of computational power are of particular concern given the rise of audit culture in academia during the neoliberal era. One of the main reasons for the publishing crisis, in fact, is the desire of academic administrators for simple, quantifiable measures of scholarly productivity.[23] Put in simple terms, books—vetted by academic publishers that assume all responsibility for peer review—are easy to count. The more of them the better, at least as far as administrators, tasked with inflating their school's brand name in a cutthroat market, are concerned. There is no inherent reason that the switch to open-access publication should not play into the audit culture's hands, leading to a remorseless intensification of pressures to publish or perish. Indeed, precisely such a dynamic is already visible in universities in Britain and Australia, where benchmarking measures such as the Research Assessment Exercise (RAE) have led to a huge proliferation of journals at the service of academics thrown into a frenetic race to publish in order to retain funding. The resulting rush to publish articles reminds one of the assembly-line scene in Charlie Chaplin's *Modern Times*. Scholars often cannot publish in experimental OA online journals because they are not counted as legitimate venues by benchmarks such as the RAE.[24] In addition, administrators were not slow to realize the powerful surveillance capabilities of the digital academy in regard to teaching. During the NYU graduate-employee strike of 2005–2006, for instance, university administrators logged onto classroom Blackboard websites secretly in an attempt to figure out which teaching assistants were respecting the strike. Unless there is a strong movement among educators to counter such baleful applications of technology, administrators are likely to seize the opportunity for speed-up and surveillance afforded by digital publication and pedagogy.

Another major issue is the infrastructure involved in publication. As Ken Wissoker, editorial director at Duke University Press, recently commented, people who argue that "information wants to be free" are rather like the money managers profiled in *Liquidated*, Karen Ho's recent ethnography of Wall Street executives: socialized into a world of high risk and outland-ish rewards, elite bankers assume that job insecurity builds character and impose these values of precariousness and instability on other businesses.[25] Wissoker's point is that the publishing industry does not necessarily operate along the lines of the gift economy celebrated by some cognitarians and that the imposition of the latter on the former is likely to do damage analogous to that wrought by speculative venture-capital funds on traditional industrial enterprises. Indeed, as Wissoker observes, Duke loses over one million dol-lars a year on its book-publishing division, losses that are only made up for by library journal subscriptions. Duke's new monograph e-publication initia-tive in fact relies on a subscription system similar to that employed for some time now to distribute journals.[26]

While multiple copies of a book cost relatively little to publish, there is a significant investment involved in the production of the first copy.[27] The cre-ation of a book is, after all, a collective enterprise, involving editors, copyedi-tors, peer reviewers, and so on. Books do not simply appear out of thin air, in other words. The same is true for journals, although more of the burden of journal production tends to be shouldered by scholars. Initiatives such as the University of Michigan Press one, which involves a partnership with the uni-versity library, promise to make the cost of book distribution far lower using electronic dissemination and print-on-demand.[28] But this will not eliminate the costs associated with producing the first copy of the book. Who, pre-cisely, will pay for this collective labor if not the university presses? Do we want individual academics to have to fund their own publications, as is cur-rently the case in the hard sciences? Or do we want publishing to be routed through university libraries, which have no experience with peer review or with the craft elements of publication? As I argued earlier, questions of immaterial labor are ineluctably tied to such practical material issues.

In addition, while a shift to publishing through university-library-hosted servers might free scholars from the vagaries of the market, it may also subject them to the political manipulation of host institutions and of fickle state legislators.[29] What would happen to publications dependent on such revenue streams, for example, in the event of a state fiscal crisis such as the one currently unfolding in California? We need to think very carefully, in other words, about how to exploit the shift online without surrendering the relative autonomy from both market pressures and political censure that we humanities scholars have hitherto enjoyed.

Gatekeeping also represents an additional quandary. At present, univer-sity presses shoulder the burden of ensuring a relatively objective system of peer review, at least in relation to book publication. Gary Hall, in his account of the future of digital publishing, highlights the fluid nature of digital texts, which lack the static quality of a printed and bound book, and asks how we can establish review standards for texts whose networked form means that they cannot be read or written in the same way twice.[30] While I agree with his conclusion that we cannot respond to the crisis in academic publishing by simply trying to put everything on the web, since the migration online changes the nature of both text and reader, I am troubled by Hall's poststructuralist-tinged reflections on institutionality, which celebrate uncertainty and instability. The digital transformation undeniably means we need to rethink the rules of the game, but it does not necessarily mean a proliferation of *différence* in textual production and evaluation.

The phenomenon of power law distribution in the blogosphere is instructive in this regard. While anyone with regular access to the Internet can theoretically write and read anything in any blog, power law distribution ensures that the more material is placed online, the greater the gap between material that gets huge amounts of attention and that which gets merely average attention.[31] So blogs like the *Daily Kos* can get literally millions of hits each day, but only a few people look at the average blog. Newcomers tend to lose out to already-established voices and sites.

This phenomenon in the blogosphere suggests that we cannot assume that simply putting scholarly materials online will get them a decent airing. Scholarly presses currently play an important curatorial function by identifying important theoretical trends and innovative scholarly interventions, ensuring that such interventions get vetted through scholarly review, and drawing attention to the works they publish through their marketing departments and through their social capital.[32] While there is no doubt a conservative aspect to this dynamic, I do not believe that we can assume that self-publishing online in a venue such as Hall's cultural studies archive CSeARCH will automatically lead to a dynamic new online incarnation of the public sphere. As power law distribution suggests, it is far more likely that, in the absence of a framework calculated to guarantee such dynamism as well as justice for junior scholars, existing inequalities in the world of publishing will be magnified. Although the institutions we inhabit today are far from perfect, they embody a century's worth of struggles for academic freedom and social justice, as well as lamentable forms of repressive State power and academic capitalism. If we are to ensure that computationalism does not reshape these institutions in ways that augment the latter characteristics rather than the former, we need to think very carefully about how to enlarge the space for autonomous thought and publication using current and fresh institutional means rather than expecting that more information will automatically mean more freedom.

The Revolt of the Cognitariat

During the mid-1990s, a group of Paris-based theorists, many of them exiles from the turbulent "years of lead" in Italy during the preceding decade, worked to develop a theoretical grasp of unfolding social struggles in the journal *Futur antérieur*.[33] These theorists examined the impact of information technology on production processes and social formations on a global scale. Particularly important in this context were the speculative writings of Marx in his *Grundrisse*, which prophesized precisely such a transformation of production. For Marx, the creation of wealth in the capitalist societies of the future would come to depend not on the direct expenditure of labor time but rather on "the general productive forces of the social brain."[34] For theorists such as Toni Negri, Paolo Virno, Maurizio Lazzarato, Michael Hardt, and Jean-Paul Vincent, the heightened significance of this *general intellect* was made possible by the ever more central role of automation and of communication networks in contemporary processes of production.

Yet Marx had rather optimistically predicted that increasing automation would diminish direct labor time and socialize production, leading inevitably to the liquidation of private ownership and wage labor. For the past several decades, however, just the opposite seemed to be happening. New communication technologies had fostered the fragmentation, outsourcing, and globalization of production processes. In much of the developed world, labor appeared increasingly intellectual as research and design grew more central to information capitalism, but workers in high-tech industries were subjected to accelerating conditions of precarious employment by transnational corporations whose footloose character gave organized labor a horrible drubbing. Neoliberal ideologies dedicated to dismantling the social compact between capital, government, and workers made significant inroads even in bastions of social democracy such as France.

Notwithstanding this rout of what Immanuel Wallerstein calls the old antisystemic movements, the hegemony of neoliberalism quickly provoked new anticapitalist countermovements around the globe.[35] Faced with these contending currents, the theorists associated with *Futur antérieur* argued that the crucial issue was not simply the automation of production, which would, after all, constitute a form of technological determinism, but rather the incessantly mutating character of the people who create and operate such technology. This variable human factor they termed *mass intellect* or *immaterial labor*. Just as the conditions of production in Marx's day had created revolutionary conditions by concentrating the proletariat in factories, so immaterial labor was linked together through the networked conditions of cognitive labor. For theorists such as Franco Berardi, contemporary conditions have produced a potentially revolutionary class in formation: the cognitariat.[36] The key question in the unfolding struggles of the neoliberal era for the *Futur antérieur* theorists was the extent to which capital could absorb and control immaterial labor.[37]

If the cognitariat had fancied themselves significant stakeholders in information capitalism, the dot-com crash, Franco Berardi argued, laid bare their precarious status as flexible wage slaves subjected to remorseless strategies of speed-up, outsourcing, and downsizing.[38] Yet an important form of rebellion had begun well before this economic downturn. If immaterial labor depends on communication and collaboration, the cognitariat has consistently asserted the noncommodified, commons-based character of digital culture from its inception. There are many facets to this culture of the digital commons, from the exchange of music using peer-to-peer file-sharing technology to the collaborative creation of Wikipedia to the creation of Creative Commons licenses designed to allow creative remixing of cultural artifacts, many of which are discussed by other contributors to this volume in far more detail than possible here. The thing that ties these diverse strands together, according to David Bollier, is an emphasis on commons-based values of participation, transparency, egalitarianism, and freedom.[39] Contemporary capitalism thrives through asserting control over information using intellectual-property regimes such as those sanctified by the World Trade Organization, hence assuring the scarcity and consequent exorbitant value of such information. Against this trend, cognitarian rebels have developed a postscarcity information economy grounded in the networked commons.[40]

This new commons movement is not, however, simply based on a shift in values away from proprietary models of intellectual property. In addition, digital technologies are leveraging new forms of social communication, removing many of the technical barriers that impeded the organization of large groups of people from the grassroots up, barriers that had helped foster relatively hierarchical and authoritarian organizational forms such as the modern state and the vanguard political party.[41] As Jeffrey Juris has documented, social networking technologies have played an important role in the global justice movement, linking geographically isolated groups such as the Zapatista Army of National Liberation (EZLN), protagonists of one of the first signal revolts against the neoliberal world order, into a global activist grid and facilitating transnational mobilizations such as the World Social Forum.[42] These new technologies have played an important role in mobilizations against authoritarian governments in nations such as Iran, with networking permitting the assembly of so-called flash mobs with little advance warning and no central planning, and the rapid global dissemination of documentation of government repression.[43] For analysts such as David Bollier, social networking technologies are thus giving birth to new forms of the Habermasian public sphere and helping to promote engaged, "history-making" models of citizenship.[44]

It seems to me that we need to approach such at-times hyperbolic claims with a skeptical eye if we are to gauge the transformative potential of digital culture and immaterial labor with any accuracy. After all, as David Golumbia has argued at great length, digitization is not necessarily emancipatory. For Golumbia, the notion that we are witnessing a complete sea change in social relations catalyzed by digital technologies with inherently progressive potential is a form of ideology, one which he dubs computationalism.[45] While recognizing and celebrating the exploits of transgressive hackers and the free/libre/open-source software (FLOSS) movement, Golumbia notes that the predominant use of computers in contemporary culture is to augment the demarcating, concentrating, and centralizing power of dominant social institutions such as the State and transnational corporations.[46] A similar point, with the statistics to back it up, is made by Mathew Hindman in *The Myth of Digital Democracy*.[47] In fact, technology permits a giddy overlap of these diverse institutions, as I learned when I attended a Joint Forces war game during which software for tracking consumer behavior was deployed to model the strategies of insurgent forces in Iraqi cities.[48] We would do well to remember, given Golumbia's trenchant critique of computationalism, that the global reach and power of contemporary capital is to a significant extent a product of precisely the networking technologies that are so often celebrated by writers such as Bollier. Moreover, repressive states such as Iran and China are adapting with alarming rapidity to their citizenry's dissident use of tactical media such as Twitter and Facebook, pushing the global corporations that own these devices into disclosing the names of dissident users. And flash mobs are not always progressive. As the *Futur antérieur* theorists might warn us, then, it is not automation but rather the general intellect that is decisive in social struggles during the era of cognitive capitalism.

In addition, there is a certain hubris to discussions of the revolutionary potential of the cognitariat among contemporary intellectuals. After all, contemporary intellectuals are hardly dispassionate social observers à la Kant. They, or, dear reader, should I say we, are instead inhabitants of some of the most exploited and ideologically benighted precincts of the information economy. Yet as deeply as we have imbibed the gall of post-Fordist austerity, we should not forget that we are not the only ones to suffer the destructive creativity of neoliberalism. The global economy is made up of multiple different sectors, not all of which can be deemed immaterial labor with any theoretical acuity. The expansion of this term by some of the theorists associated with *operaismo* no doubt stems from their reaction against the vanguardist tradition of the Communist Party. For activist intellectuals associated with the Italian movement *Lotta continua*, the Party's purported stranglehold over class consciousness had deeply authoritarian implications.[49] The concept of mass intellect is clearly meant to challenge such preemptive claims to the making of history. But, as important as it is to dismantle vanguardist posturing, there are very real dangers to expanding notions of cognitive labor to envelop the entire body politic. This is because, as George Caffentzis and Silvia Federici argue, capital has thrived historically by organizing production at both the lowest *as well as* the highest technological levels of the global economy, by exploiting both waged and unwaged labor, and by producing both development and underdevelopment. The logic of capitalism, Caffentzis and Federici underline, can only be grasped by "looking at the totality of its relations, and not only to the highest point of its scientific/technological achievement."[50] The history of the twentieth century, during which revolutionary movements found the most fertile terrain in underdeveloped, colonized nations rather than in the core capitalist countries, provides ample evidence for this critique.

By privileging immaterial labor and cognitive capitalism, contemporary theorists risk eliding the contribution of other forms of work—and other workers—to the accumulation process. To quote Caffentzis and Federici again, "the huge 'iceberg' of labor in capitalism was made invisible by the tendency to look at the tip of the iceberg, industrial labor, while the labor involved in the reproduction of labor-power went unseen, with the result that the feminist movement was often fought against and seen as something outside the class struggle."[51] To privilege one sector of anticapitalist struggle over the others is to invite defeat at the hands of capital, whose overlords are unfailingly canny in their use of divide-and-conquer tactics. Rather than privileging one sector, or even extending its terms to all other sectors as some analysts associated with theories of cognitive labor have sought to do, we need, Caffentzis and Federici argue, "to see the continuity of our struggle through the difference of our places in the international division of labor, and to articulate our demands and strategies in accordance to these differences and the need to overcome them."[52] Caffentzis and Federici's strategic warning of course also finds strong grounding in the work of critics such as Ernesto Laclau and Chantal Mouffe, whose theories of agonistic pluralism challenge precisely the erasure of difference that totalizing doctrines of a prime historical mover or revolutionary class tend to further.[53]

Caffentzis and Federici's admonitions should hardly need airing today, in the context of a global justice movement whose protagonists have been overwhelmingly based on the global South among indigenous and peasant organizations such as the EZLN and La Via Campesina.[54] Nevertheless, advocates of the networked commons almost always ignore the impact of debates about intellectual property on those who are not a part of the cognitariat but whose lives are likely to be deeply affected by legal decisions and dissident technologies.[55] As Andrew Ross puts it in a recent discussion of precarious labor that charts the overlaps and disjunctures between those at the top and those at the bottom of the labor market today,

> Because they are generally indisposed to state intervention, FLOSS advocates have not explored ways of providing a sustainable infrastructure for the gift economy that they tend to uphold. Nor have they made it a priority to speak to the interests of less-skilled workers who live outside their ranks. On the face of it, there is little to distinguish this form of consciousness from the guild labor mentality of yore that sought security in the protection of craft knowledge.[56]

For Ross, (prototypically liberal) notions of freedom endemic to the cognitariat need to be supplemented and transformed by a movement for social justice that cuts across classes, catalyzing what Caffentzis and Federici would call a political "recomposition" of the workforce.

A key element in such a recomposition will surely be the elaboration of praxis that recognizes the strategic importance of the networked commons while refusing to subordinate struggles over other instances of the commons to the perspectives and tactical orientations of the cognitariat. As Michael Hardt has recently argued, the ecological and the social commons are united by significantly similar dynamics. Both, for example, "defy and are deteriorated by property relations."[57] Nevertheless, as Hardt admits, there are significant disparities between these two commons, with the ecological sphere hinging on conservation of an increasingly depleted biosphere, while social commons discourses focus on the open and potentially unlimited character of social creation and intercourse. The point though, as Laclau and Mouffe's theoretical work suggests, should be to articulate common struggles across this differentiated but nevertheless potentially complementary terrain of struggle.

Nick Dyer-Witheford's recent model of a twenty-first-century communism as "a complex unity of terrestrial, state and networked commons" goes some way toward conceptualizing such an articulatory politics.[58] Crucial to his theorization, indeed, is a vision of the networked commons that, despite its role as "the strategic and enabling point" in this ensemble, must nevertheless be seen in its dependency on and potential contradiction with other commons sectors.[59] The successful articulation of these different commons, or their disarticulation by capital, lies, in other words, in the realm of radical democratic politics rather than in any inherent features of immaterial labor.

(Tentative) Conclusions

Academics in the humanities are woefully unprepared for digital transformations, despite the significant and multifarious opportunities it offers for scholarship. According to the landmark Modern Language Association *Report of the MLA Task Force on Evaluating Scholarship for Tenure and Promotion*, 40.8 percent of the doctorate-granting institutions that responded to the organization's survey had no experience evaluating refereed articles in electronic format, and 65.7 percent had no experience evaluating monographs in electronic format.[60] The report concludes that while scholars are willing to experiment with online publishing, what matters most in judging scholarship is peer review, and e-publishing remains tainted because peer review has not sufficiently touched it. Just as is true in the sciences, while humanities scholars may disseminate their publications online, the final, archival publication still has to appear in a traditional, paper format to be considered seriously for tenure and promotional evaluation. This means that many of the radical textual and scholarly possibilities of digital publication remain unexplored.

For this situation to change, scholars need to have a far more serious and sustained discussion about the implications of online publishing. The MLA report opens that dialogue by posing a number of important questions: Why, for example, should the monograph be the pinnacle of scholarly achievement in the humanities? Why, furthermore, should the dissertation be a protobook rather than a portfolio of essays and other forms of inquiry (data analysis, visual displays such as Moretti's graphs, maps, and trees, etc.)? Why should we cling to the isolated, atomistic model of scholarly production, a conservative tendency that seems particularly peculiar given decades of theoretical work to dismantle liberal models of sovereign subjectivity, rather than developing models for collaborative production?[61]

In my work on the editorial collective of the journal *Social Text*, I have seen that digitalization raises a series of thorny questions as well as many exciting opportunities for scholars. Recent discussions about making the journal open access have highlighted some of the complex dynamics around publishing that I alluded to earlier. Members of the editorial collective expressed hesitation, for example, about depriving their publisher of the revenues produced by the journal and trepidations about shifting the journal too far away from its archive-worthy print incarnation.[62] At present, *Social Text* is experimenting with an online presence that will explore some of the radical possibilities for digital scholarship using blogs, video diaries, and electronic forums while retaining its official paper imprimatur. We will see how long this compromise formation holds up as the digital transformation gathers steam—although this metaphor demonstrates the extent to which new technology is always framed in terms of and shaped by prior forms, suggesting that it will not be so easy to shake off the tyranny of paper even when the journal goes completely online.

A more ambitious model for the future is available in the form of the Open Humanities Press (OHP), which is using the social capital of its stellar international editorial board to leverage support for a stable of ten online journals and a constellation of five e-book series.[63] The prominence of OHP's editors is likely to solve some of the power law distribution problems that I discussed earlier, although it does raise questions about equality. Should not junior scholars have a really significant presence in any online initiative since it is they whose careers are most likely to shape and be shaped by digital transformations? Does the OHP's glamorous editorial board offer meaningful openings for scholars at all levels, or does it simply recapitulate the star system's unequal access to print publication? In addition, how sustainable is the OHP's book series, which is slated to operate through a cooperative agreement with the University of Michigan Library's Scholarly Publishing Office? Will some of the concerns voiced by the academic publishers I interviewed concerning the poor fit between libraries and scholarly publishing be borne out?

We are at the initial stages of such initiatives and of a far broader discussion about their theoretical implications. It is important, however, that we think clearly about the implications of current projects and about the processes and institutions that are driving the move online. At the moment, online teaching is dominated by for-profit organizations like the University of Phoenix that offer some of the worst examples of exploitation of precarious intellectual labor in academia.[64] Large foundations such as Mellon are promoting the shift online through initiatives such as Project Bamboo that were not initially framed in a particularly inclusive manner. As I have indicated, there is nothing to prevent administrators from using computationalism to intensify academic capitalism except our own self-organizing efforts. Academics need to assert our collective agency in establishing the contours of the digital future rather than allowing administrators and corporations to define that future for us. In addition, theories of the cognitariat have tended to be woefully myopic in their analysis of the multiple strata and divide-and-conquer tactics of contemporary capitalism. The move online certainly cannot solve the deep problems raised by academic and cognitive capitalism, but analysis of the digital humanities does need to take these material conditions into consideration in order to escape technological determinism and voluntarism. Against such problematic models, scholars need to work actively on both theoretical and practical planes to foster an inclusionary and egalitarian networked commons.

NOTES

1. Philip Pochoda, letter to author, April 2, 2009.

2. Lindsay Waters, *Enemies of Promise: Publishing, Perishing, and the Eclipse of Scholarship* (Chicago: Prickly Paradigm, 2004), 65.

3. Stephen Greenblatt, "A Special Letter from Stephen Greenblatt," May 28, 2002, Accessed 18 August 2009, http://www.mla.org/scholarly_pub.

4. Gary Hall, *Digitize This Book: The Politics of New Media, or Why We Need Open Access Now* (Minneapolis: University of Minnesota Press, 2008), 16.

5. Franco Berardi (Bifo), "From Intellectuals to Cognitarians," in *Utopian Pedagogy: Radical Experiments against Neoliberal Globalization*, ed. Mark Coté, Richard J. F. Day, and Greig de Peuter (Toronto: University of Toronto Press, 2007), 136.

6. Nick Dyer-Witheford, "Teaching and Tear Gas: The University in the Era of General Intellect," in *Utopian Pedagogy: Radical Experiments against Neoliberal Globalization*, ed. Mark Coté, Richard J. F. Day, and Greig de Peuter (Toronto: University of Toronto Press, 2007), 46.

7. Michael Hardt, "Politics of the Common," ZNet, July 6, 2009, http://www.zmag.org/znet/viewArticle/21899.

8. Waters, *Enemies of Promise*, 29.

9. Ibid., 36.

10. Philip Pochoda, personal interview, July 27, 2008; Ken Wissoker, personal interview, August 17, 2009.

11. John Willinsky, *The Access Principle: The Case for Open Access to Research and Scholarship* (Cambridge: MIT Press, 2005).

12. Kyoo Lee, personal interview, July 30, 2009.

13. Hall, *Digitize This Book*, 45.

14. Ibid., 46.

15. David Bollier, *Viral Spiral: How the Commoners Built a Digital Republic of Their Own* (New York: New Press, 2008), 285–292.

16. Hall, *Digitize This Book*, 10.

17. David Theo Goldberg and Stefka Hristova, "Blue Velvet: Re-dressing New Orleans in Katrina's Wake," *Vectors*, n.d., http://www.vectorsjournal.org/index. php?page=7&projectId=82.

18. "The Digital Humanities Manifesto," May 29, 2009, http://dev.cdh.ucla.edu/ digitalhumanities/2009/05/29/the-digital-humanities-manifesto-20/.

19. Gabriella Coleman, personal interview, May 4, 2009.

20. Franco Moretti, *Graphs, Maps, and Trees: Abstract Models for a Literary History* (New York: Verso, 2005).

21. Shlomo Argamon, Charles Cooney, Russell Horton, Mark Olsen, Sterling Stein, and Robert Voyer, "Gender, Race, and Nationality in Black Drama, 1950–2006: Mining Differences in Language Use in Authors and Their Characters," *Digital Humanities Quarterly* 3.2 (Spring 2009), http://digitalhumanities.org/dhq/vol/3/2/000043.html; Andrew Stauffer, personal interview, August 3, 2009.

22. David Golumbia, *The Cultural Logic of Computation* (Cambridge: Harvard University Press, 2009), 129.

23. Waters, *Enemies of Promise*, 14.

24. Sidonie Smith, personal interview, August 10, 2009.

25. Ken Wissoker, personal interview; Karen Ho, *Liquidated: An Ethnography of Wall Street* (Durham: Duke University Press, 2009).

26. Michael McCullough, personal interview, July 29, 2009.

27. Philip Pochoda, "University Press 2.0," *University of Michigan Press Blog*, May 27, 2009, http://umichpress.typepad.com/university_of_michigan_pr/2009/05/university-press-20-by-phil-pochoda.html (accessed August 17, 2009).

28. Ibid.

29. Wissoker, personal interview.

30. Hall, *Digitize This Book*, 67.

31. Clay Shirky, *Here Comes Everybody* (New York: Penguin, 2008), 127.

32. Courtney Berger, personal interview, August 5, 2009.

33. Dyer-Witheford, "Teaching and Tear Gas," 44.

34. Quoted in ibid.

35. Emmanuel Wallerstein, "New Revolts against the System," *New Left Review* 18 (November–December 2002): 32.

36. Berardi, "From Intellectuals to Cognitarians," 140.

37. Dyer-Witheford, "Teaching and Tear Gas," 45.

38. Berardi, "From Intellectuals to Cognitarians," 140.

39. Bollier, *Viral Spiral*, 4.

40. Nick Dyer-Witheford, "The Circulation of the Common," April 29, 2006, http:// www.thefreeuniversity.net/ImmaterialLabour/withefordpaper2006.html.

41. Shirky, *Here Comes Everybody*, 21.

42. Jeff Juris, *Networking Futures: The Movements against Corporate Globalization* (Durham: Duke University Press, 2008).

43. "Social Networking in Iran—an Electronic Forum," *Social Text Online*, September 15, 2009, www.socialtextonline.org.

44. Bollier, *Viral Spiral*, 299.

45. Golumbia, *Cultural Logic of Computation*, 1.

46. Ibid., 4.

47. Matthew Hindman, *The Myth of Digital Democracy* (Princeton: Princeton University Press, 2008).

48. Ashley Dawson, "Combat in Hell: Cities as the Achilles Heel of U.S. Imperial Hegemony," *Social Text* 25.2 (Summer 2007): 170.

49. Berardi, "From Intellectuals to Cognitarians," 133.

50. George Caffentzis and Silvia Federici, "CAFA and the Edu-Factory, Part 2: Notes on the Edu-Factory and Cognitive Capitalism," *Edu-Factory*, May 12, 2007, http://www.edu-factory.org/edu15/index.php?option=com_content&view=article&id=109:cafa-and-the-edu-factory-part-2-notes-on-the-edu-factory-and-cognitive-capitalism&catid=43:firstround.

51. Ibid.

52. Ibid.

53. Ernesto Laclau and Chantal Mouffe, *Hegemony and Socialist Strategy: Towards a Radical Democratic Politics* (New York: Verso, 2001).

54. Notes from Nowhere, *We Are Everywhere: The Irresistible Rise of Global Anti-capitalism* (New York: Verso, 2003).

55. Andrew Ross, *Nice Work If You Can Get It: Life and Labor in Precarious Times* (New York: NYU Press, 2009), 165.

56. Ibid., 168.

57. Hardt, "Politics of the Common."

58. Dyer-Witheford, "Circulation of the Common."

59. Ibid.

60. Modern Language Association, *Report of the MLA Task Force on Evaluating Scholarship for Tenure and Promotion*, December 2006, http://www.mla.org/tenure_promotion.

61. Smith, personal interview.

62. Livia Tenzer, letter to Social Text Editorial Collective, July 10, 2009.

63. Lee, personal interview.

64. Ana Marie Cox, "None of Your Business: The Rise of the University of Phoenix and For-Profit Education—and Why It Will Fail Us All," in *Steal This University*, ed. Benjamin Johnson, Patrick Kavanagh, and Kevin Mattson, 15–32 (New York: Routledge, 2003).

About the Contributors

CHRIS ANDERSON is editor in chief of *Wired*. Since joining *Wired* in 2001, he has led the magazine to nine National Magazine Awards. *Time* magazine named Anderson to its 2007 "Time 100" list. He is author of *The Long Tail: Why the Future of Business Is Selling Less of More* and *Free: The Future of a Radical Price*.

C. W. ANDERSON is Assistant Professor of Media Culture at the College of Staten Island/CUNY and the author of numerous works on the transformations of journalism in the digital age.

FRED BENENSON works in research and development at Kickstarter and previously was Outreach Manager for Creative Commons. He is the creator of *Emoji Dick* and the founder of Free Culture @ NYU. He has taught copyright and cyberlaw at NYU.

YOCHAI BENKLER is the Berkman Professor of Entrepreneurial Legal Studies at Harvard and faculty codirector of the Berkman Center for Internet and Society. He is the author of the award-winning book *The Wealth of Networks: How Social Production Transforms Markets and Freedom*. He was awarded the EFF Pioneer Award in 2007 and the Public Knowledge IP3 Award in 2006. His work can be freely accessed at benkler.org.

DANAH BOYD is a Senior Researcher at Microsoft Research and a Research Associate at Harvard University's Berkman Center for Internet and Society. She recently coauthored *Hanging Out, Messing Around, and Geeking Out: Kids Living and Learning with New Media*. She blogs at http://www.zephoria.org/thoughts/ and tweets at @zephoria.

E. GABRIELLA COLEMAN is the Wolfe Chair in Scientific and Technological Literacy at McGill University. Trained as an anthropologist, she works on the politics of digital media with a focus on computer hackers.

The COLLABORATIVE FUTURES project has developed over two intensive book sprints. In January 2010 in Berlin, Adam Hyde (founder, FLOSSmanuals), Mike Linksvayer (vice president, Creative Commons), Michael Mandiberg (Associate Professor, College of Staten Island/CUNY), Marta Peirano (writer), Alan Toner (filmmaker), and Mushon Zer-Aviv (resident, Eyebeam Center for Art and Technology) wrote the first edition in five days under the aegis of transmediale festival's Parcours series. In June 2010, the book was rewritten at Eyebeam's Re:Group exhibition in New York City with the original six and three new contributors: kanarinka (artist and founder, Institute for Infinitely Small Things), Sissu Tarka (artist, researcher), and Astra Taylor (filmmaker). The full book is freely available to read and to write at www. collaborative-futures.org.

PATRICK DAVISON is a PhD candidate in the Department of Media, Culture, and Communication at NYU. He is one-third of the Internet-themed performance *Memefactory* and has written and performed for the webseries *Know Your Meme*.

ASHLEY DAWSON is Associate Professor of English at the City University of New York's Graduate Center and at the College of Staten Island/CUNY. He is the author of *Mongrel Nation: Diasporic Culture and the Making of Postcolonial Britain*, coeditor of three essay collections, and coeditor of *Social Text* online.

HENRY JENKINS is the Provost's Professor of Communication, Journalism, and Cinematic Arts at the University of Southern California. He is the author or editor of twelve books, including *Textual Poachers: Television Fans and Participatory Culture, Convergence Culture: Where Old and New Media Collide*, and *Fans, Bloggers, and Gamers: Exploring Participatory Culture*. Jenkins is the principal investigator for Project New Media Literacies.

LAWRENCE LESSIG is Director of the Edmond J. Safra Foundation Center for Ethics at Harvard University and Professor of Law at Harvard Law School. Lessig is the author of five books on law, technology, and copyright: *Remix, Code v2, Free Culture, The Future of Ideas*, and *Code and Other Laws of Cyberspace*. He has served as lead counsel in a number of important cases, including *Eldred v. Ashcroft*.

FRED VON LOHMANN is Senior Copyright Counsel at Google, although his contribution here was authored while he was Senior Staff Attorney at the Electronic Frontier Foundation.

MICHAEL MANDIBERG is an artist and Associate Professor of Media Culture at the College of Staten Island/CUNY and Doctoral Faculty at the City University of New York's Graduate Center. He is the coauthor of *Digital Foundations: An Intro to Media Design* and *Collaborative Futures*. His work can been accessed via Mandiberg.com.

TIM O'REILLY is the founder and CEO of O'Reilly Media. In addition to Foo Camps, O'Reilly Media also hosts numerous conferences on technology topics, including the Web 2.0 Summit and the O'Reilly Open Source Convention. O'Reilly is a founder of the Safari Books Online subscription service for accessing books online and of O'Reilly AlphaTech Ventures, an early-stage venture firm. He blogs at radar.oreilly.com.

JAY ROSEN is Associate Professor of Journalism and Director of Studio 20 at New York University. He is the author of the book *What Are Journalists For?* and *PressThink*, a blog about journalism and its ordeals, located at Press-Think.org; *PressThink* won the 2005 Freedom Blog award from Reporters Without Borders.

CLAY SHIRKY is a writer, consultant, and teacher of the social and economic effects of Internet technologies. He is Distinguished Writer in Residence at the Carter Journalism Institute at New York University and Assistant Arts Professor at New York University's Interactive Telecommunications Program. He is the author of *Here Comes Everybody: The Power of Organizing without Organizations* and *Cognitive Surplus: Creativity and Generosity in a Connected Age*.

FELIX STALDER is Lecturer in Digital Culture and Network Theory at the Zurich University of the Arts, where he codirects the media arts program. He has written and edited several books, including *Open Cultures and the Nature of Networks*, *Manuel Castells and the Theory of the Network Society*, and *Deep Search: The Politics of Search beyond Google*. He is also a moderator of the nettime mailing list and can be accessed via felix. openflows.com.

SIVA VAIDHYANATHAN is Professor of Media Studies and Law at the University of Virginia. He is the author of *Copyrights and Copywrongs: The Rise of Intellectual Property and How It Threatens Creativity, The Anarchist in the Library,* and *The Googlization of Everything—and Why We Should Worry.*

Index

1% rule (the 90-9-1 principle), 190
"1984" (television commercial), 174
2600, 105
37signals, 49
4chan.org, 6, 110–111
80-20 rule, 140. *See also* Pareto's Principle

abolition, 156–157, 167
About.com, 84
action figures, 213, 216–219
Action League Now!!!, 218
Adafruit Industries, 196
Adaptive Path, 49
address book, 50
Adkisson, Richard, 26
Adobe Creative Suite, 193
advertising, 33, 38, 84, 208. *See also* marketing; media
Advice Dog, 127–133
AIGA Design Press/New Riders, 194
AJAX, 46, 47, 49
Akamai, 33, 34, 39
Albers, Josef, 193
Albrecht, Chris, 210, 220, 223–224
algorithms, 5, 36, 150
amateur, 246–247, 158, 164, 180
Amazon.com, 38, 39, 42–44, 120, 137, 140, 141, 143, 149, 164, 204
   Amazon Associates, 47
Amendments to the United States Constitution
   Fourth Amendment, 156, 161
   Eighteenth Amendment, 157
   Twenty-First Amendment, 157, 158
America's Funniest Home Videos, 213
analytics software, 190
anarchy, 83

Anderson, C. W., 5
Anderson, Chris, 5, 6, 36, 250
anime music videos, 159–160
Anonymous, 6, 110
anorexia, 252
Answers.com, 84
antiglobalization, 82
AOL, 113
Apache, 39
API (Application Programming Interface), 39, 42, 46–48, 250
Apple, 174
   Apple OS X, 183
   Apple's Powerbook, 190
   iMac, 159
   iPhone, 71
   iPod, 48, 158
   iTunes, 48, 137, 140, 141, 145, 147, 150, 158, 164
applet, 49
appropriation, 219–220
architecture, 191
art, 187, 191, 193
ASCII, 106
Associated Content, 84
Association of the Bar of the City of New York, 167
astroturfing, 246
AT&T, 25, 73, 104–105
AtomFilms, 203, 210, 223–224
attribution, 53, 130–133
augmented reality, 73
authorship, 6, 53, 56–57, 120, 130–133, 178–186

/b/. *See* 4chan.org
back-end, 8, 242, 248–251, 254
backpack, 49

Ballmer, Steve, 164
Barnes & Noble, 43, 138, 142
Bartle, Richard, 227
basecamp, 49
Battelle, John, 33, 77
Bauhaus Basic Course, 193
BBSes, 106, 114
Beastie Boys, 166
Beatles, The, 159
Benenson, Fred, 7
Benkler, Yochai, 2–3, 5, 27
Berardi, Franco, 266
BitTorrent, 33–36, 63
Black Album, 159
Blackboard (software), 262
Blair, Tony, 161
Blip TV, 166
Blockbuster Video, 138, 142
Blogger, 244
blogging, 13, 15, 34, 39–40, 53–54, 64, 75–76,
    80, 87, 239, 244–248, 271
Bloglines, 40
blogola, 246
Blue Box, the, 103
Bollier, David, 266–267
Bollywood, 138
book sprint, 194
booki, 65
books, 137, 142, 145, 160
boyd, danah, 5
Brandeis, Louis, 156
Bright Bike, 196–197
Bright Idea Shade, 191–192, 194–196
Britannica Online, 34
Brooker, Will, 221
Brothers Grimm, 209
BSD (Berkley Software Distribution), 182
burrough, xtine, 193
Bush, George, 161
"Bush Blair Endless Love", 160
business. *See* economics
business-to-business (B2B), 46
Byrne, David, 166

Caffentzis, George, 268–269
Campbell, Cole, 90

Cannes Film Festival, 159–160
Caouette, Jonathan, 159, 160
Captain Crunch, 103–104
Capturing the Friedmans, 143
Carey, James, 86, 90
Carnegie Mellon, 124
carpooling, 17, 21
Cartoon Network, 204, 219
Cathedral and the Bazaar, The (Raymond),
    188
CBS, 79
CDC (US Centers for Disease Control and
    Prevention), 251
Cee-Lo, 166
Celebrity Deathmatch, 219
celestial jukebox, 158
censorship, 249
Chaplin, Charlie, 262
Church of Scientology, 110
circuit board, 187
civil rights, 157
Clear Bits, 195
Clinton, Hilary, 174
CNN, 211
Coase, Ronald, 27, 243–244
Coates, Tom, 40
cognitive surplus, 237
Colbert, Stephen, 55–56
Cole, Jeanne, 221
Coleman, E. Gabriella, 6, 82–83
collaboration, 5, 82–83, 187, 195, 258–259.
    See also sharing
    coordination of, 53–54, 61, 65
    critiques of, 56–57, 251
    political economy in, 60–66
    systems for sharing, 17, 19–21
    with the enemy, 58–59
collective intelligence, 37, 231–233
color theory, 193
commercial culture, 163, 192, 204
commit (software development), 54
commons, the, 266, 269–270
Communist Party, 268
community, 189, 243–244, 248–249, 254
community of practice, 64
compact fluorescent bulbs (CFLs), 191

280 | *About the Contributors*

computationalism, 267
computer programming, 32–51. *See also*
    web services
Concepcion, Bievenido, 214
consumer culture, 137, 147
content management systems, 34
convergence culture, 2, 163, 204–209, 225
Convergence Culture (Jenkins), 2, 8
copyleft, 180
copyright, 5, 9, 24–30, 44, 146, 159–161, 167,
    208–210, 221, 223–224
    benefits of, 158
    clearance culture, 161, 170–176
    infringement, 253
    law, 6–7, 168, 170–176, 184–186, 191, 252
    reform of, 164–165, 178, 185
Craigslist, 43
"Crank Dat" (Superman dance), 159
Crawford, Michael David, 179–181, 183–185
Creative Commons, 7, 9, 28, 47, 65, 130,
    178–179
    critiques of, 182
    license, 163, 166, 178–186, 188, 192–194,
    252, 266
crime, 253
crime map, 238
crowdsourcing, 246, 253. *See also* labor;
    long tail; Web 2.0
Cruise, Tom, 110
Crystal Method, 141
CseARCH, 264
CSS, 49
*Cult of the Amateur: How Today's Internet Is
    Killing Our Culture, The* (Keen), 5
Cult of the Dead Cow, 109
culture. *See* consumer culture; convergence
    culture; DIY; fan culture; folk culture;
    free culture; media; public culture; read/
    write culture; subculture; vernacular
    culture; youth culture
Curley, Tom, 14
Customer Relations Management Software
    (CRM), 50

Daily Kos, 264
dance (remix in), 159

Danger Mouse, 159–160, 166
data, 35–36, 51, 242. *See also* metadata
    aggregation, 56–57, 63
    value-added data, 38, 42–44
    ownership, 42–44, 248–249
Daughter from Danang, 143
Davison, Patrick, 6
Dawkins, Richard, 6, 120, 126
Dawson, Ashley, 5, 8
Debian, 66
Debord, Guy, 242, 248
Deciding What's News (Gans), 79
DEFCON, 109
Demand Media, 78, 81, 84, 88–89, 92–93
democratic theory, 81, 89–93, 267–269
del.icio.us, 45
Dell, 47
Denning, Michael, 259
Department of Defense, 261
design, 187
Desperate Housewives, 236
Dewey, John, 82, 90
DHTML, 49
Diamond, Neil, 218
Digg, 3, 190
Digital, 25
digital cinema, 203–216, 218–220
digital creativity, 157–168
digital divide, 160, 244
*Digital Foundations: An Intro to Media
    Design* (Mandiberg), 193–196
digital humanities, 261
Digital Humanities Quarterly, 261
Digital Millennium Copyright Act
    (DMCA), 7, 173, 180, 209
digital natives, 72
digital technologies, 167
disintermediation, 170
Disney, 115, 144, 209
DIY, 104, 189, 196, 204
Doctor Who, 143
Document Object Model, 49
Dopazo, Jennifer, 194, 195
Dora the Explorer, 240
Dors, Maartin, 248–249
dot-com, 4, 6, 32

DoubleClick, 33, 34, 36, 39
Dougherty, Dale, 32
Duel Masters, 204
Duke University Press, 262–263
Duncombe, Stephen, 115
Durack, Elizabeth, 222
DVD, 137, 204, 212
Dyer-Witheford, Nick, 270

e-books, 257
E-commerce, 141
e-mail sabbatical, 71
eBay, 36–39, 42, 143
Ecast, 140
economics, 6, 192, 196
    market/firm vs non-market production,
        17–22
    market theory, 86, 245
    sharing as modality of production, 17–22
Economist, The, 24
eDonkey, 63
Eilat, Galit, 58
Electronic Frontier Foundation (EFF), 253
emoticons, 124–125
eMusic, 148
enclosure, 26
Encyclopedia Dramatica (ED), 111–112, 122
Engrave Your Tech, 190
Engressia, Joe (Joy Bubbles), 102
Entertainment Weekly, 204
etchstar, 190
Ettema, James, 80
EVDB (Events and Venues Database), 34, 44
evite, 34
Eyebeam Center for Art and Technology,
    188–192, 194
Ezekiel, 88
EZLN (Zapatista Army of National Libera-
    tion), 266–267, 269

F/X (special effects), 203, 224
Facebook, 2, 59, 120
Fahlman, Scott E., 124
failure, 193, 244
fair use, 7, 29, 56–57, 160, 165, 167, 175. *See
    also* copyright

Fake, Caterina, 41
Faleux, Shane, 215
fan culture, 7–8
fan fiction, 223–225
Federal Communications Commission,
    21–22
Federici, Silvia, 268–269
feminism, 156
film, 105, 137–140, 142–144, 149–150,
    159–160
Firefox, 50, 100
Fithian, John, 15
Fitz-Roy, Don, 214
flamewar, 106–107
Flash, 49
flash mob, 49, 267
Flickr, 34, 41, 45, 49, 163, 166, 188, 190, 244,
    248–249
FLOSS (FOSS), 6, 24–30, 39, 45, 47, 65, 99,
    101, 112–113, 182, 185–188, 193–195, 238,
    247, 254, 260, 267–269
    history of, 188
    sexism in, 252
FLOSSmanuals, 65, 194
Folding@Home, 63
folk culture, 204, 206–209
folksonomy, 34, 38, 54. *See also* tagging
FOO Camp, 33
Fort Minor, 166
Fotonaut, 166
Foucault, Michel, 120, 130–133
Fountains of Wayne, 141
Fraser, Nancy, 88
Free! Why $0.00 Is the Future of Business, 6
free as in beer, 6, 192, 246, 250, 253
Free Culture (Lessig), 161, 163
free culture, 7, 8, 53, 160, 165, 178, 182,
    187–188, 192, 253
    business models of, 192
    ethics of, 181
free software. *See* FLOSS
Free Software Foundation, 26, 178, 181
free use, 160, 165
freedom of speech, 26
Freesound.org, 163
Fried, Limor, 188–191, 196

front-end, 242, 248, 252, 254
Frumin, Michael, 189
FTC (Federal Trade Commission), 246
Fungible goods, 182–185
Furtado, Vasco, 238
Futur antérieur, 265–267
The Future of the Internet—and How to Stop It (Zittrain), 120

games, 205, 227–229
Gandhi, 88
Gans, Herbert, 79
Garrett, Jesse James, 49
Gates, Bill, 25
GeoCities, 125
Gil, Gilberto, 28, 166
Gilligan's Island, 236, 239–240
Gilmor, Dan, 14, 42
GIMP, 193–194
Girl Talk, 159, 166
GIS, 46
GitHub, 184
Gitlin, Todd, 88
Glocer, Tom, 15
GNU General Public License. *See* GPL
GNU/Linux 21, 24, 27, 39, 66, 181–184, 187
Goldstein, Paul, 158
Golumbia, David, 262, 267
Google, 34–35, 39, 42, 44–45, 120, 210, 250
    Gmail, 44, 45, 49, 50
    Google AdSense, 34, 35–36, 47, 142–143, 250
    Google Analytics, 250
    Google Docs, 50
    Google Flu Trends, 251
    Google Maps, 43–46, 238
    Google PageRank, 37, 41, 57–58, 62
    as web service, 35
Gorbachev, Mikhail, 167
Gore, Al, 55
GPL (General Public License), 28, 181–183, 247, 254
Graffiti Research Lab, 189
Graphical User Interface (GUI), 49
Graphs, Maps, and Trees (Moretti), 261
Great Recession, the, 6

Green, Seth, 219
Greenblatt, Stephen, 257
Grey Album, 159
Grundrisse, 265
GTD (Getting Things Done), 74
Gutmann, Amy, 90–91
Gypsies, The, 230

Haas, Tanni, 86
Habermas, Jürgen, 82, 90–92, 267
hackers, 6, 25, 27, 47, 99–101, 108–111
Hackers: Heroes of the Revolution (Levy), 99
Hafstein, Vladimir, 29–30
Hall, Gary, 261, 264
Halon, Aaron, 217
Hamster Dance, 125–126
"Happy Birthday," 166
Haraway, Donna, 66
Hardt, Michael, 259, 265, 269–270
Harmon, Amy, 220
Harry Potter, 175
hashtag, 54
Hastings, Reed, 143
Hebdige, Dick, 101, 108
Hemingway, Ernest, 157
Henderson, Cal, 45
Here Comes Everybody, 243
Hill, Benjamin Mako, 178
Hindman, Mathew, 267
Ho, Karen, 262–263
home movies, 212–214
Honig, Bonnie, 92
HOPE (Hackers on Planet Earth), 109
housingmaps.com, 43, 47
"The Hunt for Gollum," 174, 175
hybrid economies, 163
Hyde, Adam, 5, 194
Hyde, Lewis, 115

I Love Lucy, 236
IBM, 21, 24, 237
ideal-types, 78, 81
identity, 43–44, 53
IFC Films, 137
IM (instant messaging), 50

images, 249

IMDb (Internet Movie Database), 65, 138–139

immaterial labor, 265

Industrial Revolution, 236, 240

Indymedia, 78, 81, 82, 87, 92. *See also* journalism, citizen

information overload, 71–76

Inkscape, 193–194

institution, 245

Instructables.com, 189, 191–192

intellectual property, 25, 208–210, 221, 224–227

interactivity, 204–205

internet protocols, 27. *See also* networks

Into Thin Air (Krakauer), 137

Ippolita, 59

IRC (Internet Relay Chat), 27

Jackson, Peter, 174

Jackson, Samuel L., 218

Jargon File, the, 113

Jarvis, Jeff, 14

Java, 49

JavaScript, 49

Jay Z, 159

Jenkins, Henry, 2, 5, 7–8

Jobs, Steve, 103, 147

journalism, 5–6, 77, 79

    algorithmic, 6, 83–84, 87–89, 92

    citizen, 13–15, 29, 49, 77–83, 87, 92

    public, 81–83, 86, 87, 89–93

Juris, Jeffrey, 266–267

kanarinka, 5

Kazaa, 145, 147

Kickstarter.com, 196

King, Martin Luther, 88

Kirschner, Ann, 15

"Know Your Meme," 122

knowledge sharing, 64

Koster, Raph, 210, 227–229, 231

Krakauer, Jon, 137

Kronke, Clay, 216

Kutiman (Ophir Kutiel), 56–57

labor, 7, 36, 209–211. *See also* outsourcing; peer production; user generated content; wisdom of crowds

LaCarte, Deidre, 125

Laclau, Ernesto, 269

Lady Ada, 191

Lagaan: Once Upon a Time in India, 138–139

Lambert, Steve, 191–194

laser cutter, 187

Laszlo Systems, 49

Latour, Bruno, 66

Lawrence of Arabia, 217

Laws, Kevin, 142

Lazzarato, Maurizio, 265

Le Guin, Ursula, 105

Le Tigre, 166

LED Throwies, 189

LEGO, 218

Lenin, Vladimir, 100

Lessig, Lawrence, 6, 8, 209, 252

Levy, Joseph, 210–211, 214

Levy, Steven, 99, 100

life hacking, 74

Limewire, 63

Linden Labs, 164

Linksvayer, Mike, 5

Linux. *See* GNU/Linux

Liquidated, 262

"Living with Schizoaffective Disorder," 179, 183

Loki, 115

LOLcats, 127, 239

Lonelygirl15, 3, 245–246

long tail, 36, 141–143, 146, 149–150

Lord of the Rings, The, 174

Los Angeles International Film Festival, 159

Lotta continua, 268

Lotus, 39

Louvre, 183

Lovink, Geert, 59

Lucas, George, 222

Lucas Film, 166

LucasArts, 8, 220–221, 223, 227, 231

Luhrmann, Baz, 224

lulz, 6, 111–116

Macromedia, 49
Mahalo, 84
mailing lists, 179, 239
Malcolm in the Middle, 236
Malik, Om, 166
Mansfield, Joe, 190
MapQuest, 42, 43, 46
Marconi, 243
marketing, 4, 32–33, 245. *See also* advertising; media
Marx, 265–269
Marxism, 83
mashup, 33, 43
mass media. *See* media
Mather, Evan, 211–212, 218
Matmos, 166
Matrix, The, 248
Maurer, David, 113
McCracken, Grant, 205, 225–226
McGregor, Ewan, 224
McLuhan, Marshall, 242
media, 3. *See also* advertising; marketing
   audiences, 1–3, 6, 8, 13–15, 36, 42, 77–93,
      140–141, 160, 170, 236–241, 250
   children and media, 165, 168
   industries, 137–150, 166, 148, 165, 170, 194
   mass media, 13–15, 55, 138, 155, 244,
      206–207
   niche markets, 137–150
   regulation, 21
   social media, 4, 7, 8, 53, 242
Media Lab Prado, 194
Media Wiki, 54
Mellon Foundation, 272
meme, 6, 32–34, 120–133
metadata, 54, 132
metamoderation, 64
microblogging, 53
Microsoft, 25, 27, 33–34, 39, 45–46, 48, 50,
   164, 190
   MapPoint, 46
   Windows, 183
MIT, 6, 26, 100–101, 188
   media lab, 182
   OpenCourseWare, 260

Mitnick, Kevin, 100, 108–109
MLA (Modern Language Association),
   257, 270
   Report of the MLA Task Force on Evaluating Scholarship for Tenure and Promotion, 270
MMORPG (Massively Multiplayer Online
   Role-Playing Game), 227–228
mobile computing, 48, 71–76, 206
modders/modding, 208, 228–231
Modern Times, 262
Moleskine, 190
Mona Lisa, 183
Monde, Le, 211
Moretti, Franco, 261, 270–271
Mouffe, Chantal, 91–92, 269
Moulin Rouge!, 224
mountain climbing, 137
Movielink, 149
MP3, 203
MP3.com, 34, 148
MTV, 219
Murdoch, Rupert, 15
music, 28, 140–143, 145–150, 155–156, 158
   remix in, 159
My Morning Jacket, 166
MySQL, 39
Myth of Digital Democracy, The (Hindman), 267
mythology, 225

Napster, 33–36, 39, 42, 205, 209
NASA, 21
NavTeq, 43
NBC, 79
Negri, Toni, 265
neolibralism, 264–269
Netflix, 137, 140–143, 149–150
Netscape, 33–35, 39, 40, 50
Network Solutions, 42
networks, 5, 45, 59, 120, 146
   and copies, 161, 164–165
   infrastructure, 39, 139
   network effects, 36–37
New Line Cinema, 174–175

New York Times, 137, 211, 220, 231–232
Newsweek, 79
NextLevelGuitar.com, 56
Nickelodeon, 218
Nine Inch Nails, 166
Nissenbaum, Helen, 77
NNTP (Network News Protocol), 41
No Doubt, 149
nonfungible, 183
NPR (National Public Radio), 211
Nussbaum, Martha, 112
NYU (New York University), 262
    Interactive Telecommunications Program, 194, 238
    library, 260

O'Brien, Sebastian, 218
O'Reilly Media, 33
O'Reilly, Tim, 2–5, 237
Obama, Barack, 159–160
Ofoto, 34
Open Humanities Press (OHP), 271
Oink, 65
Olmstead, Roy, 156
Olmstead v. the United States, 156
online video
    copyright in, 170–176
    remix in, 159–160
open-access (OA), 258–262
open licenses. See Creative Commons; GPL
open source. See FLOSS
Open Web, the, 120
operaismo movement, 258, 268
Oracle, 39
organized crime, 157
Orkut, 49
Outing, Steve, 83
outsourcing, 247. See also labor
overshare, 72
Overture, 36

Pareto, Alfredo, 140
Pareto's Principle, 140
Parsons (The New School for Design), 190
participation, 8, 36, 48, 156, 166, 204, 222–225, 237, 238, 242–244. See also collaboration

party lines, 103
patent law, 184. See also copyright
PayPal, 44
PBS (Public Broadcasting Service), 143
Peachpit Press, 194
Pearson, 194
pedagogy, 193
peer-review, 258, 263–264
peer-to-peer (p2p), 36, 65, 161, 165, 252, 266
peer production, 2, 3, 7, 27, 28, 63–66, 181–182, 184, 189, 238. See also labor
Peirano, Marta, 5
the people formerly known as the audience, 13–15, 77, 80–81
permalink, 40
Peretti, Jonah, 189, 191–192
Perl, 39, 45
Peters, John Durham, 88
Pfizer, 184
Phiber optik 100, 108
phonographs, 155
Photoshop, 110, 212
PHP, 39, 45
Phrack, 100, 107–108, 111
phreaking, 6, 101, 102–105
physical computing, 188–190
Picasa, 166
Pink (musician), 149
piracy, 165, 167. See also copyright
    war of prohibition on, 161
podcast, 13, 80
Politiburo, 167
politics, 6, 101, 115, 159. See also democratic theory
Powazek, Derek, 2, 3
Powderly, James, 189–190, 191–192
power law, 8, 141, 263
print-on-demand, 257
privacy, 44, 71, 75, 158, 161–163
Probot Productions, 218
Processing, 194
Prohibition. See abolition
Project Bamboo, 272
proprietary software, 24–30, 44
Proust, Marcel, 157
Provos, Niels, 100

public-relations (PR), 245, 246
publishing, 8, 83, 137–150
  book, 137, 193
  online booksellers, 137
  open publishing, 83
  university presses, 257–265, 270–271
Purdie, Bernard "Pretty," 56
Python, 39, 45

R.R. Bowker, 43
Rademacher, Paul, 43
RAE (Research Assessment Exercise), 262
radio, 243
Radiohead, 166
Raiders of the Lost Ark, 217
Random House, 137
Raymond, Eric, 38, 188
read/write culture, 156
ReadyMade, 191
RealNetworks, 141
ReCaptcha, 62
recommendations, 137
record label, 148
Recording Industry Association of
  America (RIAA), 140
*Reel Families: A Social History of Amateur
  Film* (Zimmerman), 212
remix, 47, 56–57, 158–160,174, 180, 185,
  189–191, 197, 260, 266
  copyright law in, 165–166
Remix (Lessig), 8, 161, 163
Republica, La, 211
REST (Representational State Transfer), 46
retroreflective vinyl, 196
Rhapsody, 137, 141, 142–143, 146, 148–150
Rice University's Connexions, 260
Ritchie, Lionel, 160
rival goods, 17–18, 243. *See also* economics
Roberts, Drew, 180–181
Robertson, Michael, 148
Rosen, Jay, 2, 3, 5, 80, 89
Rosenbaum, Ron, 103
Rosenblatt, Richard, 89
Ross, Andrew, 259, 269
Ross, Diana, 160
Rossiter, Ned, 59

Roth, Daniel, 84, 92
Roth, Evan, 189–192
Rowling, J. K., 175
RSS (Really Simple Syndication), 40–41,
  47, 73
Rubio, Kevin, 204
Ruby, 45

St. Francis, 88
St. Louis Post-Dispatch, 90
Salesforce.com, 50
sampling. See *Remix*
SAP, 39
scholarly productivity, assessment of, 262.
  See also surveillance
Schroeder, Hassan, 45
Schudson, Michael, 86
scripting languages, 45. *See also* computer
  programming; web services
Scrubs, 239
search engine, 84. *See also* Google
Second Life, 110, 164, 232
"Secrets of the Little Blue Box," 103
Seed, 84
Selector, 149
Selfish Gene, The (Dawkins), 120
SEO (search engine optimization), 34, 57
"September That Never Ended," 113
SETI@home, 17, 21, 63, 163
Shakespeare, William, 115, 157
Shakespeare in Love, 210
sharing, 5, 163, 179–181, 187, 195. *See also*
  collaboration
  versus collaboration, 53
Shirky, Clay, 5, 8, 243, 244, 252, 253
Simpson, Jo, 137
sitcom, 236–237
Smith, Dana, 214
Smith, Mark, 164
Skrenta, Rich, 40
Slashdot, 3, 63
SOAP (Social Object Access Protocol), 46
social contract, 55–56, 66. *See also* politics
social media. *See* media
Social Text, 271
Soderberg, Johan, 160

software. *See* computer programming

Soulja Boy, 159

source code, 25. *See also* computer programming; FLOSS

Sousa, John Philip, 155, 159

spam, 38

Spears, Britney, 149–150

Spielberg, Steven, 215

Spoon, 166

SQL (Standard Query Language), 42

Squire, Kurt, 229–230

Stalder, Felix, 5, 8

Stallman, Richard, 26, 100, 178, 181, 182, 188, 246

Star Trek, 222

Star Wars (fan culture), 8, 203–233

Star Wars (films and characters), 166, 203–233

Star Wars Galaxies (video game), 227–228, 230–231

Stein, Danny, 148

Steinkuehler, Constance, 229–230

Sterling, Bruce, 110, 112

Studio Foundation, 193

Stutz, Dave, 48

subculture, 6, 101, 106–109

Sun Microsystems, 45

Sundance Film Festival, 143, 144

Super-8, 159, 213, 215

Supreme Court, 156, 161

Surowiecki, James, 41

surveillance, 8, 108, 156, 250–253, 262

Sxip, 44

syndication. *See* RSS

Taft, Chief Justice, 156

tagging, 34, 38, 54. *See also* folksonomy

TAP (*Technical Assistance Program*), 104–105

Tarka, Sissu, 5

Tarnation, 159

Taub, David, 56

Taylor, Astra, 5

technology, 72–73, 243
   changes in, 156- 160
   critiques of, 73, 265–269

techno-utopia, 3, 178, 180, 182–186, 242–243

television, 236–237

terms of service, 166

TheForce.net, 203, 212

Thievery Corporation, 166

Thomas, Douglas, 107

Thompson, Dennis, 90–91

Thompson, Mark, 14

"ThruYou–Kutiman Mixes YouTube," 56–57

Time, 79

TiVo, 48, 205

Tolkien, J. R. R., 174, 175

Toner, Alan, 5

Torrone, Phil, 190, 196

Torvalds, Linus, 27, 100, 181–184

Touching the Void (Simpson), 137

Tower Records, 138, 142

Toys "R" Us, 46

Triplets of Belleville, The, 138

trolls, 6, 110–116

Turow, Joseph, 78

Twentieth Century Fox Film Corporation, 216

Twitter, 71, 73, 80

ubiquitous computing, 48, 71–76. *See also* mobile computing

United States Congress, 155

university library budgets, 260

University of California, 260

University of Michigan
   Libraries, 257
   Press, 8, 257, 263
   Scholarly Publishing Office, 271

UNIX, 182

UNIX Terrorist, 100–102, 107, 114

upcoming.org, 34

Urban Outfitters, 192–193

Urban Dictionary, 100, 122

Usenet, 41, 114

user generated content, 2, 53, 77, 227–230. *See also* labor

Userland, 40

USSR, failure of, 167

Vaidhyanathan, Siva, 5
Valenti, Jack, 158, 161, 165
VandenBerghe, Jason, 217
Vann-Adibé, Robbie, 140–141
Varian, Hal, 42
VCR, 214
Vectors, 261
Verisign, 42
version control system, 53–54
vernacular culture, 204, 225–226
Via Campesina, La, 269
Viacom, 173, 221
video, 159–160, 170–176
videogames, 145
Vimeo, 64, 188, 190
Viola (browser), 49
viral licensing. *See* copyleft
viral marketing, 38. *See also* advertising
Virginia-Pilot, 90
Virno, Paolo, 265
VoIP (Voice over Internet Protocol), 50
von Lohmann, Fred, 6, 7
"Vote Different," 174

Wallerstein, Immanuel, 265
Walker, Rob, 111
War Games, 105–106
Ward, Jim, 220
Warner Brothers, 175
Warner Music Group, 253
Watergate, 78, 82
Wattenberg, Martin, 237
Web 2.0, 3–4, 6, 32–51, 77, 248, 250, 252
    critiques of, 139–150, 242–254
Web 2.0 Bullshit Generator, 4
web application. *See* web services
web design, 4, 32–51
web services, 33- 36, 44, 46, 48, 50, 51, 53.
    See also computer programming
Weber, Max, 78
Weems v. United States, 156
Wei, Pei, 49
Wellner, Damon, 218
"What Is an Author?," 130
What Would Google Do?, 4
White Album, 159

White House, 76
wiki, 34, 44, 50, 53, 65, 194–195, 238, 244
Wikipedia, 3, 8, 29, 34, 38, 53–56, 64, 71–72,
    100, 122, 130, 158, 163, 166, 184, 187, 237,
    239, 246, 250, 254, 266
Wilkinson, Jamie, 190
Williams, Dianne, 224
Williams, John, 216
Winer, Dave, 15, 40
Wired, 84, 211, 215, 246
wireless spectrum, 22. *See also* networks
wiretap, 156. *See also* surveillance
wisdom of crowds, 5, 41. *See also* labor
Wishnow, Jason, 203
Wissoker, Ken, 262–263
Witchita-Eagle, 82
WordPress, 187
World of Warcraft, 231, 239
World Social Forum, 267
World Trade Organization, 82, 266
Wozniak, Steve, 103
WWF, 219

Xanadu, 41
XML, 46, 49

Yahoo!, 36, 42, 44, 49, 137, 163, 166, 249
Yelp, 163–164
Yeltsin, Boris, 167
"Yes We Can" (video), 159
YIPL (Youth International Party Line),
    104–105
Yippies (Youth International Party), 101,
    104–105
Young Indiana Jones Chronicles, 215
youth culture, 71–76
YouTube, 2, 3, 7, 56, 130, 159, 170, 173, 174,
    190, 244, 245, 253
YouTube's Content ID, 253

ZDNet, 45
Zer-Aviv, Mushon, 5
zine, 107
Zelizer, Barbie, 79–80
Zimmerman, Patrica R., 212–213
Zittrain, Jonathan, 120, 132

convert them into goals according to the SMART formula. I am sure that the SMART formula from project management is certainly familiar to you. As a reminder, SMART is the acronym for

Specific
Measurable
Attainable
Relevant
Timely
A goal is defined as "smart" only if it meets these five conditions.
The SMART formula has proven itself to set clear, measurable and verifiable goals.

The Greatest Hurdles when Defining SMART Goals

There are, of course, times in which people on a virtual team don't think about the others on the team or the common goals of the team; they focus on themselves. Every member of the team has their own personal ambitions and goals – some of which they have not even shared with anyone else. This is normal. These personal ambitions and goals are known as **Hidden Agendas**. If these hidden agendas, however, are not in line with or begin to conflict with the team's goals, problems arise, and they can sabotage the entire process.

Hidden agendas can be very diverse. They can be related to career or professional goals. They can be related to personal or relationship goals. They become harmful to the functioning of the team when they are in conflict with the team or its goals, *The three most important development areas of the team are converted into goals according to the SMART formula. Be careful! Hidden agendas, micromanagement and know-how often cause unexpected challenges.* and the transition from harmless to harmful hidden agendas, or intrigue, is fluid. For example, if one team member tries to get more recognition in the team or if a team member tries to extract money for personal purposes, trust is broken, and the team is in danger of falling apart. It is often difficult to recognize the destruction until it is too late.

The best way to overcome destructive hidden agendas is to assure that a transparent target goal process is in place in which regular feedback occurs. Also, allow team members to speak openly about their personal and professional interests, while making sure that each team member has clear goals that correspond to the team's goals. It is for precisely this reason that we involve all team members in doing both the strengths exercise and the exercise to determine the three most important topics for the team. The strengths exercise helps you as team leader to get to know the team members better, so that you can begin to anticipate possible hidden agendas. The top three topics exercise allows all team members to participate and give input as to the direction and goals of the team. Because everyone is involved in the process, everyone owns the results. As you work with your team, it is important that you give praise only for the accomplishment of team goals, not individual goals. This reminds the team of its focus. If no goals have as of yet been reached, praise all behavior that promotes cooperation and cohesion within the team.

The second greatest hurdle in virtual teams is one that we have already discussed in detail: micromanaging. Even if all of the team members have committed themselves to the team and its goals, the boss can destroy the team's motivation and therefore hinder the team's ability to reach its goals through excessive control and micromanaging. I cannot emphasize enough how important this point is. No matter how great an expert and how experienced the team leader is, their purpose is to remind the team of its mission, not to get involved in the details of each team member's responsibilities. The only exception to this is when a team member asks for the team leader's input or advice.

In addition to hidden agendas and micromanagement, there is a third major hurdle on the way to reaching your team's goals. These are the **critics and know-it-alls** on the team. They always find something to criticize. How do you ensure that these critics do not block or de-motivate the other team members? The best way to do this is to have clear goals and to give positive feedback each time the team makes progress towards its goals. This positive feedback from the boss reassures team members that they are on the right track, and it overshadows any negative criticism that they may have received from the critics.

Virtual teams easily bring top performance to the project once the potential of each team has been established. Working independently is easy once each individual team member is clear about their goals and mission.

This being said, there are cases in which the critics and the know-it-alls just have to find fault with something. They simply can't let it go. If you find yourself in this situation, speak to the critics and try to figure out their motivation for being so negative. Speak openly and forthrightly to them about their behavior and explain how the negativity hurts the morale of the team. Work with them to find other ways for them to express their concerns if the concerns are about genuine problems. You may find as team leader that you actually have to intervene while the critic or know-it-all is criticizing something or someone and call them on this behavior.

Fortunately, I have had very few problems with critics on the virtual teams I have led in the past. By carefully selecting your team members, letting them work responsibly on their own, and giving recognition at key moments, you can help otherwise very critical people to offer valuable, but limited, constructive criticism. Once again, if you want to lead your virtual team to achieve top results with ease, they need three things: 1) the knowledge that you know and respect their talents, experiences, and unique potential, 2) for you to set clear goals for each individual as well as for the team as a whole, and 3) for you to give everyone the opportunity to work independently and be personally responsible for their results. If you do these three things, you will be successful.

Chapter 4

When goals are interlinked,
Each Team Member is Accountable

The workshop was in full steam.

As the morning sun spread its powerful rays across Hamburg, bathing the hotel conference room at "Le Meridien" with bright streaks of light, Paul took off his jacket and rolled up his sleeves. He knew the workshop was going into the decisive phase. Claude and Linda were standing in front of a flipchart. They were speaking loudly and gesticulating energetically. They were one of two groups of two working on key issues for the team. Every few minutes, everything got quiet. Then, Linda would write a new idea on the flipchart.

Bernd sat at a table in front of his open laptop. He was also fully engaged in conversation, although he was speaking in a much calmer fashion. He looked alternately at Anne on the screen with WebEx and *Paul continues with the workshop for the team. The team members work on the crucial themes of "empowerment" and "integration of external resources."* then back to his computer. The two of them posted their ideas on a virtual whiteboard.

Paul stood quietly, watching everyone from the back of the room. Every now and then he would go quietly to one of the groups to make a suggestion or ask a question. As a facilitator, his job was not to give answers but to help them come up with their own ideas and solutions.

Claude and Linda worked on the subject of "empowerment." The two discussed what they would feel and experience if the goal of maximum self-responsibility had already been achieved. Claude was once more reminded of how important this subject was to him. His excitement showed. Bernd worked with Anne via WebEx on the topic of "Integration of External Parties." They were working on the question of how the construction workers, the government, and the professor from New York could best be incorporated into the team.

After a short while, all four of them were ready to report on their results and to share their conclusions, goals, and roadmaps with the other group. Claude and Linda began.

"I want absolute freedom," Claude said loudly and clearly. Bernd had to smile. "This is Claude," he thought. The Canadian stood by the flipchart, and Linda stood next to him ready to interject her thoughts at any time.

"This means I can make decisions without first checking with Bernd." Claude continued; "As long as I remain within the budget and the timeline is not affected by my decisions, I should be free to do my work unsupervised. If each of us acts responsibly on our own, we will be able to check our progress on our weekly phone calls. Each of us can report what we did during the past week. If problems arise, they don't have to be solved by the entire team; the person responsible for that area should be responsible to come up with the necessary solutions for the problems. If that person needs additional assistance, they should contact only the specific team members necessary to find that solution."

Linda nodded in agreement. She hated it when others wanted to unload their problems on her without thinking about a solution.

"Bernd, you can ask questions or give advice," continued Claude, giving Bernd a friendly look. "But the operative decision for each individual goal should be made by the immediate person responsible. If I need your help in prioritizing or negotiating with external parties, I'll come to you."

Everyone nodded approvingly. Next, Bernd and Anne presented the SMART goals that they had worked out. This was followed by the others asking questions and giving feedback. Bernd kept a protocol of the feedback given.

Then Paul asked everyone to get up and get ready for the roadmap exercise. Claude and Linda went into their corner of the room and Bernd moved nearer to the video screen. They had just started to define milestones when Anne raised her voice over the video conferencing sound system.

"I'm so sorry to interrupt. Even though my primary role is participating in our meeting, I am also required to check for anything urgent coming in on e-mail. Just now an e-mail arrived from our local construction companies. They are sharing the results of a new cost estimate, and state that they will need about 25 percent more budget than initially requested, due to a new detailed plan using the results of the new MOOC design."

"What ?!" Bernd screamed. He hit the table with his fist and jumped up from his chair.

A Sudden Shock: Anne gets an e-mail that the government wants 25% more money. The project no longer seems financially feasible.

Linda remained unmoved. She watched Bernd's reaction, then said with calm consideration, "I'm afraid we cannot finance this additional cost by expanding our crowdfunding campaign. You are already aware that the campaign is stagnating. We found only a few investors. People have participated in small numbers, and with small amounts, and there is no more coverage coming in via the media to strengthen our push for this funding."

"What, damn it, is going on?" Bernd shouted. He was so angry that he had not even heard Linda. "This endangers our entire project!"

"Unless you build more efficiently and thus more cost-effectively" came the calm voice of Paul from the back corner of the room. Everyone turned to Paul. "I have experienced larger and more negative surprises than this one. What I see here before me is a team of top experts who are beginning to trust each other. I'm sure you'll find a way. There must be someone in this world that can do this for a lower cost."

After the coffee break, Bernd was still upset. He realized that they would need to find some help, and with this caliber of team members, a solution would be found. He was becoming timidly optimistic.

Drawing the group back together, Paul said "I suggest that we continue with the first two roadmaps and then work as a whole team on a third new roadmap that is about cost-efficient construction!"

Shortly thereafter, Claude and Linda were standing in the middle of the room writing every milestone on a metaplan card and laying the cards on the floor. Today's date and the end date of the project were marked, allowing team members to lay the cards along the timeline and walk back and forth between them. This enabled them to test the points of the timeline to see if the task written on the card was the right task at the right time and if the order of the cards was accurate.

As everyone began slowing down, lunch was announced. Anne timed out for an hour, ate a little, and went looking for her daughter.

Following lunch, Paul gathered the group together and said they would now go into the next round of the roadmap exercise using the timeline Linda and Claude had worked on. "Let's work on this example: Empowerment."

Paul was in a position so that everyone could see him well, including Anne on VTC. "Imagine, today is the day when you have fully achieved your goal."

He asked Linda and Claude to stand on the spot on the floor that marked the end point. "At this moment, all team members have acted independently and self-reliably. They feel fully empowered!"

For the next round of the workshop, Paul asks everyone to imagine what it would be like if the team had already fully achieved its goal.

Paul looked around. Everyone nodded. "So, what are you missing from the perspective of the goal? Be spontaneous. Write down what you think."

Paul moved over to the screen where Anne and Bernd were working on the topic of "integrating external parties." He looked at the digital whiteboard and asked the two to imagine they had successfully integrated all external partners.

Paul asked, "Now that you have achieved this milestone, what advice would you give to today's team that is just beginning to integrate the external parties?"

Anne immediately had an idea: "Bernd, let's name an ambassador for every key party we are dealing with. This includes the external parties. We will invite the ambassadors to the monthly telephone conference. In turn, our ambassadors will take part in the most critical meetings of the external parties and will have a brief moment to speak when appropriate."

Bernd nodded approvingly. Claude overheard Anne's comment and started listening with great interest.

"I'm sure there are others like Claude who would be delighted to be the liason," Anne added. "That person would provide information about the state of progress but would also provide information on issues which affect the respective organizations." After everyone had briefly added their opinion, the topic "ambassador" was added to the whiteboard.

Paul then announced the last round and asked both teams to present their roadmaps. Each team had to decide among themselves who would take responsibility for which of the intermediate objectives. The other group would ask questions, make suggestions and, if necessary, even challenge the decisions. Paul also encouraged everyone to actively intervene for certain interim goals when that person believed they had the necessary and perhaps more relevant personal strengths to achieve it.

There were heated discussions, and Bernd went so far as to describe some of Claude's ideas of empowerment as "nonsense." Bernd still seemed to want as much control as possible. Finally, however, he gave in. He began to realize that in future he would have much more time for overview of the essentials, and he could provide support on a more senior level.

Claude, Linda, and Anne did their best to make Bernd's role as a senior adviser seem appealing, and Linda and Claude gladly volunteered to be ambassadors. At the end, Linda and Claude held up several cards with the goals for which they were immediately responsible. Anne and Bernd had marked their goals on the whiteboard.

Paul explained that soon everyone would realize that these goals of the individual team members were interconnected with each other. "Imagine the individual targets intertwining like gears. No one person can achieve his or her goal without others reaching their goals."

Paul advised Bernd to remain largely free from operational targets, because he needed to be available to the team at all times as a guide and supporter.

After the last round, each team member is then responsible for setting several intermediate goals. The groups have to agree on who will be responsible for each goal.

Then Paul said, "Now, let us all tackle the issue of how to build more efficiently and cost-effectively."

Everyone in the core team is responsible for one of the most important team goals: articulating their vision. Teams in corporations often fix their vision in writing. Very often, these are three or four sentences in typical manager jargon, which don't trigger any emotions and with which the team members cannot identify.

As leader of a virtual team, you have two options to make it better. You can be charismatic and stand before your team like Martin Luther King: "I have a dream," painting your vision vividly and passionately, reaching your employees through their emotions. Or, you let the team work out their vision themselves. In most cases, this is the better alternative. In this so-called "bottom-up" approach, there are simple coaching techniques to guide you and your team. While doing this exercise, it is important to be creative, to stay focused on the targets, and to address all of the five sensory channels.

In virtual teams, it does not work if several people are responsible for one goal. Each team member should be assigned on large goal for which they are responsible.

Once the vision is clear, it should be broken down into annual targets. One huge difference between local and virtual teams is that, in local teams, the vision can be translated into three or four major strategic goals, and several people from the team can be designated to be responsible for tracking these goals.

In my experience with virtual teams, however, having several people responsible for a common goal has never worked well. It works much more efficiently when the vision of the virtual team is broken down into many individual annual goals. Then everyone on the core team can take responsibility for a single goal.

Method:
    Together with the core team members, or Leadership Team, define the most important team goals. Do this in such a way, that each core team member is responsible for exactly one of these team goals. This ensures that each core team member carries the same high responsibility as every other core team member. Through this, they own the project.

Virtual teams need intermediate targets and one member of the core team should be responsible for each goal. The core team, known as the "Leadership Team," consists of those who report directly to team chief. Everyone decides together, however, how to achieve the goals within the prescribed time and budget framework. All of the members of the core team are responsible to achieve their goals, and as a result, when they reach their goals they get the credit and the glory.

Avoid the Propensity to Hide in Virtual Teams

Have you ever worked really hard on a project, and it seemed like other team members were not nearly as motivated as you were? This is much more common in virtual teams than in local teams. In a virtual team, it's possible to ignore phone calls or not answer e-mails. This ends up frustrating and angering other team members. The result of such behavior is that the productivity of the team will drop rapidly. A virtual environment opens up a lot of possibilities to hide, and often, no one is able to control what each team member is doing.

Let me tell you about my own personal experience. I love sports, especially track and field. At age 40, I started to compete again. I don't know if it was a mid-life crisis, or whether it was due to one of my daughters saying, "Papa, you're getting older." At any rate, I returned to competitive sports, and I soon was the Bulgarian master in spear throwing and discus throw. In addition, I won the Balkan Championship in 2014, which includes competitors from 18 nations. One year later, I was second in the European Masters Games in the discus throw.

I am not writing about this to brag. It drives home, rather, my point of how much performance dominates my approach. Performance is my most important motivator. For my personality type, performance plays a much more important role than power or money might for someone else. Can you imagine how frustrated I was when I was working at my peak performance level on my team while other team members were shirking their responsibilities and commitments? I learned a lot about leading virtual teams from these experiences. As a result, when I lead a virtual team, I break down the team goal into many individual goals, and each core member can take responsibility for one of these goals. If everyone has their goal and has to deliver results for this goal, no one can hide.

Each Employee on a Virtual Team Needs Clear Goals

As we have discussed before, micromanagement does not work in virtual teams. Even in local teams, micromanagement reduces productivity. In virtual teams, such intervention is completely counterproductive. Team members of virtual teams need full freedom and self-responsibility to achieve their goals. This freedom and self-responsibility is what is meant by "empowerment."

The core team members should define their goals in such a way that they match the personal strengths of each team member.

Members in virtual teams are separated by time zones and cultural differences but are linked by technology; therefore, they need freedom to align their performance with clearly defined goals. Here is where the importance of clarity is manifested. How do you define goals for individual team members to match personal strengths? When the boss assigns the goals, enthusiasm and real commitment are missing. Team members should choose their own goals in a synchronous process. What do I mean by "synchronous"?

In virtual teams, there are two types of collaboration: synchronous and asynchronous. That is, either all or a majority of team members work together at the same time, (synchronous) or the collaboration over time in a series of events (asynchronous). Examples of synchronous collaboration are presence meetings and all types of video or telephone conferences, with live interaction among team members. Asynchronous collaboration takes place via e-mail, chat programs or the electronic exchange of documents. This is where each individual member of the team decides when they will react and when they will complete a task.

The defining of objectives requires synchronous collaboration. If the team members are to agree on common goals, it must be live and interactive, because it depends on the whole person, their potential and their ideas. The best format for working out objectives is in a workshop. Here, the team can brainstorm, debate, and discuss, allowing each team member to defend their opinions and positions directly with the other team members.

Bottom-Up Goal-Setting: With Roadmaps It Works Well

When it comes to setting goals of a virtual team in a group, it is rarely a good idea to exclusively refer back to existing goals. This should be obvious, but if the team leader tries to lead from the top down, this reliance on preexisting goals inevitably happens. If the team leader sets the goals and communicates them "from the top," the team members usually cannot identify with them. Of course, it is important that the team goals match the goals of the entire company. Each virtual team, however, needs to consider a lot of things that are not applicable to the whole company: the specific mix of people, the unique problems in their day-to-day business, expressed or unexpressed problems, dreams, individual concerns, and so on.

Be Careful of this Trap!
Team members have a difficult time identifying with goals which are determined from "above," from the organization or from the boss. They identify well with goals that they themselves have established.

In Chapter 3 we enumerated the three things to consider for the definition of goals according to the SMART formula:

First, individual desires, worries and emotions. Second, the opportunities and problems for the entire team. Third, a picture or symbol that serves to identify the success of the team. This "bottom-up" approach, combined with a democratic process in deciding which issues are most important, ensures a much greater commitment when everyone gets on board.

If you have defined the three most important goals for the virtual team according to the SMART formula, then these three goals summarize the team's success. This provides the basis for developing roadmaps. Roadmaps, in turn, are the series of the many intermediate objectives necessary to achieve these three major goals.

As Paul showed Bernd's team during the workshop, there are four steps to creating effective roadmaps. The team works in three groups. Each group adopts one of the most important objectives defined by the SMART formula.

I recommend the "Timeline" technique using moderation cards to mark the timeline and each step on the timeline on the floor. We call these floor or room anchors. This method is from NLP, and it activates the subconscious mind. It is important to activate the sub-

Four major steps lead to a roadmap in a workshop. I recommend the "Timeline" technique, because it activates the subconscious which helps create a stronger commitment from each team member.

conscious, because in doing so, you enhance thought processes, and you help the participant to free up the conscious mind to be more creative. Workshops are the ideal place to do this. In the teams with which I have worked, the timeline exercise has often led to new and surprising ideas. In addition, this exercise helps you get a deeper and more loyal commitment from your team members.

The Four Steps to a Roadmap with the Timeline Technique

A timeline is simply an imaginary line on the ground that symbolizes a time axis. For example, if you're working in virtual mode, paint the timeline on a digital whiteboard. If the participants are in the same room, they can position themselves at different points of the timeline and distribute floor anchors along the time axis using moderation cards.

Timeline Exercise:

Step 1: Here and now. The team members decide where on the timeline "Today" or "Here and Now" is, and they lay down a moderation card with the word, "Today" or "Here and Now" on it. From the perspective point of "Today," the participants describe the goal. In describing the goal, two things are very important: 1) the goal should be concretely and positively expressed in the present tense (i.e., "We remain focused and reach 10,000 new customers." Not, "We will not let the competition distract us and take away our customers.") and 2) define the goal according to the SMART formula with all the associated criteria, measures, involved parties, etc. This exercise does not work abstractly. On the contrary, the participants make a journey through time in their minds and should be completely transformed into the state that will reign when the goal is reached. Everyone should associate an image with the goal they want to accomplish, and they should have an emotional attachment to this goal.

Step 2: Achieved goal. The group now walks along the timeline to the end point, where the target goal has now been reached. Everyone imagines what this is like and asks themselves now that our goal is reached, what events have occurred? Ask the team members to express what they are experiencing with all their senses. What do they feel? What do they see? What do they hear? Taste? Smell? Then ask what have we missed? What have we possibly overlooked? The team looks back from the perspective it's success to the starting point, the "Today" card. What advice would the successful team give itself, if it could speak to the team members at the point where it started with the project? All of these notes are written down.

Step 3: Setting intermediate targets. The events that were mentioned in step 2 each get a moderation card, and these cards are laid down on the timeline roughly at the points when these targets need to be realized. Once these initial intermediate targets are laid down, the team should stand on each target looking back at "Today" and ask if there are any other targets we need to consider to get to this point. Once the team is certain that all of the necessary targets have been placed on the timeline, proceed to step 4.

Step 4: Responsibility for intermediate targets. Everyone now looks at the intermediate targets and milestones which have been thus far recorded. Who will take responsibility for which intermediate destination? The team then decides which specific team member will be responsible for each intermediary goal. The criterion for this decision should not only be connected to their functional role in the project. More important is the individual strengths of each person. These strengths should be the primary deciding factor in distributing the responsibilities for the goals.

Step 5: Integration. Each of the three groups has now worked on one of the three goals defined by the SMART formula, and using the Timeline technique. Through this exercise, each group has agreed on the intermediate goals and who will take responsibility for them. These results are presented by each group to the other two groups. Members of the other groups give feedback. That is, they debate both the intermediate goals as well as the decision of who will be responsible for each intermediate goal. This brings together the collective wisdom of the entire team and it allows the entire team to be responsible for the decisions made.

The outcome of the workshop is that it provides answers to the questions of *what* to do, *how* to do it, and *who* does it. The goals defined according to the SMART formula are the *what*. The roadmap using the timeline exercise determines the *how*. And distributing responsibility for each of the intermediate goals determines the *who*. This method produces two important results: First, a clearly defined plan is decided upon at a very high level. Second, team members are motivated, and they now know what they will be responsible for.

Empowerment and Cultural Differences

Empowerment plays a central role in virtual teams. Empowerment means empowering people to act independently, transferring responsibility solely to them.

Through many years of experience, I know virtual teams work best when all team members have as much autonomy as possible. In practice, this means developing topics "from bottom to top," equating the team members with the boss and strengthening self-initiative at all levels. In many Western countries, such as Germany, Great Britain, the Netherlands, or Scandinavia, this autonomy mirrors today's current culture and the prevailing values. This approach, however, contradicts the culture and values in many Eastern countries, such as Russia, China and Japan. How does these cultural differences impact the style of work in international and multicultural teams? How do team members from authoritarian or hierarchical cultures react and work on virtual teams, where leadership is autonomous for each member of the team, and each person is empowered to make their own decisions?

To shed some light on this matter, I refer to the work of Erin Meyer and her book *The Cultural Map*. The author distinguishes the cultures of the world according to a total of eight key dimensions. Empowerment is the key to the eight dimensions. In an extreme case, one team member may be from a culture that is entirely authoritarian while another is from a culture with an egalitarian style of leadership. In a purely authoritarian culture, for example, in Russia, power and decision-making are exclusively in the hands of the boss. The employee must accept decisions from above completely and without question.

In a very egalitarian culture, for example, in Sweden, all the members of a team are equal. Each team member can start initiatives and make their own decisions independently, as long as they stay within set boundaries.

Team members from authoritarian cultures will slowly accept democratic leadership. If you have patience and empathy, these transitions go very well.

In my experience, it is much easier to lead people from an authoritarian culture into an egalitarian leadership style than to convince people from an egalitarian culture to accept authoritarianism. Those who have not experienced democratic structures can get used to them relatively quickly. In turn, team members who are already accustomed to a democratic approach will never accept authoritarian power. If you do it right, you can lead teams of Europeans, Asians and Africans, and no one country of origin or style of leadership will dominate. I have led many such teams, and in all of these teams, I was successful with a markedly egalitarian leadership style.

When your team of mixed cultures comes together the very first time, it is important and essential to announce the rules of leadership immediately. This should be done in a synchronous team format, preferably a workshop. After you have all explained how the leadership will work, you should apply your leadership style consistently and demonstratively from that point on. Everyone should communicate regularly and on an equal footing with everyone else. In these regular communications, everyone should receive feedback, praise their own initiatives, and empower team members to make their own decisions within the set framework. You will observe that the team culture begins to superimpose over the respective cultural background of individual team members. The longer the team works together, the more homogenous the team becomes. Individual cultural characteristics disappear, and the team begins to create its own cultural dynamic.

How to Successfully Integrate Team Members from very Authoritarian Cultures

You may find that team members from very authoritarian cultures need additional support to get accustomed to egalitarian and democratic ways of working together. It may take some extra encouragement here and there to help them make their own decisions and solve problems independently, instead of relying on you for the answers. I have had the most success with my teams when I have been consistent in my attitude, have had patience with individual team members, and have given them the courage they needed to work independently. There are some cultures, Russians and Chinese in particular, where you should expect the process to take a little longer and to have a somewhat flatter learning curve. In workshops and other synchronous formats, it is important to treat all cultures with equal respect. It also helps to highlight the advantages of authoritarian cultures.

When necessary, be flexible and plan to give a little more guidance at the beginning to team members from authoritarian cultures. This is, of course, more challenging than it would be leading a team of more homogenous colleagues. You will find is that with people from more authoritarian cultures, you can create very disciplined and committed teams that are quick to act without lengthy discussions. Under certain circumstances this is a great advantage. Nevertheless, I always recommend an egalitarian leadership style for multicultural virtual teams.

Method:
   Treat all cultures with respect. Recognize that each culture, no matter how different or how authoritarian, have strengths that may help your team. One strength from authoritarian cultures is, for example, discipline. You will need to give more instructions to team members from authoritarian cultures at first. It doesn't take too long, though, until they begin to adjust to a more democratic style of leadership.

Some time ago, I worked for a customer who exported everyday consumer goods to Russia and was suddenly confronted with new, very strict market regulations. As a reaction, the company had to completely change its marketing strategy for Russia, in comparison to their Western markets. It was very difficult in Russia to define turnover targets, because the state made it increasingly difficult for Western companies. Russian culture is very authoritarian, so the company held their first meeting with its Russian top managers alone. The managers discussed the problem and prepared a first draft for the new strategy on the Russian market.

It is a break-through experience for people from authoritarian cultures or from less developed economic situations to purposely discover and apply their personal strengths and talents.

The company initially brought me in to lead a team workshop with their middle management, working with those who were responsible for one single business unit. When we were doing the exercise to the personal Lifeline, the participants were amazed at how little they knew about colleagues with whom they had been working for years. The employees discovered their own personal strengths, worked out the three most important topics, defined goals according to the SMART formula, and finally created their roadmaps. When the top managers saw the results, they were positively surprised. They realized that there was once again valuable input for the new strategy, which very closely matched the market. They were also amazed at how much commitment to the new strategies had developed in just one day. One top manager spoke of this exercise as providing a "breakthrough" for companies with challenging market conditions.

What Interlinked Goals Can Achieve

If you work out the three most important topics of the team, define goals from the SMART formula, and create roadmaps based on these objectives, where all team members assume responsibility for intermediate goals, then in the end all goals connect together like a set of gears in a machine. Through this system of "interlinked goals," you ensure a high commitment of all team members, and you prevent individual team members from hiding and not contributing. The more responsibility a single team member owns to reach his or her goals, the better. This means additional collaboration, more interaction, and strengthened attractiveness of the virtual team.

The three main effects of interlinked goals:

1. **Empowerment.** All team members have their own goals and can shine when they have met them. Self-initiated, bold decisions, and action orientation are seen and valued by the others. In addition, team members have the freedom to ensure results within their defined limits. This reduces the dependency on the boss, and stimulates cooperation with other team members at the same level.

2. **Increased performance**. Each team has three groups: approximately 10-15 percent are high performers. These are the team's performers. Between 70 and 80 percent are reliable team workers. They achieve their goals and secure the basis for success. About 10-15 per cent are low performers. These low performers do not necessarily have to leave the team, but know that they will deliver less than the average, reliable team member. If the lower-performance members do not have their own strategic goals, it is very likely that they are hiding. This means, for example, that they do not reliably answer calls or e-mails.

   If, however, all the objectives are interlinked and if the less reliable members have defined goals, the achievement of which is linked with the goals of the performers, then no one can hide. As soon as all the goals are interlinked, a healthy kind of group pressure is created, which at the same time forces these weakest links to perform at the level of reliable team members. One of the biggest advantages of interlinked goals is that the boss does not have to exert any pressure on the less-reliable team members, because the group does this for him. Together the team pushes toward an increase in performance. Of course, the boss should always keep an eye on the situation and should offer help if it is needed. I will deal with this in more detail later.

3. **Gravity.** The third effect of interlinked objectives is a substantial increase in gravity, or the "gravitational force" of the team. Interlinked goals ensure that the individual team members have to communicate and work together more intensively. Since everyone is in some way dependent on everyone else to achieve their goals, the team's cohesion increases enormously.

You have seen in this chapter how to develop shared goals in workshops with your virtual team, and the results of these interlinked goals for the team as a whole. I have always been surprised at how well this method works with my teams. If this is done correctly, individual team members will not be able to hide. The performance of the entire team will increase, because low performance members will be forced through peer pressure to improve their performance level to match those of their colleagues.

Chapter 5

When Team Roles Meet the True Strengths of the Team Member, Work is Enjoyable

Bernd felt the sweat running down his neck. He ran faster. His body felt good. He was pushing himself and his body was synchronizing perfectly in rhythm. His breathing flowed smoothly. The muscles, the joints, everything harmonized. Bernd liked to go to the gym, and he especially liked the phase at the end of endurance training when the body feels lighter and the even movements balance the mind. This evening it was particularly intense. "These must be the endorphins," thought Bernd. "No matter what, it does me good."

Suddenly, the financial problem came back in his mind. They had to build more efficiently and, ultimately, less expensive. Bernd remembered the discussion at the end of the workshop with Paul. They agreed that they had to find someone who had already built such houses extremely cheaply. In a way, Bernd was spoiled. Money had never been an issue on all of the construction projects he had lead in Germany. Obviously, he had to present himself as being efficient and frugal in order to win contracts, and every budget he had worked with had proven to be enough money to see the project through. He had never had to reconsider or change plans in the middle of a project before.

"I guess Claude is as spoiled in Canada as I am here in Germany," thought Bernd. "We'll have to find someone else."

Bernd was seriously determined to find someone to make this work. Feeling fit and full of energy from the fitness studio, Bernd was ready to go! "A little research, several phone calls," he thought, "then I'll have someone who can build these houses cheaply." Bernd suddenly stopped right in his footsteps. Wait! I can't do this! I have a team of stars each of whom wants to shine. Why should I try to get involved again? After all, Claude is a born networker. He knows people all over the world, and he seems to enjoy finding them and staying in contact with them.

The team needs to build more efficiently and save costs. Bernd resists the temptation to find a solution on his own. Instead, he trusts the "master networker" Claude to find someone to help.

Bernd finished his workout on the treadmill. He cleaned the handles with disinfectant and set off for the shower. The shower room was empty. He turned the water on and felt the jet stream massaging his head and body. Several times he switched between hot and cold. How refreshing! He dressed and went to the front desk, where he stopped briefly to write an e-mail to Claude on his iPhone:

> *Claude, would you be willing to activate your fantastic network again for our project? We need to find someone with experience and expertise in building low-budget, high-quality, safe houses. Would you please see if you have someone in your network that might qualify? Thank you and good luck!*

Bernd finally reached home at 8 p.m. He, his wife, Wiebke, and their daughter, Lena, have lived in their simple, spacious, modern house just north of Frankfurt for over fifteen years. As usual after his workout, Bernd was famished. As soon as he opened the front door, the wonderful scent of dinner engulfed him, and he followed the scent to the dining room. The table was romantically set, and lit candles cast shadows on the walls. Wiebke greeted him with a kiss, and they sat down to eat.

One week later, just before one o'clock in the morning, Bernd was sitting in his office waiting to begin a telephone conference with the team. As always, he had made an agenda and sent it to everyone. WebEx, the new web conferencing tool, was much more stable than Skype. Bernd opened the program five minutes before the meeting was to begin.

The light and clear voice of Anne came first.

"Good afternoon, Bernd. How are you?"

"Oh, thank you, Anne. I'm fine. It is nice that you are always so punctual. How are you?"

"I'm fine. My little daughter has recovered from the flu. In the meantime, I have also had some talks with the government. They are waiting to hear from us about the budget adjustment. Did I understand correctly that we will be joined today by someone who can help us with this?"

"Hi folks!" This was the confident voice of Linda calling in from Africa. Bernd looked at the clock. It was 12.58 clock. They would be able to start on time.

"A hearty bonjour from sunny Montreal!" Claude was there too.

"Hello and welcome, everybody," Bernd cheerfully began. "As you can see on the agenda, our main focus today is how we will build the houses for cost-effectively. Thanks to Claude, we have been able to get in contact with an internationally award-winning Brazilian architect. She has built houses for the people in the favelas of São Paulo made of recycled materials. Her name is Pilar Ruiz, and she seems interested in joining the team. I am curious about whether her know-how can be transferred to our project. This is what we will discuss with her today. Claude, is Pilar ready join the conference?"

Pilar, an award-winning Brazilian architect, joins the team. In the Favelas, she built houses made of recycled materials. She certainly will have ideas and suggestions for the project.

"Yes, she's on standby and can join us at any time," Claude said.

"Okay, then please bring her in!" After a beep, Pilar was there.

"Good morning, good evening, wherever you are, ladies and gentlemen," Pilar said.

"May I call you Pilar?" Bernd asked.

"Please do!"

"We're glad you're on board, Pilar. Would you please introduce yourself?"

"With pleasure. My name is Pilar Ruiz. I am an architect, a city planner and an expert on housing construction. My home country is Brazil. I studied in the USA and worked for several years in Lisbon. Since I have been back in São Paulo, I have been working on several innovative projects. I was immediately fascinated by your project when Claude explained it to me on the phone. I would very much like to participate. It is a matter of heart to help the people of Transmontania after this terrible catastrophe."

"Thank you, Pilar," Bernd said. "I've got a question for you: What was your most important project so far? "

"I don't have to think about that for long! This was the favela project, for which we also received the sustainability award in Davos. We rebuilt a complete district in a very poor section of São Paulo with small houses made of recycled materials. And at minimal cost. For many of the children there, this was the first time that they had a roof over their heads. The houses contain everything a family needs to live. It's not luxurious, but it's not nothing."

"Wow, great!" Linda said. "We're glad you're joining us."

The solution proposed by Pilar allows the team to react immediately. Linda reminds Claude that Pilar is new and may need some guidance. She offers to take Pilar under her wings and explain everything necessary about the team and the project to her.

"Well, you are aware of our problem," Bernd said soberly. "What do you suggest?"

"I've looked through the MOOC plans, and there are quite a few possibilities. It's quite possible to build the houses using other materials without compromising the designs. We should discuss this with the professors who have organized the MOOC. In addition, we should involve local builders in the process, so that the solution fits their traditions. Would it be possible to form a small virtual team where we can discuss these ideas and where I can explain my experiences in further detail?"

"That sounds good. Claude, can you please take the lead? You have the contact to the university in New York anyway. And, Anne, can you involve the local builders? "

"I'll discuss it directly with the professor," said Claude. "This could mean more time for me than I originally agreed to, Bernd, but that's not so bad. We are sailing in unknown waters. I am looking forward to the solution we will find together with Pilar in our expanded team."

"Thank you Claude," said Bernd.

"It is a pity," added Claude, "that we cannot use our original plans, because they were awesome! I am sure our houses would have dusted the first prize at the world exhibition for architecture in the "Smart Designs" category. But - c'est la vie."

"We're working with some really great people here, Claude!" Linda interrupted. "Yes, exhibitions and glittering awards are nice, but we should keep our goal in mind. Our goal is to help thousands of homeless people get a roof over their heads before winter comes."

"Yes, you are absolutely right," said Bernd. "We will keep our eye on the prize. You can count on it."

"Excuse me," Claude interrupted. "I just wrote an e-mail to the professor, and he agrees."

"You know my attitude to multitasking during team meetings, Claude," Bernd said in a slightly reproachful tone. "But I'm glad the professor is on board. Thank you."

"Sorry, may I suggest something?" Linda asked. "Since Pilar is joining our team and doesn't really know us yet, I would be glad to meet with her alone to explain who we all are, what each of us does, and what we've accomplished so far. I could also show how she can access the individual documents online."

"That's a very good idea, Linda," Bernd said. "Thank you for volunteering."

"I would appreciate that, Linda," Pilar said, relieved.

"Let us set up a time this week to talk. And if you have any questions beforehand, just call me or write me a text message."

"I'm making an appointment for the new workgroup," Claude said. "Pilar, the professor, and the builders from Transmontania should talk to each other next week."

"Looks like we have a plan," Bernd said, smiling. This was the first conference at which Bernd had little to talk

Bernd noticed that he had less and less to do. The team members were working independently and absolutely reliably. They were willing to take the initiative and find solutions themselves when challenges arose. It is a wonderful feeling.

about. Nevertheless, the ball rolled. The project made great progress. All the team members were bright and ready to take the initiative.

Nonetheless, Bernd felt like he ought to be doing more. He thought about why he had started this project. It was going to be the international breakthrough for him. In addition, he was going to be the savior for those in need, those who were traumatized and homeless in Asia. Now the team did the most work without him. And yet for the first time in a long time, Bernd felt like his life had a meaning and purpose greater than anything he had ever known. And he knew that this was only the beginning. For the first time, he felt a sense of being part of something greater than himself. It was more than his previous successes. It was even more than mere disaster relief. There was something new, something exciting, and he and his team were right in the middle.

Working with Ease and Pleasure in the "Flow Corridor"

In virtual teams, people predominantly work alone. They rarely, if ever, see the other team members. Because of this, the ability to motivate oneself becomes one of the most decisive success factors. So, what motivates people regardless of where they live or what they do? They want to have fun! They want to enjoy what they do. The light feelings of joy, happiness, and fulfillment are universal and not bound to any culture.

And when do we feel joy, happiness, and fulfillment? We usually feel joy, happiness and fulfillment when we do something that uses our personal strengths and that fits to our personal value system. When we work on something that interests us, uses our talents, and fits to our value system, we come into the so-called state of flow. Flow means that our tasks and our abilities fit together perfectly.

You may already be familiar with the flow theory. It goes back to the Hungarian American psychologist and fortune teller Mihály Csíkszentmihályi -- a name which cannot be pronounced correctly outside of Hungary, but this is not really so important. The decisive point in Mihály Csíkszentmihályi's theory is the so-called "flow corridor".

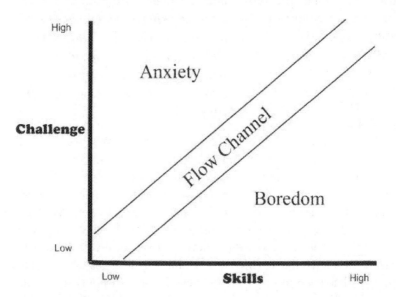

Illustration 3: The "Flow Corridor" from psychologist Mihály Csíkszentmihályi is the middle between anxiety and boredom. It is the state in which a person finds their task to be both pleasurable and motivating.

The "flow corridor" is an ideal state somewhere between challenge and overburden. In this state, we find the task that we are working on fulfilling, and while we are working on this task, we are in our center. We are focused, energized and committed. We enjoy doing this activity.

Flow Means to be Completely and Positively Absorbed by the Task at Hand.

If the required activity is too difficult or if there is too much pressure, a team member may become overstretched, frightened, frustrated, and unable to perform the task. If, however, the reverse situation is true, the team member becomes bored, unfocused and distracted. The optimal flow, the "flow" as Mihály Csíkszentmihályi describe it, is the area where the requirements of the given activity fit together with the skills, talents, and interests of the team member.

The best way to help your team members to excel and work independently is to help them come into this state of flow; and the best way to help them come into this state of flow is to know their true strengths and interests. By knowing this and helping them to take on tasks that fit their skills, you help them to be fulfilled. They will enjoy their work and feel light and energized as they work on your project. They will be willing to go above and beyond to give their best.

Methods to Discover the Strengths of Team Members

As I mentioned in Chapter 2, there are unique digital tools to help you discover the strengths of employees. One such tool is the Gallup Strength Finder 2.0. With the Gallup Strength Finder, you will be able to discover the five greatest strengths of each team member and then develop an action plan to better use these strengths in the work process. This is a very comprehensive approach. There are, however, simpler techniques for discovering these strengths. Some of them are also amazingly precise and can trigger a motivational thrust for your team members.

In my time as a manager, I often asked every team member to write down their greatest strengths in a plain Word document. For those who have difficulty identifying and describing their own strengths, there are some simple coaching questions which you can use to help them find their strengths. You can also ask your team to work in pairs, either live or online. The two team members can then ask each other questions such as these:

- What do you find easy to do in your job?
- What gives you energy and fun?
- What event in your past do you consider to be your greatest success?
- When do people come to you and ask for help?
- With whom do you often work together?
- If you asked colleagues about your greatest strengths, what would they say?
- What do you consider to be your greatest strength?

At the end of a questionnaire the respective questioner can also express his own opinion: "After all that you have answered, I believe your greatest strength is ..."

These guided self-reflection exercises always bring new insights and are often a direct energy boost for team members. The energy is created by more awareness and by the strengths of others being seen. At the end of this coaching exercise, you and the team know the greatest strengths from the internal perspective, from the point of the interviewees themselves, and also from the external view, namely as assessments of the questioners. This results in a "map of resources," which should be made available to all team members, so that everyone knows the strengths of their team colleagues. Through this exercise, the awareness that everyone on the team is uniquely gifted grows. The map of the strengths can and should be used as the guide for any decision about which persons take over which responsibilities. In addition, this exercise gives the team transparency. No one has to wonder why another team member was given preference for any given position. This can be seen from the strength profiles.

Method:

Go through the exercises mentioned to determine the individual strengths of your team members, and then put together a "Map of Resources," which your team may access at all times. This will help the team members get to know each other better, and it will provide them with an excellent resource if they need extra support.

How to Use Natural Strengths to Distribute Additional Roles

In each team, the team members can be divided into three large groups. In the first group, you have the team members who have a wide range of skills. They see the big picture and understand how things are related and influenced. If you have subdivided your customer base by geographic region, these **Generalists** are ideal for keeping connections with key figures in the respective regions. Generalists have an open ear for new needs for products and services and report them back to the team. Generalists are necessary in all teams that have direct contact with the end customer or as an internal service provider for employees in the company An example of the latter are IT departments. They are an internal department which serves internal customers, namely, the employees of the corporation.

Of course, there are also entire departments in companies whose job it is to be in customer contact, for example, sales and marketing. Nevertheless, you can divide the internal and external customers from each team and assign them to the generalists. In this way, you promote the gravitational force both within the team itself and with customers.

The second group consists of experts or **Specialists** who have a great deal of expertise in a specific field. These people are champions in their field of expertise. Before a new product is delivered to the customer or a service is provided, the specialists should give feedback and possibly make suggestions for improvement.

> *In each team there are Generalists, Specialists and Team Players. If you know who belongs to which group, you can distribute roles accordingly.*

This quality assurance is often not their real role in the company, but an additional task. The additional role is derived from their strengths and abilities in their particular area of specialization. When specialists give feedback, it gives the virtual team an additional opportunity to touch base about the project and the product. This, in turn, strengthens the interactions of the team and its gravitational force. It helps the team to further overcome the geographical distances.

The third large group consists of people who have a very good sense of the needs of other people and who contribute much to the positive atmosphere of the team. These are the **Team Players**. As an additional task, team players gladly look after new team members, just as Linda did with Pilar. They are ideal to organize trips or parties, and in doing so, they strengthen the cohesion of the team.

When I explain in my seminars that team members are to take on additional roles and other tasks, the first reaction is always the same: "We are all already 150% full! How can we possibly do even more?" In practice, however, it looks completely different. If the team members have discovered their true strengths, then they actually enjoy taking on new activities. People who are enjoying themselves don't look at the clock. For many, being in the flow ensures that they actually do not experience the extra task as being work.

The Positive Effect Additional Roles based on Strengths will have on Your Team

When team members take on additional roles on the basis of their strengths, it has three positive effects: First, everyone has more fun, because what they find easy and rewarding to do is fun. Second, those taking on additional tasks get more recognition from the rest of the team. Each team member is seen by the others with their individual strengths, which gives the team a motivational thrust. This motivation is particularly important when people work alone. Third, there are additional interactions between the team members, which cause more intense bonding for the virtual team. Generalists, specialists and team players all contribute, each in their own way to the cohesion of the team as they take on additional roles.

Taking on additional roles have three main effects: more fun at work, more recognition for each individual and more interaction. The team continues to bond and grow.

One of my clients was a globally active consumer goods manufacturer. The corporation had recently established a new IT Project Delivery Unit for all internal projects. It was essentially a pool of project managers that were assigned to different business projects throughout Europe, and they were expected to operate as a single internal business unit. This unit consisted essentially of a pool of 30 project managers, each of whom was at his home somewhere in Europe. In other words, it was not only a virtual team, it was an entire virtual unit. After analyzing the strengths of each of the team members, we found out who the generalists, the specialists and the team players are. Although all of them worked equally as project managers and were constantly involved in the project business, each of them voluntarily took over additional roles according to their strengths. The prospect of recognition made it easy to take on further roles and identify with them.

We gave four generalists the responsibility for four large geographic regions, according to the management units from a group perspective. The generalists established intensive relations with the local representatives, recognized the need for new projects, communicated them to the entire department, and developed problem solutions. The specialists were "champions" either in ERP (enterprise resource planning), in CRM (customer relationship management), or in IT infrastructure. They regularly gave feedback on individual project plans, business cases, and so on. They thereby contributed a lot to improving the quality of the work. The team players finally set up a Buddy system and looked after all the new arrivals in the department as well as the freelancers who joined the team over the course of time.

After some time, this internal unit had excellent key performance indicators in all areas measured by the corporate headquarters. The financial data agreed, the customer feedback was outstanding, and the questionnaires were full of praise from employee surveys. When the division leadership compared this department's performance to that of those for North America, Asia, Africa and other regions, the Europeans were by far number one. But the best thing was that everyone felt like a team, although they were from different places and different projects. There was intensive communication and strong cohesion. This effect was mainly due to the acquisition of additional roles according to their own strengths.

Personality Profiles Help to use Strengths and Solve Problems

As an executive coach, I often work with a relatively new personality test, the Visual Questionnaire, abbreviated VIQ. The VIQ works equally well for people all over the world and cannot be manipulated because it works exclusively with images.

The test runs in such a way, that the participants always have two pictures to choose from and click on that they like better. Sounds simple - and yet highly effective. Why?

The Visual Questionnaire is a personality test that works equally well for intercultural teams, because it works with images. It is Ideal for global virtual power teams.

For most personality tests, the results depend strongly on the quality of the translation of the questions. In addition, most of the candidates in conventional tests consider what results they would like and how they would like to be evaluated. Many test questions are, to a certain extent, transparent and one can answer them approximately as one would like to be seen. This does not work with the VIQ because the connection between the images and the personality structure is not intuitive.

The VIQ is based on the type theory of the psychologists C. G. Jung and Julius Kuhl. The basic framework consists of four dimensions:

1. Introvert or Extrovert
2. Rational or Emotional (Thinking or Feeling)
3. Sensing or Intuitive
4. Judgmental or Perceiving

The first dimension (introverted or extroverted), is about how people perceive the world. Extroverted people, for example, are more playful and more interested in new experiences. The second dimension (rational or emotional) shows whether people are more logical and objective or emotionally controlled and subjective. In the third dimension (sensitive or intuitive), people differ primarily in whether they are more detailed and thorough or if they intuitively grasp the whole. Finally, the fourth dimension (judging or perceiving) shows whether someone is more long-term and unambiguous, or open, flexible, and quick to change situations.

For a virtual team, this personality test reveals many possible findings: Where does someone have special talents? Where could they improve? How do they behave in conflict situations? Are they more a leader or a loyal follower? On the Internet, you will find much more information about the VIQ. You can try out the test online and contact me or another coach who is certified for the VIQ. Here I would like to limit myself to the practical consequences of this personality test. If you have the personality structure.

Better understanding of your team members helps you solve problems faster and overall increase the efficiency and effectiveness of team collaboration.

Method:
   Use personality analyses to better determine the strengths of your team members, to learn about their develop potential, and to know how they may react in conflict situations.

   According to the results of the VIQ, each team can be divided into four groups depending on their way of thinking and acting: **Visionaries, Planners, Doers and Critics.** By doing this, they consciously form groups of people with similar characteristics. These groups of similar personality traits should then exchange ideas and develop possible solutions. In my seminars, I am always surprised at how quickly and smoothly people with similar personality structures work together.

   If during this exchange of ideas, a problem arises or if you need some new, creative ideas, you can get suggestions from all four groups. The four groups consider the same problem from a different perspective: the **Visionaries** look to the future and define new goals to motivate the team. The **Planners** develop a clear process to solve the problem. The **Doers** quickly decide who takes care of what and are usually immediately ready to get started. The **Critics**, in turn, have identified all of the risks and pitfalls and are developing strategies to avoid them.

Depending on how people think and act, there are Visionaries, Planners, Doers and Critics. Identify the groups and use their different perspectives to strengthen your team.

   The next step is to reassemble the four groups. Let each group present their findings and suggestions to the others. It is always amazing how different the approach of each of the four groups is. In the joint round, each team member is now confronted with three completely different views - those of the groups to which he does not belong. This is a tremendous enrichment for all. In the last step, the whole team discusses all approaches presented by the individual groups. The aim is now to integrate the proposals into an overall plan which takes account of all aspects.

   The trick with this method is that the discussion just comes to an end. If you arbitrarily classify the team members into groups, where different characters meet, then you will be immediately debated and important aspects will fall under the table. In the method proposed here, with groups of similarly structured people, the group work runs very harmonically. In the end, everyone in the respective group is satisfied with their results. Only afterwards in the big round the results are controversially discussed. So there is qualified input from four different perspectives and then the synthesis. They not only ensure a good result, but also ensure that the team members do not argue all the time. When people within the team meet again and again on the same level, this also significantly increases team cohesion.

The Fuel for Management Based on Strengths

There are many different methods to help leaders recognize the individual strengths and thought styles of their team members. The key, however, to all of these methods is always the same: it is recognition. If team members are recognized for their strengths, they become excited and are willing to invest these strengths in the team. Unfortunately, most companies are not willing to recognize the strengths and talents of individual employees.

Just ask yourself: Have you already received so much recognition in your life that you do not want to ever be praised again? Probably not. And maybe you can even remember situations in which you did something special but did not receive any recognition at all.

The most frequent reason employees give for leaving their company is not lack of identification the company or its vision. Neither is it too little financial compensation. The most common reason given for leaving their job is that they cannot get along with their immediate boss. When they asked exactly what they meant by this description, they answer that their boss never gave them recognition for the work that they did. Some even say that it has been years since their boss has praised them or recognized their work. Many different studies have come to the same conclusion: Employees do not leave the company. They leave their immediate supervisors.

You cannot Praise Your Team Enough

People often think that too much praise spoils the receiver, but in my experience the opposite is true: You cannot give too much praise. Praise is especially important for virtual teams, because the daily personal contact with other team members doesn't exist. A daily smile or nod which happens automatically when a team is together doesn't happen when the team is so far apart. As the team leader, it is important to consciously allow for praise to be said at each team meeting. It should be a fixed point in your agenda.

In large virtual teams, which can be scattered all over the world, the situation can be even more aggravating. The team members work alone and rarely have contact with their supervisors. Again and again, I hear about virtual teams, where praise and recognition have fallen completely under the table. Often the team leader has even less understanding for his employees than a large corporation has for theirs.

I have always made a conscious effort to act differently with my teams. Praise is a focal point. Perhaps this comes from my experience at home: I am the father to five girls. Five. In our family, there is my beautiful wife, our five daughters, and me. Both as a father and as an international manager, I have the same secret recipe: First, praise. Second, praise. And third, praise.

What do I mean by the word "praise"? The first and foremost prerequisite for praise is attention. Be attentive and watch every little progress your team makes. Praise every positive contribution of every single team member, even if it has not brought the project decisively further. In addition, also praise any form of good cooperation. Give recognition to everything that contributes to a positive team culture.

Because members of virtual teams rarely see each other in person, and there are few opportunities for informal talks, you should make praise a fixed program point in your meetings. I will go into more detail about this in the second part of the book.

It is important that you also praise all team members for small contributions. There are "secret heroes" in every team. "Secret heroes" are employees who are quite far down the organizational hierarchy, and yet they still make decisive contributions to the

> *In virtual teams, the members hardly see each other and almost never receive praise in informal conversations. Therefore, recognition should be a fixed point on the agenda in the regular team meetings.*

success of a project. The performance of these secret heroes is often hardly noticed by the other team members.

One example of how I incorporated the use of secret heroes in my work is when I headed an IT team for a large corporation, which was in charge of facilities in Eastern Europe, the Middle East and Africa. As IT administrators, our job was to install radio antennas on a roof in Uzbekistan where the temperatures reached over 40° C (104° Fahrenheit) in the shade, while our employees in Moscow had to figure out how to lay fiberglass cable in the frozen ground at temperatures below -20° C (-4° Fahrenheit) In many virtual teams these difficult conditions go unrecognized. The members of the IT team are often so focused on the software that they do not realize the difficulties people on the ground are having. A short e-mail from the top manager which simply says, "Well done!" can work wonders in building a strong team spirit. And through this recognition, these secret heroes, who make the project possible, feel valued and respected. This, in turn, motivates them to continue to work hard for the team.

What is the best way to praise and recognize your team members? First of all, honesty and sincerity are important. Praise only what you believe is actually worthy of recognition. Then, you should pay attention to the language you use, so that you can express different degrees of recognition, depending on how much your team members have achieved and how hard they have worked. Otherwise, the praise will quickly wear out and lose its effect.

PART II

COMMUNICATION

Chapter 6

How Technology Helps Bridge Continents and Time Zones

Bernd was feeling increasingly annoyed. He was sitting in his office, and although it was almost noon, he had to switch on the desk lamp. The grey, rainy skies outside only served to darken the office -- and his spirit.

He had wasted over a quarter of an hour on the computer, looking for the most current plans and status reports from the local Transmontanian builders. Several hits had come up after entering the term "blueprint" into the search function, but after clicking and opening all sorts of files, the right one had not yet surfaced. Instead, older versions or files with similar names had come up first. And this was not the first time he had had to deal with poor search results! After a great deal of wasted time and energy, he opened the latest version of the MOOC design and latest status report on the crowdfunding campaign.

The team had chosen Google Drive for Work as their cloud storage document management provider. Initially it seemed like the ideal solution. Google Drive worked equally well on all PCs, Macs, and mobile devices. It allowed

After three months of the project, Bernd is annoyed with the chaos when filing documents. There is a urgent need for document management. And he wants a personal assistant.

simple uploads and had convenient features that allowed multiple people access and the ability to edit the same document. But after three months, things were not looking good. All possible file presentations were on the virtual drive: Excel spreadsheets, photos and videos; everything. Originally, there had been a logical storage structure, but now so many new folders had been added that the team members stored their files in any number of possible places.

"I do not know how people manage to deal with this chaos," Bernd muttered angrily, annoyed with himself. "I will just ask Anne where the plan is; she should be able to send me the link."

Then he questioned himself. Should he call her? It was early evening where she lived. No, he decided; its best to write her an e-mail and CC all the others. We must solve this problem once and for all!

Bernd composed the e-mail with two essential points: He asked Anne for the link to the latest version of the construction plan, and he asked everyone for ideas on how to solve the problem with the file folders. He vaguely wondered if he was really asking for someone to optimize the storage structure and take care of the cloud storage going forward. First, he decided, it would be best to hear opinions from the others.

Only a few days went by before Bernd came up against the same problem again. He could not find the file he was looking for. He was further annoyed that no one had responded to his question about to how to solve the problem. I urgently need an assistant, he thought. I cannot waste my time searching for files! Bernd already had a part-time assistant who supported his projects in Germany. She was around 40, competent, friendly and very well organized. Unfortunately, her English skills were not advanced enough for an international project. I'll ask Claude, decided Bernd. He knows all sorts of people. Bernd quickly sent out a Skype message:

Hi Claude! I need URGENT assistance for tackling this filing problem. Do you know someone?

During lunch, Bernd's mobile phone pinged, and Claude's reply came on the screen:

Assistance is the right keyword. But not just for you - we all need this assistance, not only in Hamburg, but virtually, for the entire team. The best thing would be a crackerjack on the computer who could bring order to our storage structure and look after our digital tools.

At the next WebEx conference with the team, virtual assistance was at the top of Bernd's agenda. Bernd worked from home that day, and was dressed very casually. He started WebEx five minutes before the appointment. Anne and Pilar immediately connected.

"Hello Anne, Hello Pilar! What is the current weather in Transmontania, Anne? "

"It's summer. We now often have 25° to 30° C. Ideal conditions to begin construction of earthquake-proof houses. "

"How is it in Rio, Pilar?"

"Hello Bernd! Today, we have some rain for a change."

At this moment, Claude and Linda joined the conference. Everyone was ready to start on time.

Bernd asked Claude and Pilar to report on the latest changes to the blueprints. How had Pilar's know-how from her project in the favelas worked in their favor with this project?

"Ladies first," said Claude.

"First, thank you, Claude, for bringing the professor and his team back onto the team so soon. We had a very productive workshop, and were quickly able to clarify what needs to be changed to implement my ideas for greater cost-effectiveness. The professor was extremely cooperative. He immediately got to work and promised that he and a colleague would deliver the revised blueprints within three weeks."

"Pilar has very clear ideas about what needs to be changed," added Claude, and "I think we'll get there very quickly."

"Thank you, Pilar, for working so quickly," praised Bernd.

Pilar responded, "I extend my gratitude to Linda,

Pilar has quickly become involved on the project and has clear ideas about what needs to be changed in the construction plans. Claude brought the Professor from New York and his team on board. Everyone is pulling together.

who acquainted me with Anne and Claude. They both took time to bring me up to speed, and explain everything I needed to know. "

"Gladly," said Linda. "It was my pleasure."

"You've all done a great job," Bernd summed up. "I'm glad you can function so well on your own," he added, smirking.

"I have an important concern," Bernd continued. "Do you remember my e-mail from last week? I still struggle to find documents, and often I have to ask one of you for a specific link to access it. Last week, I asked if anyone could provide ideas on solving this, but I did not get an answer. It is also important to note that we have wonderful commentary in these documents. Nevertheless, I am continually getting comments by e-mail, Skype and in all possible ways, and then in the final version on Google Drive, the comments are never complete."

Bernd paused, and clearly no one seemed to want to respond.

"I've discussed this problem in detail with Claude," continued Bernd, "and I think we need a virtual assistant. Someone who can organize well and who also understands IT. We need someone to care for our systems and our storage."

Then Linda spoke up: "In one of my recent projects I worked with a young woman from Eastern Europe. Her name is Stella, and she is from Bulgaria. Stella still studies economics at University, but has already proven herself in supporting virtual teams. In our project, she was more than just a virtual assistant, she provided efficient file management and knowledge management. This increased our productivity enormously. In addition, her fees are extremely favorable. Should I contact her? "

Linda brings the young Bulgarian Stella onto the team as a virtual assistant for. Her specialty is efficient file management. And that for very little compensation.

"That sounds like a good deal," said Claude. "I have never worked with someone from Bulgaria."

"Please send me Stella's CV and fee requirements," said Bernd. "I'll arrange an interview with her."

Two days later, Bernd sat in the Lufthansa Business Lounge at Munich Airport. He had entered one of the separate work areas and where he could talk to Stella on his iPad. He had hardly pressed the green button, and she was there.

"Good morning, Mr. Schmidt. I am pleased that you are interested in my services. "Stella was in her early twenties, spoke a bit slowly and had a slight Eastern European accent. Nevertheless, she was very self-confident and assured.

"Good Morning! We're all on a first name basis in our project. Would that be okay for you? I'm Bernd."

"Yes of course. I'm Stella. "

The young woman smiled at the camera, but Bernd felt as if she was smiling directly at him. He sensed that he immediately trusted Stella. The three-second test had already been achieved. Bernd was convinced that in the first three seconds of an encounter we decide whether we would like to work with someone or not. Similar to viewing a YouTube video, when we decide if we want to continue watching after three seconds have passed.

"Stella, we turn to you because we have a storage problem," Bernd explained in a factual tone. "We have more and more files constantly being generated for this project and we are losing the overview and connecting commentary.

In their first telephone conversation, Stella convinces Bernd that she has the necessary expertise, structured approach, and independence. The self-assured young woman is also now on board.

Additionally, we are working on a deadline and have little extra time. We must be innovative and creative and build our new buildings as quickly and efficiently as possible. Potentially, there are a lot of people who can contribute to our knowledge - MOOC students, a professor and his team, the local builders and more. Over the past three months, we have generated a lot of files, and in recent times, I find it increasingly difficult to find anything that I really need or want. In addition, people working on these various teams use all possible channels - WhatsApp, Skype, Viber, and so on - to send messages, changes, and updates. I believe that we must now arrange and unify all this at once. Otherwise everyone will soon have their own idea of the project, and we will be lost."

"Bernd, Linda has mentioned that her Google Drive for Work is used as a cloud storage. How do you deal with static documents that are processed by several people at the same time? Is there always a final, coordinated version? And how do you work with dynamic content - new ideas, useful links, personal updates? "

"Quite honestly, so far we have not distinguished between these. Everything is a jumble in the cloud. "

"And who is responsible for the individual areas? Who for the design, who for building and who for the tests? "

"There are responsible persons for each aspect of the project, but we have no superordinate structure and no organizer for the whole. "

"Okay I understand. I am familiar with such challenges from other virtual teams. In fact, your problems are common. I think you can keep the static documents on Google Drive, but with a little more process and discipline. For your online discussions and personal updates, however, you need something else, for example, a closed Facebook group. I can make suggestions for this. In such a project, knowledge management is crucial. "

"That sounds good. Can you be available for our next telephone conference next week? "

"Sure, Bernd. I'll just need someone to familiarize me with the project first. Do you have someone who can do that?"

Bernd liked Stella's structured approach. Within a very short time Stella had proved her competence.

"I'll ask Linda. You already know her, and she loves doing this type of thing!"

The Combination of Technology and Human Passion

We are becoming more and more dependent on digital technology. Can you even imagine traveling by car without first programming the navigation system or looking at the route on Google Maps? Almost any kind of information is accessible via the Internet, whenever we want it. There are also more and more digital helpers that make life easier for us. It is a very small step to total networking. The "Internet of Things" is coming. What already applies to every area of our everyday life is even more applicable to global business. Digital technologies are indispensable. An international project has long been inconceivable without the use of e-mail, web and video conferencing. Digital tools for real-time collaboration are increasingly sophisticated.

Any technology, however, is only as good as the people who use it. How can technology improve collaboration? From my point of view, there is only one answer to this question: anyone who really wants to achieve outstanding results must combine the latest technology with passion. In private life, we prefer to use digital technologies to stay in touch with friends and relatives or to read the latest news about our interests. Many people use Skype, for example, to communicate with friends around the world to learn about what is happening in their lives.

Similarly, Facebook and other social media allows us to keep in touch with many more friends and acquaintances. We use these technologies privately, so we are very enthusiastic and passionate. But what does it mean in a business context to combine technology and passion? How can you encourage people to share their knowledge with others through digital technology and create a living and productive community?

In our private lives, we use digital technology enthusiastically to be in touch with people we care about. In business, we should create the same enthusiasm by combining the latest technologies with deep passion.

What is at stake here is knowledge management in its various forms. In my experience, knowledge management through digital technology is only successful if the individual participants passionately contribute their personal strengths. Knowledge management works best when you have top experts on the team who know a lot in their respective fields and are passionate about their specialty. These experts see their knowledge as a personal strength and have a natural urge to share it with others. They love to conduct discussions and help others through their skills. The head of a virtual team needs to set a good example here. By sharing his knowledge at any time via digital media, he motivates other experts on the team to do the same.

When you have the right experts on the team, enlist and encourage them to share their knowledge, then you can then create the appropriate technical environment to use this knowledge in productive ways for your business.

Which Technologies are Essential for Communication and Collaboration?

When you have team members who do not meet in the same physical office location, you need digital collaboration technology. This is true even if your core team uses the same office, but some members (occasionally or constantly) work from their home office or as freelancers who support your team selectively. What kind of technology do you need to build a strong foundation for a team over geographical distance?

Initially, e-mail and instant messenger are easy and essential. Today, both are a self-evident part of our professional and private life. It is worth taking a little effort to organize e-mail and instant messaging more efficiently than might be the norm for personal use. In this way, you can greatly increase the productivity of your team. E-mail traffic is always increasing, and includes enormous amounts of spam mail. Despite many disadvantages, e-mail remains an indispensable tool for business. As I've already described in Chapter 4, it is essential for a virtual team to agree on a timeframe in which each e-mail needs to be answered. A standard guideline is 24 hours.

Method:
    Write relatively short, concise e-mails and use clear, strong subject lines, so that the recipient of your e-mail knows immediately what

the e-mail is about. Also, be very precise about the actions that you wish for the recipient to take.

Equally indispensable as e-mail today is chat, or one of the numerous forms of instant messaging, such as WhatsApp or Facebook Messenger. When team members turn off their e-mail program (including e-mail notifications) in order to focus and be creative, they are usually still accessible via chat or another instant message program. A virtual team can agree that instant messaging is only used for urgent messages, or to provide information that requires a quick and fast response. Using one single instant messaging tool, such as iMessage (if everyone uses Apple devices), WhatsApp, Facebook Messenger, Skype, Telegram, etc., for the entire team is best. A fixed response time should also be set with instant messaging. In this case 2-3 hours is the usual maximum, since it is normal to have a break from concentrated work every few hours and meetings rarely last longer than that. Some companies are also limiting instant messaging to specific times, for example stopping between 20:00 and 6:00 local time. This is to ensure sufficient recovery and downtime, since constant accessibility can also add stress and reduce productivity.

E-mails and instant messengers are now indispensable to business. Whiteboard and Workflow Tools have also gained in importance. If the team agrees on how to deal with technology, it becomes an invaluably effective tool for success.

Two other technologies that are increasingly important in business are whiteboards and collaborative workflow tools (groupware). A digital whiteboard is designed to enable the participants of a web or video conference to work on a document in real time as it is viewed by each conference participant. For interactive brainstorming, break-out groups and the like, such virtual whiteboards are ideal. There are different products available, ranging from very specialized tools like the Ricoh Whiteboard, to simple and free versions such as Google Apps for Business.

Google Apps can also be linked to Google Drive to share documents and collaborate in real-time. With tools for workflows, I do not mean the heavy-weight enterprise resource planning (ERP) systems, such as SAP, which normally represent workflows. Rather, I have my smart digital to-do apps that allow delegating certain tasks to other team members. In these apps, the entire work progress (before and after delegation) can be stored and tracked later at any time. Trello is an example of such an app. In my seminars, I am often asked which system is best suited to manage vacation times. If you do not already have a mature HR management system for your team, I recommend a simple Google Calendar.

It is sufficient in the range of functions and the flexibility to enter the vacation times of all team members and to keep an overview.

How to Choose the Right Digital Technology for Your Team

There are two basic approaches to the selection of digital tools: "Best of Breed" or "One Stop Shop." "Best of Breed" means that you are looking for the best product for all your individual requirements. "One Stop Shop" means that you choose one of the largest IT vendors, for example Microsoft, and from this vendor use all, or almost all of their products. There have been several evolutionary cycles in recent years and decades. In the early days of the software, there was often only one vendor who had the best solution for a particular need. If you could afford this often very expensive solution, that was the best option. Then came the great time of the complete providers, such as SAP. They could provide everything from a single source, which made the integration of IT much easier. If you could afford it, that was the best solution. Today the world has changed again. We are living in a time when there are millions of apps and cloud solutions and integration among these is no longer a problem. This means you can choose almost any app or program you like and integrate it into your IT landscape.

Today, a more pragmatic approach is called for. Look for the app that suits you best, but keep the number of apps you use for certain tasks as few as possible. It suffices, for example, to have an instant messenger and a video conferencing system. The less apps you use, the smoother your communication runs and the

> *Today, you have unlimited possibilities to use apps and integrate them into your IT landscape. However, to do this effectively, keep the number of apps for individual tasks as low as possible.*

less IT support you need. In large corporations, of course, the digital strategy of the organizations as a whole is important. But for the most part, there is a certain selection of shared apps available for individual teams. I advise you to use the apps that are desired by the majority, but then periodically, for example annually, to check whether there are better solutions which have become available.

The Limits of Digital Technology

Digital technology makes it possible to bridge continents and time zones, but do they connect people effectively? Is everything possible through digital technology? Or, is there sometimes no substitute for actual personal contact? As noted in Chapter 1, effective collaboration in virtual teams requires that all team members have at least met each other one on one once. Methods recommended by me, such as the "Personal Lifeline," ensures that people meet each other and lay foundations for interpersonal relationships. Technology comes into play to maintain interpersonal relationships, but does not create them! In order to maintain the relationship, it is necessary to communicate regularly about personal events via digital channels. A personal update is just as important as project information, specialist discussions, and problem solving.

I also want to remind you, as mentioned in Chapter 1, that critical feedback in virtual teams should never be public. Only criticize a team member in an one-on-one conversation. The problem of public criticism is exacerbated when web or video conferences are recorded and archived. Imagine fielding a sharp attack on a team member during a conference. Afterwards, it may be regretted, but it cannot be undone. The criticism will come out again at all subsequent reiterations of that conference.

Digital technology makes many things possible, but not everything. Personal meetings and conversations remain important. In addition, digital communication has its own traps that require careful attention.

In general, I recommend conducting regular one-on-one discussions with all team members - not only when there is something to criticize. If a problem arises and you wait to address it during one of the next scheduled conferences, it may be too late. Therefore, always communicate on the "short wire" with individual team members. I recommend that managers of virtual teams schedule more personal conversations at least once a month with all team members who report directly to them. During this conversation, you can discuss the performance over the past four weeks. If something is not running properly, you can point it out early. As soon as a really difficult problem arises, you also intervene, but again not in a public discourse, always one-to-one. The goal is to understand the perspective of the other team member.

Virtual work is simply different; this concept must be recognized again and again.

Another important point: even the most advanced technology does not change the fact that work can sometimes be uninteresting at home. Even with my long experience in virtual teams, I still experience this. I now work a lot from home and sometimes miss the personal interaction with my team members. It may be advisable to create occasions for personal encounters to keep everyone on track.

Always try to understand how individual team members are navigating their situation of virtual collaboration. It can be, for example, that very extroverted people are demotivated because they just have to work a lot from home. Initiate conversation with your team members and find out what is going on with them.

Conclusion: Technology is an indispensable part of effective collaboration with virtual teams. However, make sure that the passion of your team members is kept alive. Also, be aware of the limits of cooperation in digital technologies. You need at least one regular individual personal meeting with each team member as well as regular one-to-one calls on the phone. The good news: There is more and more technology to choose from and the integration into the existing IT landscape is easier than ever. If you agree on clear rules, how to deal with technologies, and everyone is disciplined, then digital technology becomes a key to productivity. Digital technology can erase spatial distances and enable the best experts from all cultures all over the world to be brought together.

Interview with Thorsten Jekel

As an IT entrepreneur, consultant and book author, Thorsten Jekel specializes in business success with digital technologies. During his career, the MBA has devoted himself to the topic of intelligent use of new technologies. He has the necessary management experience to integrate business and technical issues in a holistic way. Since the market launch of the iPad, Thorsten Jekel has developed innovative business models with his Berlin company, jekel & team, around the use of the iPad. He practically accompanies large sales organizations with the introduction of iPads in field service. His book *Digital Working for Managers. Work-*

ing with new technologies efficiently, was published in 2013 by GAB-AL-Verlag. I met Thorsten Jekel at the "Stuttgart Knowledge Forum."

Who are you and what do you do? Just describe yourself!

I show companies how they can become more productive with digital-working technologies. My career started in 1988 at Nixdorf Computer. Later, I was CEO of several mid-sized companies. In 2010, I founded my own company, jekel & team. It specializes in the introduction of iPads for major sales organizations, such as Coca-Cola. I work on issues similar to topics your book examines. For example, how real and virtual teams work together productively. Or, the best way to communicate with each other, especially if employees work all over the country or even in different countries.

What are the main technologies for collaboration in virtual teams?

In my experience, one needs two types of technologies: 1) one-off technologies that make each individual team member more productive, and 2) technologies or even apps to communicate well with everyone on the team. Everyone needs software for personal information management, such as for e-mails, appointments, or tasks, for themselves. It is important to be synchronized on all devices. This can be done with Microsoft Exchange. Then, the team needs software to work and communicate with each other on, such as scheduling and sharing files. The synchronization of all data is also essential here. It must work together on the same files in a uniform structure, in order to avoid duplicates in any case. Finally, there should be real collaborative platforms where employees can share ideas and work with project plans. Here I also see multimedia tools for telephone conferences and video conferences, and the beauty is that these tools are becoming more and more cost-effective. At the beginning of my career, a video conference was still really expensive, today it is even possible via the iPad or the iPhone and a fast, mobile connection. This does not yet work in every circumstance, but it is improving all of the time, and I believe mobile connectivity is the future.

Virtual teams need technologies that make each member of the team more productive, as well as those that enable good communication amongst team members. It is important to have synchronous forms of communication.

I am currently working for a company that previously held regional meetings in offices, and now they are making these meetings more and more virtual, with mobile technology playing a key role. Tools that I like are Adobe Connect or Cisco WebEx. With WebEx, Cisco is one of the international market leaders. This application is even available as an app for the iPad. For me, however, it is important that these systems function reliably in everyday life. So, try different systems, talk to your company and ask them about their experiences.

What technologies or apps do you recommend, depending on the size of the company?

There are very different options, depending on company size and other characteristics. For small and young companies, I recommend starting with free solutions like Skype or Google Hangouts. Google Hangouts are not always public, as some believe, but can also be used in a closed mode. For small projects, simple tools such as Projectplace, Trello or Wunderlist can be used.

Wunderlist, for example, once started as a simple digital to-do list, then it was purchased by Microsoft and integrated into the Outlook Exchange environment. Microsoft has since added the smart solution of a startup for its mature world, which I find quite interesting. We often suggest a mix of the small-scale world of startup apps and the large, established applications, such as Microsoft, for the larger companies. Skype was also bought by Microsoft and Skype for Business was then integrated into Lync.

Depending on the size of the company, you need to know if your systems are scalable. Where your data is placed also plays a role. For reasons of compliance, there may be a problem in some industries, if the data is in the US. Then you need to make sure that the servers are in the European Union or even in specific countries such as Germany, Austria or Switzerland. Since I work a lot for banks and insurance companies, I often face this challenge.

Virtual Personal Assistants (VPA) are becoming more and more popular. Do you have any experience with this trend?

I love virtual personal assistants! It's been about the ten years since I read the book "The 4-Hour Week" by Timothy Ferriss. His credo is: delegate, delegate and re-delegate. If you are short of staff, you should definitely use virtual personal assistants. I can also say from experience that virtual assistants are worthwhile even if there is enough staff. That way the company workers can concentrate more on their core tasks. You should, however, carefully consider what tasks you will assign your virtual assistant. If you do everything in English with your virtual team, that is the easiest. I need many things for my work done in German. To find virtual personal assistants who are fluent in German is not so easy.

It is worth having personal virtual assistants, even if you have enough staff. The PVA allows the rest of your staff to concentrate on the things that matter.

I also work with Beach Layer. This is a company from Berlin that employs assistants from Eastern Europe, which helps keep their prices low. I used to work with GetFriday and Brickworks, two suppliers from India, which were recommended by Timothy Ferriss. GetFriday is suitable for standard tasks, while Brickworks does country studies or market analyses. When I was managing director of a fruit juice producer, we did a first country study ourselves and then presented it as a template to Brickworks. They did the same study for twelve other European markets. This is an example of how you can perform research-intensive tasks with virtual personal assistants. Another example: I have a podcast, and my virtual assistant transcripts it and makes blog posts from it. The price range is between about 4.00 US dollars an hour for virtual personal assistants from South America and up to 25.00 to 30.00 Euros an hour with providers from Germany. For assistants from India or Eastern Europe, expect to pay between 8.00 and 10.00 Euro per hour.

What can be delegated to virtual personal assistants?

In short, almost everything. I always ask what do we need permanent employees to do, and what can the virtual personal assistants do. If you have employees in your office with whom virtual assistants can discuss things in person, it makes it much easier. However, I am on the road most of the time and then I would have to send permanent employees in my absence to present things accurately as possible. In my experience, it depends on the quality of the briefing, regardless of whether you have present or virtual employees. With a bad briefing, you get bad results, with a good briefing, good results. This is the essential point, and not whether the employees are virtual or present.

I use my virtual assistant for everything that can be done over the Internet. In such a situation, the only major hurdle is if they are not a native speaker. My virtual assistant is from Romania and studied in Germany, so he is very good in written German. However, one hears his accent when he speaks, which can be a disadvantage when he makes telephone calls. Generally, VPA vendors are unfortunately not particularly well-organized when it comes to outgoing telephone calls. So, that can be somewhat problematic.

Again, everything that can be done over the Internet works great with a VPA. I use them for doing research, creating slides, writing reservations for hotels and restaurants, booking flights, and anything that can be done online in writing and with forms.

Basically, it makes sense for me to delegate every-

> *Everything that can be done over the Internet can be done by virtual assistants. One exception may be telephoning, since they would need very good language skills. The deciding factor on how successful your PVAs will be is how well you explain what you expect from them.*

thing that a person with a lower hourly rate can do, so that I can concentrate on the truly value-added activities.

What do I need to do to effectively use a virtual personal assistant?

The most important thing is briefing, briefing and briefing again. The second most important is the right choice and configuration of the digital technology for the cooperation with the VPA.

For example, your VPA should be able to send and receive e-mails on your behalf. They also need a platform for file exchange and collaboration on documents. Most VPA vendors have ready-made solutions, so I already have an exchange platform for files for my VPA. If the documents are not highly confidential, I also work with Dropbox. This is one of the easiest ways to exchange documents. Confidential information requires professional solutions, such as from Fabasoft, which is an Austrian provider with a very high security standard. It is also very important to be constantly synchronized on all devices. In the case of briefings, you should follow clear rules, and the reaction times should also be agreed upon. Structure increases the effectiveness of virtual personal assistants. This means above all: well-structured briefings and well-structured digital systems.

What are your experiences with virtual teams?

I have had many different experiences. We currently have a case advising a sales organization which is represented in urban regions such as Berlin, Munich and Frankfurt, but also in rural areas which are very sparsely populated and which means long distances for the field service. The challenge is that the commutes out to the rural regions are less productive. In the big cities, the teams get together for 5-10 minutes every morning and discuss everything that is coming. This means every day at most half an hour of lost time, because the field workers are already out in the field.

We have shared with the customer how we work this out for the rural regions. We are now focusing on real virtual distribution teams that are scattered all over the country and communicate with one another, for example, through Adobe Connect.

In the field, virtual sales teams can work much more efficiently than traditional teams. Working virtually with freelancers can also be very valuable.

Another example are the many freelancers with whom I collaborate, for instance, in app development. Or another example is a food service company with whom I am working on introducing iPad technology into their workplace. We have an external app developer team, we have SAP, we have a parent company, we have a mobile device management provider, we have the individual users - and all we need is to bring everyone together. This is more and more common in companies: a mixture of internal and external team members. In the past, this has always been a bit difficult, but the beauty with the new digital technologies, is that you can integrate external team members as if they were internal employees. This works really well! I believe that in future, that you will get more and more external specialists on your internal team, which will make your team a virtual team. Fortunately, it is getting easier, cheaper and faster. The result will be that the companies become much more productive.

Which of your achievements as a leader and entrepreneur are you particularly proud of?

First, I would like to say that for me, my wife and daughter are most important in my life. If I ask myself what will remain of me on this planet, then my daughter is number one. For me, leadership and management have a lot to do with what I would like to pass on to her generation. On the other hand, I have also learned a lot from her in dealing with people, which I can apply in teams.

If I restrict my comments to purely business, the biggest success was the creation of my own company, where I earned more in three years than in all my former positions as managing director. And the companies really did not pay me badly! Interesting for your book is perhaps that I have managed only through virtual power teams, which are so fast and so successful. I started as a single entrepreneur and worked for other companies.

One of my first projects was itempus. My business partner and friend Professor Jörg Knoblauch of tempus used to sell paper-based calendar systems and we brought them together into the digital world. Long ago, the trend was for people to switch to digital calendars and apps. I said, Jörg, you have good ideas and you have a customer database with 90,000 addresses for your paper-based systems. This might be something to work with. With a team of very good app developers, we packed the proven time-schedule system into an app. This has been highly successful and is selling very well at the App Store. I could never have done it alone, because I really needed a virtual team of the best specialists.

What I have done is what Professor Günter Faltin, a very exciting man, by the way, proposes in his book, *Kopf schlägt Kapital* ("The head beats capital") as "reasons with components." Today, with digital technology and virtual teams, you can start a business very cost-effectively and still have the entire infrastructure right away. If you include external partners for each project and then work with virtual personal assistants to do the administration, you are fully scalable up and down. This is also something that large companies can learn from entrepreneurs. So, I'm a little proud of the fact that I managed to succeed with these methods so quickly.

People often fear that their employees will not work when they are not being visually supervised, so the managers risk becoming micromanagers or control freaks. How did you control your employees? How have you ensured that everyone is doing their best?

I also know a lot of people who have problems with virtual teams, because they think people do not do their job. Yes, they can become micromanagers or control-freaks. This was not much of a problem for me.

In the beginning, my problem was my lack of enforceability. I'll give you an example. I worked for the Tchibo coffee service for five years and was responsible for the service for two years. My team consisted of 25 women.

I was in my late 20's, and I talked a lot with the women. I was nice, of course, and I wanted to be liked. Then I learned that it is not about being liked, but being respected. As a manager, a clear direction must be given in order to bring the best people into a team and achieve their goals.

I am convinced today of the concept of "situational leadership" described by Ken Blanchard.

Your management style should always be adapted to the situation. Technology cannot replace leadership; it can only support it. Leading your team only through e-mails does not work.

People are different, they have different needs and do different tasks on a team. Accordingly, I must adapt my leadership style. A simple example: If someone wants to learn how to ride a bicycle, they need clear instructions about what to do - no long discussions. But if someone on a team at the Tour de France wants to refine his driving style for the next section of the track, they need quite different input and they need to discuss strategy. One should therefore always consider the whole issue of leadership based on the situation, the company, and the goals.

What I am trying to demonstrate is that technological leadership cannot replace people. Technology can help me lead, but to lead people by e-mail, for example, would not work. I was once responsible for a team of field staff who worked on their own all week. I would call them once each week. I would ask how it was going and was open to questions. Nevertheless, one worker complained about the boss always calling him. We then had a group discussion, and I asked people if they wanted more or less contact with me.

You can discuss this with employees, or external partners in virtual teams, and find a solution for your team. It is good to have the entire repertoire of communication facilities, such as telephone, e-mail, instant messenger, video conferencing and so on, but you should discuss as a group, how communication will be handled and respond to individual preferences.

How did you ensure that employees are really involved in virtual teams and that the team became more than the sum of its parts?

In different ways. First, I start with believing that everyone is doing their best at the moment, even if that is not enough for the overall team goals. Maybe someone needs support from me or someone else to perform better. This is, therefore, a value-based approach in which you get to know your people, value them, and to trust that they are not doing too little.

In my opinion, trust is the key to everything. Trust is the absolute number one. The number two is being an example for your team. Team members always look at the boss, and when the boss is really engaged, they are also engaged. I have always paid attention and made sure that I expect at least as much from myself as I expect from my employees. I think it is problematic when executives say that you have to cut costs, and then they order themselves the latest 7-Series BMW. This is simply not credible, and the employees will notice the discrepancy and not believe you.

Communicating credibly and without contradictions is important. Additionally, one must remain human. For example, I once had an employee whose daughter died of cancer. I was so glad that I could really support him in this situation. Of course, no boss in this world wants an employee to have to deal with this, but if such a situation occurs, you need to respond with real humanity and empathy.

Trust is the key to everything. It is not fair to assume from the outside that someone is not pulling their weight. And, as the team leader, I have to be an example for my team. I, myself, need to act the way that I want my employees to act, and it is important that my actions don't contradict my words.

When there is bad news, it is important to communicate this clearly and unequivocally. As managing director, I had to dismiss people, and I communicated the situation very clearly, what the reasons were, and why we had to radically cut costs. I then went forward by good example and had the 7-series BMW, which I had taken over from my predecessor, demonstratively traded in for a Citroën Berlingo. Then I asked the other managers how they wanted to save in similar fashion? One who owned a large Chrysler traded it for an economic VW Passat Diesel. Our salesmen, who had only had very cheap cars, ordered something better to motivate them to more commitment, and soon the company's position rose. When, after two years, the figures were in the black we were again profitable, the leasing contract for the Berlingo ran out. I did not return to the biggest BMW, but instead ordered a VW Multivan, the compromise in the middle. This was also a signal to the employees.

How do you see the future of virtual or even boundless teams?

Virtual and boundless teams are becoming increasingly important. The world is flat.

With modern digital technology, there are more and more opportunities to form teams on an international scale. Lower labor costs in other countries, such as South America or India, play a role, but that is not the issue. It is also about using different time zones, as McKinsey has been doing for a long time. When people anywhere in the world do things over night, the next day the other members get to work with the results. Team members from different countries can also complement each other wonderfully. In India, for example, there are outstanding software developers, but they often lack structure, while Germans are very good at project management. So, it is a good addition, for example, if project management is supplied by a German partner.

I believe it is becoming increasingly important that teams work across geographical, cultural, and business boundaries. There are external specialists everywhere, and there will be a mixture of internal and external in the future. There will also be a mix of virtual and present teams. All of these things will increase productivity. The mixture makes it best.

Chapter 7

Structured Communication Means that not only the Boss talks, but Everyone Talks — about Everything

Claude's back felt stiff and hurt. He had just finished a Skype call. 2 hours and 37 minutes. Half sitting-half lying on his sofa in the living room, his iPad was lying on his lap. He still saw Maria's face and smiled longingly. He met the Spanish architect three weeks ago at a conference in Barcelona. After three romantic days with her, he remained constantly in touch - long Skype phone calls, text messages, Facebook posts, the full program. He checked his e-mails and saw the reservation confirmation for his flight to Rome next weekend. There, he would meet Maria for the second time.

"I have to find a project in Europe, otherwise the flights across the Atlantic will ruin me," Claude thought. "I cannot afford going every two weeks." Then he saw an unread e-mail from the MOOC professor which was already two days old. There were delays with the new, more efficient blueprints. This, in turn, has caused the test buildings of the local builders to be delayed. Claude should have told Bernd immediately. "I better call him instead of forwarding the e-mail," Claude said to himself out loud. Bernd will not be happy about this delay. It affects a critical thread of the project. Claude pressed the Skype button. He had the gentle voice of Maria still in his ear and didn't even notice that it had already rung ten times when Bernd finally accepted the conversation.

"Claude, do you know what time it is? In Germany, I mean!"

Claude quickly calculated that it was 1:00 am in Hamburg. "Oh Shit, Bernd, I'm sorry!"

"Why are you waking me up?"

"Sorry, Bernd, I did not think of the time difference. We have a delay in the MOOC blueprints. As a result, the test structures will also be delayed. So, the entire time schedule has changed."

"Did you just learn that? And what do you think I can do in the middle of the night to help you?"

Claude has fallen in love with a Spanish architect. Because of his long Skype calls with her, the quality of his work seems to be suffering. Bernd doesn't understand what is going on.

"Okay, right now you can't do anything. I will set up a video conference with Pilar and the MOOC professor's team to discuss how we can speed up the process and what the worst case scenario is for the timing of our project."

"Just do it, Claude. And do it as fast as possible!" Bernd was still slightly angry. "Do you need anything from me?"

"No, no, Bernd. Thanks for asking. We're fine. I'll get back to you tomorrow at the end of the day."

"Okay, then wish me a good night!"

"Sleep well, Bernd."

Claude knew how to create a sense of urgency to activate people. He immediately started writing e-mails and sending meeting requests. Nevertheless, he was disappointed in himself. The long phone calls with Maria during his usual working hours in Canada, when it was later in the evening in Europe, steered him off. He had already forgotten dates and read important e-mails too late. "I need to concentrate more on my work and somehow separate my work and private life better," he thought. Easier said than done. It was so nice to be in love.

On Wednesday the following week, Bernd prepared for the upcoming team conference. He had just finished a telephone call with his construction manager in Frankfurt. "Comically," Bernd thought, "the team in Frankfurt is robbing me of more time and energy than my international, virtual team for Transmontania." They seemed to be reaching the "empowerment" goal that they had defined together with Paul. The workshop began to pay off. Bernd was extremely satisfied with how much self-initiative the people showed. Linda had already successfully completed the crowdfunding campaign.

The money was there. Now she helped Pilar and Claude to coordinate the MOOC architects and builders. Pilar really helped the team move forward and seemed to be accepted by everyone. Anne arranged formalities

Everything is going great! Everyone in the team shows a lot of self-initiative. The money is here. Pilar helped the team decisively. Bernd's only concern is Claude.

with the government quickly and efficiently and ensured that the local builders were kept up to date. Stella, the new team member from Bulgaria, had introduced effective file management. The team members now shared a lot more online and held lively discussions in the newly founded Facebook group. The ball was rolling - and Bernd had to do little, if nothing. He did not need to control anything either. The team actually seemed to organize itself. Bernd's only concern was Claude. He has rarely given feedback lately, which was very unusual for him. For this, Claude called in the middle of the night to bring bad news. "This has got to stop," thought Bernd. "I need to discuss this with him at the conference today."

It was a crystal-clear day. The Elbe reflected the sunlight and threw interesting patterns on the walls in Bernd's office. Bernd blinked, dropped the blinds and started WebEx. It was 12:55 pm. As usual, Anne and Linda were on time.

"Hello Ladys, how are you?"

"Great, Bernd. I see that we are really making progress!" Linda added.

"I'm fine, Bernd," Anne answered quietly. "I have some news from the builders about the test buildings."

"Good. Let's wait for the others."

At 1:00 pm, everyone was at the conference except Claude.

"I suggest we start now," Bernd said. "There is plenty on the agenda today. We have made great progress since last week's conference. Pilar, thanks for your fantastic ideas! Your suggestions are now being reviewed by the architectural team in New York. I am very happy with the collaboration between the architects and the builders."

He continued, "There is, however, some bad news. Claude reported a delay in the new designs, which is critical to our timetable. As we all know, people need their houses by the winter. For some reason, Claude thought he needed to call me with this bad news in the middle of the night!"

He paused. But no one went to his remark.

"Pilar, has your joint conference with architects and builders been held?"

"Yes, Bernd. Claude and the others were there, too, and we are now working together on the new plans. Claude should be able to describe the worst-case scenario after talking to the professor's team about the details. "

"I hope Claude will come to the conference soon. He seems very distracted lately, missing deadlines and not reported in like he usually does. Anne, how are things with the government and with the local builders? And when do we have the green light for the test buildings?"

Before she could answer, Claude interrupted. "Sorry for the delay, folks! I must have overheard the alarm clock. I'm sorry. Bernd, please give me a signal when I should report the latest news on the state of the blueprints. "

"Claude, is everything all right with you? This is not the first time you've been late lately. Please wait until Anne is finished, then you can report on the situation."

The new MOOC plans are waiting. Bernd indirectly blames Claude for this, and he calls for accountability. Later, he regrets speaking so harshly to Claude.

When Claude's turn came, he could not say how the MOOC plans would go. There was now only one team of professors working on the blueprints and they took Pilar's suggestions as a basis. But they could not name an appointment until they were ready. The professors were working parallel on different courses and projects, and they needed an additional workshop before they feel that they could make accurate predictions.

"Claude, you know me, and you know I can't rest until we have a clear deadline," Bernd said. "Should I talk to the professors in New York and encourage them to move faster?"

"Bernd, pressure is the last thing we need right now. We'll be doing the workshop this week, and then I'll tell you about the results."

"That's not enough, Claude. I want to have a status report every two days until the final date for the project is final.

Stella hooked in: "Claude, would you make sure that the current project plan is on the drive so that Anne, Pilar, and the others can watch the latest version?"

"Will do, Stella."

"People, thank you once again for your commitment. Claude, we need to talk tomorrow evening."

Bernd ended the conference with an uneasy feeling for his comments to Claude. The Canadian was a key figure in this project. Perhaps Bernd should not have criticized him so openly?

Just as he thought this, Linda called him over Skype.

"Hello Linda, nice to hear from you again. You do not call often, what's going on? "

"Bernd, I think you were a little hard on Claude. Do you know about Maria? Claude is in love. He skypes with her for hours on end and flies to Rome on weekends to see her. You might want some patience with him.

Linda finds that Bernd was too harsh on Claude. She explains what is going on in Claude's life, and Bernd is worried because he didn't know how his friend Claude was doing.

You know that love gives us wings, but it also makes us blind…"

"Oh, I didn't know. Thank you for telling me. I thought Claude and I were friends. Why didn't he tell me? How do you know about it? "

"We've been on a lot of telephone conferences together in the past months, and we always start with a personal exchange. That is how we know what is going on with the others and how we can better deal with each other."

Bernd answered somewhat surprised, "Okay, if this helps you to cooperate better with each other, then it's all right."

"Would you consider doing this for our joint conferences with the whole team as well?"

"Look, this seems unfamiliar to me, and I'm not sure if it makes any sense. But I'll ask Paul for advice. I wanted to report to him anyway."

"Thank you, Bernd." Linda hung up.

Paul had offered Bernd that he could call spontaneously whenever he needed help. Until now Bernd had not made use of the offer. Bernd was delighted at how well he and his team were doing and how independently and self-reliably everyone was working. The workshop had paid off.

Bernd wondered what he could do to improve the performance of the team. Could Linda be right? Was he giving too little room for sharing personal experiences? He decided to call Paul.

"Hello Bernd, how are you?" Paul asked on the phone with his quiet voice.

Bernd calls his mentor, Paul, and gets feedback on team communication. Paul says there needs to be more exchange with each other about personal matters. Bernd should build a relationship with everyone on the team.

"I'm fine, Paul. I hope with you as well. Before we talk about other things, I have to tell you that the results of the workshop have far exceeded my expectations. Everyone on my team is taking the initiative to get the job done, to bring others on board when they need it, and to find solutions. They are really doing great! We have not yet achieved an important milestone, but I think that is more of a communication problem than bad project management or lack of skills."

"Very good, Bernd. Your people are working together as a real team and you seem to be enjoying it. I have a question: how often are your team meetings and what is your agenda?"

"Well, we talk once a month. In the event that problems occur, we schedule an additional meeting. As for the agenda, I usually prepare and send it in advance."

"Okay. And what about the participation in your discussions?"

"Well, there are the usual suspects. Claude usually dominates the conversation. The others join in if what we are talking about is of interest to them or from their area. Linda is something like our feeling and inter-relational barometer. She always senses when someone is not doing well or if something has gone wrong. If someone does not deliver for personal reasons, then she knows the reason. She seems to have built a relationship with everyone on the team."

"And you?" Paul asked. "Have you built a relationship with everyone on the team?"

"Let me put it this way: I get along with everyone. I make sure that we can concentrate on the important things when we have our monthly calls. And I make sure that everyone delivers results. That's how I see my role. During our last conference call, I had a little run-in with Claude. He was somewhat passive, and he almost missed a deadline. He even accidentally woke me up in the middle of the night. Linda seems to think that he is in love."

"Are you not friends with Claude? I thought you told me that when we met."

"Yes, I am, actually. Perhaps, I don't show enough interest in people. Linda is of the opinion that we should allow time during our monthly calls to exchange information about our personal lives. What do you think?"

"In virtual teams," Paul continued, "it is especially important that the team members regularly talk about how they are doing personally. In my experience, it works really well to allow time during the weekly telephone conference to find out how everyone is doing in their private lives. It's best to give everyone a certain timeslot to share".

"Every week?" Bernd sounded surprised and a little unenthusiastic. "Is that not too often? And is it not boring when everyone bares their soul in front everyone else?"

"You'd be surprised. People are not boring, nor will they be bored at learning how the others are doing. Our personal lives have a huge impact on our professional lives," Paul explained. "It is important to be able to recognize the mood of the group. I'm not saying that each person should tell and endless story about their lives. Give each team member two minutes to talk about how they are doing in their private lives. Two minutes should be more than enough. But make sure that every single person gets the two minutes. Otherwise, the more introverted team members will not say anything, and you won't have any idea of how they are doing.

Following Paul's advice, Bernd wants to propose a new communication structure for the project. There should be a weekly, rather informal conference where both personal and project-oriented things will be discussed and a monthly more formal, even with the external partners.

"These two minutes make the difference between you knowing how your people are doing, and you not knowing anything about them. And not just you. The other team members need to know how their colleagues are doing, and they need to have the others know how they are doing."

Paul continued, "When you are just having update conference calls, you can just concentrate on the important topics at hand. Afterwards, people can contact each other by e-mail or get together in smaller groups to solve any problems that may come up."

"That sounds okay so far," Bernd answered, "but I am concerned that we will lose focus on the big picture and on our ultimate goals if we speak too long on personal issues and small details about the project."

That danger does exist," Paul said. "That is why I hold conferences once a month which have a different structure. These meetings are much more formal, and we do not discuss anything personal. Every person has to submit a one-page report on how far they believe they are in reaching the yearly goals we established at the workshop. I also invite the most important partners from outside the team to these conference calls, so that everyone – the core team and our partners – is informed of how things are going. If there is something confidential that needs to be discussed, we save these points for the end of the conference after the others have left the conference room. In this way, you have a weekly less formal meeting in which project details, personal issues, and the greatest challenges are discussed, and once a month you have a more formal strategic planning session to discuss the implementation of details and to make sure that no one loses sight of the big picture."

"That sounds sensible. I'm a little concerned that everything will become a bit bureaucratic."

"I highly recommend it, Bernd." Paul answered. "With this structure, you will have a better overview of everything – both where the project is and how your people are doing. And that's without an additional time commitment on your side. And do you know what yet another advantage is?" asked Paul.

"What?" asked Bernd.

"You will never again miss out on finding out if someone on your team is in love!"

"Alright," Bernd said, smiling. "It's not my usual style, but, if you say so, I'll give it a try!"

Set Up a Communication Structure as Early as Possible

Every time I am assigned to run a virtual team, I call together the core team in the first week. These are the people with whom I will be directly working, and to begin we start with a live, in-person workshop. In the first chapter, you read about how such a workshop usually goes. In this chapter, we will concentrate on to best set up the communication channels for after the workshop, so that your team keeps its momentum.

At the end of the workshop, I ask my team how often we should speak with other? By this I mean, how often should a team conference call take place. Most of the time, people say that once a month is enough. I try to provoke them by saying, "Let's try talking once every week. If you find this to be too often, we can always change it."

At the beginning of the project, roughly 60% to 70% of the team show up at these weekly conference calls. After about one month, roughly 90% to 100% of the team start showing up, and this quota stays until the end of the project. What is the secret behind these intensive meetings? It's the personal contact.

Normally, I start every weekly team conference with a general update. During the week, I receive many e-mails. I immediately direct those who require immediate action to the person who is responsible for the respective areas. But I

In the weekly conferences, not only the progress of work should be discussed, but also personal matters. This strengthens bonding and increases participation and motivation.

deliberately save the e-mails which serve to inform me about progress on the project for these weekly meetings. As manager, you will have to take part in different meetings at many different levels. Make sure that you allow time in the weekly conference call to summarize the results of your conversations with other decision makers. Discuss with your team what was decided on in these other meetings. If you don't take these few minutes to keep your team informed, you will find that rumors may start to be spread. This may lead to mistrust or other unnecessary problems.

This general update ultimately revolves around all relevant events during the past week. It gives the team members the opportunity to ask questions and get rid of false observations or rumors. After this round, everyone in the team has a fixed timeslot to report what is happening to him both personally and with regard to the project. Thanks to the first workshop, they know each other's personal and professional lifelines. During the weekly conferences, we always come back to the personal level. This creates real interpersonal relationships. A fixed timeslot is particularly important for the more quiet and introverted team members, who prefer to be silent and listen instead of sharing, if they are not assigned their own speaking time.

The more formal monthly conference is predominantly for the core team members and usually takes place through a video conference. With these meetings, it is important that each core team member reports on his or her progress on the project and how their team is. I believe it is very important and it builds trust to see your colleagues at least once per month. These monthly conferences also give us the opportunity to invite others from outside the core team to the meeting, so that they may learn first-hand how the project is progressing. If they have questions or need additional information, this meeting is an ideal place to ask. The questions that are asked are gathered in the chat column of the conference call. We then allow ten minutes at the end of the meeting to answer these questions.

In the case of a more formalized monthly conference, it is important to provide a larger body with first-hand information and to allow them to ask questions.

If there are important decisions that have to be addressed, for example, if someone wishes to give change directions and work on another part of the project, these decisions should be made during the monthly conference. This is the best platform to lay out all relevant information for and with all of the important decision makers. Afterwards all of the core team members and the extended participants should pass the results of this meeting on to their own teams, if they have employees with whom they are working. This should be done, not in a top-down fashion, but in an interactive way during a meeting or telephone conference. Everyone who has something to do with the project should have the chance to ask questions or to give feedback.

Method:
   Make sure that your weekly telephone conferences have a healthy mix between personal and project-oriented updates as well as formal and informal reports on each team member's progress.

Another advantage of holding formal monthly conferences is a healthy level of pressure. Every team member has to report on their goals and ambitions. If someone is behind schedule or does not reach their goals at all, it becomes visible to the entire team. If goals are interlinked, as they should be, the goals of one team member always depend on the goals of at least one other team member. If someone has problems, then offer support. The responsibility, however, should remain with the team member, him- or herself. Of course, there can also be conflicts, and not every conflict can be resolved during a conference call. Nevertheless, a certain pressure is important to increase the performance of the entire team.

The Art of Divvying Time at Team Meetings

Both for the weekly conferences as well as for the monthly conferences, it is crucial to have a good, clear time management. There should be a clear-cut agenda with realistic time allocations built in, so that each person knows how much time they have to speak on a particular sub-ject. It is also recommended to name someone at the beginning of each conference to the timekeeper. The timekeeper monitors the time and has permission to interrupt the others if they go too long. The timekeeper should not be the team leader or the leader of the conference. The team leader should be free to give feedback and praise team members for what they have accomplished. The team leader also needs to be free to resolve conflicts and shouldn't generally squander his authority by hav-ing to constantly refer to the time schedule.

Up to ten or twelve team members participate in a weekly conference. Since there is always a general update at the beginning of the conference and then every team member has two minutes to share personal and project-related topics, you should schedule an hour and a half for the full confer-

A scheduled, precise agenda is as important as ending the meeting punctually. It is best to appoint a timekeeper who will make sure that everyone stays in their timeslot.

ence. Conferences longer than one-and-a-half hours are ineffective. You would then need to allow for breaks, and during breaks, people check their e-mails or phone messages and are simply no longer focused on the conference call.

To finish your conference call on time is important if you want to keep participation at 90% to 100%. In absolute exceptional cases, you may ask all of the participants if they would be willing to go ten more minutes to discuss an important topic. After those 10 minutes, however, you need to stop the meeting!

At a monthly conference, up to 100 people can meet for large proj-ects. I recommend two hours for this. In virtual teams, punctuality and time allotments are even more important than in local teams. If the team members are also distributed to different time zones, bad time manage-ment is even more detrimental.

Method:
Experience has shown that you should allow the following criteria for your weekly and monthly conferences:

- **Weekly Conference** – more personal and project-related information and updates

  Length of Conference: 1.5 Hours

- **Monthly Conference** – more formal updates and participation from the extended teams

Length of Conference: 2 Hours

Time management and ending the meeting punctually are extremely important in both cases!

What Time of Day Should Conferences Take Place?

Based on my experience, a typical global telephone conference should start in Europe at noon. Then it is already evening in Australia and other parts of Asia. If the team member is already at home, then you may hear dogs barking in the background, children screaming or eating dishes. At this same time, it is early morning in North and South America. Here the team member may have just woken up and is still in his bathrobe. To recognize these differences and to openly speak about them brings the team together and helps it bond. Your team members will also appreciate it if the calling times change on occasion, so that they are not always stuck with an unpleasant time. No one, however, should have to participate too late in the evening or too early in the morning.

If you have very important news for the team members around the world, it is an option to make two identical conference calls the same day: one in the morning for Europe, Australia, Asia and Africa and one in the afternoon for North and South America. Europeans can choose whether they prefer to participate in the morning or in the afternoon session.

If they hold worldwide conferences in English, they will have to do with many people who are not native speakers and who may speak with an accent. Even native speakers speak very differently depending on where they come from, for example, England, Scotland, Texas or Australia. One complaint that often comes up is that someone else cannot speak English well. The Indian, for example, does not understand the French, while the Indians understand one another very well.

For conferences in English, the team leader should make sure that everyone can be understood. Native speakers should be asked to speak more slowly and clearly. Participants with a strong accent should write parallel in the chat.

As a team leader, you can do a lot to improve the intelligibility. For example, ask the native speaker to speak slowly and not to use too difficult expressions. In general, using simple language helps everyone to understand. If someone has proven to have a particularly difficult accent, you can ask them to submit their questions or comments in advance or to use the chat box when communicating. This creates clarity and helps to create a more relaxed atmosphere. It is important that everyone thinks not only about themselves, but also about the others and that each person does his or her best to be understood.

Simplification of communication is important. If possible, schedule team meetings on the same day of the week at the same time and over the same communication channel. The exception to this rule is with global conferences. There, as mentioned above, you should try to vary the meeting time or create two identical meetings, so that not just one party is constantly being inconvenienced.

Explore Different Points of View in Your Team

Normally in virtual teams, a lot of e-mails get sent back and forth. In most cases, something is either being asked for in the e-mail or some information is being sent. E-mail, however, is not a particularly interactive medium.

Team conferences, on the other hand, are synchronous communication tools and are therefore the ideal place to hold a discussion. A discussion means not only asking for or giving others something, but also understanding each other. Free, open discussions should be encouraged during your conference calls. Conference calls give you an ideal platform to discuss conflict situations or new challenges that have arisen. In a conference call the team is able to find solutions together.

In his book *The Fifth Discipline,* Peter M. Senge distinguishes between "Advocacy" and "Inquiry." In management, the typical behavior is to take a stand on an issue and advocate for it. The goal is to defend our opinions and influence others. We are not interested in inquiring about or understanding other standpoint or opinions. Senge argues that it is far better to begin by trying to understand the opinions of others before we establish and announce our own opinions. In a team culture, where there are many different ideas and opinions and conflicts can occur, it is important to find a balance between advocacy and inquiry. Each person on the team has a right to his own opinions, but he should try to understand the opinions of others. The team leader has to set an example here by asking questions and trying himself to understand the different opinions of different team members. He should encourage lively, constructive conversations and should be careful not to override the others with his own opinions.

An "inquisitive" attitude is the key to good team communication, especially in conflict situations. First understand others, then advocate for your standpoint.

In my seminars, participants often complain that their team leader only calls a meeting together if there are problems. Many than waste time by using the meeting to defend themselves, to blame others for problems, or to announce that they have come up with the solution. In some cultures, this authoritarian way for leaders to act is expected. In these cultures, it is expected that the boss has all of the answers when problems arise.

In virtual teams, however, this type of behavior creates many more problems than it solves. There is already a very limited amount of time available on a conference call, and when this precious time is filled with blaming others or dictating solutions, it is very counterproductive. Virtual teams have greater need to discuss about a situation with each other than in face-to-face meetings. That is why virtual teams need communication structures which allow each person to express his or her opinions. When conflicts arise or controversial discussions take place, the team leader needs to make sure that the team finds the balance between advocacy and inquiry.

How to Give Regular, Constructive, Individual Feedback

Structured communication in virtual teams is essentially three-fold: first, regular team meetings, with the right balance of personal and project-related information, alternating both in the informal and the formal framework. Second, the opportunity for genuine dialogue and exchange, beyond merely advocating for your own opinion. And third, regular one-to-one feedback with your team members on both project performance and personal development, such as team skills or soft skills. Not only team meetings, but also feedback to individual team members, should take place regularly and be very structured. Under no circumstances should the team leader give feedback only when problems arise.

Team members need regular one-to-one feedbacks on both performance and personal development. A monthly call is perfect for this.

In my virtual teams, I called every team member who reported directly to me once a month. It was important to me to discuss their progress and whether or not they were reaching their objectives. If it were necessary to give critical feedback, I always did this in the one-to-one meetings. I recommend never giving critical feedback by e-mail and certainly not during a conference in front of other team members. The one-to-one discussions, however, are not just to give criticism. The conversations are a special opportunity for each team member to get in touch with the leader. The team leader gives feedback, but this is not a one-way street. The team member should take the opportunity to seek advice and support where necessary.

Typically, the individual feedback conversations should be divided in half: 50% is about the team member progress and 50% is for feedback and support from the team leader. It is important to ask: How can I support you? Or, can I do anything to make your work even better? During these monthly one-to-one conversations, the team leader and the team member decide themselves how they benefit from the meeting. Such one-on-one conversations are also a great platform to show appreciation for the individual team member. Therefore, they should never be canceled at short notice, without immediately offering alternative dates.

I think it is good to do a formal performance assessment roughly twice a year. This can also be done during the individual feedback calls, although it is even better to do this personally in a face-to-face meeting. In this type of formal assessment, it is important to have objectively measurable achievements by means of clear indicators. These conversations should be based on a comprehensible process which gives the executive the opportunity to intervene if necessary. In addition to the performance assessment, I recommend talking about the developmental goals of the respective team member. What other competences or leadership skills would the team member want to develop in the near future? There should be a concrete plan for this

Group feedback should take place twice a year, be well prepared, and have a clear structure. Criticism can only relate to the behavior of a person present and not to the person himself.

assessment, and depending on the results, the company should ensure mentoring or training to help the team member reach his goals.

All these monthly and semi-annual individual feedback meetings are without question time-consuming, but it is an investment of the team leader in his team. The team pays back these investments manifold by being more proactive and forward-looking. Good communication is the key to greater commitment and success -- even over great distances.

Group Feedback - Opportunity in the Personal Meetings

Another form of feedback in virtual teams is the group feedback. I recommend it once or twice a year, especially if there is an opportunity is for a face-to-face meeting. For the group feedback the team members are best placed seated in a circle. Starting with team leader, each team member receives feedback on the following three points:

1. **What to do next?** What has been done well and where did some-one support the team particularly well? It is often refreshing and motivating to be told that you have accomplished a lot. Especially in virtual teams, many team members don't see their contributions to the whole hand what has become of them. These meetings give the team leader the chance to share these successes and to thank the team members in front of everyone.

2. **What to stop doing?** Where is there need for improvement? Here, for example, we are talking about so-called "blind spots." Blind spots are something that a person is unaware of which may be caus-ing harm to others, annoying others, or stopping others from reach-ing their goals. When discussing blind spots, it is important to use nonviolent and empathetic verbage. Do not let it become personal. It is always about the behavior, never about the person!

3. **What to start with?** What potential does someone have? This feed-back is about identifying skills that a team member has, but is still not using enough. The group invites the team member to develop these skills and to use them more often.

The preparation for the feedback round is very important. Each team member should answer the above questions for every other team mem-ber in advance. When they write it down, it ensures that not only do they have something to share during the meeting, but they also will tend to stick by their opinions when sharing with the other, instead of being influenced by the opinions of others.

At the end of the feedback round, each participant writes a written summary of the advice he or she was given: What to do next? What to stop doing? And what to start with? They then send this document to the team leader, so that they have it for the next individual feedback meeting.

> *A team charter gives the team some guidelines for its work together. It should always be created by the entire team. The more cultures involved, the more important it is.*

The Benefits of a Team Charter

You now have a set of principles for structured communication in your virtual team.

Each team, however, is unique in terms of its composition, its objectives and its social and economic environment. In order to take into account these factors, individual agreements for an optimal communication culture can be made. To this end, many teams are now developing a so-called team charter. This determines how members of the team have agreed to deal with each other. A team charter should always be developed jointly, preferably through a live, face-to-face workshop.

The following questions can help your team to make meaningful arrangements for regular communication in its team charter:

- What types of team meetings do we want to have?

- On which technical platform and at what times do our conferences take place?

- How often do we speak and who takes part?

- What is the agenda and what is the timeframe?

- Which one-on-one discussions are there with the team leader and when do they take place?

- What communication channels do we use with the team? (i.e., e-mail, telephone, voice-mail, text message and video conferencing)

- How much response time is allowed to answer an e-mail?

- Which communication channel do we use in urgent situations? (i.e., Voice-mail on the mobile phone or WhatsApp)

- What is the maximum response time that should be allowed on the communication channel for urgent cases?

The bigger the team is and the more cultures and different time zones are affected, the more important it is to have a team charter. We all have our personal communication style. One person likes to telephone, the other prefers to write e-mails. A third is particularly active on social media and loves WhatsApp. And so on. So that the team does not go according to the preferences of individuals, it is important that everyone agrees. In addition, there are cultural peculiarities. In Germany, for example, it is not usual to call a team member in the evening or on the weekend, unless you have explicitly agreed to. In Mexico, leaving a voice-mail on the mobile phone is an everyday communication channel. In Europe, this is only done in urgent situations. All of these different habits and cultural impressions need to be discussed in your virtual team and agreed upon. This creates standards and norms that greatly facilitate collaboration and healthy communication within your virtual team.

Chapter 8

Structure and Processes Create the Basis – Trust Unlocks the Team's Power

Bernd looked at the current status report. They have been in the construction phase for three months. The foundations and very unique, resistant structures were already in place. He was delighted as he watched the project continue to grow without him having to do much intervention.

Claude was back on track and ensured smooth communication among the various parties. Anne was responsible for the construction progress, supported by Pilar and Linda. Stella was strictly aware of the rules of document management. An extended leadership team had formed on Linda's initiative. This included all the key personnel who reported directly to the core team, for example the managers of local construction companies and engineering firms.

After the professors and students voted for the three best student contributions to the architectural contest, the professor in New York honored the winners, and they, too, were asked to be on the extended management team. They participated in the monthly video conference, asked questions via chat, and introduced their ideas.

"Wow," thought Bernd, "we are quite a lot now, and the ideas are just flowing!"

In fact, the extended team had once again given some ideas for refining the blueprints. An Asian professor, who had already been involved in the original MOOC, had set up another team that was now documenting best practices.

What was Bernd doing? He also had his own ideas for improvement and gave the team regular feedback. During the rest of his time, he devoted himself to important stakeholders, such as government representatives in Transmontania. Twice he had already flown to the capital to discuss the project and to strengthen his relationship to some of the key players. Earlier this would have been unthinkable because of a lack of time. Tomorrow he had a telephone conference with the manager of one of the most important construction companies on site, a Chinese company. Anne and the Minister for Development of Transmontania would be there. The chances for further contracts in Asia were good.

Bernd is satisfied. Everything is going steadily. Claude is back on track. Linda has created an extended team. Bernd dreams of major orders in Asia.

Bernd looked out of the window at harbor, the Elbe and the horizon. In his head, he saw the skyline of an Asian metropolis full of buildings built by his company with even larger virtual teams. Bernd was almost a little euphoric. Not only because of the business opportunities, but also because of the prospect of many new and interesting people that he could get to know and inspire. He would get to know most of them only virtually, but he would still be able to build strong relationships and collaborate very personally with them. Bernd decided to end this day sooner, just to celebrate how much he had achieved. He asked his assistant to reserve a table for two people in his wife's favorite restaurant. Wiebke was enthusiastic when she heard about it by SMS. It had been several months since they last had a romantic evening out.

Bernd had already found a parking place near the restaurant, when he decided to check his emails one last time. Immediately, he saw an email from Anne in the inbox of the iPhone, whose subject line began with uppercase letters. It read:

URGENT: Construction work will take longer.

Bernd held his breath and clutched his phone tightly, as if he wanted to squeeze the bad news out of it. "Stay calm," Bernd said out loud, as if hearing his own voice made it easier. He frantically read through the email and then read it again more carefully.

It had been proven that Pilar's new ideas reduced material costs, but now everything is taking longer. Because of this, we have two problems: First, the date of actually handing the keys over to their new owner will be threateningly close to the start of winter. Second, the additional work involved will cost additional money -- money which was to be saved by the altered blueprints and new building materials. The budget was supposed to be set. Non-negotiable. Now what do we do?

Bernd's high spirits were blown away. He was no longer in the mood to celebrate. On the contrary. "Constant changes, winter is closing in, and a super-tight budget - why do I actually do this?" Bernd asked himself. "In Germany, it is so much easier to plan and build something." Bernd hit the steering wheel with his fist.

But half a minute later, he asked himself, "Who can help us this time?" He had to think about all the problems he had already solved with his virtual team. He thought about the workshop with Paul, the very successful Crowdfunding, and the new design. Will we make it again this time? And what will I tell the minister tomorrow?

Suddenly, Bernd had an idea: "What if I just give the team a hard deadline? I can tell them that it has to be done by this deadline, no if's, and's, or but's. I can also tell them that it may not exceed our budgetary requirements. Then they will to think about it and find a solution." In Germany, Bernd had never done this before. His timetables had always been realistic and all his budgets had been met. This, however, was a completely different situation now.

Just as Bernd was about to celebrate his success, he is informed a critical delay in the construction work. He decides to trust his team.

And the minister? "Well, I will just have to tell him the truth! I will have to tell him that we still do not know if we will be ready on time, because we are breaking new ground. None of this has ever been tried before. I will tell him that I trust my team 100%."

At that moment, he saw the faces of Claude, Anne, Linda, Pilar and Stella. He also saw the faces of the young people from the MOOC, which he only knew from video conferences. This afternoon he could only think about new houses and an impressive skyline. Now he can only think about his people. His instinct told him, "Yes, I trust them. It's true. I fully trust them."

"Okay, I'm going to do it," Bernd said loudly to himself. He got out of his BMW and locked it. "Even if it means putting my reputation on the line!"

When Bernd entered the restaurant, he saw Wiebke already sitting at the table he had reserved in front of the panoramic window. The view of the evening harbor was spectacular. Wiebke turned to him as he got closer and smiled at him.

The next morning, Bernd put on an elegant dark suit and tied his tie. The video conference with the minister and the Chinese manager was the most important event on his schedule today. It was very strange to be the only person who was not physically in Transmania. The others would be in the minister's office.

At 11:00 a.m., Bernd sat in his office, drank a sip of water, cleared his throat and then started WebEx. The conference began in a very formal and cool tone.

In a video conference with the minister and a Chinese manager, Bernd promises that the work will take a maximum of four weeks longer. He still has no solution to the problem.

In a very reserved manner, the Transmontanian minister praised the good progress with which the project was forward, in particular the fact that they were using local workers and materials. He then made it clear that he could not tolerate any delays in the schedule. His credibility and the popularity of his party were at stake. They had made a promise to the people, and he wanted to keep this promise. Then he asked, "When exactly will the buildings be finished?"

Bernd made his decision. One month later than planned, his team would be ready with everything.

Anne then made a suggestion: "As a Plan B, why not first complete the schools and use them as a shelter for the families whose houses would not be ready by winter?" They agreed to make a decision about Plan B within the next two weeks.

When the conference was over, Bernd loosened his tie and leaned back on his swivel chair. He even put his feet upon on his desk, something he very rarely did. It's happened! He has given his word and risked his good reputation without having a fool-proof plan. There was only trust. There were no guarantees.

Later that afternoon, Bernd called Paul to discuss the current development.

"How are you, Bernd?" Paul asked in a good mood. "I've read your latest status report. Seems you're doing really well."

"Paul, I thought, too, that until yesterday evening. Then, out of the blue, it suddenly became clear that we needed more time and money.

With the new construction plans, we have lower material costs, but we have to spend more time. This has increased our labor costs. And do you know what I did today? I promised the minister that we would need a maximum of one month longer. My God! I don't know how we are going do it -- let alone where we are going to get the extra money! You probably think I'm crazy now. But I had a good feeling, despite the risk."

"I do not think you're crazy at all," Paul said. "You just have confidence in your team, and you are firmly convinced that you will find a solution together."

"Well, at the moment we have not even integrated the new extended team into our meetings. But somehow, I am confident that if they put their heads together, they will find a solution. "

"Bernd, I know a tool and a process that will help you with this. Would you like to try it?"

"There are many coaching tools," Bernd answered without thinking what he was saying.

"Bernd, I see that the team is making real progress," continued Paul. "My next suggestion would have been to do a feedback round anyway, with all of them giving feedback on three points: What should we continue doing? What should we stop doing? and, where should we begin? In this round, you can also use this tool and solve the new problem."

Paul advises Bernd to believe in his team and to trust that they will find a solution. He also proposes a special workshop for problem solving.

"Should I invite the extended team?" Bernd asked.

"Not for the feedback round. All you need is your core team. In order for a feedback round to work, the participants have to have established a relationship with each other and have already experienced a lot together. Your core team has this relationship.

"Later, for the problem-solving session, we should bring in the extended team. Everyone will profit from having further experience in the room."

"Okay, Paul. You convinced me once again."

The combined workshop for group feedback and problem solving was scheduled on a short notice for the following Monday. Luckily, Linda was in London anyway and could fly over to Hamburg to personally be there. Claude moved the next romantic weekend with Maria, his new friend from Barcelona, to Hamburg. He could just stay in the city on Monday to attend the workshop. Anne and the managers from the construction companies should stay in Asia and participate by video-conference. The professor and a young Asian colleague would join in from New York. Pilar, Stella and Paul would stay at home and log in to WebEx via their computers. The budget was tight. Therefore, the team did everything to keep the travel costs low.

The workshop takes place in Hamburg and by videocon-ference at five other locations. Bernd explains the situation, and everyone are ready to go the extra mile.

When the day of the work-shop came, Bernd, Claude and Linda gathered in Hamburg in Bernd's conference room. It was a sunny day, and through the large windows one could see how the sunlight made the Elbe sparkle. The interesting light play repeated itself on the ceiling of the room. All three were sitting at the conference table, their laptops were opened, and they were ready for the video conference. Bernd went through the agenda once more, while Claude and Linda had already begun a robust discussion.

At 1 p.m., Bernd started the conference.

"Hello and good day in the round! I am glad that everyone is on time. We are now in six places: in Hamburg, Rio, Transmontania, in Sofia, in Georgetown on the Cayman Islands, and in New York City. There are twelve of us here. This is truly a global conference! As we all know, we are making great strides in the construction of earthquake-proof houses. However, the adjustment of the blueprints has led to some delays. On the one hand, we have to speed up the construction process and, on the other hand, save money on the unavoidable additional working." Bernd took a deep breath.

"In this situation, I have done something that I have never dared to do before in my entire career as an entrepreneur. On behalf of the entire team, I have announced a completion date without having a detailed plan. In concrete terms, this means we have one additional month to get everything ready. This has already been decided. The government will pay the construction workers their salaries one month longer. We have to pay for all other additional costs.

"This means that we need a whole new approach. We need a break-through! We need to find a way to catch up on the delay and save money at the same time. We've got to win this fight. It is the fight against the onset of winter. When winter comes, all the families need to have a roof over their heads. We have already set priorities again and are finishing the schools first. There, we can accommodate the families whose houses are not yet finished before the cold sets in. By then they have to be out of the tents. I am convinced that as a team we will win this fight. I put my good reputation on the line by making this promise, because I know we will find a solution together. Can I rely on you all? Are you ready to fight against the winter and all technical hurdles?"

Bernd heard some say, "Yes." He saw others agree by nodding, both in the room and on the video screen. He knew that their "Yes" was not just a "Yes." Their "Yes" means: "Yes, we are willing and ready to go the extra mile, so the project becomes a success. We stand behind this 100%!"

Bernd felt the feeling of ease and gratitude come back. They had reached a new level of trust and commitment in the team. And that felt really good.

Now it was Paul's turn. He explained his special method of brainstorming.

"For our meeting today, each of you has completed the Visual Questionnaire. On the basis of your profiles I divided you into four groups. I call these the virtual brainstorming groups, and I have already set them up on our new online tool.

Paul directs the brainstorming to find a solution to the problem. The team works in four groups formed according to their personality profiles. In the end, they have groundbreaking ideas and new scenarios.

"Please look at the group to which you belong. Each of you in your group should brainstorm on the following question: How can we speed up the construction process while staying on the original budget? You have 45 minutes to discuss it and to come up with a solution. Afterwards, each group will present their results. Do you have any questions?"

You could tell that the team was getting excited. The regular conferences of the extended leadership team now paid off. All of them had the essential construction principles in mind and knew the status of the current construction progress.

Bernd, Stella and the professor were part of the strategic group. They were visionaries, saw the big picture, thought in different scenarios and were passionate about the subject. Bernd saw the other two on his laptop. Despite the distance, there was a lively discussion. The group wrote their ideas on a virtual whiteboard. Bernd has no become very good at giving others space in their creativity and taking every idea seriously. Even if he disagreed completely, he did not immediately object, but asked questions to understand the intention behind every proposal.

After 45 minutes the group had an action plan. They knew what additional research would be necessary. They could even quantify the efficiency gain. It was time for the presentation.

The creative group, consisting of Claude, Pilar and Edwin, the junior professor from Asia, suggested to test whether certain components can be produced in a 3-D printer. This would save time and money. A group of students, led by Professor Tan, has already done research in this area. The students had discovered this new trend themselves. In China, they were already having great successes with the 3-D printing of similar parts, which remained largely unknown in the West.

For Bernd, it was the light at the end of the tunnel. The best thing was that all four groups presented their results from different perspectives. There was a groundbreaking new idea for the use of materials, there were new scenarios for risk management, and there was a communication strategy to gain the full support of the population, government and non-governmental organizations.

Bernd fell a stone lifted from the heart. His team was fantastic! People had once again surpassed his expectations. Still deeply moved, Bernd finished the conference in words he'd never used before: "I'm proud to lead this team. And I am firmly convinced that this team will surpass itself. We'll write history."

Processes are Good, Trust is Better

What do a virtual team and the universe have in common? Well, the universe consists of only 10% matter. These are the planets and stars. 20 percent is nothing - black holes and other phenomena which cannot yet be explained by science. And 70 percent of the universe is invisible energy. This includes, for example, the gravitational force. It holds the universe together. A virtual team is quite similar. Only 10% of the team is its members and the infrastructure. This is, so to speak, the matter. 20% are undeveloped potentials.

And 70% are the relationships, the trust, that is, the gravitational force that holds the virtual team together. The art of running a virtual team is to focus on this 70%. Make sure that the gravitational force is strong. You will be amazed at how much you can improve your results by focusing entirely on relationships and trust.

Trust is the main factor that holds virtual teams together. Anyone who wants better results should focus on this.

Now, you may disagree: A team needs efficient structures, processes, rules and procedures. This is not wrong. There are various methods for process optimization. For example, Lean Management, Agile Management, Scrum or Kanban are such methods. But more importantly are the interpersonal relationships on the team, the ability to work independently, and self-discipline. With all of these there is a common denominator: Trust.

Structures and processes are unquestionably important. The more virtual the team, the more the interaction between the team members has to be institutionalized. A process, an agenda or a certain role distribution ensures efficiency.

In Chapter 7, I presented you with various forms of regular team interaction, which provide both a clear structure and content flexibility. This includes the informal weekly conference with its personal and project-related updates, as well as the formal monthly conference, which focuses on the state of the progress of the team in working toward its goal.

At the monthly conferences, the extended management team is present, which consists of everyone who reports directly to the core team. This ensures that strategic guidelines penetrate all hierarchical levels and that everyone is informed of the progress of the project. In Bernd's team, this was a prerequisite for a breakthrough, when a solution was urgently needed for faster construction progress.

Without the use of regular, trusted processes, virtual teams cannot function. The deciding factors, however, are interpersonal relationships and self-discipline. Moreover, it is more important to have clear objectives and to promote individual respon-

The more virtual a team, the higher the need for commitment. Processes are important; however, flexibility and individual responsibility are even more vital.

sibility rather than to hold on to pre-defined processes. Processes can become tedious. What I mean by this is that they build on the results of the previous step and take into account the feedback from customers and other stakeholders for the next step.

In virtual power teams, it is essential that everyone has a clear annual goal and that they can decide for themselves how best to achieve it. At the same time, there must be processes which ensure a constant exchange with the most important stakeholders. The customer perspective is enormously important and should be constantly considered before going on to the next development stage. Scrum defines roles, for example the "product owner." The "product owner" acts as if he were the client's lawyer. He takes the perspective of his client and explains his needs to the team. The "Scrum Master", in turn, organizes the communication and ensures compliance with agreed rules in the individual phases of the project.

The Process Master should be the Primary Coordinator of the Team

In order for processes to run smoothly, there should be a "process master" or coordinator who ensures that everyone adheres to the agreed rules. This person can, at the same time, be responsible for the agenda and the observance of the time frame during meetings. In my teams, I have often assigned this role to the person who was also responsible for the document management and the electronic directories.

The person responsible for document management in virtual teams is often also well suited to be the team coordinator.

The coordinator then defines the conventions, such as the naming of documents or the filing, to which the team agrees and ensures that everyone respects them. The coordinator is also responsible for the smooth functioning of the conferences, and they ensure that each person has time to express his or her thoughts on issues. In Bernd's team Stella took over the role of the coordinator. She has very good IT knowledge and has enough authority to enforce the agreed upon rules.

Giving team members specific roles is even more important in virtual teams than in local teams. It creates clarity and ensures smooth processes. These roles, however, must not distract from the fact that everyone should be goal-oriented and individually responsible for achieving these goals.

Individual responsibility on the basis of trust is always more important than to be a slave to certain processes.

Helpful regular questions for a week conference:

- How did I help our team achieve its goals last week?

- What do I want to do this week to help the team achieve their goals even better?

- What hurdles do I see that make it harder for me or the team to achieve the goals?

A wonderful story which illustrates what I mean is the victory of Admiral Nelson against the Spanish armada. At the beginning of the 19th century, naval battles were always the same. The ships floated parallel to each other and shot at the other side with cannons. The "process" of how a naval battle was to be conducted was precisely defined, and there were whole libraries which described it.

The formation of the fleet and the command chains were, as well, defined as the question of when to shoot and what was targeted. Admiral Nelson did it differently. He allowed his commander to make his own decisions. The English ships did not line up, as usual, parallel to their opponents, but drove straight to the opposing line, broke through, causing chaos on the opponent's ship. Each commander under Admiral Nelson could make his own decisions as to how to best attack the enemy. This created a new leadership culture which was based on trust rather than on orders. Virtual teams are more scattered than ships in a sea battle. Therefore, trust and individual responsibility play an even greater role for the motivation and implementation of a strategy.

The Art of Building Trust

As you have already read in a previous chapter, trust has two sides:

First, trust your team members personally and second, trust in their ability and experience. The sympathy factor plays an important role in developing a personal trust. We tend to trust people who have similar values. When this happens, the chemistry seems to be right, and intuitively we like the person. It is therefore very important that people in virtual teams can show their personal values. Allow ample time for your team members to get to know each other and the values of the other person. This allows them to bond at a deep, personal level. This alone, however, rarely suffices.

In order to establish a deep professional trust, it helps for the team to overcome a conflict situation. In his book *The Five Dysfunctions of a Team*,[7] the American management expert Patrick Lencioni describes five "killer factors" for a team performance. If you flip each of these to the positive counterpart, they automatically become the success factors for each team.

Illustration 4: The five Dysfunctions of a Team from Patrick Lencioni

Lencioni represents the five dysfunctions or "killer factors" of a team in the form of a pyramid.

The base of the pyramid is trust - or the absence of trust - as the foundation for everything. In order for grow trust and become resilient, the team has to endure conflicts. Fortunately, confidence increases after every successful conflict. You have already read in this book about how executives can succeed in creating a culture which tolerates – even encourages – making mistakes.

Creating this type of culture is about encouraging people to take calculated risks and being willing to support them if things go wrong. This is the key to innovation. It is important not to blame them for setbacks, but instead to ask what can be learned from the experience. What this means in virtual teams is that no one should accuse or blame another person by email or messaging for mistakes which have been made. Instead, encourage both parties to come together and invite them to a personal conversation in which they can discuss what has been learned from the situation.

In order to resolve conflicts on a lasting basis, wise leadership is necessary. The "inquisitive" style of communication from Peter M. Senge,[8] which we discussed in Chapter 7, is important for effective leadership. Do not be naïve:

Virtual teams must develop a foundation to deal with conflicts. Trust is the most important. Intercultural competence and an "inquisitive" communication style are also necessary.

Conflicts always happen. They cannot be totally avoided. Different working styles, different personalities, and different priorities alone create the potential for conflict.

For example, imagine that you have on your team one person who finds it important to keep a strict appointment schedule. You have yet another person on your team who finds it more important to create and maintain interpersonal relationships but being on time to meetings or meeting deadlines is not as high a priority. This will, over time, cause conflicts.

Intercultural factors also play a significant role on virtual teams and should not be underestimated or ignored. In some cultures, tasks count more than relationships - in others it is the other way round. This is just one example of many possible intercultural conflicts. I would like to recommend Erin Meyer's *The Culture Map*,[9] already mentioned, to better understand intercultural conflicts. It is very helpful for team leaders and the entire team to know the eight dimensions of cultures. It is thus possible to classify where the cause of the respective intercultural conflict may lie. Through these types of resources you can find specific solutions.

Method:
Learn how to distinguish professional, personal and intercultural conflicts. In the understanding of intercultural conflicts, for example, *The Culture Map* by Erin Meyer

Not all conflicts have their roots in character or cultural differences. It may also be that some team members avoid taking responsibility. Or that certain team members want to exercise power and try to dominate their peers. Another situation which may lead to conflicts is if team members lose sight of their goals. Or if they do not identify as strongly with their goals as they may have initially claimed.

To be a strong team in the long run, all these conflicts need to be resolved. Here, again, the "inquisitive" communication style helps to identify the source of the conflicts. The better you understand what drives people and their behavior, the easier it will be to solve the conflict. Conflicts escalate when people stubbornly hold onto their position instead of changing perspective and opening themselves to the needs and intentions of the other team members. If the team members manage, however, to come together and solve the conflict, their trust in each other will grow and deepen.

In virtual teams, commitment and individual responsibility are encouraged primarily through interlinked goals. You encourage individual responsibility in that you allow your team members both to set their own annual targets and to have the freedom to make their own decisions. In addition, these annual goals have to be dependent on other team members and their goals. I described this in detail in Chapter 4.

Where team members themselves assume responsibility, they are also capable of creating conflicts and, as a result, are able to exercise a healthy degree of group pressure. The decisive factor is always the team culture. Where tolerance for making mistakes and an "inquisitive" communication style prevail, and where the team leader is an excellent role model, team performance automatically increases.

The Typical Four Phases of Virtual Teams

Maintaining high levels of commitment in virtual teams is not always easy. The team members work in different places and often there are different organizational levels. It is important to establish how strategic decisions will be communicated to all team members at all locations and at all levels. And, as we have already mentioned, it is important to link individual goals to the goals of other team members and, of course, to the team goal. Emails are often used as the medium to announce decisions to the team members, but this alone is not sufficient to keep everyone on board. It is also important to explain the decisions that have been made during telephone or video conferences in order to give team members the opportunity to ask questions.

It is also important that everyone has the same level of information at all times. The monthly conference with the extended team is an excellent way to keep everyone informed. Allowing for comments or questions at the end of the conference help to involve everyone and give everyone the chance to voice their opinions. Decisions will only be supported and implemented at all levels if you have given everyone the opportunity to ask questions and provide feedback.

Having a single, clear goal for the entire team helps enormously to produce results. In Bernd's team the goal is clear to everyone: The homeless earthquake victims need new houses before the win- *Maintaining high commitment over a long period of time is especially challenging in virtual teams.*

ter sets in. This objective is the number one priority. Everything else is secondary to this goal. Teams with such clearly defined goals have a much easier time focusing, setting other priorities, measuring the progress of the project, and engaging with full force. It is also true here: Trust is the basis of everything. It is the one common denominator bonds together all of the resources and activities of the team. Trust, however, is always in danger of being violated. It is not automatically retained once it has been won. It has to be earned time and time again.

Every team - whether present or virtual - goes through certain phases in its development. A number of authors have described these phases scientifically. A classic you may be familiar with is Bruce Tuckman's Four Phase Model.[10] It was first published in 1965 and became known by the names of its four development phases: "Forming, Storming, Norming, Performing." The model can also be applied to all team development, especially the unique development of virtual teams.

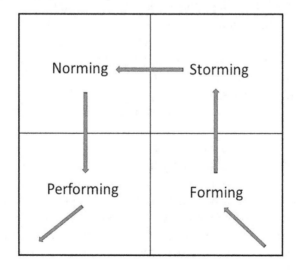

Illustration 5: Bruce Tuckman's Forming Storming Norming Performing (Four-Phase) Model

In the first phase, **Forming**, trust is established on the basis of how we perceive the other person and what we assume about their personality. Because on virtual teams, team members don't usually know each other at the beginning of a project, a workshop can provide the basis for the beginning of trust. Where this is not possible, the personal and professional lifeline exercise should be done for all team members during a video conference.

Bruce Tuckman's classic Four Phase Model can also be applied to virtual teams. Virtual teams are still trying to avoid the conflict phase. Or they want to resolve conflicts by email.

Some teams never leave this first Forming phase. They remain in the comfort zone, polite to each other, but they never realize their full potential. Tuckman observed that only about half of all teams are involved in real discussions about the resolution of conflicts. Only by doing this, can they enter the next phase, the phase of Storming. This is even more extreme in virtual teams. Team members avoid conflicts either completely or try to resolve them by email.

At this point in the development of his team, the team leader plays a decisive role. He should be accessible at all times, communicate intensively both individually with individual team members as well as with the entire team, and he should be able to recognize and call out conflicts. For example, if he realizes that through email communication, a conflict is escalating, he should immediately intervene and draw attention to the situation. The team leader does not need to know the solution to the conflict, but he should ensure that the conflicting parties talk to each other by telephone or in a video conference. While doing this, the team leader should show understanding and openness. Through his own behavior, he signals to the team that it is important to be open and understanding with each other.

The third phase, the **Norming** phase, is about roles and processes. Processes are important but only the basis for the success of the team. True peak performance is created where people are inspired, where they trust each other, and where they give everything they need to succeed. Efficient processes are not a goal unto itself; they are the means to a goal. Norming is best done in virtual teams by transferring responsibility to individual team members. In Bernd's team, Stella is the key figure for the stage of norming.

Watch out, trap!
Conflicts in virtual teams escalate extremely quickly when they are emailed. The Teamchef should have the e-mail traffic in mind and in the event of a conflict make sure that the participants talk in a telephone or videoconferencing.

While the team leader is crucial in the first two phases of team development, he should have less daily influence during the third and fourth phases. During the third and fourth phases, the team leader should modify his communication style. At this time, he should give even fewer instructions and see his role as being more motivating, keeping an eye on the big picture and encouraging the development of individual team members.

Psychologists have found that in a somber and controlled state of consciousness, we can only get a maximum of 60% of our potential. Only in a state of enthusiasm and inspiration can we give 100%. That is why, in the last phase, the **Performing** phase, when the team's maximum performance is important, one of the team leader's most important tasks is to inspire his team.

Regular, structured communication sets the foundation for excellence. At the crucial moment, the commitment is there and new ideas emerge.

In our story, Bernd instinctively trusted his team and was ready to risk his reputation. This risk was rewarded. He was able to see how a top team finds a solution for absolutely every problem. This is Performing. He created the prerequisites for this by providing regular structured communication. At the decisive moment, his people were passionate about the project and reaching their goal. Because of this, they understood the challenges confronting them, and they came up with creative, constructive ideas for the solution.

In a climate of trust, the positive expectations of everyone on the team automatically rise. You come to a point where you believe: With this team, everything is possible! The course is set for outstanding performance and exceptional results.

Part III

Culture

Chapter 9

Virtual Power Teams Can Quickly React to Changes and Take Advantage of Opportunities and Trends

The sunrise was gorgeous. Bernd looked up from the iPad on his lap and looked out the airplane window. Thin clouds lay beneath them like a violet ocean, touched by the first rays of the sun. On the horizon, the violet turned into a bright red. Behind it, one could see the first tiny piece of the rising sun. Bernd was on his way to Munich to visit the biennial trade fair for Architecture, Building Materials and Systems. He hoped to discover new trends and make some interesting contacts.

He hoped to retire to a quiet corner at 11:00 a.m. He was planning a video conference with Anne and Edwin, the junior professor from China, who worked for the MOOC in New York and who, with his team of students, developed the idea to use the new building materials. Bernd had brought Edwin into the extended project team. Now, he wants to find out how the new building materials are working out.

The morning went well. Bernd made his way through the crowds in the exhibition halls. The colorful activity at the attractively designed stands, the many conversations, the hostesses giving out flyers, all the colors, lights, and faces made him curious and aroused his desire for new projects.

Bernd visits a trade fair for architecture and building materials in Munich. Thanks to the independent work of his team, he finally has more time for new contacts and new ideas.

At 11:00 a.m., Bernd is sitting in an armchair in the café area with a fresh coffee in his hand and he starts the WebEx to talk to Anne and Edwin. "Good evening Anne, good evening Edwin, how are you?"

Anne replied, "Good morning, Bernd! I am fine. I am working from home today. We have exciting news for you."

"Good morning Bernd," said Edwin. He sounded calm and reserved. "I am delighted, and I am honored to be speaking with you personally. After many discussions in the expanded team, I can tell you today where we are with the new materials and how they will affect our plans. "

"Outstanding! Today, I am concerned about the completion date of the houses with the new materials. How does our time schedule look?"

"We have made great progress with local builders," said Anne. "Claude, Pilar, Edwin and some of his colleagues and students from the MOOC have been supporting us intensively. Since Edwin has coordinated all the talks, I suggest that he also present our results."

"Excellent," said Bernd. "The virtual stage belongs to you, Edwin."

"First of all, thank you, Bernd, for letting me be the head of the virtual sub-team for the integration of the new building materials," Edwin began. "We will do our utmost to speed up construction."

"I'm glad," said Bernd, smiling. "Welcome on board! I hope you enjoy the work, and I wish you all the best."

"Okay thanks! I've been leading my own virtual team for several weeks now," Edwin said. "We have already had several conferences, and we've managed to speed up the process. In the beginning, we met in in a large round with Claude and Pilar, as well as the chief engineer and construction site coordinator of the construction company. At this point, my core team consists of the engineer and the three MOOC students who won the prizes. Their plans were already included in the final blueprints for the houses. From time to time, Anne helps us coordinate with government agencies. But she is not a permanent member of our team."

Bernd speaks with Edwin, a Chinese associate professor and a new team member, under whose leadership innovative building materials have been developed. The first results have been positive.

Bernd nodded contentedly and took a sip of coffee.

"Together with the three students, I have developed a detailed plan that has been reviewed by the chief engineer and is being tested on site," continued Edwin. "It's a long story, but in short we believe that the houses can be finished by the middle of December. We would then be able to meet your deadlines, Bernd. In order to be 100 percent sure, however, the test buildings would have to be finished first. Only then will we know whether all our calculations are correct and the buildings are resilient."

"Apparently, a lot of progress is being made without me having to get involved. This is great! And if the government still knows who am I, it's even better!" Bernd joked. "Speaking of the government, Anne, do you have any new information about the governmental crisis?"

"Well, Bernd, I wanted to wait until after we talked today, so that I knew what Edwin had to say. Tomorrow I will report to the Minister on our progress, and I will inform him that the houses will most likely be finished in mid-December. On the condition that the test buildings are a success, of course.

"Very well," said Bernd. "Edwin, would you please report on the current plan at the extended team conference next Wednesday? I would like everyone to be up to date. Excellent work so far!"

Bernd closed WebEx, stood up and felt a burst of energy. Yes, indeed, it was true: If you find the right people, bring them together, and give them the freedom to individually take responsibility, everything is possible. He could hardly believe that everything was running so smoothly and quickly, without him having to intervene or put people under pressure. This project was more satisfying and pleasant than any project he had ever worked on before. Relieved and exuberant, he continued through the exhibition halls in search of possible strategic partners for the future.

The next Wednesday Bernd was sitting in his office in Hamburg. The rain drops mingled as they ran down the large windows, and they blurred the view of the large cranes on the other side of the Elbe. Despite the murky day, Bernhard's thoughts were crystal clear: What can our team do to accomplish even more and to finish even sooner? At the fair in Munich, Bernd had seen many new, innovative ideas for smart houses, but they were too expensive for Transmontania. What simpler, more efficient methods could be developed? If the extended team put their heads together, Bernd knew that they would be able to find solutions.

With this in mind, Bernd started WebEx. As soon as he logged in as an organizer, he saw that some members of the extended team were already in the conference.

"Hello, everyone!" Bernd wrote in the chat.

He started the conference punctually at 11:00 a.m.

"A warm welcome to everyone! Today is our fourth conference in the expanded team and we have already come up with many tangible results. You all have really done some outstanding work! As usual, everyone from the core team will tell us where they are in their progress. By doing so, we all will get an overview of how the project is going. If there are questions from the extended team, please ask them in the chat. We will answer your questions at the end. Today, Edwin's contribution is also on the agenda. He will report on the progress made in the use of the new building materials. So, let's go!"

The members of the core team reported on the current status of their target. It was a combination of hard factors about the project and soft factors, such as self-discipline and the integration of external partners. The agenda was just as they had agreed upon in their workshop with Paul.

The efforts for the soft factors were already paying off. One of the most obvious and beneficial rewards from this was the extended team. The "Buddy System" from Kurt Faller,[11] which Linda had introduced to integrate new team members, worked perfectly. Likewise, it proved to be the case that important partners attended some of the regular conferences. Thus, the gravitational force in the team was maintained, although geographically, the team members were further apart than ever before.

Now it was Edwin's turn. "Hello everybody! I am honored to be able to present the results of my work to you. I am an assistant professor in New York, but I also spend a lot of time in my home country of China. For our project here, I lead a sub-team of the award-winning MOOC students and local contact persons in Transmontania to integrate the new materials. First of all, on behalf of my team, I would like to thank Claude and Pilar for their great support. The two gave us many suggestions, shared their experiences with us and linked with important people."

Edwin continued, "Linda has also taken on the task of introducing new members to our project. She explains our goals and purpose to them, so that they can understand what we do and why we do it. Many thanks also to Stella, whose excellent document management makes our ability to collaborate much easier.

With the new sub-teams, the network has grown considerably. This fosters innovation and new ideas. One of these new ideas is to equip the houses with inexpensive solar roofs.

"As you all know, we have opted for new materials in 3-D printing to speed up the construction progress. We are still in the test phase, while the construction work continues uninterrupted." Edwin continued with a detailed report on the milestones of the plan and all they needed to complete the test phase successfully. The first comments and questions were coming in the chat box.

"We have now activated a large network," Edwin said. "The members of my team are talking to various suppliers and potential partners. And from this network yesterday came a whole new idea! One of our students reported that cheap solar roofs in China are on the rise. The whole thing is not yet very well known, but our network has managed to get some figures and calculate what the installation would cost and what efficiency gains would be achieved by solar roofs."

"Interesting!" Bernd was astonished.

"Our assessment is that the solar roofs, especially in the remote areas of Transmontania, would see to it that the government would have much less to invest in the reconstruction of the electricity grid. We therefore propose to take up this trend and at least to equip some of the houses with solar roofs. On the basis of figures from China, we have sketched a business plan. Regarding the funding, with Anne's help we could go directly to the government."

"Why didn't I think of that?" said Claude.

"If we can build the solar roofs as cheaply as in China," Edwin said, "we save not only building costs, but also operating costs. That should be very attractive to the government. "

"Extremely exciting," said Pilar. "I can't stop wondering if that might not be something for South America."

"And for Africa," Linda added radiantly.

"What are the next steps?" Bernd asked.

"I am sending the entire business plan to the core team," explained Edwin. "I'm looking forward to feedback from Claude and Pilar and, of course, from you, Bernd. Once we have considered your feedback, Anne and I will present the plan to the government. Bernd, you should be at this meeting, too, so that the matter has sufficient weight."

"I'll gladly give feedback, of course," said Bernd. "And I would also like to take part in the meeting. At the same time, Edwin, I would like you to continue to be in charge here. Perhaps we really have something here, which could be interesting for all emerging countries."

The team decides to add the solar roofs. Edwin is in charge of developing a business plan. After this, they want to get the government on board. This solution could save a lot of money.

"Please keep me informed," Claude said. "I am active in a great many networks in the construction industry. New materials and methods are always a big issue. We might be a real trendsetter here."

Bernd was enthusiastic. Just a few days ago, he'd shattered his head about how to build faster and more efficiently. Now the ideas were bubbling. They are already in the process of developing a business plan for solar roofs. What the advanced team did through the networks of each member, surpassed all his expectations. So many creative ideas were being discussed without him having to be directly involved, and yet everything was moving exactly in the direction he wanted.

After one week Bernd received an email from Anne which invited him to a conference with the Minister of Energy and Development, the highest-ranking officer for infrastructure development and the director of the state energy company. The aim of the conference was to fix the final completion date for the houses and to discuss the business plan for the solar roofs. The financing and the necessary permits were also to be discussed. From week to week, it became more exciting now! And the team did more and more. Bernd knew intuitively that he could still build a lot in Asia. And he felt grateful for his wonderful team. Yes, he was becoming more grateful every single day. The team was constantly discovering new trends, and because of the high individual responsibility and motivation they could be put their ideas into practice almost immediately.

Virtual Power Teams are able to React Quickly to Trends

Virtual teams are inherently beneficial when it comes to developing rapidly and picking up new trends. If the team culture is right, then the ideas start bubbling up and new trends can be picked up and integrated very quickly. What makes virtual teams so strong?

First of all, there is the difference in the team. If the team members are scattered across different continents, time zones and cultural areas, they also have very different perspectives. Being multi perspective is, according to creativity research, a decisive factor for coming up with new ideas and being innovative. In addition, the more the team members are scattered, the more access they have to networks and thus different information, new trends, and achievements. When different cultures blend in the team, that also makes it creative. The team members bring their understanding of markets and customer needs on different continents. This makes the perspective much broader. Added to this is a very practical advantage: Multicultural teams have access to information in many languages, both online and offline.

If the team culture is healthy, above all, there is individual responsibility and the team members have the feeling that they can assess situations and make their own decisions about them. This, in turn, makes a team eager to reach its goals and more willing to experiment with new things to achieve these goals. The team *Diversity in virtual, multicultural teams encourages creativity. There is access to information in many languages. Together with a strong sense of individual responsibility, innovation grows and new ideas develop.* members take the initiative, use their personal networks to gather new ideas, and to bind other partners on their own. By the time team members present their ideas to the larger team, they often already have results to report on. This makes it easier for the team to understand the ideas and faster for the larger team to make decisions. In Bernd's project, there is an extended leadership team. This includes all project staff who have distinguished themselves through outstanding achievements. Like Edwin, you get the chance to manage virtual sub-teams and to involve other partners and suppliers.

In hierarchical organizations, for example, globally active groups, the extended leadership team consists of those who report directly to the members of the management team. In smaller organizations, on the other hand, the trend is increasingly that the entire project work is done by self-organizing teams with flat hierarchies. Whatever the initial situation, it is crucial to increase the reach of the virtual team in order to capture and integrate new trends. The further the sensors of the virtual team reach into different networks, the easier it to learn about new trends and innovations, which can be implemented quickly.

This is precisely the goal: innovation. Fast innovation. The question is: what promotes rapid innovation and ensures short innovation cycles? How can trends be detected even earlier and integrated more quickly into projects? In my experience, there are three key factors for rapid innovation:

1. Team structure

2. Communication culture

3. Team culture, in particular performance culture

These three factors are closely related. Where they work together, new trends can be picked up quickly and innovations can emerge.

Team Structure: Traditional or Flat Hierarchies?

In virtual teams, increasingly flat organizational structures are emerging. There is a team leader who calls the team together and organizes the initial team funding. What sets the team's agenda, however, and how it evolves evolutionarily today, depends to a large extent on the entire team. In flat hierarchies, there is no middle management. Everyone reports to the few top managers. This is a model particularly suited to small and medium-sized enterprises (SMEs). In Germany and Western Europe, it is a trend for SMEs to completely eliminate entire hierarchical levels. Of course, it saves costs to forego superfluous management levels, but the greatest advantage is the higher speed of innovation. Companies with flat hierarchies are faster on the market with key projects. They decide more quickly, have a better flow of information and, as a rule, have more committed employees.

Fast, proactive innovation is a question of the team structure, the communication culture, and the team culture. Flat hierarchies tend to be much more innovative.

Surprisingly, SMEs are increasingly focusing on flat hierarchies. An Internet giant like Google is almost completely flat. At Google, there are partial teams with more than 150 people reporting directly to a single senior vice president. The flat structure allows for quick decisions and almost immediate feedback in both directions. The ideal climate for innovation! In such flat hierarchies, completely different reward systems are necessary. At Google, the payment is strictly based on performance, or rather, on the value of an individual's contribution to corporate objectives.

Communication Culture:

Transparency and the Principle of "Followers"

Transparency is everything if you want a good flow of communication and committed employees. Not only do the strategic objectives have to be clear to everyone in the team, but all of the team members should have an active role in defining these goals! Flat hierarchies favor rapid decision-making. There are not so many people who have to agree to a single decision. But for the decision-making to work, total transparency is necessary.

All strategic decisions and their justifications must be publicly known. Usually, important decisions are always made in a synchronous format, typically during a telephone or video conference. This is the only way to ensure that all team members are always behind the team's goals and initiatives, and that all external parties are involved.

Many successful and innovative companies, such as W. L. Gore, are now organizing their project work according to the principle of "followers." Projects are no longer pushed from above, but everyone in the company can start a project and advertise for followers. Individual employees are therefore looking for new ideas in their network, they are researching and looking for fellow employees with whom they can present their concept to others in the company. The better an idea, the higher the probability that others are willing to follow. Everyone in the company makes their own decisions about who they want to follow and which projects they are willing to commit to. The projects which find the most followers will be financed by the company. The number of followers also determines how much management responsibility the project leader will be given. For example, Terri L. Kelly, the CEO of W. L. Gore, is simply the person in the company with the most followers.

In the follower principle, not only the brilliant ideas and concepts are the deciding factors. An employee must also demonstrate the ability to inspire and lead other people. Sometimes, this leadership position is shared between two people: the one is the creative genius and the other more the business leader. Famous examples of such successful tandems are Bill Gates and Paul Allen or Steve Jobs and Steve Wozniak.

In the "followers" principle, projects are no longer top-down. Everyone in the company can advertise their ideas and initiatives to gain followers. The best ideas are determined by those with the most followers.

In virtual teams with flat hierarchies, people come together and organize themselves through individual responsibility. They communicate and find solutions without the Team leader having to intervene each time. For self-organization to work well in the long term, there should be structured group forums that allow people to share, support, or brainstorm creatively. The project management method "Scrum" even provides for a daily conference to start the day. Each team member quickly realizes what their focus is today and who can help them in their work. Often, ideas are already being exchanged at such conferences. In small teams with about five people, a quarter of an hour at the start of the day is enough to come together and share some creative ideas. This method can even work in big teams.

With some internet companies in the Silicon Valley, there is the rule that on one day per week employees should be free to explore their own ideas and projects. The companies give the employees rooms in which they can do their research, test their new ideas, and inspire others in the company. Now you can say that this is typical of Silicon Valley, where product innovations depend very much on the creativity, expertise and productivity of each individual employee. This approach, however, also proves successful in traditional industries because innovation is the key to survival. Self-organization, self-responsibility and the principle of "followers" are taken over by many companies, regardless of their size and product field. It pays off.

Team Culture:
Free and Self-Determined Brings Top Performance

The third decisive factor for rapid innovation is the team culture. This is about values.

Virtual collaboration allows for great freedom. Each person may choose when and where they would like to work. As a result, freedom automatically becomes a core value of any virtual team. In my experience, freedom happens automatically. The team leader does not have to talk about it or officially implement it. It should be a given. In virtual teams, it is far better to grant a great deal of freedom and to measure the employees' results rather than measuring how many hours they have been working. In addition to freedom, autonomy and self-realization are important values in self-organizing virtual teams. The basic principle of virtual teams with flat hierarchies is that top experts work most productively if they are directly involved in the decision-making process and are not constantly monitored by "top". The role of leadership in virtual teams is far from the traditional top-down approach. Managers are now more "enablers" than anything else. Their quality is measured by the extent to which they succeed in inspiring and motivating people.

In flat hierarchies, career is no longer a great motivation factor because there are hardly any formal leadership positions to fill. Much more tempting is the opportunity to quickly take on responsibility on projects and to have appropriate decision-making competences. In Bernd's team, Edwin took advantage of this opportunity. The subject of new building materials is now

Freedom is almost always one of the core values of every virtual team, since each team member has the freedom to choose when and where they will work. Working independently is often a higher value for many than having a traditional career path.

"his." Being an integral part of high-speed innovation and an intensive exchange of ideas is often more motivating than aspiring to become "boss" in a formal hierarchy.

There is a close link between self-determination and innovation. Innovative research says that innovation is usually the result of a spontaneous exchange of ideas. Highly innovative companies, such as Google or Apple, consciously make a point of informally bringing people together as often possible so that they have the opportunity to exchange creative thoughts and ideas. The many cafés and lounge-like areas in Silicon Valley companies are not just a luxury; they exist to promote the informal and unplanned creative exchange. Spontaneity and "controlled chance" are certainly a good approach. I believe, however, that the structured communication processes of virtual teams can also stimulate creativity. It is necessary to set up appropriate slots at regular conferences to allow informal discussions. You have already read a lot about these structures in Part II of this book.

Not only cultural differences, but also self-determination is, according to innovation research, a decisive factor for the rapid development of many new, creative ideas. Structured communication can also promote innovation.

Some companies that I have advocated follow a very exciting approach: they rely on "virtual cafés." Team members agree to informally meet via video conference with a cup of coffee or tea in their hands to simply converse with each other. It is important that everyone has access to a digital whiteboard to write down and keep track of ideas. For most video conferencing applications, a whiteboard is included. Whether such formats ultimately lead to innovation, ultimately depends less on the technology, but on the extent to which those in leadership positions recognize how useful these informal approaches can help team creativity and innovation and how much they encourage their use. Of course, you can also invite a network partner to a "virtual café". Thus, the creative exchange becomes even more diverse - and the results may become even more interesting. A virtual team has an unbeatable advantage over a live team, because it is much easier to invite interesting, innovative people from the outside to the meetings. In a "normal" team this just wouldn't be possible without having to fly the visitors in.

In "virtual cafes" team members agree on meeting for a coffee or tea by videoconference so they can brainstorm and exchange ideas in a relaxed setting. They write down their ideas on a virtual whiteboard. Guests are allowed to attend, and they greatly enrich the discussion.

You can also learn from the open-source movement in the IT sector. Here, too, the principle is usually that someone initiates a project and "follower" searches for it. These edit and refine the open source code, which is put online by the initiator of the project. Companies can take a look at this, for example, by integrating important partners into a project virtually and allowing them to work out individual steps independently. High-speed innovation and extraordinary success are possible where people can enjoy freedom, experience autonomy and realize themselves and their dreams.

Chapter 10

Whoever Promotes Diversity Instead of Combating It, Raises Potential

The autumn holidays with the family were very relaxing. Bernd spent ten days on Tenerife with his wife and daughter. Blue skies and sunshine gave him energy, quite different from the dreary weather in Hamburg. During the entire ten days on Tenerife, there was only one day where there was a short but violent downpour. Perhaps it was the last remnants of a storm far out at sea? Soon afterwards a magnificent rainbow appeared over the Atlantic.

Every day, Bernd played tennis with his daughter, Lena, and then took long beach walks with Wiebke, during which the two conversed intensely. He had promised both Wiebke and Lena not to read a single email during the holidays. If anything urgent should occur which requires his immediate attention, Bernd asked his team to contact him on his cell phone.

Going without any digital communication was refreshing and rejuvenating. But as the days passed, however, Bernd's curiosity grew. He wanted to know how things were going in Transmontania. The team had made two important innovative decisions shortly before Bernd's departure: the new building materials

On vacation Bernd did not read any emails. After he returned, however, he saw that the Asian director wants Bernd's signature on the amended contracts. No big deal, Bernd thinks.

and the solar roofs. Bernd really wanted to know how these two things were affecting their timetable and the quality of the results.

Bernd slept most of the way on the return flight. He decided he would wait to retrieve his emails after landing in Hamburg. Once he reached the baggage claim, he could wait no longer! He took out his iPhone and quickly scrolled through the new emails. His daughter had to pull him by the sleeve, so he did not miss one of her heavy suitcases on the baggage belt.

At first glance, there appeared to have been no emergencies during the ten days. There were a few new emails from Edwin about the first experiences with the solar roofs and the new building materials. In some of the emails had the subject line "decision needed." Bernd opened these emails first.

When they reached the car park, Wiebke offered to drive, so that Bernd could continue to read through his emails. Normally, she was not quite so generous, but the beautiful days in Tenerife had brought them closer together, and she realized how important this project is for Bernd. Out of gratitude for her understanding and in the attempt to extend the vacation just a little longer, Bernd offered to cook dinner for her this evening. "Besides," he joked, "Maybe it will win me some more points for the next time I screw up!"

Wiebke laughed and said, "Keep on dreaming!"

As far as the emails were concerned, new tools and new suppliers were needed for the new materials. Decisions had to be made. Bernd had agreed in principle for the team members to spend additional money as long as they remained within the budgetary restrictions. It looked, however, as if the Asian construction company wanted to see Bernd's signature on the new contracts. "Okay, we'll get that done quickly," thought Bernd, and he asked Edwin to organize a videoconference with the manager of the construction company and his most important employees.

Two days later the video conference was on while Bernd himself was on the road. There was an unexpected problem on a construction site in Germany, and he needed to meet the site manager on short notice. Bernd had agreed to the meeting only reluctantly, knowing that this would mean that he would have to do the video conference with the Asian construction company from his car. At 10:30 a.m., Bernd pulled over at a rest stop on the highway and opened WebEx on his iPhone.

This was far from his first conference on the road, but he was a bit nervous this time. After he started the conference, he could see Anne immediately. She sat in the office of the construction company next to the director of the construction company, an Asian business man of middle age, and two of his closest associates, the chief engineer and the construction site coordinator. Edwin took part in the videoconference from China, this time with a suit and a tie. Bernd had never seen the assistant professor wearing a tie.

"Good evening, everyone together," Bernd began the conference. "I apologize for taking our conference from my car. I have to go to an urgent meeting on one of my construction sites, and there was just no other way. I hope everyone can see and hear me."

"Good morning, Mr. Bernd," the construction manager replied dryly. Bernd was accustomed to the fact that Asians called him "Mr. Bernd", because it was difficult for them to meet foreign business partners with their first names. Normally, it took a long time before they said anything but Bernd.

"I am delighted to discuss the consequences of the last two innovations with you," continued the director. "On the one hand, we are familiar with more efficient technologies that speed up construction. On the other hand, we need to involve new suppliers, train employees and integrate more people into the team. This means more overhead and more costs for us. I would like to talk with you about how we divide these costs."

"So, with all respect, Mr. Director, I had asked Edwin to steer the introduction of the two innovations and do not know what to discuss between us. If I have understood Edwin correctly, then the new materials as well as the solar roofs are ultimately cost neutral, because the productivity gains correspond approximately to the investments. This means that you will invest a bit more now but gain that back as soon as the solar roofs are functioning. Did Edwin not discuss this with you during my vacation?"

During a telephone conference, strong cultural differences between Bernd and the Asian director become apparent. Bernd says that Edwin could have clarified everything with the director.

"Professor Edwin has discussed this with my chief engineer and my construction site coordinator. I am attached to your personal commitment, Mr. Bernd. With regard to this as well as future cooperations."

"Mr. Director, may I tell you a little about me? I used to do what you are proposing with my teams in Germany. I took care of everything myself and signed every bill. Now I'm head of a great virtual team. I trust my team and I delegate important competences, also with regard to the budget, as long as we remain within the agreed framework. Edwin is your contact. And by the way, why do not you actually try that? Give your people more options to make decisions! Then we will actually progress even faster with the project. Believe me, it pays off."

It is scandalous when Bernd gives advice to the Asian director about how he should lead his team. The director puts the project on hold and threatens to end his business relationship with Bernd. Bernd can hardly believe his ears.

While he spoke, Bernd saw Edwin looking irritated at the camera and then lowering his gaze. Anne listened, but seemed alerted.

Bernd felt that he had gone to a muddy ground, but he was not sure why.

Before Bernd could ask, the director had already intervened.

"Reverend Mister Bernd, I'm afraid we will have to postpone a week and consider our business relationship." His voice was frosty. Although he was totally under control, Bernd could see that he was tormented. He could hardly believe his ears.

"What do you mean to postpone a week?" He shouted into the microphone. "We have valid contracts and thousands of people need to move into their homes before winter!"

"We'll be back in a week. Until then, we are interrupting the construction work. The contractual penalties for this are known to us."

"But that's ridiculous!" Bernd shouted. "What's your fucking problem?"

At the moment Bernd saw a personal message from Anne in the chat: "Bernd, please stop pressuring him. If possible, please apologize immediately for interfering in the affairs of the other company. Let us discuss the next steps immediately after the conference."

"Mr. Director," said Bernd in a quiet voice, "If I have offended you in any way, I beg your pardon. I was just glad that we were finally able to speed up the construction work and were on the verge of catching up to our proposed timeline. I regret very deeply that you would like to suspend construction for a week, and I am very sorry if I have caused you to make this decision. I am already looking forward to our next meeting. If there is anything I can do to help you resume the work earlier, please let me know."

"I'll get back to you as soon as we're ready. Goodbye, Mister Bernd."
This ended the conference.

Although it had become cold in the car, Bernd felt his sweat sweating through his shirt. "What's wrong here?" He asked himself. "Why did Edwin not do his job? And why did the engineer and the coordinator not simply bless the matter? "

Bernd stepped out of the car to catch a breath of fresh air. "What just happened?" he asked himself. As soon as he got back into the car, he called Anne on her cell phone.

"Anne, hopefully you have a reasonable explanation for what has just happened?"

"Bernd, I do not know if you are aware of it, but all Asian cultures, especially Transmontania, are very authoritarian. The supreme boss always has the last word and must be involved everywhere. When we enter into cooperations here, it goes strictly according to the hierarchy of who talks with whom. Edwin and I were able to discuss a lot with the chief engineer and the construction site coordinator. But when it comes to investment, the agreement has to be signed by the two bosses. You need to respect this hierarchy and speak directly to the director without involving us. Because you were on holiday, the new contracts have already been delayed. This is not a good sign.

Taking vacations is not as sacred in Asia as in Europe. The real problem here, however, is that you have now given the director advice on how to lead his team better. I am afraid he has interpreted this as a personal criticism. He might just have swallowed it just now, but you publicly criticized him in front of his own people. He has lost his face. In Asia, this is the worst thing that can happen in a conversation."

Anne explains to Bernd why his communication was offensive from the Asian point of view. She explained that in Asia, only the bosses can sign agreements, whereas in Europe this task may be delegated to someone down the line.

"So, what you are saying is that because I gave him some tips, is he now angry and is stopping construction for a week? In addition, he's questioning our entire business relationship and all our contracts?

"Yes, Bernd, that's about it. Look, I also think that he overreacted. This is a large project, and there are potentially a lot more contracts coming. So, my guess is that things will soon calm down. I suggest you ask him for a personal phone call for day after tomorrow. If you would allow, I would like to help you to write an appropriate email for this."

"You know, I'm a German. We're rather direct, and we tend to stick to the facts rather than to worry about what everyone is feeling. But our project is in danger. Therefore, I would like to take you up on your offer."

Bernd drove back onto the highway and started to reflect on what just happened. Why did this problem have to happen right now, as they are all ready for the final sprint? The more people coming onto the team from all over the world, the greater the risk of intercultural misunderstandings.

Anne also finds the reaction of the Asian businessman a bit exaggerated. At the same time, she understands where he is coming from. Bernd realizes that he has underestimated how important intercultural relations are.

"I have to be careful," thought Bernd. "Diversity is obviously a risk. I have to get this risk under control. But how?"

At once he thought of Paul. Probably it was once again time for a telephone call. This man always had an ace up his sleeve. Bernd and Paul arranged to skype on the following evening.

Bernd was still in his office when he started Skype. He had made himself comfortable with his laptop in his seat.

"Good evening, Bernd. Please tell me what all has happened." Paul began. He sounded as fresh as ever.

"So, first of all, my holiday was fantastic! Probably you have also read the reports that we are now slowly catching up the delay? The tests with the new materials were all successful. I thought we were ready to begin the final sprint."

"All the information that I have seen also looks quite like things are going well and about to wrap up."

"That is all well and good, but brace yourself for the latest. I had a phone call with the director of the construction company the yesterday, and I managed to put my foot in my mouth. "

"What happened?"

Bernd told Paul that he wanted to give the Asians a few tips. The director, however, understood this as personal criticism, and he completely overreacted. His subordinates, Anne and Edwin, just sat there and said nothing.

"Oh, I see. That's how it is in Asia, Bernd. It is so important to respect the cultural differences, and you should never criticize anyone in front of the others -- especially not in front of their subordinates. That undermines their authority."

"Yes, yes, Anne explained that to me. The question is what we can do now? Anne suggested that I call the man again privately. She is also willing to help me write the email asking to meet with him."

"That's a good idea. Anne knows how to hit the right tone. As for your team, I would like to propose an intercultural workshop so that something like this won't happen again in the future. In this workshop, you and your team will become familiar with all the different cultures which are represented in the project, and you will learn the *Anne helps Bernd to smooth everything over, and Bernd decides to contact Paul for more advice. Paul proposes that the team do an intercultural workshop to learn more about each other's culture.* most important ways of interacting with each other. It is, by the way, very similar to the personal Lifeline: you just ask people what they are proud of in their culture. You can do this over a video conference, so do not worry about the cost. But make sure that everyone in their culture brings something to show the others - photos or a short video or sing a song."

Diversity as a Challenge and an Opportunity

We live in a time when more than 60% of all business teams are spread over more than one time zone. Often the team members come from different countries and cultures. This is a challenge and an opportunity at the same time. Multicultural teams are important to the future of our planet. I am firmly convinced of this. For the differences between people in companies and teams, the keyword "Diversity" has been established in recent years. There are different aspects of diversity, for example gender, age, or cultural background.

Global virtual teams naturally live diversity, especially with regard to different cultures. On the one hand this is an enrichment, since the different cultural experiences and values also allow for different perspectives. On the other hand, cultural diversity also carries risks, as intercultural conflicts can come to light or simmer under the surface. In this chapter, I would like to show how diversity can be understood and used as an opportunity in virtual teams. If you want diversity on your team, then you should promote it and give it space. This is the basic principle. Cultural and other differences should be allowed to exist and be shown in the team. Let's look at the most important features of diversity and its advantages.

The more diverse a virtual team is, the greater the personal and cultural differences. These differences are not only challenging. They can also be a great source of opportunity. These cultural differences should be openly discussed and shown!

First of all, the topic of *Gender Diversity*. This is about the potential of women in business. One of my success secrets as a manager was that I drastically increased the women's quota on each of my teams. For some teams, especially in the IT sector, I initially had a women's rate of 0 percent and within two years it was 50 percent or more. I just failed with my attempt to increase the men's quota at home – try though I may, I have five daughters. But back to virtual teams.

A healthy mix of men and women in a team ensures more balanced discussions and helps to better understand the needs of customers and stakeholders in the company. In each team, there are also roles that are usually filled by women rather than men. When it comes to multitasking, adhering to rules, or showing empathy, women are generally easier to deal with. When people barely have the opportunity to communicate with one another, women often recognize the problems more quickly. Women are more sensitive to the needs of the others and they can sense when someone in the team feels poorly treated.

Men, on the other hand, are generally more willing to take risks and often have more entrepreneurial spirit. It is important to recognize that there is no better or worse. The right mixture between male and female qualities in the team is important. In my experience, this mixture is what leads to better performances.

A second type of Diversity is in regard to different *Age Groups*. Incorporating people of different ages offers a wealth of opportunities in virtual teams. The technically efficient digital natives and the experienced generation X together with the older generations complement each other well. Mutual mentoring is an approach to build relationships and promote personal development. The very young, for example, can show the elderly how to deal with the Internet, apps, and online tools. In turn, the younger ones can learn a lot from the older ones about strategy and risk management.

The most important form of diversity in virtual teams is undoubtedly *Cultural Diversity*. Often more than 50% of the team members come from different cultures. How to bridge cultural differences and make positive use of them to achieve maximum performance is therefore an important challenge for virtual teams.

Building Bridges Through Intercultural Understanding

I have a very simple metaphor for intercultural management in a team: I compare it with cooking. You need a recipe, a stove, and a pot in which you cook the ingredients. Then, from these different ingredients, you create a tasty dish. The recipe is understanding the different cultures in a team. In addition, it is understanding what dish is to be created together. In other words, it is the gathering of the ingredients. The stove is the energy that we need to transform the ingredients into something new and beautiful. The preparation and stirring of the food is our rituals and structured communication. He who wants to cook should know what he wants to create. In a virtual team, the entire team needs to know what they are going to create.

The first step is to get to know the individual team members with their respective cultural backgrounds. From Chapter 1 you already know the exercise with the professional and personal lifelines. In order to get a better understanding of the cultures involved, you can proceed very similarly.

Intercultural workshops can help virtual, multicultural teams to discover and appreciate diversity. Let people present what they are particularly proud of in their culture.

Instead of representing themselves, in the intercultural workshop the team members represent and present the "lifelines" of their respective cultures. Let all representatives of a country briefly say something about its history, explain typical customs and represent the most important values. Ask each team member to present something from his culture: pictures of places or cultural events, sing or dance a folk song, tell about traditions or something that people in their country are particularly proud of. Music and videos are especially good. They should not only talk about the achievements of the countries that are presented, but also unique or witty traditions or customs. An intercultural workshop is always fun.

Examples of stories from individual countries

Kenya. In Kenya and Uganda, the bridegroom has to pay for his future wife in cows. And not only before the wedding, but for a lifetime, to secure the bride's family. It is tradition that the bridegroom and the father of the bride negotiate a corresponding "contract" for the coming years.

Malaysia. A Polish friend was transferred to Malaysia to manage a team that provides IT services to branch offices around the world. The Malaysian society consists of three large ethnic groups: Malay, Chinese and Indian. With his typical Polish cordiality, my friend went through the offices during the first week and offered his colleagues small pieces of sausage, which he had cut off with a Swiss knife. Most of the staff were friendly but said, "No, thank you." This surprised my friend. Later, a team member got up the courage to explain the situation. The Malays are predominantly Muslims and, therefore, do not eat pork. The Chinese do not eat anything that is cut with a knife. And the Indians were afraid that it might be beef of sacred cows in the sausages, but they were afraid to ask because they didn't want to offend him.

India. The famous patience of the Indians is sometimes problematic when the deadline approaches. Indians like to take their time, and it is almost impossible to rush them. If you ask them to commit to something, Indians will most likely say yes, because it is hard for them to refuse something directly. So, it can be that an Indian says, "Yes, I'll do it by tomorrow," and the task is still not done several days later. The only thing that can help in this situation is to develop a sense of trust and understanding.

Bulgaria. There are some universal body language signals that have the same meaning almost all over the world, but there are exceptions. For example, to shake your head in Bulgaria means "yes" and to nod your head means "no". So, it's the opposite of most places in the world.

Colombia. When Colombians want to point at or show something, they tend to point their noses at it. So, just as in other cultures we use the index finger to point at something, they use the nose.

From all of the workshops I have done over the years, I could tell you many stories about different cultural peculiarities. These workshops are amusing and uplifting. In going through these exercises, the team realizes that cultural differences are exactly that which brings spice into the team and helps it to be unique. But be careful: there are also a lot of prejudices and stereotypes about certain countries and ethnic groups. Make sure that no prejudices dominate, but the team members actually learn something about the different cultures. The key to this is a genuine curiosity and respect. Respect for the different cultures and respect for each other.

Common Goals Fuse Cultures

In order to unite people from different cultures in a team, a common goal is needed. The goal is like a magnet that attracts people from all over the world. In the new business world, more and more people are working on projects which are oriented toward common goals. At the same time, fewer and fewer people work in the "silos" of large companies, where they only assemble small pieces of a puzzle which somehow create a larger business process. The young digital natives are already very open to multicultural teams. They expect that there are clear goals and one can personally develop and have fun on the job. A meaningful contribution to a better world is much more important than traditional career opportunities.

Method:
   When you are setting ambitious goals for your team, do not do this alone but work with your team to develop the goals and to explain why these goals are desirable. Ask if your work improves the lives of people and is a response to the challenges of our time.

Let's go back to the cooking metaphor for intercultural bridge building. If we have a stew on the stove, we should stir it from time to time or it will get burnt. In virtual teams, this "stirring" means having regular rituals, in which team members can show how their culture would traditionally react to the given situation. Everyone should have the same opportunity to share anecdotes or aspects of their culture in meetings or in telephone and video conferences. I can only recommend putting cultural issues on the agenda. Reserve a slot during meetings, where team members can talk about the different cultural aspects of the whatever the subject may be.

Intercultural topics should be regularly placed on the agenda. For example, make a timeslot at conferences, where team members talk about their culture.

If more than one person from a specific culture is present, the group should name a speaker to represent them and their respective culture during the meeting. They may perhaps even play a suitable piece of music. It has also proven to be useful when a virtual team also exchanges social media on intercultural topics. For example, the team could have a closed Facebook group where the team members can post their contributions to cultural topics. There may be photos of the Chinese New Year, the Muslim fasting month of Ramadan or the Diwali, the Hindu light festival.

Often misunderstandings are also caused by the different languages in the virtual teams. Different language usage even has an effect if the working language is English.

In English, for example, "not too bad" means that something is "pretty good," just like you say in German "not bad". This type of "double negation," however, is not known in many other European languages. The team members, therefore, may not understand what is meant here. In other cultures, people sometimes say yes and mean no. And when a Briton says "interesting", then that does not necessarily mean that he finds something really interesting. He can also mean "terrible" and not want to say it out of politeness. In multicultural teams, it is important to avoid subtle allusions, double entendres, and implied meanings. These only cause confusion and, for the team members not "in the know," frustration. Be as clear as possible and use the chat function to communicate in writing.

In virtual teams, different cultures melt together, because everyone is working towards a common goal.

In my image of cooking, the stove is the third element to bridge cultural differences. We bridge differences by bringing the different cultures together in one pot and allowing them to melt together, the so-called melting pot. What then comes out is something new and exciting and very unique. We create something that would not have been possible if we had left even just one of the "ingredients," just one of the cultures out of the mix. If everyone realizes this, then they realize how important each team member is to the success of the team. What is created from this melting pot is the character of the team, and this character is also what adds emotion to the team. The team goal is the magnet that pulls the team together, but emotion is what drives a team to an outstanding success. And this emotion comes from the melting pot, from heating the ingredients to get them excited. And this excitement is the element that gives your team power and energy. Make sure the team members have fun and can be proud of who they are and what they have done. Keep the stove hot. In other words, keep the emotion and excitement going to help drive your team to the finish line.

To take the cooking metaphor one step further, recognition is like the spice when cooking. Make sure everyone is seen. This spice goes into the cooking pot, and reinforces the excitement. In the end, everyone should feel appreciated and should feel like a hero. Appreciate the uniqueness of each team member and give them the feeling of being a star. Praise them as much as possible for their contributions, skills or attitudes.

Working with the Culture Map according to Erin Meyer

If you have multicultural teams, you should work with *The Culture Map*. In her book *The Culture Map*,[12] Erin Meyer distinguishes eight dimensions, in which the countries and cultures of the world differ on a flowing scale. These eight dimensions are: communication, performance assessment, conviction, leadership, decision making, trust, criticism and scheduling (see graphic).

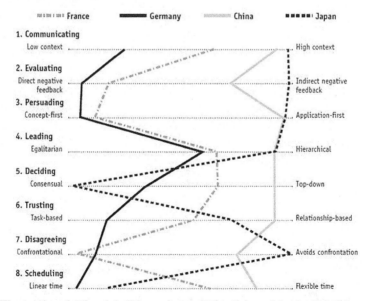

Illustration 6: The eight Dimensions of *The Culture Map* by Erin Meyer

In my experience, leadership (leading), deciding and disagreeing are the neuralgic points in virtual teams. I have already dealt with various leadership styles in the previous chapters. In some hierarchical cultures, for example, it is not customary to contradict the boss in the presence of others. Also, here the boss has to be asked for permission for every important step. The boss is expected to answer all questions of the team. The communication is also hierarchical here, that is, team members have different hierarchy levels, which are not directly related to each other. Information is passed strictly along the command chain.

As you have already read elsewhere, I recommend an egalitarian team culture based on individual responsibility for virtual teams. All team members should make decisions for themselves and find their own solutions - as long as they comply with the agreed upon timetables and budgets. The team members must also be allowed to object in the team. The boss, in turn, should be seriously interested in the views of others. In the team, everyone is talking to everyone, as it is objectively necessary. It does not follow the hierarchy.

The neuralgic points in virtual teams are leadership, decision-making, and criticism. A multicultural team needs its own team culture with regard to these topics.

Now, if you have people from Japan, Korea, India, Russia or other strictly hierarchical cultures in your virtual team, and at the same time, you have team members from Denmark, Sweden, Norway or Australia, so extremely egalitarian cultures, then you should initially be in a synchronous format in order to create a common team culture. I have already described this in a previous chapter.

The team culture is best created on the basis of respect for the cultural backgrounds of each of the team members. Everyone should know and appreciate the advantages and disadvantages of the other cultures. It is best to use stories about the characteristics of the different cultures. Only if the team members are aware of what is unique about each other's cultures does real understanding arise.

As soon as such an understanding of the cultures exists, the team will be able to agree on the team culture to be based on the eight scales described by Meyer. As you already know, I encourage all virtual teams to position themselves more on the egalitarian side. Virtual collaboration naturally requires freedom and individual responsibility. Authority, hierarchy and command are very difficult over long distances. This does mean that once a certain direction for virtual teams has already been set, your job is to help the team go in this direction despite being pulled in other directions.

Let's take a closer look at how decisions are made, what Meyer labels "Deciding." With deciding, the Meyer scale ranges from pure top-down decisions to decisions which are made with complete consensus from everyone.

My recommendation is to reach as much consensus as possible early in the project, for example in a joint work-

In developing your project with your team, try to reach as much consensus as possible. One way might be, for example, in a joint strategy workshop. The team leader should only step in and make a final decision when the team disagrees and come to an impasse.

shop on strategy and objectives. In virtual teams, it is important that all team members be involved in strategic decisions and objectives. Even if later there is a strategic change of focus or a major change which affects the work of the entire team, the team should come together again to reach a joint consensus as how to move forward. The team leader should only make use of a top-down decision when there is not clear consensus from the group. This creates clarity and brings the team back on track.

If the team leader makes a decision, he should be receptive to feedback and be able to revise his decision as the project progresses. This is especially true when things do not go according to plan.

Another intercultural challenge is the way different cultures express criticism. On the Meyer scale, the two extremes are confrontational and avoiding confrontation. As soon as there are team members from cultures which express criticism very differently, conflicts can arise very quickly. This especially occurs in meetings where controversial issues are discussed and it is expected that everyone contributes to the discussion.

I advise virtual teams to make criticism as confrontational as possible in order to make quick decisions. For team members, for example from Japan, China or Saudi Arabia, this is hard to bear. Luckily, there are some tricks to help team members who want to avoid any confrontation, nevertheless, to participate in discussions. For example, make it clear before each discussion that there is always only dissent in the matter and never about the rejection of a person. In some cultures, these two are considered one and the same. A Japanese or Chinese person may feel personally attacked if you criticize his point of view. If this happens, try to increase awareness that it is in fact possible to separate both - as you find in most European cultures.

As a team leader, you should ensure that conferences do not lead to extreme confrontations. Make sure that the discussions are objective and not subjective. If there are difficulties with this, ask your team members to submit their points of view in writing.

Another trick is to avoid the direct clash of different opinions in conferences. Simply ask the team members to submit their positions in writing ahead of time. This gives everyone plenty of time to deal with different opinions and to prepare the discussion. For people from cultures where it is extremely difficult to take criticism, you could even create the possibility that team members post their opinions anonymously. As a team leader, you should also avoid discussing your opinion. Ask everyone else about their opinion. Otherwise, many team members, especially those from authoritarian cultures, will be guided by your point of view.

Team Culture, Yes – Compartmentalization, No

As we have already discussed, over time a team culture emerges, and it begins to override the cultural differences in the team. It is also important to ensure that team culture does not become so strong that it conflicts with the corporate culture. I once had a case in which this happened. I was leading a team of 20 project managers in a corporate organization. We had fantastic figures, and yet my boss called me to the office and accused me of creating a state within the state. He found that my team was too different from the other employees in the company and we should change that. Our very good results did not help me at all. I learned a lot from this situation.

The Team Newsletter

How about a team newsletter that everyone can subscribe to? Through this, outsiders remain informed, get to know their team members better, understand the cultural differences, and develop understanding for their special team culture.

To avoid a negative attitude towards your team from the rest of the company, it is important to stay in regular communication with important stakeholders, including your supervisors and the personnel division.

The corporate culture should be respected first and foremost. Just as you communicate changes and decisions within your team, you should always do the same externally. Let your corporate partners know what your team is doing, where you see them going, and why your team may take a different cultural stand at certain times. Always remain open for feedback from others in the corporation and be prepared to change course if conflicts with the corporate culture arise.

One good idea to help with this is to name ambassadors who represent the team to the outside and regularly communicate with other departments in the company. These ambassadors should take part in corporate events and present the progress of the team. Conversely, you can invite stakeholders to your own project meetings from time to time. By doing this, you avoid the impression that you are pulling a fence around your garden and excluding the others.

Interview with Cemal Osmanovic

Cemal Osmanovic, born in 1958, is the founder and CEO of smile2 GmbH in Schweinfurt as a platform for people who want to continue developing professionally and personally. Today, the platform is one of the market leaders in the field of professional live online seminars in the B2B area in the German-speaking world.

After completing his studies, Cemal Osmanovic led a successful IT service company for 11 years and, starting in 1994, accompanied numerous IT companies as a consultant and entrepreneur coach. In 1999, he sold the company. Together with his co-managing director Rüdiger Sievers, he developed the iTeam system house group by the end of 2008 into the largest IT network company with a total of more than 330 locations and 9,000 employees. By the beginning of 2009, he focused even more on his core themes of training, development, and inspiration for people. With this goal in mind, Cemal Osmanovic founded smile2 GmbH.

Who are you and what do you do? Just describe yourself!

In my youth, I was a professional musician. As someone who is half-turkish, Oriental passion is already in my blood. Nevertheless, I studied mathematics and later computer science. So, I am both an emotional type and a structured computer scientist.

All the important decisions I have made in my life have been value-oriented. My professional mainstays are people who develop and create great things, have power, create lasting benefits and have fun at the job. Therefore, I became an entrepreneur at a very early age and have always remained so.

I am currently running smile2, a market-leading company for professional live online seminars on all non-professional topics, such as marketing, online marketing, communication and rhetoric, time and self-management and, above all, leadership and sales. Personally, I am an expert for success. This means that I support people in finding the right goals for themselves, which guarantee success and quality of life for a long time and whose implementation I also like to accompany.

This is done either through open seminars or for entrepreneurs and executives in a 1: 1 weekend coaching. This is what I call "Entrepreneurial Clarity."

What are the main technologies for collaboration in virtual teams?

To properly understand my answer to this question, let me briefly summarize what is, according to my philosophy, most important in a company. First, does the company have a tangible spirit or culture which can be sensed by everyone who comes into contact with the company? Is everyone involved with the company aware of this spirit, and do they act in congruence with it? Second, is there a clearly defined goal and a daily strategy? Third, are there best practices and successful business models to learn from and incorporate into the company? And is there a target group that really needs these products? Finally, communication, communication, and once again communication!

Virtual teams need to communicate clearly, and they need to be more sensitive to what other team members are saying in order to avoid misunderstandings.

In a modern organization, all of these elements should be supported and carried out by not only the employees in the regional offices but also by the virtual teams. Of course, with virtual teams there are challenges to overcome, especially in regard to communications. Communications need to be even clearer than in teams that meet in person, because it is more difficult to read the body language or to directly ask other team members about something than when the group is in the same room. We need to be more acutely aware and sensitive in virtual teams to avoid misunderstandings. As a prime example, do not carry on conflicts or disagreements through emails. This rule should apply to conventional teams as well, but the temptation to do this is even greater in virtual teams. And finally, a clear documentation of all results and decisions is even more important for virtual teams.

What technologies or apps do you recommend, depending on the size of the company?

Since the customer should always be the focus of our interest in a modern company, a CRM system – especially the willingness to use it - is absolutely essential. For excellent transparency and effective communication, it is necessary to have a synchronized portal, such as a wiki, a web-based project management software such as Trello or the like. More important than the tool itself is the fact that this tool is consistently and uniformly used by all parties involved, and that it is so perfectly structured that all relevant information is easy to find quickly. Otherwise, no one will use it!

In virtual teams, of course, it is important to have ways to bring the team together as a substitute for being physically in the same geographical place. There are modern solutions for this using software which allows the team to see and hear each while conferencing. One such program for this is Skype. It is important that the team has a high-quality video conferencing system with a very good camera quality, an absolutely disturbance-free sound transmission, and screen sharing, so that the participants in meetings can work together, for example, to create a Mindmap. We are currently using Adobe Connect as an online seminar company.

What are your experiences with virtual teams?

I would say good to very good! I can start with the fact that when I work with virtual teams, I get better more highly qualified people, because I am not limited to choosing people from my geographical location. And somehow,

In virtual teams, you have to find a substitution for people meeting in person. In my opinion, this can be easily solved through modern technology and software developed for this purpose.

I feel that with virtual teams, the employees are more hungry and flexible in their thinking than team members who get up and go to work every day in the same place with the same people and sometimes fall into the same old trot. It can also be that with a virtual team, I subconsciously lead differently. I strive to communicate more clearly, because I know that the communication channels are more limited than with a convention team.

Which of your achievements as a leader and entrepreneur are you particularly proud of?

That I managed to become market leader in all three companies that I founded and raised. Admittedly, this is not always measurable. But that aspect is not as important to me. Just to know that we are one of the market leaders in our field makes me proud. I am not so much about being the absolute number one. I am about creating something great, something essential, something that has importance for many people.

As for myself, I once again realize how important it is to create a tangible company spirit and philosophy which reflects our values and to live both of these in my company. I want this on the one hand, because I want to live this philosophy intensively. On the other hand, I also want this because in times when competition is so high, this gives the company a unique positioning on the market. With this philosophy, I have managed to create three successful companies, two of which I sold for a considerable amount of money. This success proves, in my opinion, that we were on the right track.

Successfully founding and growing a company is something that lasts forever. As a young musician, I worked really hard to save up enough capital to found my first company. Everything I had went into it, and the success of the company showed me that I was on the right path. This may sound old-fashioned, but I found it very rewarding.

People often fear that with a virtual team, their employees may not work when they cannot regularly see or control them. Thus, they become micromanagers or control freaks. How do keep your employees under control? How do you ensure that everyone is giving their best?

Again, from my point of view everything begins with the selection of the right employees for the right place. You want employees who love the upcoming tasks and are focused on their goals. Having fixed appointments to discuss the team's progress greatly helps. The consistent and thorough documentation of what has been discussed and the clear scheduling of objectives and tasks ensures that everyone knows what they have to accomplish. Above all, I signal that the cause and the people involved are important to me. I believe that the problem of control is largely defused if I really transfer competence and responsibility to all participants. But as I said, it needs the right staff.

If I have these things, the next most important thing is the attitude of everyone involved. On the whole, it does not matter to me how many hours an external employee works. From my point of view what matters is that they get the task done. I don't care about effort; I care about results! Look, in the end, the most important thing is that everyone is focused on the goal. In the best-case scenario, everyone gets his recognition through helping the team accomplish its goals. When this is the case, you don't need to control people.

I should say that having fixed dates to meet and confer is in its own way a control function. But because everyone is self-motivated, it doesn't feel like control.

How did you ensure that employees actually get involved in virtual teams and the team is more than the sum of its parts?

The answer to the first part of the question I have already given to the previous question. A team can only achieve more through communication than through the sum of individual skills. It is only when employees exchange ideas that the individual is inspired to be creative. Even in virtual teams, the direct communication is the salt in the soup, which makes a team of top experts a team that is far better than the sum of its individual team members.

Where do you see the future of virtual teams or teams without borders?

Virtual teams are going to become a matter of course, even in areas where they are not found today. With virtual teams, we will be able to overcome the shortage of qualified employees. The world is becoming more and more complex, and the need for specialists in every area is growing. Because of this, companies need to be more flexible than ever before. The classical model of employing hundreds of workers in one geographical location is dying out, and virtual teams are the best solution to give companies this flexibility.

Chapter 11

Extraordinary Achievements
Deserve Extraordinary Rewards – for Everyone

Bernd began to sweat. The thermometer in the gym sauna showed 90 ° C. After an extensive round on the equipment and 2 km on the treadmill, he enjoyed relaxing. He lay on his towel, his eyes closed, and felt his body begin to heat up. In that moment, he had to think of the winter in Transmontania and of the people who should be warm and dry inside when it is cold outside.

In the latest construction site photos Anne had sent him by email, the mountain peaks on the horizon were already white. The sight of the shells of unfinished buildings with snow in the background worried Bernd. The winter was getting closer, and they had to be faster. Fortunately, the conflict with the head of the Asian construction company had been taken care of, and everything was back on schedule. But the time was short. By the middle of December, everything had to be finished, otherwise the winter would take over.

In some of the photographs, there were women and even children who helped the construction workers by carrying ready-made parts or even buckets of water. In other pictures, there were villagers standing around the construc-

The houses in Transmontania must be finished by the winter. Bernd is still not sure if they will succeed, but the team is ready for the final race.

tion sites and amazed at what was going on. Suddenly it hissed loudly

- someone had pressed the infusion button. Bernd opened his eyes. The pictures from Transmontania disappeared, and he was back in the sauna in his gym in Hamburg.

A video conference with the extended team was set for the next morning. They would look at the complete project status and the current state of all the team members' goals. Bernd was looking forward to it. He already knew that the members of his core team were on their way to achieving all the goals. The people from the extended team, like Edwin or the other professors from the MOOC, also gave gas and solved many problems independently. The most important suppliers were now familiar with all processes and were constantly kept up to date on the project progress. Bernd could be satisfied. Everything was moving in the right direction. If only winter were not coming so quickly!

The next day, Bernd decided to work from home. In the past months, he had changed a lot. For his German projects, Bernd was now more and more involved by telephone and video conference. Their suppliers and partners had become accustomed to Skype and WebEx. There were still live, personal meetings. But these went more into the depth than before, so that they subsequently regulated much more over the Internet. Even with his German projects, Bernd had made an astounding observation: since he had been showing more interest in his German employees' and partners' personal lives and interests, they have been answering his emails much more quickly and also calling him back more reliably. It was an uphill spiral. The better Bernd knew them, the less friction there was and the more time was spent on fun and personal things on the sidelines. And through these shared positive experiences, you got to know each other even better.

Through this project, Bernd has changed his leadership style. Even with projects in Germany, he works more from home and does more video conferences, and his partners acknowledge that he seems even more interested in them than before.

Whenever Bernd had to carry out strategic or creative tasks, he preferred to do so from home. He enjoyed the convenience and was happy about the extra time he would otherwise have spent in the car. On most days when he worked from the home office, he offered to cook dinner in the evening. Today was one of those days. Wiebke offered to go to the fresh market during her lunch break to get what they needed. He was already looking forward to their dinner together.

Bernd started WebEx as scheduled at 11:00 a.m. All members of the extended team were already logged in. Some said brief hellos, others wrote a greeting in the chat and added a smiling emoticon.

"We are now in the final phase of our project," Bernd began. "Very soon, we will be able to celebrate finishing the first houses and begin the interior decoration. At this point, my very big thanks to Anne, Edwin, Claude, Pilar and their teams, including all suppliers and professors in New York. Together they have managed to speed up the construction work. It is also thanks to them that our relationship with the largest local construction company is again is back on track. Moreover, the relationship has grown more deeply and become more resilient. Now we have to concentrate all our forces once again for the final pace. It is now early November, and we only have six weeks to complete the project."

Claude learns about the competition for an architectural prize. In order to participate in the competition, the team would have to finish two weeks earlier. An enormous challenge.

"Hello again, everyone, and excuse me for interrupting you, Bernd," Claude said. "Are you aware that the International Architecture Summit in Stockholm will take place on December 20th? There are two main prizes to win, one for innovative architecture and another for social responsibility. The closing date for the contest entries is November 30th. And do you know something amusing? All the nominees will be on a large video screen during the conference - live from where they have built their projects, of course. I have already looked at projects on the website from Brazil, Mexico, and the Philippines. Some are similar to what we are doing, but the projects are also more commercial and none of them has to do with helping people in distress. Do you think we should apply?"

"Why not?" Said Bernd. "You know me, Claude. You know I love to win. If this is the one with the greatest social responsibility, that's even better. "

"Unfortunately, there is a catch," Claude explained. "The projects must already have come to an end before the contract is submitted. This is important for the jury to know the exact budget, the time required, and the scope of the project. They also attach importance to a first feedback from the builders, or in the case of more socially-oriented projects, the residents. We would have to hurry and finish two weeks earlier if we want to participate in the competition."

"That would be a miracle," moaned Bernd. "Anne, Edwin, Linda, Pilar what do you think?"

They voted. They would have to spur the construction workers and the local population once more, was the unanimous opinion.

"It just so happens that December 20th is a religious holiday," Anne said with her calm voice. "Perhaps it might be an incentive to tell people the following: If everything is finished by November 30th, and you help us and try really hard to finish early, then you will have time to move into your new homes and set everything up in peace, so that you will be able to celebrate on December 20th together with your Family in your new house. I can well imagine that the construction workers would be glad to give more overtime for this goal."

"Anne, in your photos I see a lot of people who help the construction workers," Bernd said. "There seems to be a strong sense of togetherness in Transmontania. How would it be if we were to organize the already available help a bit better? For example, we could recruit whole groups of volunteers who commit themselves to do a certain number of hours of work. The construction workers can assist the volunteers and give them clear instructions on what to do. Not in a typical German manner, but if everything had an orderly framework, these volunteers could contribute a lot more."

In order to be able to cope more quickly, the team decides to involve more local residents. Volunteers help with the project so that families can celebrate an upcoming holiday in their new homes.

"I will contact the mayors and the religious leaders," Anne replied. "The population is very enthusiastic about the matter, we can count on that. But we need the support of the local authorities. Also, I'm not sure if the construction workers alone will be able to get the people involved. We may need a few coaches and organizers with specialized organizational skills."

"We have students from Transmontania in our MOOC!" Edwin cried. "I guess that's about 25 people. Let me make contact with them, and I can see if I can activate them. I would be thrilled not only work on the blueprints alone but to be able to help with the practical execution."

"Great idea, Edwin!" said Bernd. "On the one hand, we need experts who are familiar with the new buildings and the special construction method, and this is only possible if we know our blueprints. On the other hand, we need people who speak the language of the people in Transmontania. The students would be ideal for this!"

"Edwin, could you physically be here during the intense phase?" Anne asked cautiously. "I know you are in China and, well, Transmontania is not exactly around the corner, but it would be great if you could be here on the ground. "

"I will definitely stay there long enough to find enough volunteers and to hold a workshop with the students, so that they know what we expect them to do. We should probably first develop a plan of how best to involve the volunteers, how to train them, how to distribute their duties, and to determine who will be managing their whole involvement. Once our team has established which duties the volunteers will have, I will have to fly back to China for a week, but I'll remain in close contact with the project from there."

"Thank you very much," Anne said tightly, in her usual sober and reserved manner. "We can communicate the details as soon as you have arrived here."

"Hey, I have an idea!" That was Stella. "So far, we have made quite conventional status reports - bar charts, pie diagrams, and explanatory texts. Why do not we visualize project progress much more? There are some interesting, new trends. You can show the status of the proj-

With the help of local MOOC students, Edwin wants to recruit volunteers. Stella also has a novel idea for a more motivating form of the status report.

ect on a slide with a picture so that everyone can see with a glance where we stand. It could, for example, be a tree and hang on the tree fruits in the traditional colors of all places in Transmontania where we have building sites. The size of the fruit indicates the percentage of the houses completed in each location. I was once in a project where they worked with such a visualization, and it worked out very well. For weeks, people kept looking at the site to see how we were progressing. It is really motivating to see how a project is progressing. If you all agree, I will create a slide for it. "

"I like your idea," Linda said. "If you like, I'll send you some suggestions within the next two days."

Stella agreed. And Bernd felt great. He was proud of his team. At the same time, he felt humbled by how engaged and thoughtful his was. He knew his team had done a great job over the last few weeks. It had organized itself and mastered all the challenges. He himself had contributed very little to it. But that did not matter, because he had given his team members the authority they needed to act independently and with passion.

"Let us go with this," said Bernd. "We are a great team, and I have no doubt that we can finish the houses by the end of November. If we win one of the two main prizes in Stockholm - or even the shortlist - then that will be a top reference for us all, and we may get a lot of new assignments. In addition, perhaps even more of our budget will remain intact if we finish two weeks earlier. Then we can use this money to bring everyone to Transmontania so we can celebrate together on December 20th. After all the problems that we have already mastered, it is now an enormous challenge to finish two weeks earlier. But with the passion you have shown up until now and with the enthusiasm of local people for their homes and the religious festival, I am firmly convinced that we can do it!"

There are more Effective Rewards than Money or the Usual Bonuses

Several times in this book I have dealt with the importance of recognition and a functioning reward system for virtual teams. Every team member needs genuine and honest recognition. Lack of recognition is one of the main reasons people leave a team. At this point, however, I am not asking for recognition in general but for exceptional team performance. Such a special prize should never simply be money or some other conventional bonus, such as stock options. The reward should be a highly emotional experience for the entire team. It has to be an event that every single team member is looking forward to. Because the members of virtual teams rarely see each other personally, a community event is often a very good reward for everyone.

A special prize, which is to motivate the team to top performances, must also be something very special. Money is not enough. It should be a unique experience for everyone!

Questions for Reflection:

What special event would inspire all of your team members? To which extraordinary place would everyone like to travel together in order to celebrate their success?

Ideally, the event or the trip should have something to do with your business or the particular character of the project. For example, a team from the automotive industry could visit the Grand Prix in Monaco after successfully completing a project. People from the advertising industry might enjoy a visit to Hollywood. There are virtually no limits to the imagination. No matter what, the desire for a community experience from people who work separately over a longer period of time is great. This is especially true when a team has grown together and worked intensively with each other as they do in virtual power teams. What could be more beautiful than celebrating an extraordinary success together? Be aware, however, that this is a very special reward for absolutely exceptional achievements, and the reward should not be expected by the team members as a given. Only when they realize how special it is, does it mobilize people and motivate them to go the extra mile. Let me tell you about a personal experience.

Work Hard, Play Hard – A Personal Success Story

In 2006 and 2007, I was a project manager in an international company. Our project was part of a global program, and I was responsible for the roll-out of this program in Europe. The aim of the project was to transfer the IT service management of 20 European national companies into the newly created global service management of the Group. The project touched on three areas: The first area was personnel, a new organizational structure was to be created. The second area was legal, since there would be completely new service contracts. And the third area was taxes, since IT services would be billed across international borders in the future. At the beginning of 2006, I had only two full-time employees available for the project: There was a German, who for the sake of this story I will call Klara. She spoke five languages and was extremely well organized. To this came Jamschid, an Uzbeke, who lived and worked in Moscow. Jamschid was a great, bullish and energetic type with an over-reaching self-confidence.

Five global experts were at our disposal, one for HR, two for law and tax, and two for design sovereignty, a typical role in IT projects. In addition, there were 20 IT service managers who were scattered all over Europe and were working part-time on the project. It was my first big international project, so I wanted to prove myself. I felt personally responsible for the success of the whole project.

In the first three months, everything went perfectly, and I was completely enthusiastic. I traveled to many countries and met many great people. Then the virtual team meetings suddenly became tenacious. The project co-workers were no longer so involved. Today, I know why: I behaved like a professor in the virtual lecture hall. Because I thought I knew everything myself, I always instructed my people about what they were to do. Although I acted this way, I should have noticed that I was sometimes envious of the expertise in my team. In legal and tax issues, for example, I was far from being as good as the relevant experts. And yet, I acted like I knew best. It became increasingly difficult to motivate my team and drive top performance. One day I looked into the mirror and I wondered. What are you doing here? You've turned from a productive factor in this team to someone who is hindering the entire project. And you are slowly but surely heading for a burnout. Can this team not be lead differently?

Shortly thereafter, Jamschid, the Usbeke, left the project. He accepted a job elsewhere. He was replaced by Pilar, a Spaniard with a lion's mane and a hoarse voice. She brought fresh air into the team and contributed to the fact that things turned positive. When the project really took off in February 2007, two more people were added full time, so that we were now a total of five in the core team. We came together to do a live workshop, similar to what I described at the beginning of the book. We looked at each others' personal "Lifelines" and discovered our greatest strengths. I was completely taken aback when I realized what great people I had, how much experience they had, and the great challenges they had already mastered in their lives. I felt that it was a great gift to work with these people.

So, I finally managed to turn down my ego a bit. The whole team concentrated again on the project. We had a clear goal - and unfortunately a time problem: if we were to continue as we had been, we would never be ready on time. We also competed with the teams of the other continents within the global program. Should we Europeans be the only ones to fail? A terrible idea! At the beginning of May 2007, we had so much momentum that I made a bold proposal to the Group's supervisory board, the so-called Project Board: If we were finished three months ahead of schedule, then all 30 members of the extended team should be flown to Tenerife for a 2-day celebration. This trip would be financed by itself. I reckoned: The personnel costs for the project amounted to roughly 1 million Euros per year. That at least was my estimate, going from the salaries of full-time employees. I did not include those working part-time on the project in the bill. If we were finished a whole quarter earlier, the company would save € 250,000 in personnel costs. For 50,000 euros, one fifth of the total, we would all fly for two days to Tenerife.

To my great pleasure the board agreed with the plan and gave the green light for the 50,000 Euros. When I told the news to the team, the mood changed instantly. To understand this, it is perhaps important to know that my team included members in Belarus and Uzbekistan. Employees who could never have afforded such a trip privately. I said, "Okay, folks, if you want to go to Tenerife, you need to all deliver. Each country has to make its contribution and finish on time."

We also had a weekly status report, which worked with a special visualization tool. On the slide was an island and 20 parachute jumpers. Whenever a parachute jumper approached the island, a milestone was reached. So, the tension rose week by week, day by day. On the one hand, there was an exciting competition between the individual countries. Whose parachute jumpers would land on the island first? On the other hand, we could only reach our goal together and would only fly to Tenerife if all parachute jumpers landed on the island in time. The results? On December 30, 2007, one day before the deadline, the parachute jumper from Uzbekistan was the last one to land on the island. We made it! That we were finished on time was only one thing. We also received great feedback from our internal customers. And finally, we saved the company 200,000 Euros. Actually yes, 250,000, but 50,000 of it we took as agreed and flew for two days to Tenerife. There, we celebrated and had the party of our lives!

A Reward must be Great - and Communicated Early

Now you know my greatest success story. And the moral of the story? There are two: First, if you promise a reward, be bold and be generous. If you choose something that does not seem special, it will hardly provide an additional motivational thrust. Being generous should not be a problem. As in my situation, if your team completes its project early, it will save money and, at the same time, pay for the reward. Second, inform the team about the reward early. In my experience, you should tell them at least half a year before the announced end of the project. In a virtual team, people need a little more time for the reward to become tangible for each and every person. Because the team members do not see each other often, it takes longer for everyone to exchange ideas about how cool it would be to get that reward and celebrate the success together.

In virtual teams, people need more time to work toward a special reward. Therefore, make the reward known early, at least half a year before the deadline.

One more thing: it is worthwhile to think about how the project progress can be visibly and vividly visualized. The usual slides with numbers and text are usually not motivating enough. Bernd's team chose fruit on a tree. In my first major international project, we chose parachute jumpers landing on an island. Let your imagination play! The visualization should be fun, and everyone should be able to identify with it. And if you do not know which reward might be suitable for outstanding performance? Then start brainstorming with your entire team! Ask your people what joint venture would really inspire them. Be careful, however, that your people are not too modest. Think big! Give examples of international top events in your industry or suggest places where celebrities from the business meet. Exceptional rewards in combination with creative reporting will foster superior performance and great results.

Questions for Reflection:

- Do you have a reward for extraordinary achievements in your team?

- Which jointly-attended event, which destination or other form of recognition could make your team go the extra mile?

- How could you visualize the progress your team is making in a creative, fun way?

The English entrepreneur Richard Branson is famous for driving his teams to top performances with exceptional events. On Necker Island, his private island in the Caribbean, Richard Branson regularly receives outstanding employees from all departments of his company group Virgin. Life on the island offers lots of action, water sports, parties, fun, surprises, but also recreational possibilities. A real highlight is when Richard Branson personally picks up the employees in his helicopter. It is just something special that people who work on different continents for Virgin celebrate with each other, and it gives them the chance to meet each other personally.

Can it also be a Little Cheaper?
Yes, If You are Creative Enough!

A trip for 30 employees on a holiday island such as Tenerife will rarely be approved by an organization, even if it can be financed through productivity gains that the employees themselves have made possible. How can individual achievements be rewarded regularly? I have had very good experiences with my choice of "Champion of the month" in my teams. Every month, a team member, who has delivered extraordinary performance, was nominated online by the others. At the end, everyone the voted on the winner. Everyone in the team was able to nominate someone and everyone had a vote for the winner. Whoever received the most votes was the "Champion of the Month." The funny thing was, that this recognition was not purely virtual but there also tangible. No, it was not a trophy, but a beautiful African doll with a patchwork suit in bright colors. This doll was always sent by mail to the respective "Champion of the month" and he or she put the prize on their desk. Whenever someone came in and asked what about the doll, the team member could proudly tell what it was and what the prize was for. More and more, the exotic doll within the team has become a coveted symbol for exceptional performance.

In various companies and organizations, I have already experienced a whole series of rewards and prizes. Once, for example, I have had an online university offering such MOOCs (Mass Open Online Courses) for architecture as in the story about

An exciting visualization of the project progress helps your team in the final laps. Find something tangible instead of just presenting numbers and graphs.

Bernd and his team. During a MOOC, the students designed novel school

buildings for the Philippines. The professors chose the best design and
spent one week at the Faculty of Architecture and Design in Harvard. The
student, who, incidentally, came from Sri Lanka, was extremely proud
that his design was shown with his name at one of the most famous universities in the world. I can only encourage managers to think of something to give, both as tangible as well as intangible recognition to team
members for special achievements. Use your resources in the company
and your imagination to come up with and to provide something spectacular. And note that spectacular is not always expensive.

There are different kinds of moti-
vating rewards and prizes for
virtual teams. Think about what
your employees could be proud
of. And what is fun for everyone.

Let me give you one
example of this: A German
non-governmental organization for young people who did
not have a budget for great celebrations, persuaded a sponsor
to give the young volunteers
(it was almost exclusively
young men) as a reward tickets for a federal league game of FC Bayern
Munich. Of course, such a proposal needs to come from the team and
should make the team excited. A Bulgarian non-governmental organization, which provides young Bulgarians worldwide with aid projects and
also looks after social issues in Bulgaria once organized a "virtual party"
involving all of its locations worldwide. They all took part in a big video
conference, and the company arranged for everyone to have food and
drinks for the party. Even such a low-budget party works well with teenagers. The young people had a lot of fun, and the event unlocked additional energy and momentum.

Even if you don't have the
budget for an expensive trip,
you can make a "virtual
party" instead of a video con-
ference. Provide food, drinks
and music, and the team mem-
bers connect from everywhere
for the "party."

Once again: Exceptional
rewards should be given only for
exceptional performance. And
they must be fun for the entire
team. A combination of physical
activities, social activities, and
a party is usually good. Finally,
one last tip: If everyone is already
coming together for a party,
why not have a strategic session
beforehand? Then the team, if it
remains in this constellation, can set the next high goal.

Chapter 12

When a Virtual Power Team Splits Apart, a New Team is Quickly Born

Bernd's limbs were stiff. The flight from Hamburg to the capital of Transmontania lasted almost 18 hours. Bernd left Hamburg at 7 p.m., flew to Frankfurt, and was now on his way to Delhi. He would land there the next day at 9:00 a.m. local time. After a several hours stay, a small Indian airline would then take him to his final destination in another three hours.

Transmontania did not have its own airline. Bernd moaned softly. Not even half the flight was over. On the last of these flights he ordered a red wine, watched a film from Lufthansa's on-board program, and then fell asleep. Now he was much too nervous to sleep. The hours on board dragged on and his thoughts ran around in circles like on a carousel.

Bernd has now been leading his virtual team for ten months, and it felt like half a life. New pictures appeared in his thoughts. First, the destroyed houses immediately after the earthquake. Bernd felt the shock again when he had seen the pictures on the iPad that morning. Then, the first Skype conferences with Anne and Claude, the confidence and enthusiasm in their faces. He saw Linda, Pilar and Stella, who had come onto the project team one by one. He remembered the workshop with Paul - what a breakthrough! Paul had shown him how a leadership transfers individual responsibility and enthusiasm instead of having to exerting pressure. And now all the new faces in the extended team, the professors of the MOOC, Edwin and his students, the minister, the director of the local construction company, which he had almost scorned, and many more. It was a new world indeed, and it was a very different way to live and work than he had previously known in tranquil Hamburg.

After ten months, the houses are finally ready. Bernd flies to Transmontania for the dedication of the new buildings. From the capital, the team will participate virtually in the award ceremony.

Bernd knew that shortly after landing he would see the finished houses for the first time. "I can't believe it," he thought, feeling great humility. "This is my first big international project, and I was almost never on site at the construction sites. Nevertheless, everything has worked out. Over the last few weeks, the locals had often been working on the construction sites for twelve and sometimes 16 hours a day. Their training and guidance had been organized by local MOOC students and other volunteers. It had been cold and often dark. For hours, the helpers only were able to work in the light of large headlights. But the people were ready to give everything so that their houses would be ready for the upcoming religious holiday."

"My team did it," thought Bernd. "And this time the emphasis is on *team* and not on *my*." He liked this thought, at the same time, he felt his heart warm. The interior construction of the houses had actually been completed on time. The team had been able to submit the blueprints and project data for the competition in Stockholm. "We have a realistic chance of winning at least one of the two prizes," Claude had recently said at a conference. "But the matter has not yet been decided. Above all, the Mexicans and the Brazilians also have very strong contributions."

Bernd's neighbors were wrapped in blankets and slept. In his boredom, he went through the plan for the next day in his mind: Landing at noon local time. Anne and Edwin would pick him up from the small airport with its flat concrete buildings. He was already looking forward to seeing them again. The three of them would drive with Ann's car, a Hyundai SUV, to one of the newly built areas about 200 km north of the capital. They planned to have dinner with the local mayor and to stay in the village. The next morning, they would return to the capital. For the rest of his stay, Bernd would be staying in the government's guest house, a colonial mansion surrounded by a large park. The other team members were already there or would arrive tomorrow during the day. They all had developed so close ties with the team members in Transmontania that they were invited to stay in their homes. Claude and Stella would live with the parents of two MOOC students. Linda and Pilar were invited to Anne's house. This hospitality was unusual for the culture in Transmontania, but the team spirit had long been stronger than local traditions. Paul wants to attend by videoconference from the Cayman Islands as soon as the award ceremony in Stockholm starts. Deeply lost in thought and full of anticipation, Bernd finally fell asleep.

What a sight! Bernd, Anne and Edwin were in the middle of one of the new buildings, surrounded by the sustainable and earthquake-resistant houses their team had designed and built. It was bitterly cold, but cloudless, and the solar roofs sparkled in the sunlight. Anne and Edwin picked

Bernd is overwhelmed when he visits the development. He feels the warmth and gratitude of the locals. They are looking forward to celebrating the big festival in their new houses.

Bernd up at the airport. After a snack in the tiny business lounge, they drove as planned into the first accessible new building area. Bernd could hardly believe he was really here now. He struggled with his feelings. He had visited so many completed projects in his life, but this was something very special. The streets were full of people, men, women, and many children. They were dressed in thick, colorful woolen fabrics, carrying furniture, pots, pans, dishes, and other furnishings into the houses. Through some windows he could see how the houses were decorated.

As they walked through the streets, which had not yet been paved, Anne and Edwin were warmly welcomed by many people. Anne introduced them to Bernd in their mother language. Then people bowed before him in the traditional way. Some elderly people wanted to touch Bernd's hand while they bowed. He could not understand what people were saying, but he felt a wave of human warmth and gratitude every time.

"People are honored to meet you personally," Anne explained. "Many say how grateful they are that they have a warm living room and solid roof over their heads for the winter," she translated. "They are delighted to be able to celebrate the great festival tomorrow in their houses."

Then they entered one of houses, where Anne had arranged for Bernd to visit. After a warm welcome and a cup of hot tea, Edwin showed Bernd where the new materials were used. Edwin was very proud, but he tried not to let it show. Quietly and objectively, he demonstrated the solar systems and explained how the materials would behave in the event of an earthquake. "The whole house is as pliant as a reed," explained the young Chinese. "In a severe earthquake, it will swing very hard, but no parts will fall down and the window panes will not splinter."

The whole afternoon felt like the fulfillment of a dream for Bernd. In the evening, they all found themselves in the house of the mayor. His house was relatively narrow. It was festively decorated and full of people. With kindness, the mayor welcomed him in a formal and traditional manner. The mayor gave a speech in which he thanked Bernd and his entire team for the great organization. He emphasized the successful collaboration with the local builders, and he also mentioned once again the commitment of many local people in the past weeks. The festivities consisted of countless courses, all of which tasted excellent. Once it seemed to Bernd, as if one of the great Buddha statues in the room winked at him. "That must be the rice wine," he thought.

Early next morning Bernd, Anne and Edwin got in the car to drive back to the capital. The mayor bid his farewells and wished them all the best for the competition in Stockholm. He was sure that they would win a prize. At Anne's house, they picked up Linda and Pilar. The two women had been in the country for three days, and Anne had already shown them one of the new buildings. Claude and Stella visited another new development project, accompanied by their hosts. At noon, they were all together again. The whole team met for lunch in one of the most beautiful places in the capital. After ten months of virtual cooperation, with their ups and downs, everyone enjoyed being here together. The felt very close to each other, and there was much laughter. As they were talking, they exchanged ideas about what they had learned during the project for the future.

When the whole team is finally together, they feel very close to each other. At 5:00 pm the video conference begins for the award ceremony. Claude presents the project.

The video bridge to Stockholm was planned for 5 p.m., when it was still in the morning in Europe. At half past five, everyone had already gathered in a governmental conference room. Anne and her staff had prepared everything perfectly. A large video screen hung in the middle of the room. Three webcams were installed in different new building areas and could send live pictures from there. The hall was full. High officials from the government had come; all of Anne's employees, representatives of the construction company, including chief engineer and coordinator, members of the extended team, as well as all MOOC students from Transmontania were there. Bernd now understood better why the project had worked so well. He had become acquainted with people whom he had never known before, and yet, they and their expertise were essential to the success of this project. It all seemed to him to be a miracle.

To just before 5 p.m., everyone started staring at the video screen, which showed live pictures of the prize ceremony in Stockholm. You could see a well-filled hall, different cameras, cabins for the simultaneous translators - it was a really big international event. At exactly 5 p.m., they were then switched in live. In Stockholm, only the hall in Transmontania could be seen, then the live pictures from the webcams from the new construction areas. One saw the houses and the many people, who went in and out and were in the process of setting up. The presenter gave the floor to Transmontania and asked them to present their project. First, an official from the government spoke, expressing his gratitude. This had been discussed in advance with the locals.

Claude then took over the microphone and named in his polished English the most important figures, data, and facts of the project: how many houses were built at what time, what innovative materials and techniques, how many people in all of the regions were involved, what budget, what a Type of financing, and so on.

Bernd himself did not want to be on the stage. It was enough for him to see the glow in the eyes of his team and the locals. When the presentation was over, there was great applause in Stockholm. They were the last competition contest, which was presented, so afterwards they went directly to the award ceremony. It was perfectly quiet in the Transmontania hall, when the presenter in Stockholm came to the microphone with two envelopes. Nobody moved. Anne held her hand to her mouth. The moderator opened the first envelope.

"The prize for the most Innovative Architecture of the year goes to Manuel Vargas and his team from Brazil."

Disappointed faces everywhere in the conference center in Transmontania. Especially with the Asians. In Stockholm, a Brazilian architect entered the stage with great joy. Bernd looked at the other team members.

"We are neither the first nor the only ones to build resiliency houses," Claude said soberly. "But let's wait, who gets the second main prize."

The host in Stockholm was alone again on the stage and opened the second envelope.

"The prize for Social Responsibility goes to Bernd Schmidt from Germany and his international virtual team for earthquake-proof houses in Transmontania."

The team cheered. Claude, Pilar, and Linda jumped up. Anne gave Stella a hug. Edwin clapped the shoulders of his students. In the meantime, Bernd's wife Wiebke went to Stockholm to take the prize on behalf of the team.

Bernd was ecstatic. He shook hands with everyone in the hall, and hugged all of the members of the core team. He gave Paul a "thumbs up" over the video camera and saw a satisfied smile on his face. Suddenly, loud music sounded: "We are the champions, my friends." Claude had connected his iPhone with the music system. After half an hour of joy and hugs, Bernd asked for peace and stood at the front of the microphone.

"Ten months ago, I started this project to help the needy here and at the same time, start my first international experience as a contractor. Until that time, I had always worked in Germany and was proud of always having adhered to schedules and budgets. I had been convinced that this was mainly due to my leadership skills and my sophisticated processes. But what has happened over the past ten months has surpassed my wildest dreams. You are all shining stars. It is an honor for me to lead this team, and I am convinced that the work you did here will go down in history. "

Bernd now honored every single team member. He started with Anne, who was standing on the far left of the room, and pointed out what a support she had been to the team from the beginning. Then he wanted to say something about Claude when his mobile phone rang. To Bernd's horror, Claude began speaking on the phone. Somewhat irritated Bernd continued with Stella. He spoke to each individual team member personally and looked into their eyes. While he praised each one, he saw how some eyes were red, others had tears of emotion in their eyes. Everyone was aware that they had been part of a big cause. Finally, Bernd wanted to come back to Claude, who had finally ended his phone call. The Canadian himself took the floor.

"Listen, everyone," Claude said with a wide grin on his face. "I have just received a call from an international relief organization, which is part of the Architectural Summits in Stockholm. They have been watching us for some time now, and now that we have won one of the two prizes, they would like us to build a refugee camp in Africa on their behalf. It is supposed to be a dignified place for the refugees and we should use the innovative construction methods, new materials and solar components, which we also installed here in Transmontania. Well, what do you say? Are you in, Bernd?"

Bernd's irritation over Claude's cell phone was like blown away, "Of course," he replied, laughing. "And how about you?" Linda, Pilar, Stella and Edwin also nodded with joy.

Bernd gave a speech and pays tribute to every single team member. Claude gets a call on his cell phone. The next project is waiting. This time Linda wants to take over the management of the team.

"I would like to participate," said Anne. "You are a fantastic team. But I'm afraid I cannot be there the next time. I am working on behalf of my government and there is still a lot to be done here before the infrastructure is fully restored. Besides, I have neglected my family a little over the last ten months. But I would be very happy if we kept in touch. "

"You all showed leadership," said Bernd. "I still have some inquiries for projects in Germany. In addition, the Chinese construction company has already come to see me. It is about a mill town in China. Which of you would like to be able to lead the project in Africa?"

"I would love to do that," Linda said. "If you trust me." Her voice sounded self-confident and determined. "I am a financial expert and would like to help people on my continent. With the expertise of Claude and Pilar in the field of architecture, we can again create something great. Maximum freedom and individual responsibility for all in the team would be my motto. "

"You can count on me and my network," said Claude. Stella and Pilar also agreed with Linda as project manager.

"I've never been to Africa," Edwin said, smiling, "but my Chinese countrymen are already getting involved there. So, I'll be there."

"Great," Bernd said. "I'm very happy. And now let us all celebrate!"

High Potential as Multipliers and Hinges

And so ended the project of the virtual team from Bernd, Claude, Anne, Linda, Pilar, Stella, Edwin and the others. Together with students from all over the world, the team has designed new, earthquake-proof houses and erected them in the earthquake area after its devastating destruction. For their social commitment with the means of architecture, the team is awarded an international prize. There were some ups and downs in the project, but in the end, everyone is happy and satisfied. The amazing thing is that the project immediately continues and grows into a new project! As one project ends, a new one begins. Is this a coincidence? Probably not. The team has developed a common mission and vision. A truly powerful mission and vision continues as if by itself. It aut014;tically finds more followers. Management responsibility often goes to the next generation - or to those who have thus far been in the second row.

When I started to lead large virtual teams years ago - teams in which people around the world were involved at different levels of hierarchy in companies - I soon realized that I could no longer be the only team leader to carry the vision and mission. I needed multipliers who carried our mission and vision to other parts of the world and to other hierarchical levels within the company. How did I achieve this?

Recall chapter 4 and the interlocking goals: The method of interlocking goals is to break the team's mission and vision into so many individual objectives that each member of the core team is responsible for exactly one strategic goal. The right way to achieve this personal goal is to let each team member be as independent as possible and do what they need to succeed.

In larger teams, you need multipliers to carry on the mission and vision. This is best achieved by involving young high potentials as early as possible and giving them responsibility.

The core team members do not have to achieve their goals alone. In the ideal case, a further 3-5 high-potential team members are found for each individual target. They form another small virtual team, a sub-team working together on a goal under the leadership of the responsible member of the core team. In Bernd's team, for example, Edwin and his best students come into the boat when it comes to developing and implementing ideas for new materials and constructions. Within big international corporations it is usually so that these highly talented people, who have already proven leadership qualities in one way or another, join a project team. It is usually the task of the HR department to recognize outstanding young talent and to ensure that they are taken into account for future management tasks. Project managers can contact the HR department and ask who is eligible for a specific task, so that they can be hired onto the virtual team. Where this is not the case, for example, in many small and medium-sized enterprises, in start-ups or in non-governmental organizations, the core team has to take care of itself. It will then usually see who from the extended team is eligible to take on more responsibility for certain tasks - and finally a real leadership role.

Promoting Young Talent Instead of Executives Sitting High in an Ivory Tower

In my experience, it is always important for virtual teams to include the next level within an organization or the extended team in the strategic agenda. Not only should the core team have internalized its mission and vision; the extended team should have as well. Otherwise, the ivory syndrome threatens. By this I mean that the core team or leadership team has great visions, and also exchanges ideas amongst themselves intensively, but does not realize how it is becoming gradually decoupled from the rest of the team and the entire organization. The leaders sit in an ivory tower and push each other up, while those who are outside the tower and farther away no longer understand what their mission is. To prevent this, highly talented team members are like hinges between the core team and the rest of the team or the entire organization. Without them the team cannot function. In other words, involve younger and less experienced team members in strategic work and management. Of course, only the best are considered – the truy high potential employees.

Watch out for this trap!
In large virtual teams, it can quickly happen that the leadership circle sits high in an ivory tower and exchanges ideas and visions, while at the base no one understands what is going on. Bringing in young talented leaders is the best way to bridge the gap between strategists and the grassroots of the company.

My proposal from my experience: three to five high potential employees per strategic goal should be part of the regular online conferences of the core team. If the budget allows it, one to two of these should move for two to three months to a different location, where they are responsible for the same strategic goal. A positive dynamic emerges when there are virtual sub-teams that participate in the strategic discussions and at the same time operate in the operational business. They learn to think strategically, and they internalize the mission and vision. At the same time, they also know what is going on at the base, and they have to prove themselves there. If your young talents are sitting in different locations around the world or at different organizational hierarchies, this creates the best conditions for them to become the top leaders of the next generation.

Three to five high potential employees per strategic goal should be included in regular conferences. In addition, if possible, the junior staff should be employed at various locations.

In the course of his project, Bernd has strategically integrated more members of his extended team into the core team. He even brought in business partners and suppliers to be involved in the process to increase the speed of innovation, reach the goal more quickly and carry on the mission and vision of the project. If you are able to mobilize the entire team, the biggest advantage is that opportunities are recognized and acted upon that the core team might have easily overlooked. For this, it is necessary that as many people as possible have internalized the mission and vision of the team. For only those who have the vision will be able to see the opportunities. As soon as you have young leaders in the extended team, who push forward strategic initiatives on their own, new ideas are implemented much more quickly. The junior executives not only recognize new opportunities, but also create individually responsible virtual sub-teams in order to realize the opportunities they recognize.

When Mission and Vision Inspire the Entire Team

Young talent for new projects is best achieved by encouraging employees in the existing project. In Bernd's team, Linda is the head of the next project, because she was under Bernd's leadership - and Paul's influence – and experienced what "empowerment" means. If everyone in the extended team sees that they get chances and that they can initiate ideas to achieve their goals independently, irrespective of where in the world or where in the organization they sit, then a strong team spirit arises. Your people realize: Yes, we can do everything, we can do great things regardless of distance, time zones, or cultural differences. If such a spirit has emerged, the team vision and mission will continue, and new projects will appear.

In my work as a coach I already had companies of all sizes and industries as customers. Corporations and real global players were among them as well as international middle-sized companies and even start-ups. Everyone succeeded in incorporating the expanded team into the agenda, strategic thinking, mission and vision. They all made extensive progress. Especially last year, I was fortunate enough to work with a number of non-governmental organizations that are responsible for major international projects in the field of education, prevention for young people or the integration of different social groups. It is crucial that projects are sustainable and that there is a continuity of the mission across individual projects. Non-governmental organizations in particular have a clear mission and vision in this world and always need new people to share this vision and implement it in concrete projects. In the projects I was involved in, it was crucial to communicate effectively within large and widely dispersed groups and to keep motivation high over a long period of time.

If you want to have lasting enthusiasm and high motivation in the team, you should step by step, involve all team members in the agenda, the mission and vision, and in the strategic thinking.

In my projects, I have always ensured that stakeholders at all levels begin to think strategically and to internalize the mission and the vision. Virtual teams often fail because there are a few who think strategically, and others understand themselves as operational translators. The art of leading a team to success also consists in closely interlocking these two levels - strategy and implementation. Then neither the executives in the ivory tower nor the employees on the operational level see themselves as mere command receivers. The gravitational force of the entire team increases and exceeds geographical and cultural boundaries with ease.

Epilogue

Bernd took a deep breath. The cold, fresh mountain air filled his lungs and cleared his mind. His body felt clean. He had just passed the first fantastic descent on the ski slope. His leg muscles were still pleasantly warm. Next to him in the chairlift sat his daughter Lena. She had red cheeks, squinted in the sun, and looked at her smartphone, with which she sent WhatsApp messages to her friends at an insane pace. Immediately after his return from Transmontania, Bernd had gone with Wiebke and Lena to their favorite ski resort in the Alps. They wanted to stay there over New Year's Eve.

Bernd closed his eyes and enjoyed the gentle, warm rays of the winter sun in his face. In the front of his mind he saw again the newly built houses in Transmontania. He saw smiling and grateful locals. He saw the faces of Anne, Claude, Pilar and Linda, all lively in conversation. Then Edwin and Stella, full of enthusiasm and energy. Finally, he saw Paul with his calm, clever smile. Bernd also thought about some of the government officials and various representatives of construction companies and other suppliers. What a great community there had been during the past ten months! Bernd was satisfied. At the same time, he did not feel arrogant and proud as he used to be after successful projects; he remained humbled by the experience. Yes, he had taken the initiative. But then it was the passion, the energy and the enthusiasm of so many people in the team that ultimately led to success.

Now, after all the difficulties they had had to struggle with - funding, time pressure, new building materials, local construction companies and much more - everything felt easy and profoundly satisfying. "It was worth it," thought Bernd. And then he wondered, "Could it be that I miss all this already? Our weekly team meetings, the constant challenges, our firm belief that we will create it together, whatever happens?"

As the chairlift went uphill, Bernd also recalled the Stockholm awards, which they had watched from Asia on the monitor. After winning the prize, he received congratulations from all over the world. Bernd was not accustomed to this level of recognition and publicity. It was flattering, and quite secretly, he enjoyed it.

During this short vacation bringing in the new year, he finally wanted to focus on his family and not let the whole day be determined by his smartphone. He had therefore asked Stella, who continued to work for him, to pre-sort the emails during his vacation, and to pass on only those who required his immediate attention. Secretly, he hoped that Stella would not send him a single email. Nevertheless, he suddenly felt the desire to retrieve his emails on the smartphone halfway up the mountain station. As soon as he had taken the phone out of his jacket pocket, he saw on the display already a message from Stella and the word "important."

"Damn," thought Bernd, and immediately went into combat mode. He opened the email program and read the message Stella had passed on to him. Then he relaxed again immediately, and a broad smile appeared in his face. "I do not think so," Bernd said out loud. His daughter lifted her eyes up from her WhatsApp and looked over at him.

"Imagine, Lena," said Bernd, "a billionaire from California has bought an island in the Pacific and wants me to cultivate it! He calls it the "rainbow island" and wants to build a sustainable holiday resort, where all the great cultures of the five continents are represented with their traditional architecture, their cuisine and their art. He wants to operate the resort exclusively with sustainable energy. And he wants to hire an innovative entrepreneur instead of a multinational construction company with the construction management. It says that the investment volume should be 500 million dollars. The billionaire watched the award ceremony in Stockholm over the Internet and saw our presentation. He wrote me: 'I am deeply impressed by your work in Transmontania, and I would be delighted if you could look at our idea as soon as possible.'"

The chair had arrived at the station. It was time to get out and start the next descent. Shortly before he jumped onto the slope, Bernd stopped for a moment beside the mountain station and looked out over the surrounding snowy mountain peaks. What a great panorama! Down in the valley he saw the narrow valleys and small villages, the hotels and inns. On the horizon, he could see the next city.

He closed his eyes and imagined the next city and the next. In his mind, he traveled on until he came to the "rainbow island" in the Pacific. He saw the blue ocean, saw windmills turning and solar systems flashing in the sun. He saw the outlines of a Buddhist temple and a gothic cathedral. And he saw faces, smiling faces of people of different skin colors and cultures, all with bright eyes and all with a new world in their hearts.

Endnotes

1. Meyer, Erin: *The Culture Map. Breaking through the Invisible Boundaries of Global Business*. New York: PublicAffairs, 2014.

2. Csíkszentmihályi, Mihály: Flow. *The Psychology of Optimal Experience*. New York: Harper & Row, 1990.

3. Jekel, Thorsten: *Digital Working für Manager. Mit neuen Technologien effizient arbeiten*. Offenbach: GABAL, 2013.

4. Ferriss, Timothy: *The 4-Hour Workweek: Escape 9-5, Live Anywhere, and Join the New Rich*. New York: Tim Ferriss, 2007.

5. Faltin, Günter: *Kopf schlägt Kapital. Die ganz andere Art, ein Unternehmen zu gründen. Von der Lust, ein Entrepreneur zu sein*. München: Hanser, 2011.

6. Senge, Peter M.: *The Fifth Discipline: The Art and Practice of the Learning Organization*. New York: Bantam Doubleday Dell Publishing Group, Inc., 1990.

7. Lencioni, Patrick: *The Five Dysfunctions of a Team. A Leadership Fable*. New Jersey: John Wiley & Sons, 2002.

8. Senge, Peter M.: *The Fifth Discipline: The Art and Practice of the Learning Organization*. New York: Bantam Doubleday Dell Publishing Group, Inc., 1990.

9. Meyer, Erin: *The Culture Map. Breaking Through the Invisible Boundaries of Global Business*. New York: PublicAffairs, 2014.

10. Phasenmodell von Bruce Tuckman

11. Faller, Kurt u.a.: *Das Buddy-Prinzip.Soziales Lernen mit System*. Düsseldorf: Buddy e.V., 2007.

12. Meyer, Erin: *The Culture Map. Breaking Through the Invisible Boundaries of Global Business*. New York: PublicAffairs, 2014.

The Author

Peter Ivanov, born in 1970 in Bulgaria, is a Keynote speaker, business consultant and executive coach. He has more than 20 years of experience with international management. In the business world he has lead virtual teams with more than 100 employees, spread throughout West and East Europe, Central Asia, the Middle East and Africa, and his teams have won multiple corporate awards.

The graduate mathematician speaks five languages and has won several international discus throw championships as an athlete. Born and raised in Bulgaria until the age of 28, Peter witnessed the transformation of his home country from communism to democracy and as a student, he often held public speeches. Today, he is in demand as a Keynote speaker at business events and congresses throughout all of Europe.

Peter Ivanov shares his knowledge about leadership and virtual teams as a speaker, consultant and executive coach. He is also heavily devoted to the topic of cultural diversity in businesses and organizations. He lives with his wife and five daughters in Hamburg.

http://www.peter-ivanov.com

About Castle Mount Media

"Improving Leadership and Communication
in Healthcare and Education"

Castle Mount Media GmbH & Co. KG is a publishing company located in Erlangen, Germany, which specializes in print and online media dedicated to improving Leadership and Communication especially in the areas of Healthcare and Education. Our mission is to inspire and empower our readers and seminar participants to achieve success through value-based leadership and generative collaboration.

For further information about Castle Mount Media, our online seminars, books, and other products please visit our website:

www.castlemountmedia.com

Dealing with Divas and Other Difficult Personalities: A Mindful Approach to Improving Relationships in Your Business or Organization!

by Laura Baxter

In a world where having productive relationships and effective communication means the difference between success and absolute failure, you need tools that will help you remain calm, confident, poised, and focused on the task at hand so that you accomplish your goals, regardless of any conflict that may be going on around you.

This book helps you do just that. It gives you the tools you need to remain calm, centered, and focused when you are dealing with difficult people, and it gives the tools you need to better communicate with everyone on your team — including your "Divas" — so that you reach your goals with success.

Laura Baxter, American opera singer and performance coach, has studied the effects of the voice and the body on communication and leadership for over 25 years. The focus of her work is presence. She helps her clients master having both a strong inner presence -- even in the most difficult situations -- and a dynamic, charismatic outer presence. They own the room! In Dealing with Divas she brings this experience together to help you master dealing with your diva!

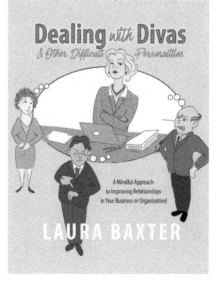

English Version:
ISBN 978-3-9818472-1-5

German Version:
ISBN 978-3-9818472-5-3

Next Generation Entrepreneurs: Live Your Dreams and Create a Better World through Your Business

By Robert Dilts

Entrepreneurs are individuals who are willing to take personal, professional, and financial responsibility and risk in order to pursue opportunity. The entrepreneurial spirit has been a driving force for social and economic growth and advancement throughout human history.

In recent years, a new generation of entrepreneurs has emerged who are interested in much more than financial gain. Characterized by people like Steve Jobs, Richard Branson, and Elon Musk, this new generation of entrepreneurs is also deeply committed to living their dreams and making a better world through their projects and ventures. By combining personal ambition with the desire for contribution, growth, and fulfillment, they have made game-changing and world-changing innovations that have transformed the way we live and do business.

In this first of three volumes, expert author and thought leader Robert Dilts shows both new and experienced entrepreneurs how to connect to their values and mission to create a thriving, value-based organization. With case studies from some of the best leaders of our time, the reader will be inspired and empowered to succeed!

Robert Dilts has had a global reputation as a leading coach, behavioral skills trainer, and business consultant since the late 1970s. The author of 28 books, he has been a major developer and expert in the field of Neuro-Lingusitic Programming (NLP). Robert has provided coaching consulting and training throughout the world to a wide variety of individuals and organizations and has influenced and improved the lives of hundreds of thousands of people worldwide.

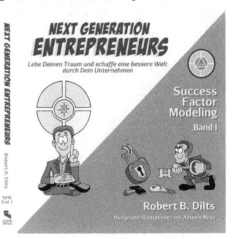

English Version:
ISBN 978-0-9962004-0-0

German Version:
ISBN 978-3-9818472-0-8

Index

Symbols

3-D Printer 156, 237

A

Allen, Paul 178, 237
Apple 67, 118, 179, 237
Asia 18, 37, 47, 97, 103, 142,
    150, 154, 156, 174, 185,
    187, 228, 233, 237
Australia 37, 142, 194, 237

B

Buddy-Prinzip 231, 237

C

Coaching 68, 82, 99, 100, 153,
    198, 236, 237
Coca-Cola 122, 237
Common Goal 11, 12, 67, 82,
    191, 192
Crowdfunding 21, 22, 25, 43, 45,
    46, 47, 48, 50, 51, 55, 59,
    60, 61, 62, 66, 79, 111, 132,
    151, 237
Csíkszentmihályi, Mihály 98, 99,
    231, 237
Culture Map 161, 193, 231, 237

D

Decisive Phase , 77

F

Faller, Kurt 172, 231, 237

Faltin, Günter 127, 231, 237
Ferriss, Timothy 123, 124, 231,
    237
Flip Chart 64, 71
Forrester Research 9

G

Gallup 53, 69, 99

H

Hidden Agendas 73, 74

J

Jekel, Thorsten 121, 122, 231,
    237

L

Lencioni, Patrick 160, 231, 237

M

Map of Resources 70, 100, 237
Meyer, Erin 88, 161, 193, 194,
    195, 231, 237
Micromanaging 19, 22, 74
MOOC 18, 19, 22, 44, 45, 46, 47,
    48, 49, 50, 60, 61, 62, 79,
    96, 111, 115, 131, 132, 133,
    134, 149, 151, 169, 170,
    172, 204, 206, 207, 213,
    215, 216, 217, 219

N

NGO 12, 13

O

Osmanovic, Cemal 197

R

Roadmaps 62, 78, 79, 81, 84, 85,
   90, 91

S

Senge, Peter M. 143, 161, 231,
   237
Skype 8, 9, 17, 18, 19, 20, 22, 24,
   30, 44, 46, 50, 54, 60, 61,
   62, 63, 94, 112, 114, 115,
   116, 118, 123, 131, 132,
   135, 186, 199, 204, 215
SMART 22, 65, 67, 73, 78, 85,
   86, 87, 90, 91, 96, 118, 123,
   171
Synchronous 84, 89, 122, 143,
   177, 194

T

Team Leader 27, 35, 38, 39, 40,
   67, 68, 74, 75, 84, 106,
   107, 129, 141, 142, 143,
   144, 145, 146, 147, 162,
   164, 165, 176, 178, 179,
   195, 196, 222
Timeline Technique 86, 87

Transmontania 7, 8, 9, 17, 18, 19,
   20, 25, 43, 47, 48, 49, 59,
   63, 95, 97, 113, 132, 150,
   154, 171, 172, 173, 181,
   185, 203, 204, 206, 207,
   208, 215, 216, 217, 219,
   220, 221, 227, 228, 237
Trust 3, 23, 24, 25, 27, 31, 34,
   36, 48, 50, 51, 53, 62, 63,
   64, 69, 73, 79, 128, 129,
   139, 149, 151, 152, 153,
   155, 156, 157, 158, 159,
   160, 161, 162, 163, 164,
   165, 184, 190, 193, 221
Tuckman, Bruce 163, 164, 231,
   237

U

Upward Spiral 52, 69

V

Virtual Power Team 3, 13, 25, 31,
   52, 57, 67, 70, 215

W

WebEx 54, 63, 64, 77, 78, 94,
   112, 123, 133, 152, 154,
   170, 171, 182, 204, 205
Whiteboard 29, 63, 70, 77, 80,
   81, 86, 118, 156, 180

CPSIA information can be obtained
at www.ICGtesting.com
Printed in the USA
LVHW081327220219
608463LV00035B/690/P

9 783981 847239